ROCKS & R(

Sailing Routes Across The Atlantic
and the Copper Trade

Fred Rydholm Measures the Copper with his 6'3" Height.

LARGEST Glacial "Float" Copper in the WORLD

Jay Stuart Wakefield
Reinoud M. de Jonge

Dedicated to Fred Rydholm

"Over and beyond mere living, the human spirit adds and creates what is better than what was before"—R. Roefield

ISBN 0-917054-20-2

$35 US
+$10 Global/US Priority Mail
MCS Inc., POB 3392, Kirkland, Wa., USA 98083-3392

Covers: Rows of Menec, Brittany, France, May, 2005

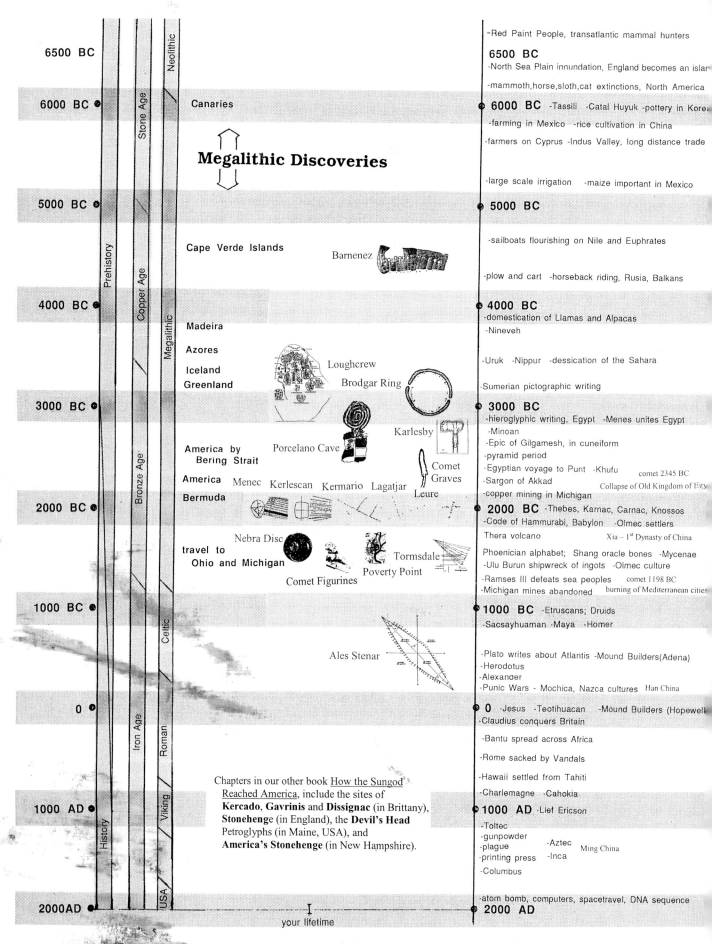

Megalithic Discoveries

6500 BC

6000 BC — Canaries

5000 BC — Cape Verde Islands

Barnenez

4000 BC — Madeira

Azores

Iceland

Greenland — Loughcrew

Brodgar Ring

3000 BC

Karlesby

America by Bering Strait — Porcelano Cave

Comet Graves

America — Menec Kerlescan Kermario Lagatjar — Leure

Bermuda

2000 BC

Nebra Disc

travel to Ohio and Michigan

Comet Figurines — Poverty Point — Tormsdale

1000 BC

Ales Stenar

0

Chapters in our other book How the Sungod
Reached America, include the sites of
Kercado, Gavrinis and **Dissignac** (in Brittany),
Stonehenge (in England), the **Devil's Head**
Petroglyphs (in Maine, USA), and
America's Stonehenge (in New Hampshire).

1000 AD

2000 AD

your lifetime

Timeline, showing dates of the megalithic sites (Chapters) in this book. The time periods at the left are generalizations that vary by location.

Right-side time markers and events:

-Red Paint People, transatlantic mammal hunters

6500 BC

-North Sea Plain innundation, England becomes an island

-mammoth, horse, sloth, cat extinctions, North America

6000 BC -Tassili -Catal Huyuk -pottery in Korea

-farming in Mexico -rice cultivation in China

-farmers on Cyprus -Indus Valley, long distance trade

-large scale irrigation -maize important in Mexico

5000 BC

-sailboats flourishing on Nile and Euphrates

-plow and cart -horseback riding, Rusia, Balkans

4000 BC
-domestication of Llamas and Alpacas
-Nineveh

-Uruk -Nippur -dessication of the Sahara

-Sumerian pictographic writing

3000 BC
-hieroglyphic writing, Egypt -Menes unites Egypt
-Minoan
-Epic of Gilgamesh, in cuneiform
-pyramid period
-Egyptian voyage to Punt -Khufu   comet 2345 BC
-Sargon of Akkad   Collapse of Old Kingdom of Egy
-copper mining in Michigan

2000 BC -Thebes, Karnac, Carnac, Knossos
-Code of Hammurabi, Babylon -Olmec settlers
Thera volcano   Xia – 1st Dynasty of China

Phoenician alphabet; Shang oracle bones -Mycenae
-Ulu Burun shipwreck of ingots -Olmec culture
-Ramses III defeats sea peoples   comet 1198 BC
-Michigan mines abandoned   burning of Mediterranean cities

1000 BC -Etruscans; Druids
-Sacsayhuaman -Maya -Homer

-Plato writes about Atlantis -Mound Builders(Adena)
-Herodotus
-Alexander
-Punic Wars - Mochica, Nazca cultures Han China

0 -Jesus -Teotihuacan -Mound Builders (Hopewell
-Claudius conquers Britain

-Bantu spread across Africa

-Rome sacked by Vandals

-Hawaii settled from Tahiti

-Charlemagne -Cahokia

1000 AD -Lief Ericson

-Toltec
-gunpowder   -Aztec
-plague   Ming China
-printing press   -Inca
-Columbus

-atom bomb, computers, spacetravel, DNA sequence
2000 AD

Left-side vertical columns:

6500 BC
6000 BC
5000 BC
4000 BC
3000 BC
2000 BC
1000 BC
0
1000 AD
2000AD

Neolithic
Stone Age
Copper Age
Megalithic
Bronze Age
Celtic
Iron Age
Roman
Viking
USA
Prehistory
History

Contents

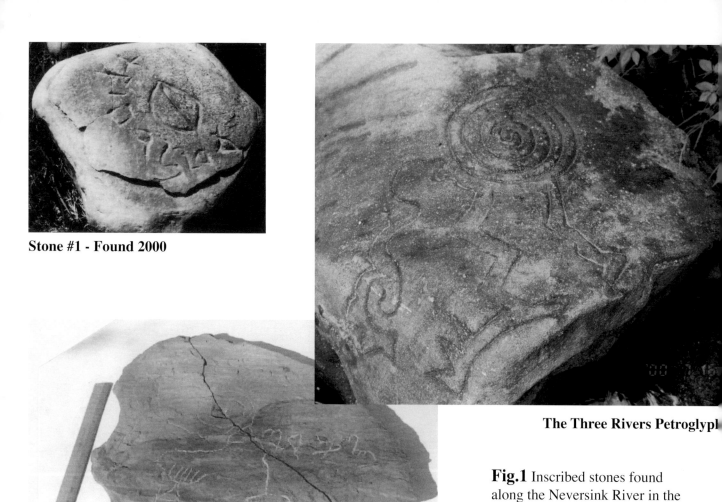

Stone #1 - Found 2000

The Three Rivers Petroglyph

Fig.1 Inscribed stones found along the Neversink River in the Catskill Mountains of New York.

Stone #3 - Found 2007, by Zena Halpern, Don Ruh and Harry Weymer

Stone #2 - Found 2004

Introduction

J.S. Wakefield, jayswakefield@yahoo.com

"Archaeology is still in the pre-Louis Pasteur, pre-Joseph Lister stage, when doctors believed that diseases developed spontaneously – as they also thought that woodworms did in waterlogged wood – instead of being carried and infected. They believed that human cultures, will, left to themselves, progress through the same stages at comparable speeds. This is demonstrably not true."
Jim Bailey, Sailing to Paradise

A new paradigm of prehistory is being built by people with a variety skills, educational backgrounds, and experiences. The new paradigm has been described as "many people, many places", meaning that there have been multiple pre-Columbian discoveries of the Americas, on both coasts by many people of different cultures. A big part of the story is the Bronze Age thousand-year trans-Atlantic trade in copper. This new understanding is building upon the previous work of many outstanding researchers: Elizabeth Twohig, Thor Heyerdahl, Barry Fell, Arlington Mallery, Aubrey Burl, Dr. Stechini, Jim Bailey, Charles Hapgood, Ignatius Donnelly, Salvatore Trento, R. Jairazbhoy, Roy Dryer and Octave Du Temple, to name a few to whom we are indebted. During the 7 years since our last book was done, a number of exciting new discoveries and advances have been made.

Phoenician Stones Discovered in New York (Fig.1)

Our friend and author, Zena Halpern of New York, and her friends Julie, Don Weymer, and Don Ruh have found Phoenician stones that substantiate our decipherment of the Three Rivers Petroglyph. Our explanation of the stone carved with a big spiral and three legs on the bank of the Neversink River in the Catskill Mountains of New York, was that it was a river map to aid travel and trading in 1500 BC (Ref.34). **Figure 1** shows the big 3-Rivers Petroglyph, and the stones they found nearby. The lettering of Stone #2 is clearly Phoenician. Donal Buchanan has identified the meaning as "living waters", so this stone is now called the "Living Waters Stone". Stone #1 has a well-known Near Eastern fertility symbol surrounded by more Phoenician letters, and has a Hebrew letter on the back of the stone. Stone #3 is called the "Goddess Stone" (Refs.31&32). These stones confirm our interpretation that the Neversink River was a trade route between the Hudson River on the East Coast, and the refuge colonies and relatively advanced "Hopewell" moundbuilding cultures of the Ohio Valley. Similar spiral petroglyphs along rivers were noted in colonial writings, but some have disappeared, with one now underwater behind a dam. Some of the Burrows Cave map stones show river routes from the Mississippi, up the Ohio, and further to the East coast, further confirming east-west routes.

Cultivated Plants prove Transoceanic Voyages (Fig.2)

A Landmark botany study was published in 2001 by John Sorenson (Emeritus Professor of Anthropology, Brigham Young University), and Carl Johannessen (Emeritus Professor of Biogeography at the University of Oregon). It is titled "Scientific Evidence for Pre-Columbian Transoceanic Voyages to and from the Americas". They have shown "conclusive evidence that nearly 100 species of plants, a majority of them cultivars, were present in both the Eastern and Western Hemisphere prior to Columbus' first voyage to

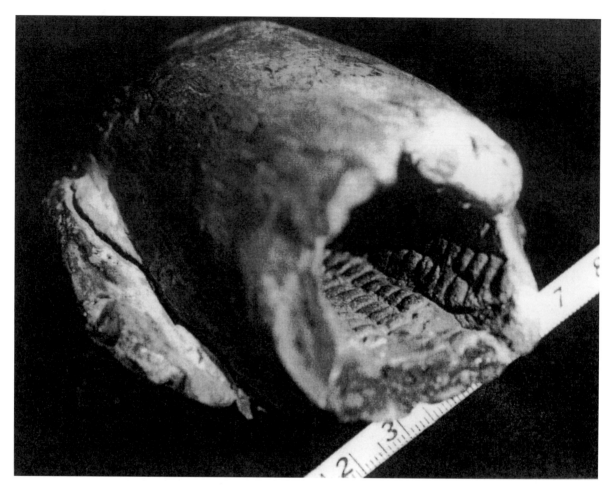

A pottery effigy of a bird, which is barely visible in this photograph, was formed of clay, shaped around a maize cob; when the clay was fired, the cob was consumed, leaving on the interior of the clay object impressions where the kernels had been. The object was from a Han Dynasty tomb (no later than AD 200.) near Xinxiang, Henan, China, and is now in the Xinxiang Archaeological Museum. (Photograph by C. Johannessen.)

Fig.2 Carl Johannessen's interesting photo of a pottery bird effigy from a Han Dynasty tomb is from page 206 of their landmark study. Many photos of Indian temples with corncob carvings, pepper plants on Java, and many other Asian photos of American nuts, fruits, and flowers are to be found in this report (Ref.1).

the Americas. ... Additionally, 21 species of micro-predators and six other species of fauna were shared by the Old and New Worlds... Well over half the plant transfers consisted of flora of American origin that spread to Eurasia or Oceania, some at surprisingly early dates. The only plausible explanation for these findings is that a considerable number of transoceanic voyages in both directions across both major oceans were completed between the 7th millennium BC and the European Age of Discovery. ...given the apparent scale of biological contact, one would *apriori* expect substantial cultural interchange as well."

In this text, each of these plants is discussed in great detail, one by one. Their bibliography alone runs 39 pages. The study concludes that "the expressions 'Old World' and 'New World' have outlived whatever usefulness they initially possessed ... we need to move on. The time is at hand when plausible scenarios for actual voyages with believable motives, along nautically feasible routes, arriving at particular locations, can be proposed". The authors encourage more genetic research: "the evidence for transoceanic interchange of fauna and flora imply also a human gene exchange and generally a more complex biological history of mankind ... the history of disease is a connected subject that calls for new lines of investigation in the light of our findings about the unexpected ancient distribution of microfauna" (Ref.1).

Jim Bailey (Ref.4, pg.95) mentions a "blue-eyed grass, Sysirinchium Bermudiana, which from prehistoric times has grown only in Bermuda and Ireland". This is not one of the plants in the Johannessen study, but is specifically supportive of our decipherment of the Devil's Head Petroglyphs of Harmony, Maine, which recorded the discovery of Bermuda, c.2200 BC.

Warm North Atlantic Weather during Upper North voyages (Fig.3)

Paleoclimate records, drawn from deep Greenland ice cores, now reveal that at the time of the discovery of the Americas by the Megalithic Culture, the Northern Hemisphere was experiencing unusually warm conditions. "The North Atlantic was as warm in the winter as it now is in the summer... Most people think that human civilization evolved under a stable, benign climate, but that is not true ... we have found eight abrupt changes in climate during the last 10,000 years that coincide with changes in civilization" (Ref.11,12).

You can see in **Fig.3** that these warm conditions continued until the 1600 BC discovery of the crossing of the Labrador Sea, as recorded in the Lagatjar site in Brittany. Note how cold peaks coincide with the disappearance of the Norse on Greenland (1300 BC) and the population declines on Iceland (1000 BC) (Ref.10). "A runic inscription found in Helsingland told of a sailor named Vidor and his voyage to "Big Mount" near Vinland, with its long, arduous passage up many rivers to an enormous lake and a big island where copper was obtained" (Ref.36).

Recent sequencing of a mitochondrial genome from the frozen hair of a Paleo-Eskimo human found in Greenland has revealed derivation from Bering Sea populations. This also illustrates the movement of peoples in the arctic around 2500 BC (Ref.15).

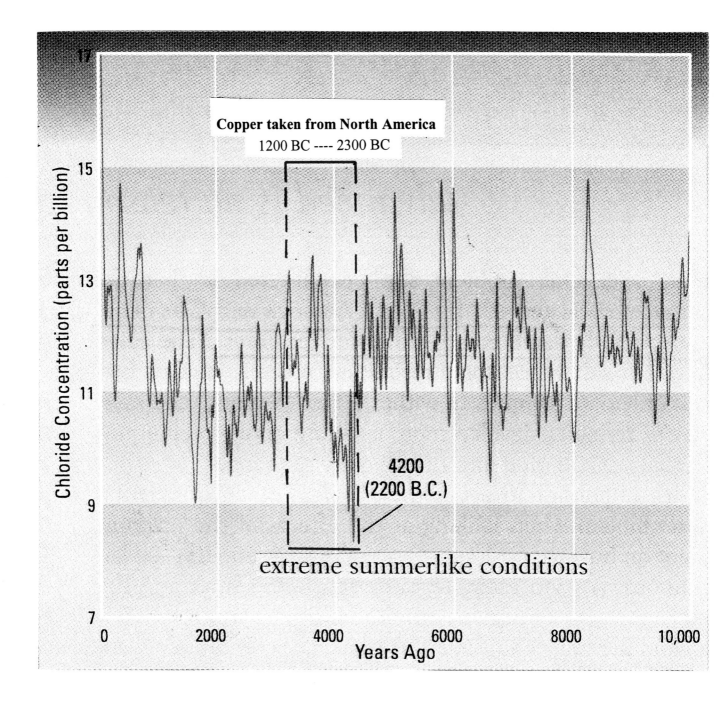

Fig.3 The concentration of windblown salt in deep ice cores in the Greenland ice sheet, showing the lowest values on record during the times of the early explorations of the Americas, and the Bronze Age copper trade (Ref.11).

Genetic Research reveals Iberian genes in Amerindians

DNA studies have made great progress, through work done at Stanford University (Ref.2). In this Journal, a table lists the "non-Indian HLA (Human Lymphocyte Antigens) content in samples of 26 American Indian tribal groups running from .01% to 24%. The atypical HLAs of the eastern Canadian and Greenland Eskimos are predominantly European (Basques have some of the highest values), and those of the Nahua and eastern Mayans are heavily southern Asian … rather than northern Asian…A rare X haplogroup of maternal DNA was found in almost 25% of tribal members of some groups of the Iroquois, in the "moundbuilder" region of the Great Lakes, and among many Algonquin tribes (Micmac at 50%). The highest frequency is in the Basques of Iberia and the Berbers of North Africa, a Caucasian race thought to be survivors of Atlantis (Ref.6). Unfortunately, the National Geographic Society's multimillion dollar Genographic Project to collect 100,000 indigenous DNA samples was brought to a halt (12/10/2006) by Indian tribes. The tribal leaders felt the Project could "undermine their moral basis for sovereignty and their legal claim, land claims, and other benefits" (Ref.5).

The work of Bolnick found that "the higher status Hopewell had a higher incidence of the Haploid X Group, indicating a legacy culture from Atlantis, Iberia, or Phoenicia in the Hopewell elite." It is also said that Native American groups who carry the Caucasian cluster of genes called Haplotype X also share, with the Berbers and Tuaregs, an underlying ancient Na Dene language (Ref.9).

New sites/studies: "Brazilian Stonehenge", Newark Octagon, Comalcalco Brick Inscriptions

Near the coastal village of Calcocene (at 2 ½ °N), in the northern Brazil State of Amapa, north of the delta of the Amazon (at 0°N), a total of 127 large stone blocks were reported by the BBC. The stones each weigh "several tons". They are spaced at regular intervals, some standing upright on end, some fallen or tilting, around the top of a hill, "like a crown 100 feet in diameter". Archaeologists with Amapa State Scientific and Technical Research Institute "believe the site was once an astronomical observatory". The site, known only to locals for a long time, had not yet been excavated or carbon dated, as of 2006 (Ref.28).

A computer study of the celestial alignments of the Newark Octagon was reported in 2007. It is claimed that the odds of the alignments being accidental are one in 40 million (Ref.27). The study did not include other "Hopewell" sites with similar alignments, which would further greatly expand the odds, if combined.

The Mayan city of Comalcalco was built on a river delta on the Gulf of Campeche, east of La Venta. It is the most western of the great Maya cities. The city is unusual, being constructed largely of fired brick. "The arches and other construction techniques are not only reminiscent of Roman construction, but nearly 800 bricks inscribed with mason's marks have been excavated, 640 of them in various ancient European and Asian languages, some mixed with Mayan, some with sketches of elephants. Only ½ of 1% of the bricks have been looked at, so there "may be more than a million inscribed bricks" (Refs.24&25). Unfortunately, we do not expect these to be on exhibit anytime soon. The

HUMAN SACRIFICE, AREA 19, TEMPLE OF THE WARRIORS
Approximately one-fourth actual size

LITH. A. HOEN & CO., INC.

Fig.4 Top, portion of wall murals found in the Temple of the Warriors at Chichen Itza by Morris, Charlot and Morris of the Carnegie Institution in 1931. The murals show the the capturing and sacrificing blond, fair-skinned sailors with beads of green seawater in their hair. The Temple is now closed to the public, the murals have disappeared. **Lower photo**, a portion of a painting on the wall of the Visitor Center was taken by the author in March, 2002. Now culturally cleansed, the mural no longer includes the blond sailors.

fresco panels of the Temple of the Warriors at Chichen Itza have been ethnically cleansed of the yellow-haired figures in the museum exhibit at the site **(Fig.4)** (Refs.26, 35). The murals depict a series of episodes concerning fair skinned people arriving in boats, being defeated in marine combat, and subsequently sacrificed to the feathered serpent Kukulcan. The fresco painters were careful to depict racial distinctions, but today, the re-painters of the Visitor's Center have eliminated the distinctions. Thousands of daily visitors are cheated of the most remarkable frescoes in America, and insight into the Pre-Columbian history of the Americas.

Egyptian finds in Brittany, England, Iowa, and Arizona (Figs. 5,6,7)

Out-of-place finds show more transport of people and ideas than previously thought. **Figure 5** shows an Egyptian "anch" symbol carved into a French menhir on the coast of France. This symbol is held by Egyptians to give them eternal life. The site is about 700m north up a paved road behind the beach at Pointe de la Torche, site of the World Windsurfing Championships. **Figure 5** also shows green faience Ouchtabi figures found in the megalithic tomb of Plougonven, near Morlaix, in northern Brittany. These figures accompany the dead, to do work for the dead person in the afterlife, as they did in life. Faience beads, also made in Egypt from a glass paste, are called "exotic" grave goods and "problems" when found in Wessex graves, England (Ref.14). Many features of Egyptian culture such as pyramids, sedan chairs, and priests illustrated wearing Jaguar skin cloaks with long tails, are found in the early Olmec Civilization of Central America, as has been illustrated by many authors, such as Jairazbhoy (Ref.16).

The Davenport Stone in the Putnam Museum in Davenport, Iowa **(Fig.6)**, which Fred Rydholm and friends had driven 800 miles to see, was declared fake and locked in the basement by the State Archaeologist and the Museum Board. So Fred was not allowed to see it, and he wondered what they were afraid of. The drawing on the stone shows the raising of a Djed column, made of bundles of reeds encircled at the top by rings, representing the Tree of Life, and/or the backbone of Osiris. It was in his honor, that the Djed column was erected each year on the day of the Spring Equinox, as shown also on a tomb drawing of the 18th Dynasty in Thebes. The rising of the sun means the crops and the Pharoah are regenerated and resurrected, showing the stability of life in the Kingdom. The Iowa stone shows that the Djed Festival was celebrated in Iowa, probably around 700 BC (Ref.25).

The Smithsonian still denies reports **(Fig.7)** of its study of tombs in the "forbidden zone" of the Grand Canyon. Reportedly, the government has made it impossible for anyone to check out the veracity of the original report, though I do not know anyone who has tried.

Corvo coins, petroglyphs and the Equestrian Statue

Frank Joseph, in his new book (Ref.18) relates this story: "The Azores were uninhabited at the time of their discovery by the Portuguese in 1427, but inside a cave on Santa Maria (one of two eastern Azores) they stumbled upon a stone altar with serpentine designs." Paul Herrmann (Ref.33), relates that a "smoke blackened old earthenware pot with a handful of Carthaginian and Cyrenaic coins was found after a severe storm-tide on the island of Corvo (one of the two western Azores Islands) amongst the foundations of a

Fig. 5 **Left**, an Egyptian "Anch" symbol (everlasting life) carved in a menhir at the Carriere de Kerharo site, Near Kerdraffic, Brittany, France.

Below, Ouchtabi Figurines, found in the megalithic tomb of Plougonven, just SE of Morlaix, in Northern Brittany. The display case is in the Departmental Museum of the City of Quimper, Brittany. This museum has stone balls in its courtyard, like the ones in Costa Rica and San Lorenzo, as does the Penmarch Museum, further down the coast of Brittany (photos by author, May 2005).

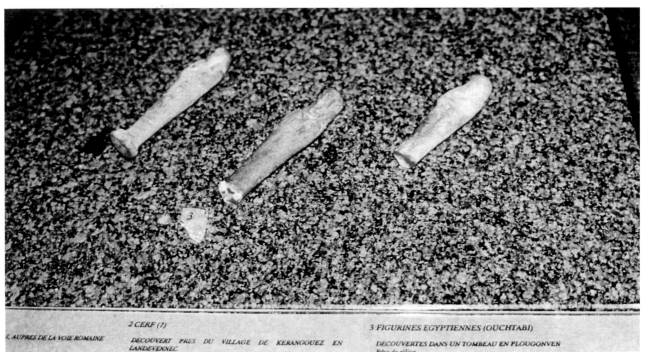

3

1, AUPRES DE LA VOIE ROMAINE   2 CERF (?)   3 FIGURINES EGYPTIENNES (OUCHTABI)

DECOUVERT PRES DU VILLAGE DE KERANGOUEZ EN   DECOUVERTES DANS UN TOMBEAU EN PLOUGONVEN
LANDEVENNEC   Pâte de silice

ruin on the beach. The coins have vanished after passing through many hands. The German geographer, Richard Hennig, propounded an argument, authoritativley confirmed by numismatics, that it would have been impossible in 1750, to have got together an almost complete set of Carthaginian coins from the decade of 330 to 320 BC. Hence there can be no question of fake or fraud" (Ref.33).

A more dramatic find was an equestrian statue atop a mountain at San Miguel (the large eastern Azores Island). The five meter tall bronze masterpiece comprised a stone pedestal with a badly weathered inscription, and surmounted by a magnificent horse, its rider stretching forth his right arm to point across the sea towards the west. When notified of the discovery, King John V ordered it removed to Portugal, but the statue slipped from its improvised halter and crashed down the side of the mountain. The rider's head, one arm and the horse's head and flank alone survived the fall. These fragments, together with an impression of the pedestal's inscription, were sent to the king. They were preserved in his royal palace in Lisbon, where scholars were baffled by the 'archaic Latin', as they thought the inscription might be read, but were reasonably sure of deciphering only a single word –*cates*. Its meaning or significance, however, escaped them. The word is close to cati, which means, appropriately enough, 'go that way' in Quechua, the language spoken by the Incas. … In 1755, however, all the artifacts removed from San Miguel were lost during the great earthquake and tsunami that destroyed most of Lisbon" (Ref.37). In 2006, Joaquim Fernandes Ph.D., Professor of History and Informatics Engineering at the University of Fernando Pessoa, in Porto, Portugal, was writing a history of the Corvo Statue (Ref.37).

Smithsonian: Orient Tablet Lost

In our previous book (Ref.34), we wrote a chapter about the inscribed Orient Tablet, which had been found at Orient, a small harbor near the eastern tip of Long Island. Because it had images of a man, a boat, an animal and a bird, it was thought the stone had petroglyphs that were recording an Indian hunting trip, and was in the collection of the National Museum of the American Indian. Barry Fell had deciphered the Egyptian and Libyan scripts on the two sides of the stone in his famous book America BC. His translation of the Libyan text was "this ship is a vessel from the Egyptian Dominions", and the hieratic text was "a ship's crew from Upper Egypt made this tablet in respect of their expedition". Fell also deciphered a copy of the Lord's Prayer written by Algonquian Indians in Micmac, a heiroglyphic writing system first described by Abbe Maillard in his *Manuel Heiroglyphique Micmac* in 1738. Fell showed it to be nearly identical to Egyptian hieroglyphics, which were not deciphered until 1823, by Champollion. The Indians had learned to use the hieroglyphs three or four thousand years earlier than the decipherment, so could only have been taught by the Egyptians themselves.

In 2006, Zena Halpern asked to see the Orient stone, and got the following reply by mail: "Your request for information regarding the former Museum of the American Indian (MAI) object numbered 9/8603, an engraved stone, has been received by the Registration Department of the National Museum of the American Indian (NMAI). After a search of the paper archives, including loan, gift and exchange documents, no trace of the whereabouts of 9/8603 can be found. The engraved stone found at Orient, Long Island

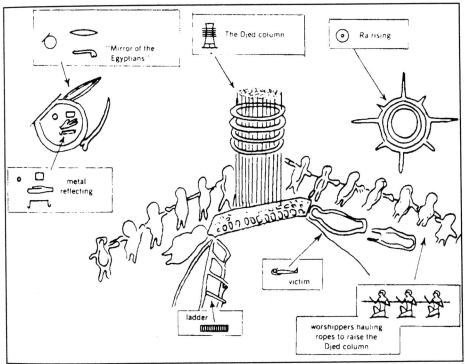

Fig. 6 Above, photo of the Davenport Stone of Iowa, the "Djed Festival Tablet". Reportedly found along the banks of the Mississippi by a Reverend Gass, it shows 3 ancient alphabets: a rare form of hieroglyphics, and others thought to be Punic and Libyan. A tomb inscription of the 18th Dynasty in Thebes explains that the column of Osiris was erected each year on the day of the spring equinox. The metal mirror was used to reflect rays of the rising sun (Ref.25).

was lent to MAI in 1920 by Daniel A. Young, along with other objects, with the intention that the loaned objects become a gift upon his death. If the engraved stone was believed to not be of Native American manufacture, then it could have been returned to the lender, although we have not found documentation to support this in the NMAI archives." This awful loss demonstrates again what many others have discovered, that the Smithsonian Institution cannot be trusted with finds.

What happened to those who came? Where are they?

This is a question I get asked. Usually I explain that DNA studies are showing that they interbred a great deal, and of course, over time "went native", such as the Mandans. We also can see from the massive stone forts in many states, that there must have been a lot of violence. Native tales speak of massive battles, such as at the Falls of the Ohio, where the "White People were wiped out". Arlington Mallery (Ref.30) reported finding heaps of very old skeletons, which he thought must have been due to Black Death brought into the communities in Ohio by new arrivals. Former US National Park Director Kennedy's chapter entitled "The Great Dying" shows how greatly the North American continent was depopulated by disease prior to the arrival of Columbus (Ref.38).

Diane Wirth's 2003 book (Ref.29), which goes into detail about beards, baldness, stocking caps, and other parallels, brings some new light on this. She says that by the time of the Spanish Conquest in 1521 there were not many men left capable of growing full beards. She reports several statements, independent of one another, that note that men with white skin were sacrificed in Mexico. Father Sahagun wrote that "when the sun is eclipsed … they hunt out men of fair hair and white faces, and they sacrifice them to the sun". She quotes the work of Lord Kingsborough: "There was a law that wherever a child was born that was very white and blond, when it was five years of age, it was right away sacrificed. This law lasted until the coming of the Spaniards." She also quotes a native historian, Chavero, "who made frequent reference to the sacrifice of white children at the center of Lake Pantitlan" …This may have been the demise of the bearded foreigners seen carved in stone all over Mexico.

References

1. Sorenson, J., and Johannessen, C., Scientific Evidence for Pre-Columbian Transoceanic Voyages to and from the Americas, Dept. of East Asian Languages and Civilizations, University of Pennsylvania, Philadelphia, Pa. 19104-6305, 2001, 257 pages, vmair@sas.upenn.edu in paper or on CD
2. Jett, S.C.,et.al., "Genetics and Language in Transoceanic Context", Pre-Columbiana, Journal of Long – DistanceContacts, Vol.2, Nos.2&3, Dec. 2000 &June 2001, Early Sites Research Society, $24, Celia Heil, POB 5731, Arlington, Va. 22205 (ISSN 1522-8495)
3. Marsh, P., "Genetics Rewrites Pacific Prehistory", Ancient American, Vol.11, No.68, pg.28-31.
4. Bailey, J., Sailing to Paradise, the Discovery of the Americas by 7000 BC, Simon & Schuster, New York, 1994 (ISBN 0-684-81297-5)
5. Harmon, A., "Alaska Natives' Concerns bring DNA Tracking Project to a Halt", Seattle Times, A4, 12/10/06
6. Hart, W., "DNA Evidence for Atlantis", precolumbian_inscriptions@yahoogroups.com, 5/20/06
7. Michael, J., "Native Americans and Mitochondrial DNA", AKHA Newsletter, 11/15/05
8. Bolnick, D.A., "Unexpected Patterns of Mitochondrial DNA Variation Among Native Americans from the Southeastern United States, American Journal of Physical Anthropology 122:336-354
9. Brown, M.D., et.al., "mtDNA Haplogroup X: An Ancient Link between Europe/Western Asia and North America?", American Journal of Human Genetics 63: 1852-1861 1998
10. Eshleman, J.,et.al., "Mitochondrial DNA studies of Native Americans: Conceptions and Misconceptions of the Population Prehistory of the Americas", Evolutionary Anthropology 12:7-18, 2003
11. Nadis, S., "Ice Man", Archaeology, Nov. / Dec. 2001

EXPLORATIONS IN GRAND CANYON

(Continued from Page One.)

which indicates that some sort of ladder was attached. These granaries are rounded, and the materials of which they are constructed, I think, is a very hard cement. A gray metal is also found in this cavern, which puzzles the scientists, for its identity has not been established. It resembles platinum. Strewn promiscuously over the floor everywhere are what people call cat's eyes or tiger eyes, a yellow stone of no great value. Each one is engraved with a head of the Malay type.

The Hieroglyphics.

"On all the urns, or walls over doorways, and tablets of stone, which were found by the image are the mysterious hieroglyphics, the key to which the Smithsonian institute hopes yet to discover. These writings resemble those on the rocks about this valley. The engraving on the tablets probably has something to do with the religion of the people. Similar hieroglyphics have been found in the peninsula of Yucatan, but these are not the same as those found in the orient. Some believe that these cave dwellers built the old canals in the Salt River valley. Among the pictorial writings, only two animals are found. One is of prehistoric type.

The Crypt.

"The tomb or crypt in which the mummies were found is one of the

contain a deadly gas or chemicals used by the ancients. No sounds are heard, but it smells snakey just the same. The whole underground institution gives one of shaky nerves the creeps. The gloom is like a weight on one's shoulders, and our flashlights and candles only make the darkness blacker. Imagination can revel in conjectures and ungodly day-dreams back through the ages that have elapsed till the mind reels dizzily in space."

An Indian Legend.

In connection with this story, it is notable that among the Hopis the tradition is told that their ancestors once lived in an underworld in the Grand Canyon till dissension arose between the good and the bad, the people of one heart and the people of two hearts. Machetto, who was their chief, counseled them to leave the underworld, but there was no way out. The chief then caused a tree to grow up and pierce the roof of the underworld, and then the people of one heart climbed out. They journeyed toward the sun, looking for the messenger. When he returns, their lands and ancient dwelling place will be restored to them. That is the tradition. Among the engravings of animals in the cave is seen the image of a heart over the spot where it is located. The legend was learned by W. E. Rollins, the artist, during a year spent with the Hopi Indians. There are two theories of the origin of the Egyptians. One is that they came from Asia; another that the racial cradle was in the upper Nile region. Heeren, an Egyptologist, believed in the Indian origin of the Egyptians. The discoveries in the Grand Canyon may throw further light on human evolution and prehistoric ages.

EXPLORATIONS IN GRAND CANYON

Mysteries of Immense Rich Cavern Being Brought to Light.

JORDAN IS ENTHUSED

Remarkable Finds Indicate Ancient People Migrated From Orient.

The latest news of the progress of the explorations of what is now regarded by scientists as not only the oldest archaeological discovery in the United States, but one of the most valuable in the world, which was mentioned some time ago in the Gazette, was brought to the city yesterday by G. E. Kinkaid, the explorer who found the great underground citadel of the Grand Canyon during a trip from Green river, Wyoming, down the Colorado, in a wooden boat, to Yuma, several months ago. According to the story related yesterday to the Gazette by Mr. Kinkaid, the archaeologists of the Smithsonian Institute, which is financing the explorations, have made discoveries which almost conclusively prove that the race which inhabited this mysterious cavern, hewn in solid rock by human hands, was of oriental origin, possibly from Egypt, tracing back to Ramses. If their theories are borne out by the translation of the tablets engraved with hieroglyphics, the mystery of the prehistoric peoples of North America, their ancient arts, who they were and whence they came, will be solved. Egypt and the Nile, and Arizona and the Colorado will be linked by a historical chain running back to ages which staggers the wildest fancy of the fictionist.

A Thorough Investigation.

Under the direction of Prof. S. A. Jordan, the Smithsonian Institute is now prosecuting the most thorough explorations, which will be continued until the last link in the chain is forged. Nearly a mile underground, about 1480 feet below the surface, the long main

feet ventilation of the cavern, the steady draught that blows through, indicates that it has another outlet to the surface.

Mr. Kinkaid's Report.

Mr. Kinkaid was the first white child born in Idaho and has been an explorer and hunter all his life, thirty years having been in the service of the Smithsonian Institute. Even briefly recounted, his history sounds fabulous, almost grotesque.

"First, I would impress that the cavern is nearly inaccessible. The entrance is 1486 feet down the sheer canyon wall. It is located on government land and no visitor will be allowed there under penalty of trespass. The scientists wish to work unmolested, without fear of the archaeological discoveries being disturbed by curio or relic hunters. A trip there would be fruitless, and the visitor would be sent on his way. The story of how I found the cavern has been related, but, in a paragraph: I was journeying down the Colorado river in a boat, alone, looking for mineral. Some forty-two miles up the river from the El Tovar Crystal canyon I saw on the east wall, stains in the sedimentary formation about 2000 feet above the river bed. There was no trail to this point, but I finally reached it with great difficulty. Above a shelf which hid it from view from the river, was the mouth of the cave. There are steps leading from this entrance some thirty yards to what was, at the time the cavern was inhabited, the level of the river. When I saw the chisel marks on the wall inside the entrance, I became interested, secured my gun and went in. During that trip I went back several hundred feet along the main passage, till I came to the crypt in which I discovered the mummies. One of these I stood up and photographed by flashlight. I gathered a number of relics, which I carried down the Colorado to Yuma, from whence I shipped them to Washington with details of the discovery. Following this, the explorations were undertaken.

The Passages.

"The main passageway is about 12 feet wide, narrowing to 9 feet toward the farther end. About 57 feet from the entrance, the first side-passages branch off to the right and left, along which, on both sides, are a number of rooms about the size of ordinary living rooms of today, though some are 30 or 40 feet square. These are entered by oval-shaped doors and are ventilated by round air spaces through the walls into the passages. The walls are about 3 feet 6 inches in thickness. The passages are chiseled or hewn as straight as could be laid out by an engineer. The ceilings of many of the rooms converge to a center. The side passages near the entrance run at a sharp angle from the main hall, but toward the rear they gradually reach a right angle in direction.

The Shrine.

"Over a hundred feet from the entrance is the cross-hall, several hundred feet long, in which was found the idol, or image, of the people's god, sitting cross-legged, with a lotus flower or lily in each hand. The cast of the

12. Mayewski, P., University of Maine, Institute for Quarternary and Climate Studies, Bryand Global Sciences Center, Orono, Maine, 04469-5790
13. Mayewski, P., and White, F., The Ice Chronicles, University Press of New England, Lebanon N.H., 2002 (ISBN: 1-58465-061-3)
14. Pigott, S., "The Early Bronze Age in Wessex", Proceedings of the Prehistoric Society, 1938, IV, 52.
15. Gilbert, M. et.al., "Paleo-Eskimo mt DNA Genome Reveals Matrilineal Discontinuity in Greenland", Science, Vol.320, 27 June, 2008.
16. Jairazbhoy, R.A., Ancient Egyptians and Chinese in America, Rowman & Littlefield, Totowa, N.J., 1974 (ISBN 0-87471-571-1)
17. Campbell, J., Historical Atlas of World Mythology, Harper & Row, New York, Vol.11, Part 3, pg 262 (ISBN 0-06-055158-5)
18. Joseph, J., Atlantis and other Lost Worlds, Chartwell Books, 2008, Edison, N.J., (ISBN 978-0-7858-2431-2)
19. Diehl, R., The Olmecs, America's First Civilization, Thames & Hudson, London, 2004 (ISBN 0-500-02119-8)
20. Sullivan, W., The Secret of the Incas; Myth, Astronomy, and the War Against Time, Random House, 1997 (ISBN 0517888513)
21. Childress, D., Lost Cities of North & Central America, Adventure Unlimited Press, Stelle, Ill., 1998, (ISBN 0-932813-09-7)
22. Letter from Smithsonian Institution, National Museum of the American Indian, Dated April 5, 2006
23. Stefansson, V., Iceland, The First American Republic, Doubleday, New York, 1943
24. Steede, N., "Comalcalco: An Early Classic Maya Site", Across Before Columbus, NEARA Publications, 1998 (ISBN 0-9663038-0-6)
25. Rydholm, F., Michigan Copper, The Untold Story, A History of Discovery, Winter Cabin Books, Marquette Mich., 2006 (ISBN 0-9744679-2-8)
26. Hyerdahl, T., American Indians in the Pacific, The Theory Behind the Kon-Tiki Expedition, Rand McNally, New York, 1953
27. Hively, R., Horn, R., "A Statistical Study of Lunar Alignments at the Newark Earthworks", Midcontinental Journal of Archaeology, Fall, 2006
28. http://news.bbc.co.uk/1/hi/world/americas/4767717.stm, 13 May, 2006
29. Wirth, D., Parallels, Mesoamerican and Ancient Middle Eastern Traditions, Stonecliff Publishing, St. George Utah, 2003, (ISBN 0-9602096-0-3)
30. Mallery, A.H., and Harrison, M.R., The Rediscovery of Lost America, The Story of Pre-Columbian Iron Age in America, Dutton, NY< 1979 (ISBN 0-525-47545-1)
31. Wolter, S., "The Catskill Mountains Inscription" & Halpern, Z., "Report on Two Inscribed Stones Found in the Catskills", Epigraphic Society Occasional Papers, vol.25, 2007.
32. Halpern, Z., "The Inscriptions on the Goddess Stone from Onteora (Land in the Sky)", Epigraphic Society Occasional Papers, Vol.26, 2008.
33. Herrmann, P., Conquest by Man, Harper & Bros., N.Y., 1954
34. de Jonge, R., and Wakefield, J., How the Sungod Reached America c.2500 BC, A Guide to Megalithic Sites, MCS Inc., Kirkland, Wa. 2002 (ISBN 0-917054-19-9)
35. Morris, E., Charlot, J., Morris, A., The Temple of the Warriors at Chichen Itza, Yucatan, Vol 1, published by Carnegie Instution of Washington, May 21, 1931
36. Rydholm, F., "Discovery of the Ancient Stone Monuments of Upper Michigan", Ancient American #29, pg 34, quoting J. Bauer, Viking Mettles, 1929.
37. personal email communication
38. Kennedy, R., Hidden Cities, The Discovery and Loss of Ancient North American Civilization, Penguin Books, N.Y., 1994 (ISBN 0-14-0255273)
39. Trento, S., Field Guide to Eastern North America, Henry Holt & Co., New York, 1997 (ISBN 0-8050-4449-3)
40. Vastokas, J., and Vastokas, R., The Sacred Art of the Algonkians, a Study of the Petersbourough Petroglyphs, Mansard Press, Peterbourough, 1973
41. Gellig, P., Davidson, H., The Chariot of the Sun, and Other Rites and Symbols of the Northern Bronze Age, Frederick A Praeger, N.Y., 1969
42. Mahan, J., North American Sun Kings, Keepers of the Flame, ISAC P., Columbus, Ga., '92 (ISBN -1-880820-03X)
43. Nadis, S., "Ice Man", Archaeology, Nov/Dec 2001, pg 31 (ISSN 0003-8113)
44. Leutze, W., "Keepers of the Secret", Ancient American, Issue #14, p.15
45. Great Ages of Man, Cradle of Civilization, Time Inc., 1967
46. Sorenson, J.L., and Raish, M.H., Pre-Columbian Contact with the Americas across the Oceans, An Annotated Bibliography, 2 Vol., Research Press, Provo, Ut. (ISBN 0-934893-14-4)

Site Photo: Reinoud next to the SE side of the Cairn of Barnenz.. This is how you first see the monument when you walk up from the Museum. (May 2006)

THE CAIRN OF BARNÉNEZ
Explorations of the British Isles
(North Brittany, France, c.4800-4500 BC)

R.M. de Jonge (drsrmdejonge@hotmail.com)
J.S. Wakefield (jayswakefield@yahoo.com)

Summary

The Cairn of Barnénez is a very old megalithic monument, located at the north coast of Brittany, France, beside the Morlaix estuary, at 49°N. The huge mound of stepped terraces of stones contains 11 corbelled passage graves. We believe these tell the history of discovery of the British Isles that lie to the north of the Barnenez site, from 50°N to 60°N. It is the oldest monument that reveals the use of latitudes in its design.

Introduction

The monumental Cairn of Barnénez is situated on the north coast of Brittany, France, at 49°N on the tip of a small peninsula (community of Plouézoch). The site is on a hilltop (45m), with views to the south and east, and in past times had open views to the north and northwest, now obscured by trees. At the west side of the peninsula, the river of Morlaix empties in the wide Bay of Morlaix, and at the east side is the small bay, which would have been a valley when the monument was built (**site photo**). The site is one of the major tourist sites in France, with a museum, and an entrance fee.

At first sight Barnénez appears to be a big, oblong mound of stones. The man-made monument has a length of 80 meters, a width of 20 to 30 meters, and a height of about 6 meters. Inside the mound of stones are 11 long passage graves. These lie side by side, at right angles to the axis of the mound (see **Fig.1**). These graves point northwest, while their entrances face southeast. Half of the front, northwest side, was quarried for quartz rock for roadbuilding in 1955. You can see the scooped-out missing portion in the attached photos.

The passage graves are the important features of the monument, not the mound of stones over them. The width of the passages is about 1 meter, and the height is about 1.5 meters. The length of the narrow passages varies from 6 to about 13 meters. At the end are the important burial chambers, which are nearly round chambers, with inside diameters of about 2.5 meters and heights of up to 4 meters. Most of them are now walled off, preventing access. Finds from the chambers, including pottery and axeheads, are on exhibit in the Prehistory Museum in Penmrc'h (Ref.34). The pots, mostly broken and undecorated, include half of a banded-decorated Beaker pot. Among larger ground axeheads, are more than a dozen early Mesolithic-style smaller flint axeheads.

The walls of most of the passages and chambers are built of flat dry stones, with no mortar, as is typical of such early construction. The burial chambers have a characteristic design, called "corbelled bee-hive", where each layer of the walls cantilevers inward a little, until a pointed center, or a small slab, is reached at the top. All the corridors have vertical sidestones covered by large capstones. To bear the enormous weight of the mound above,

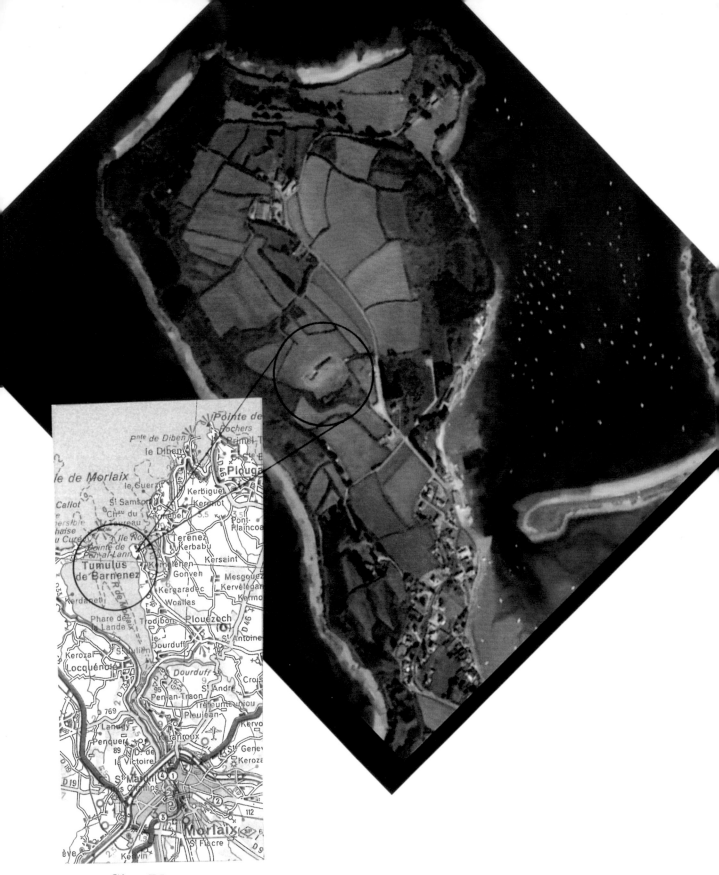

Site Photo: The Cairn of Barnenez is in the circle in this photo. The peninsula is on the east side of the estuary of Morlaix Brittany, France. The northwest face of the monument is on its left side. (Google Earth, 2006)

the sidestones have a thickness of at least 20cm. There are a few passage graves which must be more important than others because they contain more of these big stones, especially A52, as seen on the groundplan (fig.1). Petroglyphs found on stones in the passages and chambers were recorded by Elizabeth Twohig (Ref.9), now teaching archaeology at a university in Cork, Ireland.

There are 11 passage graves protected by the mound of stones over them. The sizes of these smaller stones vary considerably, but on the average these measure 30x20x10cm. When passage graves are protected by a mound of stones, such a construction is usually called a "cairn". However, the Cairn of Barnénez has two parts: it consists of an old, eastern cairn with 5 passage graves, and a later built, western cairn with 6 passage graves. Carbon-14 measurements show that the eastern cairn dates from about 4700 BC. The western cairn was built about 3 centuries later, so it dates from about 4400 BC. We have dated the explorations (in the article title) 100 years earlier, assuming that the explorations preceded the monument construction.

The two construction phases can be seen in **Photos 3&4**. The old, eastern Cairn A is made of dark green dolerith, which is locally available. The later, western Cairn B is made of the lighter colored granite, which is found on the islet of Stérec, two kilometers away. In the years 1954-'55 the north side of the west Cairn B was damaged, because of granite stones removed for road building. Fortunately, the important passage graves still remain largely intact.

The mound of stones at Barnénez has a layered structure, visible as terraces on the outside. These may have been used in ceremonial functions. The old Cairn A consists of 3 layers, and originally, the later Cairn B probably had 4 layers. However, primarily because of the roadwork, the 4th layer is almost gone on the front (northwest) side of the mound. In 1955, P.R. Giot began a two-year partial restoration of the site, as we see it today.

The Sun Religion

Archeologists now call these 11 tunnel/chamber constructions in the Cairn of Barnénez "passage graves". However, this name is a misnomer. While some grave remains have been found in them, often from later usages, these are pre-Christian churches of the Sun religion. We do not call Westminister Abbey a "passage grave" just because it has a long passage and graves in it. Just as there are many cathedrals and churches in Europe, there are hundreds of these "passage grave" structures close to the coasts of Europe, or close to rivers that flow to the sea. They are one of the characteristics of the "megalithic culture" that developed along coastal Europe during the six thousand year neolithic period that ended in a catastrophe in 1200 BC, just prior to Celtic times.

We think the passages symbolize the Land of the Living, and the burial chambers represent the Realm of the Dead. Note that all passage graves were built with their important burial chambers pointing to the northwest. This is because (as written in Egyptian hieroglyphics) the almighty SunGod has said: "The Realm of the Dead is in the west, at the other side of the waters (the Ocean), in the land where the Sun sets". In the hierarchy below the SunGod, the pharaohs of Egypt were considered manifestations of

Map 1 The British Isles, showing the latitudes of early discovery which are encoded by the chambers of Barnenez. Note the circled locations of Barnenez, at the bottom, by Morlaix, and to the right, the shallow Doggersbank, and to the left, the Islet of Rockall. (National Geographic Map, Atlantic Ocean, 1955)

sungod Horus in this world, while moongod Osiris ruled the Land of the Dead in the West. Note the two-part construction of the monument, which was labouriously built with different light and dark types of rock, in east and west halves. The light rock was on site, but the darker quartz was somehow transported considerable distance. This construction, 1500 years before pharonic times, is in keeping with the two-land dichotomy of Horus and Osiris, the heaven/hell dichotomies seen in subsequent religions, and even in the mythological structure of the dark side/ light side in contemporary Starwars movies.

The eastern Cairn A was built first. For that reason we have labeled its 5 passage graves with an "A", and the associated latitude number, as will be explained. The 6 passage graves of the later built, western Cairn B are labeled with the letter "B", and their associated latitude. The chamber of the first passage grave A50 is situated on the east-west centerline of the mound. This is also the case with the chamber of the last passage grave B60. The other burial chambers were all built beyond this centerline. This is a strong indication that both cairns are designed to be parts of a single master project, even though built 300 years apart. If the outermost burial chambers of Cairn A are connected by a line, this line A-A points 23°WSW. This direction corresponds with the latitude of the Tropic of Cancer, at 23°N. On midsummer day the Sun at 23°N is directly overhead. This is the highest latitude reached by the Sun prior to moving back south again, changing the season. This angle is seen in all major megalithic monuments, and is evidence of the Sunreligion in each of them. Even ancient China was later influenced, as a tradition states that "in the Capital of the Perfect Soverign, the sundial must give no shadow at midday of summer solstice".

The Atlantic Ocean & Latitudes

It was known that as one traveled north or south, the angle to the sun, moon and other celestial objects changed consistently. This angle was measured. Today we call it "taking the latitude". It was done using an invention called the Jacob's Staff, connected sticks which made possible consistent readings of the Sun above the horizon. Drawings of this instrument (staff) are shown twice in the petroglyphs of Barnenez (**Figs.6&7**). Similar drawings are found in many other locations, indicating the suspected origin of this instrument several thousand years earlier. This is not surprising, since we know that the Zodiac, a 26,000 year cycle, was understood. The cyclic movement of the Sun lasts a year, slightly more than 360 days, so it is known that the Egyptians divided the circumference of the Earth into 360 degrees of latitude. As of now, the eastern Cairn A of Barnénez is the oldest monument where the use of latitudes is demonstrated (c.4800 BC).

Barnénez is located on the northwestern coast of Western Europe, close to the Ocean. The placement of so many megalithic cairns so close to the ocean, pointing to it, appears to indicate that the people wanted to cross this Ocean to reach the Realm of the Dead. The line A-A points 23°WSW, indicating the place where the holy Tropic of Cancer leaves the continent of Africa, at 23°N. It was there that people most wanted to cross the Ocean, thinking that the Sun, which crossed there every day, was giving them a clue on how to do it. We think many brave explorers lost their lives in the Doldrums of the Sargasso Sea trying this crossing.

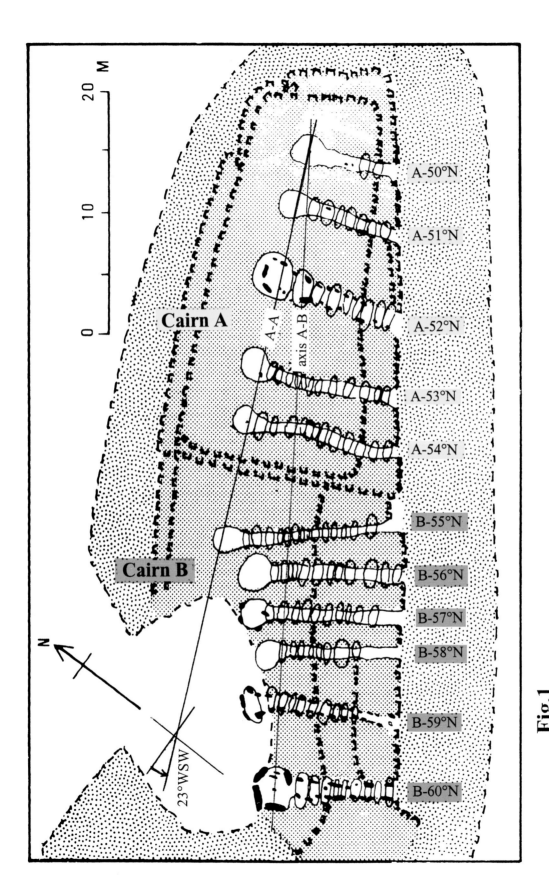

Fig.1

Groundplan of the Cairn of Barnénez (above), with frontal view (below) (Ref.8). The mound of stones is 80 meters long, 25 meters wide, and 6 meters high. It consists of 3 to 4 layers. The mound protects 11 passage graves. The eastern Cairn A dates from c.4800 BC, and the western Cairn B dates from c.4500 BC. The 11 passage graves ("churches") are labeled from east to west, corresponding with the 11 latitudes of the west coast of the British Isles, from 50°N to 60°N. The axis is line A-B, while line A-A points 23°WSW, encoding the holy Tropic of Cancer, at 23°N.

The shape of the Cairn of Barnénez might have been intended to resemble a primitive ship, as several archeologists have written. The line A-B is the axis of this ship. The stern is situated near the first passage grave A50, and the prow is near the last passage grave B60. This "ship" is sailing in the direction WSW. The prow is fortified by large, upright slabs, clearly visible in the photos. The large "deck" at this end may have served as a ceremonial platform.

The British Isles: Cairns A& B
The Cairn of Barnénez is located at 49°N. The 11 passage graves A-B are also labeled by the 11 numbers 50 to 60, for the 11 latitudes above Barnénez, from 50°N to 60°N (see **Fig.1**). These are the 11 latitudes of the west coast of the British Isles, from the Scilly Isles near Cornwall, at 50°N, to the Shetland Islands in the extreme north, at 60°N (see **Map 1**). We think each passage grave represents a degree of latitude, and each passage grave deals with the exploration of the sea at its latitude.

Chamber A50: "The Buckler"
 The 5 passage graves A50 to A54 of the old Cairn correspond with the latitudes 50-54°N. The first of these graves, A50, looks small, compared to the others, but may be represent the first discovery, of the Islands of Scilly, off Cornwall at 50°N. There is a petroglyph in A50 that archaeologists call a "buckler" (see **Fig.2**). As shown in the introduction to our 2002 book "How the SunGod Reached America c.2500 BC", this glyph is the fourth of 36 illustrated petroglyphs of this design, and one of the more common petroglyph motifs. One has even been found on Stonehenge stone 57 in recent years. This example in A50 is one of the earliest examples in a dated site. Carved in this first chamber, this petroglyph explains what the whole monument is about, the problem of crossing the ocean to see what was on the other side of the earth.

 The petroglyph appears on the first coverstone of the passage, stone RS1 of A50. We see a rectangle, one of the first maps ever drawn of the North Atlantic Ocean, an early classical petroglyph. In the east is the well-known continental land, in the south the equator, and in the west the suspected opposite side (America). In the north, the "hair" is the Polar Cap, where, theoretically, it might be possible to cross the ocean. The symmetry of the glyph shows that people assumed a symmetrical distribution of land and water, in the (well-known) east as well as in the (unknown) west. It was a great mystery, what might be on the other side of the Earth. The energy and focus of this culture was to explore the backside, by crossing the Ocean. This petroglyph shows that they knew there was a polar cap, where distance (longitude) lines converged because of the curvature of the Earth. Their knowledge of latitude distances (1 Egyptian moira = 1° of 360), provided them with the correct size of the Earth, and by the spacings in the distance lines (dl), they show they were surprisingly close to estimating the size of the ocean correctly. The spacings between the lines at the top of the petroglyph each correspond to 1 HMoira (1 big Half Moira= 5° of latitude). In the east we see 5 spacings with an overall distance of 5 HMoiras (5x5= 25° of latitude). The total width of the ocean is estimated to be about twice that amount, which is 5+7 spaces= 12 HMoiras (= 12x5°= 60° of latitude= 3600 nautical miles (NM). This estimated width of 60° is similar to the distance of Cornwall (50°N) from the equator. This is the reason this ocean petroglyph was made almost square.

Fig.2

Petroglyph of the North Atlantic Ocean. In the east the well-known continental land, in the south the equator, and in the west the suspected opposite side (America). On top the Polar Cap. The width of the Ocean is estimated at 12 Half Moiras= 3600 NM.
(Stone RS1, Grave A50, Ref.9, Barnénez, c.4600-4500 BC)

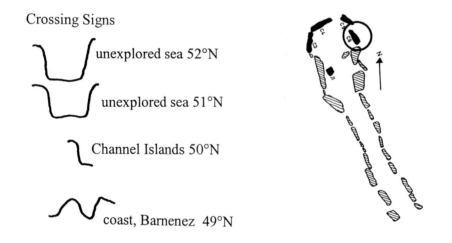

Fig.3

From bottom to top: The coast of France (Barnenez) at 49°N, the discovery of the Channel Islands at 50°N, and the still unexplored sea at 51° and 52°N.
(Stone C6, Grave A52, Ref.9, Barnénez, c.4500 BC)

Chamber A51

During the construction of Barnénez, A51 was the second and most important passage grave of Cairn A, corresponding to the crossing of the Strait of Dover, at 51°N. The shortest sailing distance to England is 18 NM. No petroglyphs have been found in A51.

Chamber A52: "U's" and Triangles

Grave **A52** has the highest number of big stones, so clearly it is the most important passage grave of Cairn 1. This chamber corresponds with Dunmore Head, SW Ireland, at 52°N, which is the westernmost point of Western Europe. Westernmost lands are always very important to them, of course. A variety of petroglyphs were found in the chamber of A52. **Figure 3** shows the layout of the stones of this chamber, and shows petroglyphs on stone C6, in the east side of the chamber (in the circle). These upside-down "U's" are a common petroglyph motif. We call them "crossing signs" because they show the depth of the waters, and land at the sides. In **Figure 4**, we see a primitive map of the west coast of Normandy, France (the vertical line at the right side below the waves), the crossing of the Channel to Cornwall (the waves), and a coastal route along South England. The 3 spaces between the waves might correspond to the length of both crossings, 3x1/2moira= 1.5 moiras= 90 NM. In **Fig.5**, is another image of this, showing an exploration further west and north, into the Irish Sea. In **Fig.6**, on stone C4, is another image of the crossing of the Channel, this time showing the waters as wavy lines, with several spacings.

Also in **Figure 6** is another motif in early megalithic "art", the triangle. This is a representation, fairly correct, of England and Scotland. Note there is a crook, a detail of the Thames River or the Humber/Trent, on the eastern shore. What is notable, is that there is no big lump on the east side of the triangle, as is sometimes seen, representing the dry Doggersbank, which shows, that by this time, this huge land area had gone below the rising seas of glacial meltwater.

At the right side of **Figure 6** is a copy of a glyph documented in eight Iberian passage graves which Twohig calls "The Thing", which she says "must have had a specific meaning". This is an earlier representation of the British Isles, which does show the Doggersbank as dry land, on the east side of England. You can see the shallow Doggersbank today on **Map1**. Stone tools are frequently dredged up from this area, which is thought to have been forested, with several river mouths, a very rich area that was heavily populated in ancient times. The Iberian petroglyphs illustrating dry land show that these coastal people had been exploring the British Isles by sea long before the construction of the Barnenez Cairn in 4400 BC. So the Cairn was probably built to commemorate major socially-endorsed expeditions that followed a long period of explorations by individuals and traders.

A pillar was found (J1) in A52, as shown in the circle of **Fig.7**. The photo shows a replica of the pillar standing in the Museum near the site. These deep carvings are the most important petroglyphs of Barnénez. We see 3 petroglyphs of England/Scotland (the 3 triangles). Triangles like this are the usual convention for illustrating Birtain in early European petroglyphic rock maps. They can be seen in Twohig's book "The Megalithic Art of Western Europe". The curved lines of the triangles, like other curving lines in

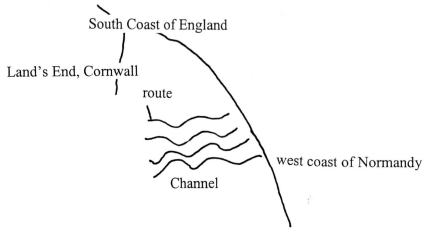

Fig.4

The crossing of the Channel (the waves), from the west coast of Normandy (right, below), to the south coast of England (above), to Land's End, Cornwall (left, above). The sailing distance is 3x0.5= 1.5 moiras= 90 NM.
(Stone C3, Grave C52, Barnénez, Ref.9, c.4800-4500 BC)

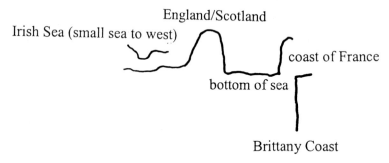

Fig.5

Center: A height profile of the English Channel, the coast of France, and the bottom of the sea, with indication of the Irish Sea and the Brittany coast.
(Stone C5, Grave A52, Ref.9, Barnénez, c.4800-4500 BC)

Megalithic sea-drawings, show that the people were very aware of the curvature of the Earth.

The lowest "Britain" triangle on the pillar must refer to the earliest cairn, Cairn A of c.4800 BC. At that time the explorations were dealing with the western coastal area around the southern latitudes of 50-54°N (South England and Ireland). Above it, another "Britain" triangle refers to more northern explorations, so now new Cairn B of c.4500 BC. These explorations covered the western coastal area around the northern latitudes of 55-59°N (Scotland). At the left side we see a boat, sailing along the East Coast of Ireland to the north. It appears that this boat is evidence that serious sailing along the shores of the Atlantic was already underway seven thousand years ago. It may be, when Ireland was explored, that the boat was seen as being west of Ireland (the triangle), so a new triangle needed to be added on the east, to show Scotland, and its islands to the north.

The third "Britain" triangle on the pillar, to the right, around the corner of the stone, also is a part of Cairn B. The explorations had by then extended to the Shetland Islands, at 60°N., the last latitude of Cairn B. Separated around the corner, its position on the stone symbolizes the out-of-sight Shetlands. Above the triangle is a Jacobstaff. This is a simple, wooden instrument to measure the latitude. The symbol is also called a "Mediterranean Sign". It starts appearing in petroglyphs of about 8500 BC. It was carved because people wanting to cross the Ocean from the Mediterranean (the vertical line), did not know which way to go. The left branch leads down the coast of Africa to Cape Verde, and the right branch runs up the coast of Iberia to Brittany. (For a thorough explanation of this, see our book How the SunGod Reached America c.2500 BC.) This sign is at the right side above the petroglyph of England/Scotland, suggesting the location of the Shetlands. This is as far north as these voyages had gone at this time.

Chamber A53
This chamber would be about features and landmarks at 53°N.

Chamber A54
The next grave A54 suggests the discovery of the Isle of Man, at 54°N.

Exploring Britain: Cairn B
The six passage graves 55-60 of the later built Cairn B correspond to the latitudes 55-60°N. These six latitudes along the west coast of the British Isles are explored again, more thoroughly. Cairn B is slightly broader than Cairn A, indicating the original exploration was broadened.

Chamber B55
Passage grave B55 celebrates the discovery of Ireland from the Kintyre Peninsula, Scotland, at 55°N. The tomb resembles the last passage graves of Cairn A, which are dealing with the west coast of Ireland, too.

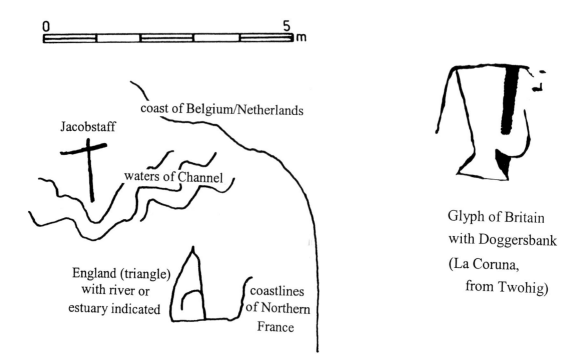

Fig.6

Above: Coast lines of Northern France, with a Jacobstaff/Mediterranean sign. Below: Map of England/Scotland, and the coast of Belgium/the Netherlands. To the right, is the "Thing" glyph from Iberian sites, that shows the Doggersbank as dry land.
(Stone C4, Grave C52, Ref.9, Barnénez, c.4800-4500 BC)

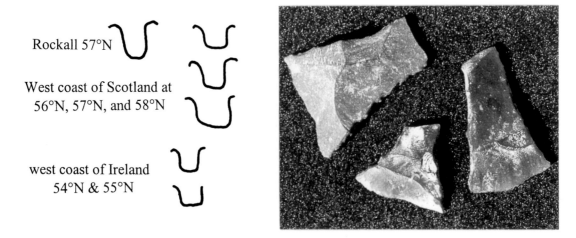

Fig.8

Left: Five crossing signs (height profiles). The discovery of the Islet of Rockall, at 57°N, the west coast of Scotland at 56°N, 57°N, and 58°N, and the west coast of Ireland at 54°N and 55°N.
Right: Three of the more than a dozen early Mesolithic-style axeheads found in B57.
(Stone R1, Grave B60, Refs.2&9, Barnénez, c.4100 BC)

Chambers B56, B57, & B58
At these latitudes are the Isle of Mull, the Hebrides, and Northern Scotland (Caithness). Three very nice small wide-bladed flint Mesolithic axes were found in B57. They are not chipped on the blades, so are clearly grave goods, very early ones **(Fig.8)**.

Chamber B59
Grave 59 has many big stones, and a big coverstone, because the newly discovered Orkney Islands, at 59°N, are considered particularly important, extending known land further north. Enormous monuments will be built there 1700 years later.

Chamber B60: "Crossing Signs"
The last passage grave has even more big stones, because of the importance given to the Shetland Islands, at 60°N. We think the many big stones indicate that this place is considered to be promising for making new discoveries in the west from here. This chamber has at its base large upright slabs, but it is almost 4 meters high. The discovery of the Shetland Islands, at 60°N, was the last important discovery before the construction of the Cairn of Barnénez (c.4800 BC).

Our other studies (Ref.11) show that later, the Islet of Rockall (57°N) (see **Map 1**) was discovered by expeditions from St. Kilda (58°N). Rockall is located 4 moiras= 240 NM west of the Outer Hebrides (Scotland). We think this discovery had a great influence on Barnénez. Suddenly, grave B57 became more important, so it appears that at that time the base of the burial chamber was strengthened at the inside with the large, upright slabs shown in Fig.1. Explorations of the sea west of Rockall were then undertaken to try to find more new land in the west. Probably the explorations looking for more lands west of Rockall lasted more than 5 centuries (c.4100-3600 BC). The many archeological finds in B57 (Ref.34) show prolonged use of this chamber.

On stone R1 **(Fig.8)** in this last chamber, petroglyphs are seen. These are Crossing Signs (height profiles), 5 in a column on the right, and one on the left. The right ones form a western coastline. The two lower signs form the west coast of Ireland at 54°N and 55°N, and the three upper signs form the west coast of Scotland at 56°N, 57°N, and 58°N. This petroglyph shows the newly discovered the Islet of Rockall, slightly above 57°N (the 6th crossing sign, at the left side above). (For more documentation on Rockall, see How the SunGod Reached America, c.2500 BC). The carving might have been made in grave B57, because Rockall is situated at 57°N. However, people rejected this location, because the Shetlands are situated at 60°N, and are big and important islands, also in this glyph, so it was carved in B60.

Discussion
The Cairn of Barnenez is a partially restored monument that is a popular tourist site, because it is conveniently close to Morlaix, and because it is so large. There is a bookstore and museum by the parking lot, close to the site. The site is impressive, and is very unusual, in having so many chambered passage graves in one Cairn complex. Scientifically, it is important because it is the earliest megalithic site that demonstrates the use of latitudes in its design. It is a shame that the public visiting the site each day are not

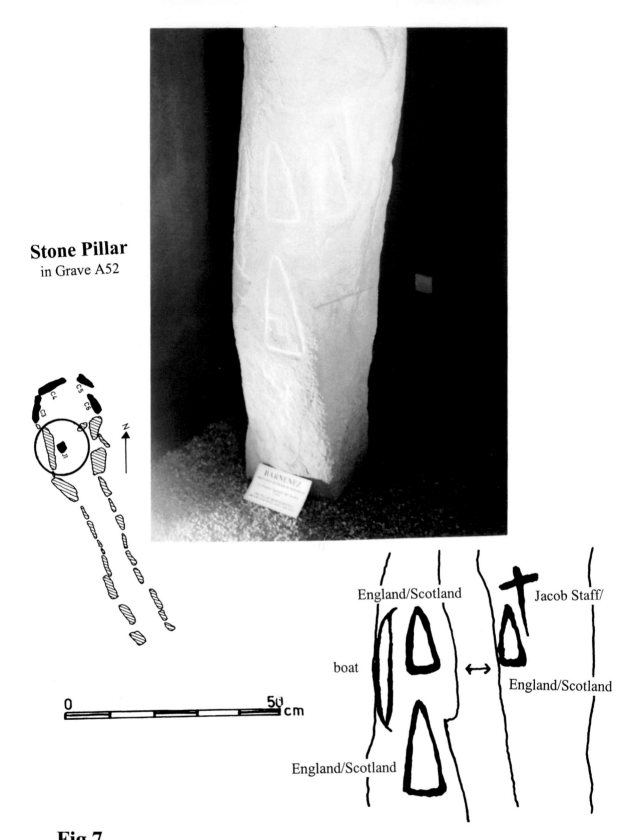

Stone Pillar
in Grave A52

England/Scotland

Jacob Staff/

boat

England/Scotland

England/Scotland

0 50 cm

Fig.7
Three triangles on stone pillar in A52, with groundplan showing the location of the pillar. Three coast maps of England/Scotland. Note the boat, sailing along the east coast of Ireland. (Photo by authors of Stone J1, in site museum, 2005, and petroglyphs from Twohig, Ref.9, Barnénez, c.4500 BC)

Photo 1
Dr. de Jonge taking a photo of the Cairn of Barnenez from the N, showing the NW face and NE end of the monument (May, 2005).

Photo 2
The west end of the monument, showing the four terraces, and larger stones at the bottoms of the first and second terraces, with the upper ones standing on end, like the prow of a ship. (Photo by authors, May, 2005)

Photo 3

View of the new portion of south side of the Cairn, showing the 4 terraces at the west end, and the entrances to some of the chambers. Chamber B57 can be seen through, while others show the entrances blocked off. The joint between Cairns A & B is visible at the right. (Photo by authors, May 2005)

Photo 4

Enlargement of the joint between the Cairns A & B. You can notice the darker rock of the older cairn A at the right (east half of the monument). (Photo by authors, May, 2005)

Immédiatement après la découverte, un premier débroussaillage de la butte
montrait que des murs de parement étaient décelables dès la surface.

Photo 5

1955 photo of the north side of the Monument, with the newer portion on the right,
showing removal of stone for road building. (Photo of Photo in Museum at the site)

Photo 6

Same view as Photo 5, showing removed section, same view, closer up. Dr. De Jonge's
left hand is pointing to the stone chamber of B59, with the stones of B60 beyond. The
two open chambers at the left in the photo, are B58 and B57 (seeing through to the
other side again). (Photo by authors, May, 2005)

yet able to associate the eleven northwest-facing passage graves with the explorations of the British Isles. This is the earliest of the big megalithic monuments commemorating oceanic sailing voyages of discovery, documenting the courage and curiosity of man. Soon, other discoveries off Iberia, such as Madeira, were to follow, which eventually led to the discovery of the Americas on the other side of the world.

References

1. Giot, P.-R., Barnénez, Ed. Ouest-France, C.N.M.H.S., 1991 (ISBN 2-7373-0933-6) (French)
2. Briard, J., Barnénez, Ed. J.-P. Gisserot, 2000 (ISBN 2-87747-499-2) (French)
3. Giot, P.-R., Prehistory in Brittany, Ed. JOS, 1995 (ISBN 2-85543-123-9)
4. Giot, P.-R., Aimer La Bretagne des Mégalith, Ed. Ouest-France, 1995 (ISBN 2-7373-1672-3) (French)
5. Briard, J., The Megaliths of Brittany, 1991 (ISBN 2-87747-063-6)
6. Les Dossiers de l'Archéologie, Bretagne Préhistorique, No 11 Juillet-Aout 1975 (French)
7. Masset, C., et Soulier, P., Allées Couvert at autres Monument Funéraires, Ed. Errance,1995 (ISBN 2-87772-104-3) (French)
8. Balfour, M., Megalithic Mysteries - An Illustrated Guide to Europe's Ancient Sites, Collins & Brown, 1992 (ISBN 1-85-585-3558)
9. Twohig, E. Shee, The Megalithic Art of Western Europe, Clarendon Press, Oxford, 1981
10. People of the Stone Age: Hunter-gatherers and Early Farmers, The Illustrated History of Humankind, Weldon Owen Pty Limited, McMahons Point, Australia (1995)
11. De Jonge, R.M., and Wakefield, J.S., How the SunGod Reached America c.2500 BC, A Guide to Megalithic Sites, 2002 (ISBN 0-917054-19-9). Available: MCS Inc., Box 3392, Kirkland, Wa 98083-3392, also CD
12. Website: www.howthesungod.com, De Jonge, R.M., and Wakefield, J.S.
13. De Jonge, R.M., and IJzereef, G.F., De Stenen Spreken, Kosmos Z & K, Utrecht/ Antwerpen, 1996 (ISBN 90-215-2846-0) (Dutch)
14. De Jonge, R.M., and Wakefield, J.S., "The Discovery of the Atlantic Islands", Migration & Diffusion, Vol.3, No.11, pgs.69-109 (2002)
15. De Jonge, R.M., and Wakefield, J.S., "The Discovery of the Islands in the Atlantic" (StoneC8,CairnT, Loughcrew, Ireland, c.3200 BC), Vol.13, No.81, January, 2009
16. De Jonge, R.M., and Wakefield, J.S., "The Passage Grave of Karleby, Encoding the Islands Discovered in the Ocean, c. 2950 BC", Migration & Diffusion, Vol.5, No.18, pgs.64-74 (2004)
17. Old World Civilizations, The Rise of Cities and States, The Illustrated History of Humankind, Weldon Owen Pty Limited, McMahons Point, Australia (1995)
18. Adams, B., and Cialowicz, K., Protodynastic Egypt, Shire Egyptology, Princes Risborough, 1997
19. Hart, G., A Dictionary of Egyptian Gods and Goddesses, Routledge, London, 1986 (ISBN 0-7102-0167-2)
20. Kemp, B.J., Ancient Egypt, Anatomy of a Civilization, London, Routledge, 1991
21. Rolt-Wheeler, F. Ed., The Science-History of the Universe, Current Literature Publishing Co., 1917
22. Wallis Budge, E.A., Osiris and the Egyptian Resurrection, 2 Vol., Dover Pub., N.Y., 1973 (ISBN 0-486-22780-4)
23. Wheeler, R.L., Walk Like An Egyptian, Allisone Press, 2000 (ISBN 1893774-21-X)
24. Ancient Egypt, National Geographic Maps, Supplement to the National Geographic Magazine, April, 2001.
25. Casson, L., Ships and Seafaring in Ancient Times, British Museum Press, 199
26. Wachsmann, S., Seagoing Ships and Seamanship in the Bronze Age Levant, College Station, Texas, 1998
27. Heyerdahl, T., The Ra Expeditions, George Allen & Unwin, London, 1971
28. Heyerdahl, T., The Tigris Expedition, George Allen & Unwin, London, 1983
29. Website: www.bbc.co.uk/history/timelines
30. Website: www.iomguide.com/castletown/events/billown-dig.php
31. Burl, A., Megalithic Brittany, Thames & Hudson, GDR, 1985
32. Gordon, C.H., Before Columbus: Links Between the Old World and Ancient America, New York, Chilton Book Co., 1971
33. Critchlow, K., Time Stands Still, St. Martin's Press, New York, 1982
34. La Musee de la Prehistorie Finisterienne, Station scientifique de L'Universite de Rennes, Penmarc'h, Brittany, France
35. Ashmore, P.J., Neolithic and Bronze Age Scotland, B. T. Batsford Ltd / Historic Scotland, London, 2000 (ISBN 0 7134 7531 5)

THE DISCOVERY OF THE ISLANDS IN THE ATLANTIC

(Stone C8, Cairn T, Loughcrew, Ireland, c.3200 BC)

R.M. de Jonge, drsrmdejonge@hotmail.com
J.S. Wakefield, jayswakefield@yahoo.com

Summary

The megalithic complex of Loughcrew is located at the Boyne River in County Meath, Ireland. On top of the central hill is the most important passage grave inside the large Cairn T. On the westermost Stone C8 of this grave are deeply carved, famous petroglyphs. The images are a unique form of picture writing, and are the most historically important and most beautiful megalithic petroglyphs of Europe. They describe the discoveries of the islands in the North Atlantic Ocean, including the dates of discovery. The petroglyphs were carved c.3200 BC, when the megalith builders gave up their efforts to cross Davis Strait, on the west side of Greenland.

Introduction

Our initial work on the C8 stone of Loughcrew started with a single page drafted by Dr. De Jonge ten years ago. Our book with a chapter about the site was published in 2002, and that same year, an article appeared in the Journal "Migration and Diffusion" under the title "The Discovery of the Atlantic Islands" (Ref.4). A photo of Dr. De Jonge explaining the site to a visitor is shown on the front cover of our book (Ref.1), and a photo of the best C8 glyphs is shown on the back cover, both in color. In the articles, our decipherment of the petroglyphs was supported by sensible decodings of more petroglyphs across the roofstone of the same chamber using the same methodology. We have made further progress in recent years, producing new articles while working on sites in Sweden ("The Passage Grave of Karleby", and "The Monument of Ales Stenar"), and near the Orkneys ("The Rings of Stenness, Brodgar, and Bookan", and "The Stone Rows of Tormsdale"). What we have learned from recent work has led us to revisit the Loughcrew material, and brought some new insights, which are presented in this article.

The megalithic complex of Loughcrew (Sliabh na Caillighe) is located at the Boyne River in County Meath, about 40 miles (60km) from the east coast of Ireland **(Fig.1)** (Refs.5-7). The oblong complex is spread over three hills, and extends from east to west over about 3 miles. Each of the hills has an altitude of c.800 meters. On their tops are a total of about 30 passage graves, which are situated inside separate cairns. They contain a total of 120 decorated stones. These cairns consist of mounds of smaller stones, which protect the more important passage graves. Loughcrew is situated at 54°N, 25 miles west of the famous complex of Newgrange of about the same age, which also comprises the cairns of Knowth and Dowth (Refs.8,9).

Megalithic monuments always have religious and geographic meanings (Refs.1-4). The passage graves of Loughcrew are "churches" of the SunGod Religion, which is known to have developed by the beginning of the Old Kingdom in Egypt (c.3200 BC). The round cairns represent the round Sun, symbol of the SunGod Ra **(Fig.2)**. They also resemble the "wheel of the law". For that reason they are also dedicated to Maat, the goddess of law and order in the universe. People wanted to spread this religion to the unknown back side of the planet Earth. That is why these constructions are located along the West Coast of

1

Photo 1 Dr. Reinoud de Jonge explaining the "Story of Loughcrew" inscription, July 8, 1998. The flashlight points to the discovery of the Azores in the middle of the Atlantic (c.3600 BC). (Cairn T, Loughcrew, Co. Meath, Ireland)

Western Europe, not far from the Ocean. The round cairns also represent the round Earth. Important passage graves with large cairns are found on both the central and western hills of Lough-crew. These graves point with their important burial chambers to the west.

The Azores

The 3 hills of Loughcrew represent the 3 island groups of the Azores (Refs.1,2). The eastern hill symbolizes the East Azores, 1 degree of latitude above the Strait of Gibraltar, at 36+1= 37°N. The central hill represents the Central Azores, 2° above Gibraltar, at 36+2= 38°N. And the western hill is the West Azores, 3° above Gibraltar, at 36+3= 39°N. Loughcrew itself is situated at the complementary latitude of the Strait of Gibraltar, at 90-36= 54°N.

The famous passage grave of Gavrinis in Brittany shows the Azores were discovered c.3600 BC (Refs.1-4,14,15). All carbon-dates of the Loughcrew-complex point to values in the second half of the 4th millennium BC, which is just after this date (Refs.2,10). The number of cairns on top of the hills increase from east to west, emphasizing the western orientation. The western hill possesses a very big passage grave to emphasize the importance of the West Azores. For 300 years the Azores were the westernmost islands of the then known world.

South Greenland

The 3 hills of Loughcrew also represent the 3 important latitudes of South Greenland (Ref.13). The eastern hill symbolizes Cape Farvel, the south point of Greenland, 1 degree of latitude above the Orkney Islands, at 59+1= 60°N. The central hill represents the SW Cape of Greenland, 2° above the Orkneys, at 59+2= 61°N. And the western hill is the West Coast of Greenland, 3° above the Orkney Islands, at 59+3= 62°N. The Orkneys, in the north of the British Isles, are situated at the complementary latitude of the northern Nile Delta, at 90-31= 59°N.

Cape Farvel and the SW Cape are discovered c.3250 BC (Refs.1-4). The central hill possesses an important passage grave in the large Cairn T, to emphasize the importance of the SW Cape of Greenland. From this Cape people thought they had the best chance to reach the unknown land at the back side of the Earth. The western hill has most of the passage graves to emphasize the important west coast of Greenland. On that location, at 62°N, people had to give up their efforts to cross Davis Strait. This information was also used in the design of the monument of Stonehenge I, in South England, of the same date (Refs.1-5,10,16,17). These monuments show that the prime social concern across the British Isles in 3200 BC was about the discovery of new lands to the west, and the question of what might be on the other side of the Earth.

Cairn T

The round Cairn T has a base diameter of 26 meters, and a height of almost 6 meters (**Fig.2**). It contains the most important passage grave of Loughcrew. The groundplan resembles the figure of a man lying on the ground: the SunGod (Fig.2). The 6 rooms of the grave encode Cape Farvel, the south point of Greenland, 6° above Loughcrew, at 54+6= 60°N. The grave is built of walls of 30 upright stones, which confirm the complementary latitude, at 90-30= 60°N. The tomb is oriented to the west, and the

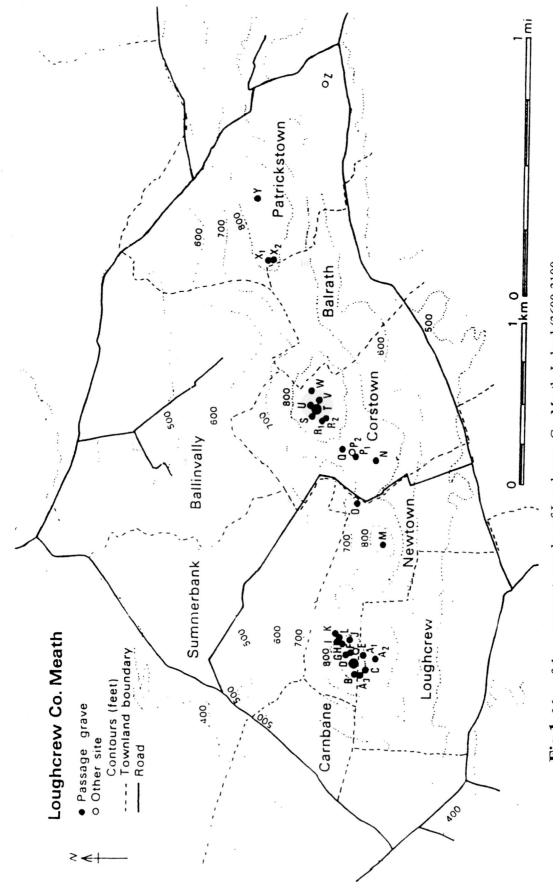

Fig.1 Map of the monument-complex of Loughcrew, Co. Meath, Ireland (3600-3100 BC) (Ref.5). The passage graves (cairns) lie on the tops of three hills, which resemble the East, the Central, and the West Azores, but also Cape Farvel, the SW Cape, and the West Coast of Greenland at 62°N.

westernmost chamber will be the most important one. And of course, within this chamber, the westernmost Stone C8 will be of special importance. In accord with this statement, the endstone C8 has been engraved in a surprisingly beautiful fashion **(Fig.3)** (Refs.6-10).

This is a story in ideograms, a quantitative picture writing, actually the oldest written history on Earth. It is the story of the attempts to reach the other side of the world - that is, to cross the Ocean (c.3200 BC). These images are a unique form of picture writing, and are the most historically important and most beautiful megalithic inscriptions of Europe **(Photo 1)**. As in many other examples of cave and stone art, the natural shape of the stone has been used as part of the work, the surface of the stone being an endless sea that is now called the North Atlantic Ocean. As drawn in detail in **Fig.3**, note the coast of Europe on the right, Greenland in the north, and the other, unknown side of the Ocean on the left. The proof of the story lies in the inscriptions themselves. Each figure has a number. In some figures, you count the petals of the "daisies", while in others, you count the waves, or the spaces between the lines. By adding the numbers, the actual and true degrees of latitude of the discovered landpoints are obtained, and all, except the oldest ones, are in historical order!

The Discovery of the Islands in the Ocean

This is the decipherment and translation of the "Story of Loughcrew", as it appears on Stone C8 in Cairn T, dated c.3200 BC **(Figs.3,4)**:

"A very long time ago, we travelled with **a sailing boat (A)** from the **Strait of Gibraltar (A)** along the coast to the south, and we discovered the **Canary Islands (B)**, at 28°N (A+B+G+G'= 6+6+8+8= 28). At about the same time we discovered near **Great Britain (G+G')**, the **Scilly Isles (G)** near Cornwall, at 50°N (A-H= 50), and due north of Loughcrew, in the west of Scotland, the **Outer Hebrides (G')**, at 58°N (A-H+G'= 50+8= 58)."

"Slightly later, we discovered at the latitude of the Outer Hebrides (G'), 4° (G'b) above **Loughcrew (G'a)**, at 54°N (A-H+G'a= 50+4= 54), the islets of **St. Kilda (G'b)**, at 58°N (A-H+G'a+G'b= 50+8= 58). At the same time, we discovered from the **Orkney Islands (J)**, at 59°N (A-H+J= 50+9= 59), the **Shetland Islands (J')**, 1° (J'= 1) above them, at 60°N (59+1= 60). This archipelago belongs to the British Isles (J' points to G+G'). In all cases discussed so far the sailing distances were less than 1 Egyptian Moira= 1°= 60 Nautical Miles (J'= 1)."

"The 3 **Western Canary Islands (Z'= 3)**, at 28°N (A+B+C+Z'+E+F= 6+6+3+3+9+1= 28), are located just below the **Eastern Canary Islands (B)**, at 29°N (A+B+D+E= 6+6+8+9= 29). Later, people also discovered the small **Selvagens Islets (Z)**, 2° (Z= 2) above the Western Canaries (Z'), at 30°N (28+2= 30). The sailing distance was 2 Moiras= 2°= 120 NM (Z= 2)." (Z and Z' were later carved: notice that they are oddly fitted into the layout, and more lightly carved, at a somewhat larger scale.)

"Later, we sailed from the **Canary Islands (B)** to **Cape Verde (C)** at 15°N (A+B+C= 6+6+3= 15), and further south to the Bissagos Islands (also C), at 11°N (C+D= 3+8= 11). We wanted to cross the North Atlantic Ocean (the surface area of the stone) at the

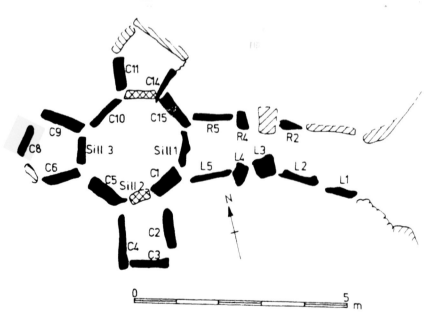

Fig.2 Photo of Cairn T, on the central hill of Loughcrew (Summer 1998), and groundplan of the passage grave in this Cairn (c.3200 BC) (Ref.5).

latitude of the holy Tropic of Cancer, at 23°N (A+B+C+D= 6+6+3+8= 23), in honor of the **SunGod Ra (D),** but we were not able to do so. This is the latitude of the Southern Egyptian Empire, the center of the Sunreligion, at 23°N. However, from Cape Verde we discovered the **Cape Verde Islands (also C)** at 15°N, 16°N, and 17°N (B+D+C1,2,3= 6+8+1+1+1). The sailing distance was 6 Moiras= 6°= 360 NM (previous glyph B= 6). But still we were not able to cross the Ocean."

"Later, we discovered from the Canary Islands (B), the two **Islands of Madeira (E and F)** at 33°N (A-F= 33). At about the same time we discovered from the British Isles (G), west of Scotland and its Outer Hebrides (G'), the islet of **Rockall (G''),** at 57°N (A-G+G'+G''= 41+8+8= 57). In both cases the sailing distances were 4 Moiras= 4°= 240 NM (previous glyphs G'a= G'b= 4). These islands gave a little bit hope that more land would be found (E and G'' are stars)."

"Then, after some time we discovered from **Madeira (E)** the three island groups of the **Azores (F, H, and I)** at 37°N, 38°N, and 39°N (Aa1,2,3+Ab+B+E+F+H+I= 1+1+1+3+6+9+1+9+8= 39= 1+1+1+36) (F has double meanings.) The sailing distance was 8 Moiras= 8°= 480 NM (previous glyph G= 8). The Azores consist of 9 islands (H= 9). We believe these islands must lie in the middle of the Ocean (H and I are glyphs of the Ocean with latitude lines, and vertical lines in the middle of them). But still we were not able to cross the Ocean!"

"Finally, we discovered from the **Orkneys (J)** at 59°N (A-H+J= 50+9= 59) the **Faroes (K)** at 62°N (A-I+K= 58+4= 62), and from the Faroes we reached the **SE coast of Iceland (L)** at 64°N (A-I+L= 58+6= 64) (Figs.3,4). Both sailing distances are 4 Moiras= 4°= 240 NM (G'a= G'b= 4). **Iceland (L)** lies like the Azores (H and I) in the middle of the Ocean (L resembles H and I). When we sailed around Iceland to its **NW peninsula (L',** the edge of L) at 66°N (64+L'= 64+2= 66), we reached a more western position than Rockall (the line from L' to G")."

"Thanks to the SunGod (M resembles D), we discovered from the **NW peninsula of Iceland (L'),** at 66°N, **Cape Holm (M)** at the SE coast of Greenland, which lies on the holy **Arctic Circle (M),** at 67°N (A-I+M= 58+9= 67). This is the northernmost line the Sun still shines at midwinter day. The sailing distance is 5 Moiras= 5°= 300 NM (the waves go up and down 5 times). We also reached Cape Brewster, the east cape of Greenland, 3° (the 3 waves) above Cape Holm (M), at 70°N (67+3= 70). Cape Holm (M) can be reached from **Cape Raven (M',** the 2 marks of M), at 69°N (67+2= 69), in the easiest way. The sailing distance from Iceland (L) to Cape Raven (M') is only 4 Moiras (the lowest wave goes up and down 4 times)."

"The islet of **Jan Mayen** (on top of the stone) is located 2° (**JM**= 2) above Cape Raven (M'), at 71°N (69+2= 71). It can be reached from Cape Brewster, at 70°N (the highest wave, near the edge), by sailing a distance of 4 Moiras= 4°= 240 NM (3+1= 4 spacings along the edge)." (JM and the different "Oot" glyph were carved 250 years later, as will be discussed below.)

"From Cape Holm (M) we went 1° (N= 1) to the south, to the **Eric the Rode Island (N),** at 66°N (67-1= 66). Next we went 6° (O+P= 1+5= 6) to the south to **Cape Farvel (P),**

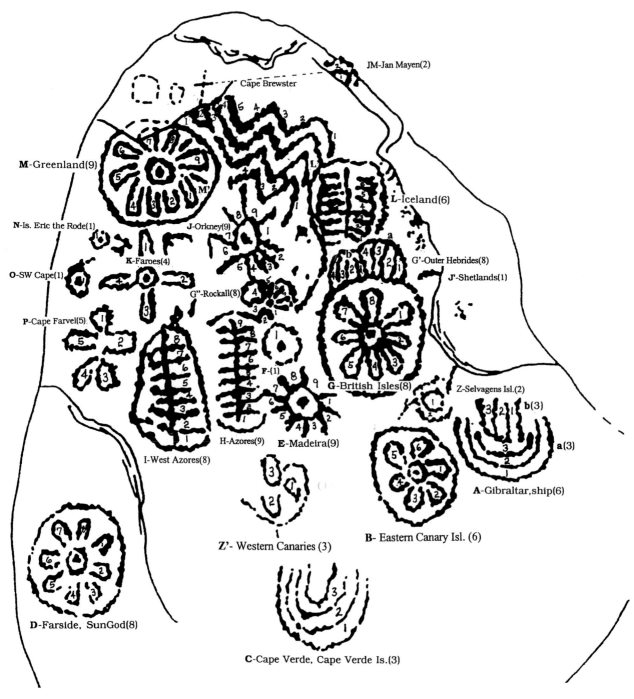

JM-Jan Mayen(2)

Cape Brewster

M-Greenland(9)

N-Is. Eric the Rode(1)

O-SW Cape(1)

K-Faroes(4)

J-Orkney(9)

L-Iceland(6)

G'-Outer Hebrides(8)

J'-Shetlands(1)

G"-Rockall(8)

P-Cape Farvel(5)

F-(1)

G-British Isles(8)

Z-Selvagens Isl.(2)

b(3)

a(3)

A-Gibraltar,ship(6)

H-Azores(9)

E-Madeira(9)

I-West Azores(8)

B- Eastern Canary Isl. (6)

Z'- Western Canaries (3)

D-Farside, SunGod(8)

C-Cape Verde, Cape Verde Is.(3)

Fig.3 The petroglyphs on Stone C8, with author's labels, geographic names, and corresponding numbers. The first glyph A is one of the oldest images of an ocean going sailing boat in the world. The last glyph P is a man, telling us that the megalith builders gave up their efforts to cross Davis Strait. (Cairn T, Loughcrew, Ireland, c.3200 BC) (Ref.5)

C8

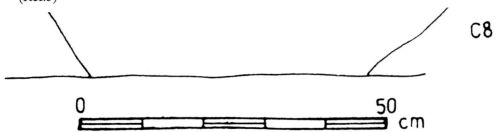

0   50 cm

the south cape of Greenland, at 60°N (66-6= 60). From there we went 1° (O= 1) to the north (P, head) to the **SW Cape (O)** at 61°N (60+O= 60+1= 61). But at these places we gave up **(P, the little man)**. We did not explore the west coast of Greenland above the latitude of the Faroes (K), at 62°N."

Dates of Discovery

Stone C8 also provides the dates of the discoveries in the Ocean **(Figs.3-5)**. The methodology used for date encoding turns out to be similar to date encodings first noticed at the Karleby Passage Grave in Sweden (Refs.11,12). Here at Loughcrew, we find similar results if each important petroglyph represents a century, or 100 years. To find these dates, we have to go back in time from Cape Farvel (P, the little man glyph in **Fig.3**). The waves on top of the stone do not count, because these represent water, and the little circles N and O (and also J') are too small. The vague inscriptions Z and Z'do not count either, because these glyphs were carved into the stone at a later date.

We start with the most recent discovery, shown at the top of the table in **Fig.5**. Looking back at the glyphs of **Fig.3**, notice that above the big daisy SunGod symbol for Cape Holm (M), there are the three "Oot" dotted glyphs, referred to earlier. We think the two circles represent the cycles of full centuries, and the horizontal stroke cut in half represents half a century, showing that the small islet of Jan Mayen (JM), situated above Iceland (L), was discovered 2½ centuries after the construction of this passage grave, so 250 years after c.3200 BC, which is c.2950 BC (Refs.11-13). This interpretation is supported by a similar date for this discovery from Karleby (Ref.11).

Carbon-dates indicate, both this passage grave of Loughcrew and Stonehenge I were built c.3200 BC (Refs.10,16,17), because at Cape Farvel, the south point of Greenland, (P), people gave up their efforts to cross the Ocean (Refs.1-4,18-20). A century earlier (M), c.3300 BC, Greenland was discovered at Cape Holm (M). Another century earlier (L), c.3400 BC, Iceland (L) had been discovered. A century prior to that (one glyph, K), c.3500 BC, the Faroes (K) were discovered. The late discovery of the Faroes, only 4 Moiras from the Orkneys, and located due north of Loughcrew, was caused by their northern, remote situation.

In the glyph of the Faroes (K), the NS and EW directions are carved in an unusually clear manner (see **Fig.3**). This may indicate that the Faroes were the first islands discovered with the aid of a magnetic compass (c.3500 BC). Megalithic petroglyphs of Chao Redondo (Portugal) and Liverpool (England) prove the use of such a device as early as c.2200 BC, and c.2700 BC, respectively (Ref.1).

Finally, another century earlier (I), c.3600 BC, the West Azores (I) were discovered (Refs.1-4). The passage grave of Gavrinis, in Brittany (c.3500 BC), through archaeological dating, as well as its design characteristics and petroglyphs, confirms the discovery of the Azores, one century earlier (Refs.5,14,15). It appears that the Gavrinis passage grave was built a century after the discovery, following careful exploration of all the coastal waters surrounding the islands, as illustrated in the petroglyphs.

The glyphs J, G", H, and E are attached to each other. Together with carving F in the center (or G), they form a group of 5 glyphs. The connection line from Iceland (L) to

Megalithic Explorations, Atlantic

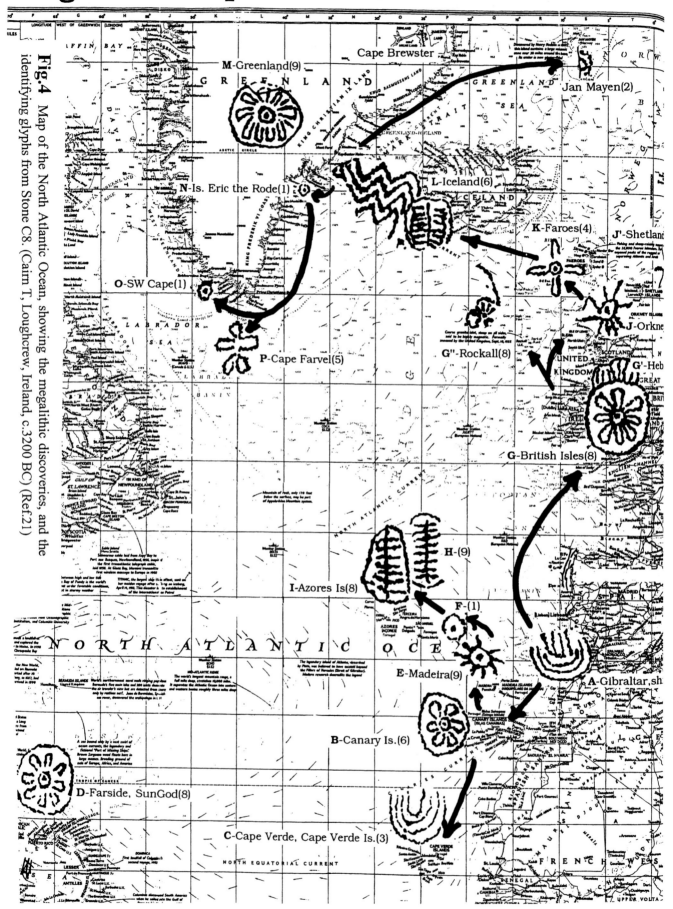

Cape Brewster

M-Greenland(9)

Jan Mayen(2)

L-Iceland(6)

K-Faroes(4)

J'-Shetland

N-Is. Eric the Rode(1)

J-Orkne

O-SW Cape(1)

G"-Rockall(8)

G'-Heb

P-Cape Farvel(5)

G-British Isles(8)

H-(9)

I-Azores Is(8)

F-(1)

E-Madeira(9)

A-Gibraltar,sh

B-Canary Is.(6)

D-Farside, SunGod(8)

C-Cape Verde, Cape Verde Is.(3)

Fig.4 Map of the North Atlantic Ocean, showing the megalithic discoveries, and the identifying glyphs from Stone C8. (Cairn T, Loughcrew, Ireland, c.3200 BC) (Ref.21)

Rockall (G") in this group indicates the discovery of this island, Rockall (G"), 5 centuries earlier, which is c.4100 BC. Porto Santo (F) was not attached to the group just mentioned, which indicates the special position of this little island. Madeira (E) is carved more to the right (east), so this island was discovered earlier than Rockall. The center of glyph G resembles the one of E. So, the Islands of Madeira (E and F) were discovered one century (G or F) earlier, c.4200 BC.

The shortest sailing distance to Madeira (E) equals the distance to Rockall (G"), 4 Moiras, so these islands were discovered at about the same time. The tablet of Paredes, Spain, as well as the petroglyphs of Dissignac, Brittany, confirm the fairly close discovery dates of Madeira and Rockall (Refs.1-5). In Dissignac, both discoveries are shown with a single glyph.

The 4 remaining glyphs D, B, A, and C give the discovery of the Cape Verde Islands (C), as well as the Bissagos Islands (also C), 4 centuries earlier, c.4600 BC. The passage grave of Kercado, Brittany (carbon dated to c.4500 BC) confirms the discovery of the Cape Verde Islands (C), one century earlier, c.4600 BC (Refs.1-5). The Bissagos Islands are located offshore Guinee-Bissau, and they form the important SW Cape of North Africa. Dissignac confirms the simultaneous discoveries of the Cape Verde Islands and the Bissagos Islands in a single glyph (Refs.1,5).

The vague glyphs Z and Z' are both different from all the others. For this reason they were probably carved in the stone at a later date. Apparently, the carver was irritated that the small Selvagens Islets (Z), situated above the Canary Islands (B and Z', the scratch from B to Z), had not been included on the stone. Note, that the 3 circles in Z' represent the correct geographic locations of the 3 islands of the Western Canaries (Z'), southwest of Madeira (E).

Today, the main Selvagens islet has a diameter of less than 3 miles (5km). The date of discovery is calculated just like the date of the Shetlands (J') (the top scratch from the edge to Z resembles J'), as will be explained. The Selvagens Islets (Z) were discovered 2 centuries (Z and Z') earlier than the Cape Verde Islands (C) (the scratch from Z' points to C), which is c.4800 BC.

The Early Discoveries: Orkneys, Canaries, and Shetlands

Up to here, the dates over 15 centuries, between 3200 BC and 4600 BC, have been given by the 15 original petroglyphs. What remains are the discoveries of the Shetland Islands (J') near the Orkneys, and of the Canary Islands (B) near Madeira. Between the inscriptions of the Orkneys (J) and Madeira (E) are 4 simple glyphs J, G", F, and E lying on a straight line. These are clearly less beautiful glyphs compared to the others. So it appears these do not play a role for the early datings.

Of the remaining 15-4= 11 nice carvings, there are 9 large glyphs, indicating the discovery of the Shetland Islands (J'), 9 centuries before the Cape Verde Islands, so c.5500 BC. The Shetlands are located 43 NM (Nautical Miles) from the Orkneys. It appears, that the islets of St. Kilda (G'b), with a maximal diameter of 2 miles, located 32 NM west of the Outer Hebrides, were discovered as well.

Fig.5
Date Table: The Discovery of the Islands of the Atlantic Ocean
(Stone C8, Cairn T, Loughcrew, Ireland, c.3200 BC)

kind of time glyphs	number of time glyphs	corresponding number of years	corresponding geographic glyph	island or location	date of discovery	comment
"Oot"	2.5	+250	JM	Jan Mayen	c.2950 BC	carved 250 years later
P & O	reference	reference	P & O	S & SW Capes of Greenland	c.3200 BC	date of the monument
M	1	-100	M	Cape Holm, Greenland	c.3300 BC	
L	1	-100	L	Iceland	c.3400 BC	
K	1	-100	K	Faroes	c.3500 BC	
I	1	-100	I	(West) Azores	c.3600 BC	
J,G",H,E, and F or G	5	-500	G"	Rockall	c.4100 BC	
G or F	1	-100	E and F	Madeira and Porto Santo	c.4200 BC	
D,B,A,C	4	-400	C C	Cape Verde Islands Bissagos Islands	c.4600 BC	
[Z',Z]	[2]	[-200]	[Z]	[Selvagens Islets]	[c.4800 BC]	carved later
A,B,C,D,G,H, I,L,M	9	-900	J' G'b	Shetlands St. Kilda	c.5500 BC	large glyphs
K,P	2	-200	B G G'	Canaries Scilly Isles Outer Hebrides	c.5700 BC	smaller glyphs
E,F,G",J	4	-400	J	Orkneys	c.6100 BC	smallest glyphs
all	15	-1500	J'/Ga	Isle of Man Ireland	c.7600 BC	
A,B,C,D,G,H, I,L,M	9	-900	J'/G	England/ Scotland	c.8500 BC	large glyphs

The 2 remaining small glyphs K and P give the discovery of the Canary Islands (B), 2 centuries earlier, c.5700 BC (Refs.1-5,11,12). The Canaries are located 49 NM from the African coast. It appears, that the Scilly Isles (G), located 22 NM from Cornwall, and the Outer Hebrides (G'), 12 NM from the island of Skye, Scotland, were discovered as well.

These five archipelagos had been discovered much earlier than all the others, because they contain islands close to the coast. The shortest sailing distances to the Shetlands and to the Canaries are only c.1 Moira= 1°= 60 NM (the scratch J'). Halfway to the remote Shetlands is a small islet, Fair Isle (with a diameter of about 3 miles), which facilitates the crossing. However, the mountainous Canary Islands can be seen from the African coast on a clear day, and probably due to their closeness to the Mediterranean, and warm seas, they were explored at an earlier date. The 2 glyphs A and B at the right side of the stone, confirm the discovery of the Canaries (B), 2 centuries before the Shetlands (J').

Loughcrew shows, the first important discovery on the Atlantic was the Canary Islands (B), at 28°N (A+B+G+G'= 6+6+8+8= 28). However, this first latitude encoding points to the carving of the Shetlands (J'), NE of the British Isles (G+G'), which appears to be the second important discovery. The simple carving J' of the Shetlands also resembles one of the beams of the glyph of Madeira (E). This island had been discovered after the Canaries (B), like the Shetlands (J'), which confirms the order again, through comparison of the similar shapes.

The dates of all these discoveries, as shown in **Fig.5**, are the same as the dates found in the passage grave of Karleby (Falbygden, Sweden, c.2950 BC) (Refs.11,12). Significantly, those time encodings were also in centuries. All these dates have an uncertainty of half a century, or 50 years. However due to various reasons, like the monument construction date, the uncertainty may be slightly higher.

The 4 glyphs E, F, G", and J, which are along a straight line, have not been used in the datings discussed above. However, Loughcrew suggests the discovery of the Orkney Islands (J), 4 centuries before the discovery of the Canaries, which is c.6100 BC. The prominent position of glyph J on the stone justifies this calculation. The Orkneys are located only 5 NM from mainland Scotland, in the north of the British Isles. They are clearly visible on a normal day. To our knowledge, there are no other megalithic monuments or petroglyphs which report the very early discovery of this important archipelago, where huge megalithic monuments were later built (Ref.13).

England and Ireland

The date of discovery of the Shetland Islands (J') was determined by the 9 large glyphs. This use of large glyphs indicates this small J' is important. This is because J' also represents the shortest crossing from Scotland (the Kintyre Peninsula) to Ireland, at 55°N, 1° (J'=1) above Loughcrew (Ga), at 54°N (A-H+Ga=54). The edge of the stone to which J' is attached represents Scotland, with J' running west. If we add all the glyphs, they total 15, perhaps indicating the 15 centuries prior to the discovery of the Orkneys, which is c.7600 BC. This date matches the date for the discovery of Ireland and the Isle of Man in the current literature of c.7500 BC (Refs.22,23).

Glyph J' may also represent the crossing of the Strait of Dover, at 51°N, 1° (J'=1) above

7

the Scilly Isles/Cornwall (G), at 50°N (A-H). Here, the edge of the stone represents the continent of Europe, and G is England. Note that the petals of G are carved so that they contact the central circle with the dot in it. This is different from the other "daisy" glyphs, showing that something is different about this one. Since J' (1) points to G (8), this suggests that G (England) was discovered 1+8= 9 centuries before Ireland was reached, or c.8500 BC, which matches the literature (Ref.22).

Discussion

Glyph A is one of the oldest images of an ocean going sailing vessel in the world. Note, that the innermost hull line has dots at both ends of the deck **(Fig.3)**. This is an indication, that the expeditions may have been carried out with papyrus boats, as suggested by Thor Heyerdahl. The seaworthiness of these boats is based on the washing-through principle. On board water runs easily back to the sea, through and around the bundles. Apparently, both ends of the boat were attached with ropes to the top of the mast, preventing the papyrus bundles from sagging in the waves (Refs.18-20). It is known that the later built Egyptian sewn wood planked vessels were also strengthened by this technique.

The 9 beautiful glyphs in Loughcrew are carried out in three types: the boats A and C, the sails H, I, and L, and the Suns B, D, G, and M. These 3 types refer to the 3 ways they thought it might be possible to cross the Ocean to the Realm of the Dead in the west (glyph D, behind a natural relief of the stone).

In view of the north-eastern winds and currents, a possible route to the other side starts at the Cape Verde Islands (boat C). Only 2 glyphs (A and C) of this type were made, because this is the easternmost departure point, appearing to be most difficult. Probably any early exploratory vessels taking this route were not heard from again, because a route back was unknown at this date. The wind and current patterns of the Earth were not understood yet.

Because of the winds and currents from the west, the West Azores (sail I) were very difficult, but due to their apparent mid-ocean location, they were considered important for a possible return route. It is thought that they had been discovered by sailors reaching northwest from Madeira, trying to find winds to take them home to Brittany. A total of 3 sails (H, I, and L) were made (one more than the previous type), because the West Azores are located west of the Cape Verde Islands.

Finally, in view of its very western situation, Greenland (the Sun M) is most promising for reaching the unknown land at the back side of the Earth (America, D). A total of 4 Suns (B, D, G, and M) were made (one more again), because Greenland was by far the westernmost land of the then known world.

Stone C8 in Loughcrew shows that the attempts to cross the Atlantic Ocean lasted from c.5700 BC to c.3200 BC, which is 2500 years. Sailing the Ocean started c.6000 BC, which is an incredible 8000 years ago. The discovery of the Azores was relatively early (c.3600 BC), because of its favourable latitude, to the Strait of Gibraltar. The discovery of the Faroes was relatively late (c.3500 BC), because of its remote situation, north of the British Isles. The west coast of Greenland was reached c.3250 BC. Fifty years later, people gave up their efforts to cross Davis Strait, c.3200 BC. This was a firm decision of the megalith builders, illustrated by the little man glyph P. The discovery of America via the Atlantic did not happen earlier than c.2500 BC, which is 700 years after this decision (Ref.1).

The megalithic petroglyphs of Dissignac, France, illustrate that it was decided that it might be less risky to extend explorations to the east (Ref.1). These glyphs include a coast map of Australia (c.2700 BC), and stylized coast maps of the Americas (c.2600 BC). Recent discoveries of huge pyramids constructed at Caral, Peru, carbon-dated to c.2700 BC, illustrate first megalithic contact on the Pacific side of the Americas, despite all the early voyages of discovery in the Atlantic.

References

1. De Jonge, R.M., and Wakefield, J.S., How the SunGod Reached America c.2500 BC, A Guide to Megalithic Sites, 2002 (ISBN 0-917054-19-9). Available: MCS Inc., Box 3392, Kirkland, Wa 98083-3392, also on CD

2. Website: www.howthesungod.com, De Jonge, R.M., and Wakefield, J.S.

3. De Jonge, R.M., and IJzereef, G.F., De Stenen Spreken, Kosmos Z & K, Utrecht/ Antwerpen, 1996 (ISBN 90-215-2846-0) (Dutch)

4. De Jonge, R.M., and Wakefield, J.S., "The Discovery of the Atlantic Islands", Migration & Diffusion, Vol.3, No.11, pgs.69-109 (2002)

5. Twohig, E. Shee, The Megalithic Art of Western Europe, Clarendon Press, Oxford, 1981

6. Twohig, E. Shee, Irish Megalithic Tombs, Shire Archaeology, 1990 (ISBN 0-7478-0094-4)

7. Eogan, G., Knowth, and the Passage Tombs of Ireland, Thames and Hudson, 1986.

8. O'Sullivan, M., Megalithic Art in Ireland, Country House, Dublin, 1993 (ISBN 0-946172 –36-6)

9. Balfour, M., Megalithic Mysteries - An Illustrated Guide to Europe's Ancient Sites, Collins & Brown, 1992 (ISBN 1-85585-3558)

10. Dames, M., Mythic Ireland, Thames & Hudson, London, 1992 (ISBN 0-500-27872-5)

11. De Jonge, R.M., and Wakefield, J.S., "The Passage Grave of Karleby, Encoding the Islands Discovered in the Ocean, c. 2950 BC", Migration & Diffusion, Vol.5, No.18, pgs.64-74 (2004)

12. De Jonge, R.M., and Wakefield, J.S., "The Passage Grave of Karleby", to be published.

13. De Jonge, R.M., and Wakefield, J.S., "The Rings of Stenness, Brodgar & Bookan, Celebrating the Discovery of South Greenland, c.3200 BC", to be published

14. Briard, J., The Megaliths of Brittany, 1991

15. Le Roux, C-T., Gavrinis, Ed. Gisserot, 1995 (French)

16. Richards, J., Stonehenge, English Heritage, 1992

17. Atkinson, R.J.C., Stonehenge, 1979

18. Casson, L., Ships and Seafaring in Ancient Times, British Museum Press, 1994

19. Wachsmann, S., Seagoing Ships and Seamanship in the Bronze Age Levant, College Station, Texas, 1998

20. Heyerdahl, T., The Ra Expeditions, George Allen & Unwin, London, 1971

21. "Atlantic Ocean", map by National Geographic Society, Dec. 1955

22. Website: www.bbc.co.uk/history/timelines

23. Website: www.iomguide.com/castletown/events/billown-dig.php

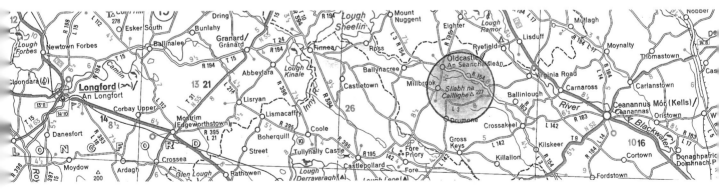

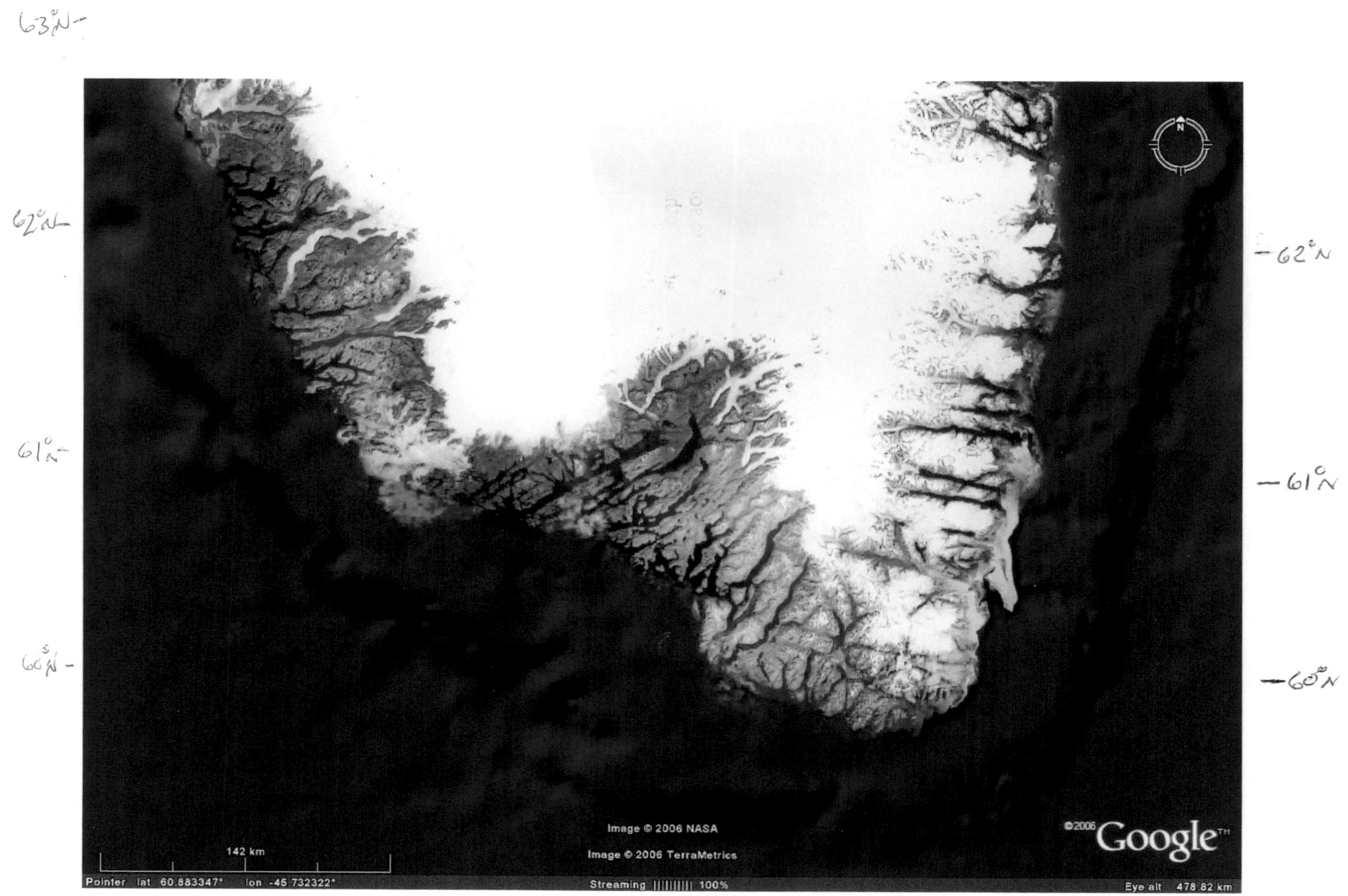
63°N
62°N
61°N
60°N
62°N
61°N
60°N
Image © 2006 NASA
Image © 2006 TerraMetrics
©2006 Google™
142 km
Pointer lat 60.883347° lon -45.732322°
Streaming ||||||||| 100%
Eye alt 478.82 km

THE RINGS OF STENNESS, BRODGAR & BOOKAN
Celebrating the Discovery of South Greenland
(Orkney Islands, Scotland, c.3200 BC)

R.M. de Jonge, drsrmdejonge@hotmail.com
J.S. Wakefield, jayswakefield@yahoo.com

Summary

The Stones of Stenness and the Ring of Brodgar are the largest of the many prehistoric ruins in the Orkneys, and among the premier megalithic remains in the world. The Orkney Islands were the jump-off point from coastal Europe to other islands being discovered in the north as the people looked for the home of the SunGod in the west. These two henge monuments, dated c.3200 BC, represent Greenland's South and Southwest Capes. The Ring of Stenness was originally built of 12 stones, also to commemorate the discovery of a new island in the north, Jan Mayen, 12° of latitude above the Orkneys. The larger Brodgar Ring was originally built of 61 stones to celebrate the area around the SW Cape of Greenland, at 61°N. Today, the reduced number of stones encode the later crossing (c.2500 BC) from West Greenland to Baffin Island.

Introduction

The Orkney Islands are located in the north of Great Britain at a latitude of 59°N (**Fig.1**). The small archipelago has a diameter of about 30 miles (50km), and the southerly shores are situated 10 miles (16km) north of the Scottish mainland, at the other side of the passage called the Pentland Firth. The Orkneys (and the Shetlands further north) are the most north-western islands of Western Europe. Most of the megalithic monuments are located on the largest island, called "Mainland". These three Rings are situated on one of the most beautiful megalithic sites in the world, a narrow neck of land called the Ness of Brodgar (**Fig.2**). This is an isthmus between the Loch (Lake) of Harray on the northern shore, having fresh water, and the Loch of Stenness on the south-western shore, with brackish water. The lochs are connected by a short stream of fresh water under the Bridge of Brodgar (**Fig.4a**), and situated about 4 miles NE of the town of Stromness (**Figs.1,2**). Since 1999, the Rings have been protected by the World Heritage List of UNESCO, because of "their outstanding universal value" (Ref.5).

The Stones of Stenness

Originally, the Ring of Stenness had 11 to 12 huge stones set in a circle, with a diameter of 32 meters (105 feet) (see **Fig.3**) (Refs.4-12). Today it has only 3 of the big stones, which range in height from 4.8m to 5.7m, one smaller bent menhir of 2m, and a small group of 3 stones inside the Ring. The three standing flagstones are huge, and only 30 to 40cm thick, which is surprisingly thin. The tops of the largest stones are angled about 45°. At the north side of the circle is the shorter "elbow stone", with the top half bent to the left, when seen from the center of the ring (**Fig.3a**). This special stone appears to be quite squarely and intentionally cut.

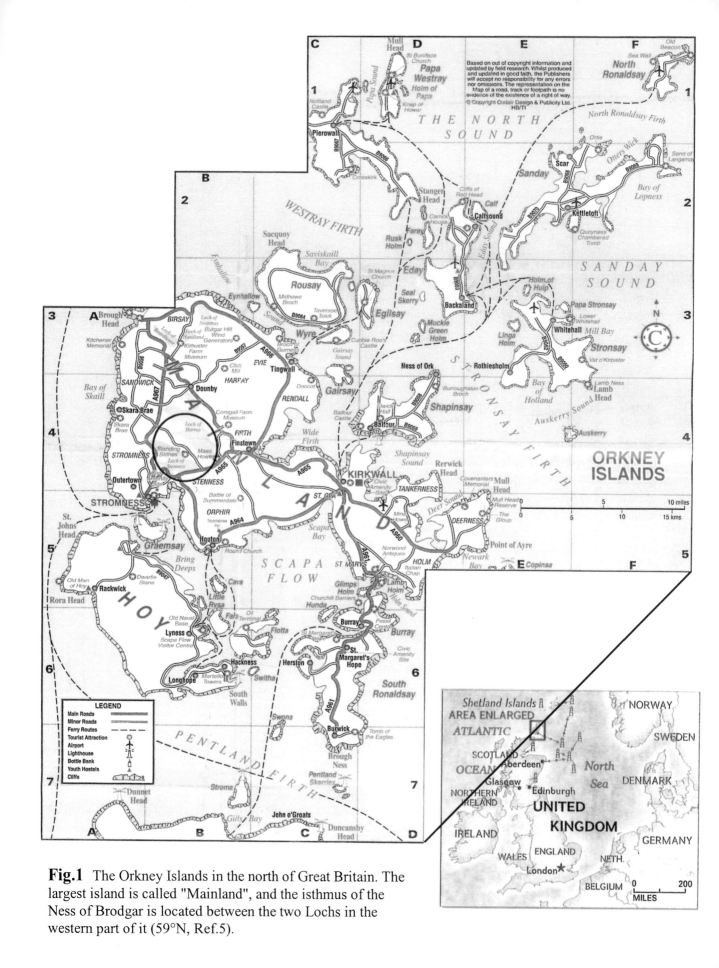

Fig.1 The Orkney Islands in the north of Great Britain. The largest island is called "Mainland", and the isthmus of the Ness of Brodgar is located between the two Lochs in the western part of it (59°N, Ref.5).

Around the stones was a ring-shaped ditch with a diameter of 50 meters, originally 6m wide and 2m deep, with an outer wall, no longer visible. About 2,000 cubic meters of solid sandstone bedrock had to be removed to shape the ditch. There was only one entrance and exit, on the northern side of the monument. Organic material for radiocarbon dating the site, which was obtained from the ditch, provided a date of c.3000 BC (Refs.4-8). The bottom of the ditch was found to be beneath the water table and was therefore probably originally filled with water, apparently a deliberate element of the design. However, both ditch and outer bank are barely visible today.

The 12 original flagstones are indicated in their correct positions in the center of **Fig.3**, as revealed by the clumps of "setting stones", once crammed around the base of these big stones. Number 12 may have been a small stone. Small excavations in the Ring in 1973 revealed a stone lined rectangular hearth at the center (**Fig.3**), with burned bone, charcoal, and grooved ware (early) pottery (Refs.4,16,17). It also contained a quantity of "cramp", which is burned seaweed, still used as fuel in the Orkneys. About halfway out from the center is the group of three "altar stones", that were re-erected in their original positions (**Fig.3a**). Other "holes" full of debris for stone or wood uprights have been discovered nearby. The whole area has been subject to small archaeological projects, but no major excavations have been done.

Opposite the northern exit, at a distance of about 200 meters from the Ring of Stenness, was a Neolithic settlement with a large ceremonial building (in part, **Fig.4b**) called "Barnhouse Village" (Refs.4,5,9-12). It is located on the shore of the Loch of Harray. Archaeological excavation has revealed the remains of about 15 free-standing Neolithic buildings. Each house had a central hearth and beds set against the walls. The site seems to have been in use for about 400 years from around 3200 BC. Approximately 30 meters to the east, a menhir near the loch holds up a wire fence (**Fig.4c**), illustrating the extent of the undocumented richness of the site.

About 120 meters NW of the Stones of Stenness, at the southern edge of the Bridge of Brodgar, stands the magnificent Watch Stone (**Fig.4a**) (Refs.4,5,9-12). This menhir is awesome, the largest standing stone in the Orkneys, 5.6m (18 ft) tall, 1.5m wide, but only 40cm thick. Before 1930, a socket for another stone was recorded close to it during roadwork.

About 140 meters NNW of the Ring, toward the loch, stood a "holed" menhir, 2.5m high and 1m wide, called the Odin Stone (**Fig.2**). It was destroyed by a tenant farmer in 1814, angry that visitors to the site were damaging his fields. "As late as the 18th century, men and girls plighted their troth by clasping hands through the hole, and a contemporary report stated that "after this they proceeded to Consummation without further Ceremony" (Ref.14). Recent excavations which located the Odin Stone pit revealed another, similar pit earby.

The Ring of Brodgar

This Ring is located on the isthmus, about 1 mile (1.5km) WNW of Stenness (**Fig.2**). It is one of the largest henges (stone circles with ditch and wall) of Western Europe (**Fig.5a**)

Fig.2 The isthmus of the Ness of Brodgar (59°N, Mainland, Orkneys) between the Loch of Harray in the north (fresh), and the Loch of Stenness in the SW (brackish). The isthmus symbolizes the narrow south coast of Greenland: The Stones of Stenness are Cape Farvel, at 60°N, the Ring of Brodgar is the SW Cape, at 61°N, and the Ring of Bookan is the West Coast of Greenland, at 62°N (c.3200 BC, 1 grid-length= 1km, Ref.25).

(Refs.4-12). The stones are arranged in an impressive, nearly perfect circle. It measures 104 meters (340 feet) across, the same as the two Avebury inner rings in South England (Ref.15). It has been reported that, originally, there may have been 60 stones. However, in May 2004 we visited the site, and after close inspection we found evidence for correcting this number to 61 stones. It seems the number of stones was greatly reduced a long time ago. After archaeological restoration in 1908, the Ring was said to have a total of 27 menhirs, 23 of these standing, and 4 lying down.

The upright stones of Brodgar vary in height from 2.1m (7 ft) to a maximum of 4.6m (15 ft) (**Figs.5,6**). Like the Stones of Stenness, the thin stones have pointed tops at 45°, and are oriented with one of their flat sides facing the center of the ring. The slabs are long planks split from local sedimentary flagstone. There is quarry a mile to the north near Brokan Farm, where the stones may have been removed (Ref.8). Some of the tall slabs might have been split from the sandstone bedrock with wooden wedges when the ditch was cut (Refs.4,5). The henge of Brodgar is not scientifically dated yet, although most archaeologists estimate its date between 2500 and 2000 BC (Refs.5-8).

Around the stones is a vast circular ditch with a diameter of 121 meters, 9m wide, and originally 3.5m deep. It was battered and hacked out of the sandstone bedrock with great labor. The broken rock, with a volume of 12,000 cubic meters, was heaped onto a surrounding outer bank, which has since long disappeared. Renfrew, who dug a 3 foot section across it, has calculated that at least 80,000 man-hours went into the original construction, equal to three months of continuous digging by 100 laborers (Ref.8). Today, the ditch is clearly visible, though somewhat reduced in depth (**Fig.5**). Across the ditch are SE and NW causeways with azimuths of 38°SE and 38°NW, respectively. It is a pity that an accurate groundplan drawing of the site is not available. From the aerial photo in **Fig.5**, the causeways can be seen to be parallel with the road, running NW up the peninsula. The interior of the Ring, thickly covered with heather, has never been excavated (Ref.5).

The Ring of Brodgar is not quite on the crest of the ridge, which it could have been, had the builders just moved the Ring about half its diameter to the west. Instead, it all rests on the slightly east-facing slope. The circle presents therefore a dramatic face to the rising morning sun. This strikes the visitor as clearly intentional. Folktales describe the Ring of Brodgar as the "Temple of the Sun", while the Stones of Stennes form the "Temple of the Moon" (Refs.4,9-12). There are at least thirteen burial mounds near the Ring, two being very large, while nine are in a group south of it (Ref.5). Some of these were probably added later onto the holy ground around the Ring. Four big Neolithic passage graves are located within a radius of 7 miles (11km), which illustrates the importance of the whole area.

To the ESE, 137 meters from the edge of Brodgar, stands the Comet Stone (**Fig.8b**), 1.7m high, 0.7m wide, and 30cm thick (Refs.5,11). It is on a low oval platform measuring about 14 meters across, and 0.8m high. On the same mound and at both sides of the Comet Stone are the stumps of two other stones.

Fig.3 Center: Groundplan of the Stones of Stenness, representing Cape Farvel, Greenland (c.3200 BC, Ref.4). Photos May 2004: (a)= view W: The "altar stones" showing a narrow passage to more land in the west. The "elbow stone" shows the sailing route from Cape Farvel to SW Cape. (b)= view SW. (c)= view NNW. (d)= view SSW: The 4 stones encode the crossing from Greenland to Baffin Island at 59+4= 63°N.

The Ring of Bookan

Another massive earthwork is located 1 mile (1.6km) NW of Brodgar, called the Ring of Bookan (**Fig.2**) (Refs.5,9-12). It consists of an enclosing ditch, 13m across and 2m deep, surrounding an oval raised platform, measuring 45 by 38 meters. The Ring overlooks the Loch of Stenness, as shown in the photo of **Fig.8a**. There are no stones on the platform and no causeway. For that reason, it is not included in tours, and unnoticed by visitors.

These three rings are sited in a biologically rich area, with rich surrounding agricultural lands, and a very near natural harbor. This would have been an obvious and spectacular site for early occupation by a maritime people. It is known from Greenland ice core studies that in Neolithic times the climate was warmer. Physical evidence for this has come through archaeological excavations of Orkney sites. "Wheat as well as barley was grown by the people of Skara Brae, whereas the farmers of recent times have not risked a wheat crop, preferring hardier barley and oats. Many bones of the corkwing wrasse were found in the chambered tomb at Quanterness, and a red sea bream was found in the tomb at Midhowe. These are both fish which are rare in such northern latitudes today" (Ref.13). Today, the land is remote, and used for farming and protected anchorage in the Scapa Flow naval harbor. Its people have gone all over the world, many recruited as employees of the Hudson Bay Company in Canada. The walrus herds are long gone, but curlews, oystercatchers, and other seabirds nest in the fields, the ruins, the seacliffs, and sand dunes along the beaches. Seals abound. The near-absence of trees and new construction have helped preserve the many ancient sites.

The Sun Religion

Barnhouse Village was populated between 3200 and 2800 BC, and the nearby Stones of Stenness are dated c.3000 BC. These dates coincide with the start of the Egyptian civilization. We know that the megalith builders were followers of the Sun Religion, which became most developed during the Old Kingdom in Egypt, and was centered there, as shown by encoded latitude references to it in many megalithic monuments (Refs.1-3). Stenness, Brodgar, and Bookan were originally henges – stone circles with circular ditches and outside walls. Let us first look at their religious and geographic meanings.

These henges are located at the west coast of Western Europe, close to the Ocean. That is because the megalith builders wanted to spread the Sun Religion to the unknown back side of the planet (Refs.1-3). So in the largest sense, the henges symbolized the circular Earth. The inner circular platforms represent the well known Old World, and the ditches around them, which may have been filled with water, represent the huge Atlantic Ocean. The meaning of the outer walls is interesting, because these would represent newly discovered land in the west, on the other side of the Ocean.

The henges have the shape of the circular Sun, dedicated to the Egyptian SunGod Ra. In the hierarchy below this supreme God were two other gods, the sungod Horus and the moongod Osiris. The circular outer walls of these monuments were dedicated to the sungod Horus, and the inner circular platforms were dedicated to the moongod Osiris. The ancient Egyptians believed that their kings and pharaohs were earthly substitutes or representatives of these two gods (like the Pope in our time). Brodgar was called the

Fig.4 a) The Watch Stone (5.6m) near Loch Stenness at the start of the Bridge of Brodgar. (b) A portion of Barnhouse Neolithic Village north of the Stones of Stenness near Loch Harray. (c) A menhir 100 feet east of Barnhouse Village. (Photos May 2004)

a

b

c

"Temple of the Sun", and Stenness was called the "Temple of the Moon", illustrating the influence of these two gods. However, the whole circular henge also resembles the "wheel of the law". For that reason it is also dedicated to Maat, the goddess of law and order in the universe.

Cape Farvel, Greenland

Northwest of the Orkneys, the Faroes and Iceland are located. These islands had been discovered c.3400 BC (Refs.1-3). After Iceland, Neolithic people, following the holy Arctic Circle, at 67°N, discovered Cape Holm, Greenland, c.3300 BC. Along the east coast of this continent they voyaged slowly to the south (**Fig.7**). They hoped they had discovered the other side of the Ocean. However, Greenland turned out to be an island. They reached Cape Farvel ("Farewell"), the south cape, at 60°N, and later the SW Cape, at 61°N. These successes were recorded in the famous monuments of Stonehenge I, in South England, and in Loughcrew, Ireland (Refs.1-3, 21-23). Both monuments date from c.3200 BC, when they gave up their efforts to cross Davis Strait.

Barnhouse Village and the Stones of Stenness were in use during the centuries around 3000 BC, just after this dramatic decision. So, it appears that the isthmus between these two lochs is a model of the narrow south coast of Greenland (**Fig.2**). The fresh water of the Loch of Harray symbolizes the huge ice cap of Greenland in the north, and the salt water of the Loch of Stenness represents the unknown Ocean in the southwest. Note, that the Stones of Stenness are placed just west of the southernmost tip of Loch Harray, at the coast of the Loch Stenness, named after these Stones. So the Ring of Stenness is positioned to represent Cape Farvel, the south cape of Greenland.

The original groundplan of the Ring shows only one causeway in the north (**Fig.3**). So, except in the north, the platform was at all sides surrounded by water (in the ditch), just like Cape Farvel. Look also at the so-called "altar stones" (**Fig.3a**), and the reduced (dotted) western end of the ditch. It is a view west. So, in western direction, there is a narrow passage (the narrow space between the two upright stones), leading to more land in the west (the slab lying behind them on the ground). This is correct, because in western direction people could sail through a narrow strait, between the Islets and the mainland, to the SW Cape, and beyond.

The pointed tops of the huge menhirs #2, #3, and #5 resemble a coast map of South Greenland, confirming this interpretation (**Fig.3**). Seen from the center of the Ring, the "elbow stone" (#7) bends to the left, or NW (**Fig.3a**). The shape of the stone closely resembles the coastal sailing route from Cape Farvel to the SW Cape (see **Fig.7**). The menhirs are placed with their flat faces toward the center of the Ring. So the monument resembles the spherical Earth as closely as possible. Originally, the Ring of Stenness possessed an outer circular wall (not shown on the groundplan). This wall represented Greenland, the westernmost land of the then known world, located at the other side of the Atlantic Ocean (the ditch).

The stone circles of the henges deal with the edge of the Old World, and the ditches beyond them represent the surrounding seas. The Ring of Stenness contained 11 to 12

Fig.5 (a) The Ring of Brodgar looking north. It represents the SW Cape, at 61°N (the original 61 stones). (b) The tops of the stones, like this one, resemble South Greenland. (c) The "elbow stone" near the NW exit shows the sailing route around the SW Cape. (Photos May 2004) Center: An aerial photo of the Ring of Brodgar looking north (Ref.5).

stones, because stone #12 was a small one (as indicated on the groundplan, **Fig.3**). The 12 stones had been placed to celebrate the discovery of the island of Jan Mayen, above Iceland in the north, 12° above the Orkneys, at 59+12= 71°N. This happened three centuries after the discovery of Cape Farvel, c.3250 BC (c.2950 BC, Ref.30). So this circle of 12 stones was placed in the center, about 300 years after construction of the earthwork.

The small stone #12 may have symbolized the islet of Jan Mayen. The other 11 stones represented Cape Farvel, 11° below Jan Mayen, at 71-11= 60°N. This cape was more important, of course. The whole Ring continued to symbolize Cape Farvel. These early discoveries in the Upper North may be surprising. However, recent ice core studies in Greenland show the seas around these areas had more of a Mediterranean climate during this time period (Ref.20).

When Neolithic people walked from Stenness along the isthmus to the Ring of Brodgar, they thought about the coastal sailing route from Cape Farvel to the SW Cape of Greenland. After 120 meters, we arrive at the Watch Stone near the Bridge of Brodgar (**Fig.4a**). This enormous menhir of almost 6m high shows that the area around the SW Cape, which we are about to reach, was considered of the utmost importance. Note, that the monolith is situated at the side of the salt water of Loch Stenness. Remember, that people wanted to cross the Ocean from the SW Cape of Greenland, so this stone may commemorate major expeditions that departed to the west from this point, and never returned.

Before 1814, the Odin Stone, with the round hole in it, was located about 140 meters NNW of the Stenness Ring (**Fig.2**). Looking from the Odin Stone, the Ring of Brodgar is 29° to the northwest. This is the complementary latitude of the SW Cape of Greenland, 90-29= 61°N. So the location of the "holed" Odin Stone shows it was at least partially connected in meaning to the Rings.

At the other side of the bridge, near Brodgar Farm, are two menhirs 8.3 meters apart (**Figs.2,8c**) (Ref.5). A geophysical survey undertaken for the Orkney Archaeological Trust has indicated extensive settlement remains in the vicinity. The SE-stone is 1.7m high, and the NW-stone is 2.7m high. The first menhir could represent Cape Farvel, 1° above the Orkneys, at 59+1= 60°N, and the second, taller menhir could represent the SW Cape of Greenland, 2° above the Orkneys, at 59+2= 61°N. Perhaps archaeological excavation of the surrounding settlements will suggest further meanings.

SW Cape of Greenland

The circular inner platform of the Ring of Brodgar symbolizes the well-known Old World, and the stone circle around the outside is about the edge of that world (**Figs.2,5**). Originally, this circle contained 61 stones, corresponding with the latitude of the important SW Cape of Greenland, at 61°N. The SE entrance shows this cape could be reached from the southeast, and the NW exit illustrates sailing could be continued to the northwest.

Fig.6 Some pointed stones of the Ring of Brodgar (2.1m-4.6m). Their tops resemble South Greenland (below). The lower left photo (c) is looking north up the Loch of Harray. The other photos are looking into the dark heather of the center of the Ring.

All the Brodgar menhirs were placed with their flat faces toward the center of the Ring (see **Fig.5**), just like in Stenness. In this way the monument resembled the spherical Earth as closely as possible. The circular platform represents the Old World, which is surrounded by the vast Atlantic Ocean (the huge ditch). The outer wall, which has disappeared, symbolized Greenland, the westernmost land of the then-known world. The pointed tops of the menhirs (**Figs.5,6**) resemble a coast map of South Greenland, confirming the interpretation. Seen from the center of the Ring, the top of the "elbow stone" (**Fig.5c**) bends to the right, or north. The shape of this stone closely resembles the coastal sailing route around the SW Cape of Greenland (see **Fig.7**).

The round platform of the Ring of Brodgar has a diameter of 112 meters (367 feet), which is equal to 1 milli-Moira, or one thousandth of a Moira. The Moira is an ancient Egyptian unit of length, corresponding to 1 degree of latitude. So, 1 Moira= 1°= 111km (69 miles, or 60 NM) = 365 thousand feet, and 1 milli-Moira equals 111 meters (365 feet) (Refs.1-3). This huge size of the monuments stresses the importance of finding the new lands. Including the ditches, the Rings of Stenness and Bookan have average diameters of 56 meters and 55 meters, respectively, equal to half a milli-Moira (55m), so these Rings were considered less important than the Brodgar Ring.

The Ring of Brodgar is split in two by its two causeways across the encircling ditch. The SW half contained 31 menhirs, corresponding to the northern Nile Delta in Egypt, at 31°N, and to the Orkneys, at the complementary latitude of 90-31= 59°N. The NE half contained 30 menhirs, encoding the southern Nile Delta, at 30°N, and Cape Farvel, Greenland, at the complementary latitude of 90-30= 60°N. All these striking "coincidences" are not accidents, but are features of a complex site carefully designed by the mind of man.

At a direction of exactly 45°SW of the Ring of Brodgar is the "SW Cape of Brodgar" (**Fig.2**), which symbolizes the important SW Cape of Greenland. At the opposite shore of Loch Stenness is the chambered cairn of the "Knove of Onston" (or "Unstan", Ref.4, **Fig.2**). Seen from this chambered cairn, the "SW Cape of Brodgar" is located at a direction of 61°NE, encoding the latitude of the SW Cape of Greenland for the third time, at 61°N. This SW Cape was considered to be the most promising point of departure for reaching unknown land at the back side of the planet Earth.

West Coast of Greenland
Seen from the "SW Cape of Brodgar", the Ring of Bookan is located at a direction of 62°NW, encoding the latitude of the West Coast of Greenland, at 62°N (**Fig.2**). This particular location did not coincide with an important cape. In spite of this, however, it had some importance. According to Stonehenge I in South England, and Loughcrew in Ireland, it was the westernmost point the megalith builders reached, before giving up their efforts to cross Davis Strait, c.3200 BC (Refs.1-3).

The central platform of the Ring of Bookan, an important earthwork, symbolizes the Old World, and the ditch represents the Atlantic Ocean (**Fig.8a**). The outer bank, which has disappeared, symbolized Greenland, the westernmost land of the then-known world. It is

Fig.7 Map of Greenland (Ref.26), showing Cape Farvel (Stenness), the SW Cape (Brodgar), and the West Coast of Greenland at 62°N (Bookan) (c.3200 BC). The 4 Stones of Stenness encode the crossing of Davis Strait, at 59+4= 63°N. The stones of the Ring of Brodgar support this crossing (c.2500 BC).

reasonable to assume that early pathways and roads in this area were constructed simultaniously with the henges (see **Fig.2**). The main road due east of the Ring of Bookan points 62°NW, confirming the West Coast of Greenland, at 62°N. The small road due west of the Ring points 62° SW to the coast of Loch Stenness. It confirms this coastal area of Greenland again.

The first monument on the isthmus, the Stones of Stenness (**Fig.2**), symbolizes Cape Farvel, 1 degree of latitude above the Orkneys, at 59+1= 60°N. It appears that the second monument, the Ring of Brodgar, symbolizes the important SW Cape of Greenland, 2° above the Orkneys, at 59+2= 61°N. Finally, it appears that the third monument, the Ring of Bookan, symbolizes the West Coast of Greenland, 3° above the Orkneys, at 59+3= 62°N (the three circles in **Fig.7**). Note, that the west side of this Ring is situated due north of the chambered cairn of the "Knove of Onston", just mentioned (**Fig.2**).

A series of menhirs (now horizontal or being used for corner fenceposts) lie along the shore of the Loch of Stenness between the Ring of Brodgar and Ring of Bookan (**Fig.9**). These may indicate early voyages of exploration from the West Coast of Greenland, dated c.3200 BC.

A nice photo of the Comet Stone is shown Fig.8b. Seen from the center of the Ring of Brodgar, this stone points 14°ESE to Maes Howe, a magnificent stone Tomb of 3000 BC (**Fig.2**) (Ref.4). This famous tomb is situated about half a kilometer east of the southernmost part of Loch Harray. On the Maes Howe platform "has been found at least one socket for a very large standing stone", and around the platform is a ditch, originally 14m wide and 2m deep, with a bank outside (Ref.5). The meaning of this easterly alignment to Maes Howe and its standing stone(s) is not clear, but it appears that the Comet Stone and the Tomb may be related to the dramatic decision to give up the efforts to go further west across Davis Strait (Ref.1). The geographic position of Maes Howe east of Loch Harray shows that Greenland was considered the westernmost land for a long time.

Prior Western Lands: The Azores

The main road leading to the Stones of Stenness, and along the shore of the Loch Harray to the Ring of Brodgar, points 39°NW (**Fig.2**), which references the monument of Stonehenge I in South England at the complementary latitude of 90-39= 51°N. Stonehenge I (which at this date did not yet include the huge "Sarsen Stones"), is the most important monument in Europe, which was built for the discovery of South Greenland (c.3200 BC) (Refs.1-3).

However, the direction of 39°NW is also coincident with the 39°N latitude of the West Azores (**Fig.2**). So the isthmus of the Ness of Brodgar also represents the long archipelago of the Azores, and both lochs now symbolize the vast Atlantic Ocean. These islands were discovered c.3600 BC (Refs.1-3). It was the westernmost area of the known world during the three centuries prior to the discovery of Greenland.

Fig.8 (a) The Ring of Bookan, view south across the Loch of Stenness toward the Knove of Onston. (b) The Comet Stone, view SE across the Loch of Harray toward Maes Howe (behind the top of the stone). (c) Two Standing Stones in the yard of a house SE of the Ring of Brodgar, with Loch Harray in the background (c.3200 BC).

The three big Rings symbolize the three island groups of the Azores, in keeping with the traditional representation of the Azores by 3 circles or 3 joined spirals (Refs.1-3). The first Ring, the Stones of Stenness, symbolizes the East Azores, 1° of latitude above the Strait of Gibraltar, at 36+1= 37°N. The second, and largest monument, the Ring of Brodgar, represents the important Central Azores, 2° above Gibraltar, at 36+2= 38°N. Finally, the third construction, the Ring of Bookan, stands for the West Azores, 3° above the Strait of Gibraltar, at 36+3= 39°N (Refs.1-3).

The entrance of the Ring of Brodgar (the causeway across the ditch) points 38°SE, and the exit on the other side points 38°NW, twice confirming the purposeful intent of encoding the Central Azores, at 38°N. The group of 9 small mounds just SE of the Ring of Brodgar symbolizes the 9 islands of the Azores (Ref.5). These mounds have base-diameters of 5 to 13m, and are up to 1m high. The Azores became very important after the discovery of America, c.2500 BC, because of the return route from Newfoundland in the west, with the wind and current.

Changing Times – Monuments altered

As shown by the famous petroglyphs at Dissignac, Brittany, new lands in the west were discovered by the Egyptians via the Bering Sea, c.2600 BC (Refs.1-3). In the next century people crossed the Atlantic Ocean via the Southern Crossing, from Africa to South America, c.2500 BC. In the same century, they crossed the Ocean via the Upper North, from Greenland to Baffin Island. All these developments had a tremendous influence on the peoples of the Old World. The attempts to cross the Atlantic Ocean had lasted for 3000 years, from 5500 to 2500 BC (Refs.1-3, 21-23). Finally, the unknown back side of the Earth had been reached. After this event a completely different world vision became shared among the peoples of the Old World. From 2500 BC forward, megalithic monuments had a different character.

The three Rings on the Ness of Brodgar were modified, and updated. We have seen that this was done with other monuments, for instance Kercado in Brittany, and Stonehenge in South England, where Phases II and III followed Phase I by a thousand years (Ref.1). Aubrey Burl, an expert on stone ring design, has stated that "changes of mind were common". We should not be surprised, since these were the visible civic monuments for such long spans of time. We don't believe the drastic changes that have occurred to these Rings in the Orkneys were caused by vandalism in the 19th or 20th century, as sometimes suggested. Vandalism is not a typical characteristic in this remote, and thinly populated part of Scotland. On the contrary, it is well-known that the survival of the remains of the Neolithic period on the Orkneys is exceptionally good (Ref.5).

With the new understanding of the world, the central platform of each of the Rings now symbolized all the land on Earth (not just the Old World), and all this land is surrounded by sea (the ditch). The outside walls, which previously represented Greenland at the edge of the earth, were removed from all three rings. The new paradigm of geographic understanding led to further remodel of these old sites. Stones were removed, to encode new meanings.

a
b

Fig.9 Standing Stones along the shore of the Loch of Stenness, between Bookan and the Ring of Brodgar (barely visible at the horizon, photos b,c). Stone d is furthest from the Ring, a is closer, b is closer yet, and c is nearest to Brodgar.

c

d

The Ring of Stenness, which represents Cape Farvel, was reduced to today's 4 western menhirs. The small "elbow stone" (#7 in **Fig.3**) confirms Cape Farvel, 1° of latitude above the Orkneys, at 59+1= 60°N. The other 3 menhirs, which are more than twice as tall **(Fig.3d)** can count for two! So, they describe the important crossings of Davis Strait. The southern crossing, 3° above Cape Farvel, has a length of 2x3= 6 Moiras= 360 NM. The northern crossing, 2x3= 6° above Cape Farvel, has a length of 3 Moiras= 180 nm. Both sailing distances are correct. Next, the ditch of Stenness was filled in, because at 63°N and 66°N the Ocean could be crossed, so the ditch symbolism became meaningless. The Ocean was not a barrier anymore.

The large Ring of Brodgar was reduced to today's 27 menhirs. This number is much higher than the 4 at Stenness, which means that after the discovery of America, the SW Cape was considered to be much more important than Cape Farvel. All crossings to the new continent proceded through the SW Cape. The remaining 27 menhirs correspond with the complementary latitude of the south point of Iceland, and with the most important crossing from Greenland to Baffin Island, both at 90-27= 63°N. So, the Ring of Brodgar confirms the southern crossing indicated at Stenness (Refs.32-35). Added together, the Rings then had 27+4= 31 menhirs, encoding the latitude of the Nile Delta, the Northern Egyptian Empire, at 31°N, as well as the important latitude of the Orkney Islands, where these huge Rings are located, at 90-31= 59°N.

The "altar stones" in the center of the Ring of Stenness receive a broader meaning now **(Fig.3a)**. It is a view west. So, in western direction there is a narrow passage (which might be around the south coast of Greenland, or might be the whole crossing of the Ocean, both represented by the narrow space between the two upright stones), leading to more land in the west (America, the slab lying behind them on the ground). The large standing stone at Maes Howe may have been removed as the easterly alignment, which indicated no further possible passage to the west, had been shown to be a mistake.

Dating

The discovery of Greenland is firmly dated to c.3300 BC (Refs.1-3), and the discovery of its south coast probably happened 50 years later, c.3250 BC. In view of their similar design, the shapes and orientations of the stones, and, last but not least, their meanings, the Rings of Stenness, Brodgar, and Bookan must have close construction dates, but of course after the discovery dates (Ref.4). Most monuments related to Greenland, like Stonehenge I and Loughcrew, are dated c.3200 BC, when the megalith builders gave up their efforts to cross Davis Strait. Barnhouse Village was populated during this time. It is very probable that most of the monuments on the Ness of Brodgar have the same age. The supposition that the Ring of Brodgar is of a much later date, between 2500 and 2000 BC, is definitely wrong (Refs.5-12).

The two corrected Carbon-14 dates from the ditch of the Ring of Stenness provide an averaged date of c.2960 BC (Refs.1,4,6). This later date supports the discovery of the islet of Jan Mayen, encoded by the old stone circle of Stenness. It is probable, that some organic material was dropped in the ditch during the construction of this circle. The discovery date of c.2950 for Jan Mayen was recently confirmed by the passage grave of Karleby in Sweden (Ref.30).

On the Shetland Islands, north of the Orkneys, there is evidence of land having been cleared and divided by walls between 3200 and 2800 BC (Ref.11). This is just after the important discovery of Cape Farvel, at 60°N. Shetland, also sited at 60°N, became important because of the discoveries in the west. Ales Stenar is a large sunship monument in Sweden, constructed of 60 stones (Ref.35). This megalithic monument of later date also encodes Cape Farvel, at 60°N.

The name of the "Watch Stone" near the Bridge of Brodgar (Fig.4a) may indicate it has a time encoding. If we add it to the near 4 Stones of Stenness, you get 1+4= 5. There are also 5 huge trilithons in the Horseshoe of Stonehenge III, which is the monument for the discovery of America, as explained in our book, "How the Sungod Reached America, c.2500 BC" (Ref.1). This discovery via the Atlantic occurred during the 5th Dynasty of Egypt (2518-2371 BC). Is it possible that the 5th Dynasty is encoded by these monuments?

Discussion

The Megalithic Culture of Western Europe started about 5500 BC, more than two thousand years before the Old Kingdom of Pharonic Egypt, which became the center of the Sun Religion. People wanted to spread the old Sun Religion to the west, because their supreme god, the SunGod, had said (in Egyptian hieroglyphics): "The Realm of the Dead is in the west, at the other side of the waters, in the land where the Sun sets." For that reason, people were looking for the unknown other side of the earth. This search lasted thousands of years, because of the huge size of the Atlantic Ocean. This is the main reason the Megalithic Culture lasted so long, some 4 millennia, from 5500 BC to 1500 BC. The ring monuments of the Orkneys document an important part in this story of the exploration of the backside of the earth.

There must be a need in man, springing from the spatial ability of his large brain, to create maps. Birds are thought to find their way during migrations by memorized star patterns, wolves use smell markings, and memorized land features, but people make maps to communicate with each other. We have found that many megalithic petroglyphs are actually maps (Ref.1-3). The design of this Ring complex in the Orkneys is a good example of a walk-in map laid out in large stone constructions. The most complex example of a walk-in map site is the American Stonehenge site in New Hampshire, dated c.2200 BC (Refs.1,32). These stone maps are a tribute to man's ability to conceptualize his environment, and symbolize it in grand public monuments.

One may wonder about the origin of the name of "Brodgar" or "Brogar" (Ref.10). For years, the origin of the placename has been explained as being from the Old Norse brúar-garðr meaning "Bridge Farm". However, there is another intriguing possibility. Bearing in mind the local pronunciation, broadyeur, the name could actually stem from "brúar-jorð" - the "earth bridge". The Ring of Brodgar turns out to play a prominent role in man's discovery of the "Bridge" between the Old World and the New World. Now that

11

we again understand this old meaning, perhaps this will encourage further study of these important sites.

References

1. De Jonge, R.M., and Wakefield, J.S., <u>How the SunGod Reached America c.2500 BC, A Guide to Megalithic Sites,</u> 2002 (ISBN 0-917054-19-9). Available: MCS Inc., Box 3392, Kirkland, Wa 98083-3392, also on CD
2. Website: www.howthesungod.com, De Jonge, R.M., and Wakefield, J.S.
3. De Jonge, R.M., and Wakefield, J.S., "The Discovery of the Atlantic Islands", Migration & Diffusion, Vol.3, No.11, pgs.69-109 (2002)
4. Garnham, T., <u>Lines on the Landscape, Circles from the Sky, Monuments of Neolithic Orkney,</u> Temple Publishing, Great Britain, 2004 (ISBN 0-7524-3114-5)
5. <u>Nomination of the Heart of Neolithic Orkney for Inclusion in the World Heritage List by UNESCO,</u> Historic Scotland, 2000 (ISBN 1-900168-54-5)
6. Balfour, M., <u>Megalithic Mysteries - An Illustrated Guide to Europe's Ancient Sites,</u> Collins & Brown, 1992 (ISBN 1-85-585-3558)
7. Burl, A., <u>The Stone Circles of the British Isles,</u> Yale University Press, London (1976) (ISBN 0-300-02398-7)
8. Burl, A., and Piper, E., <u>Rings of Stone, The Prehistoric Stone Circles of Britain and Ireland,</u> Ticknor & Fields, New York, 1980 (ISBN 0-89919-000-6)
9. Website: www.undiscoveredscotland.co.uk/westmainland/stennessstones/
10. Website: www.orkneyjar.com/history/standingstones/
11. Website: www.stonepages.com/ancient_scotland/sites/stenness/htm/
12. Website: www.maeshowe.co.uk/maeshowe/standing.html/
13. Burl, A., <u>From Carnac to Callanish, The Prehistoric Stone Rows and Avenues of Britain, Ireland, and Brittany,</u> Yale University Press, New Haven and London, 1993 (ISBN 0-300-05575-7)
14. Burl, A., <u>Prehistoric Avebury,</u> Yale University Press, London, 1979 (ISBN 0-300-02368-5)
15. Bullock, T., and Burnham, A., <u>Stone Circles and Stone Rows, Photographic Tours</u> (2 CD discs, revised 2nd Edition, 1989-2003)
16. Ritchie, A., <u>Prehistoric Orkney,</u> B.T. Batsford Ltd. / Historic Scotland, London, 1995 (ISBN 0-7134-7593-5)
17. Thom, A., <u>Megalithic Sites in Britain,</u> Clarendon Press, Oxford, reprinted 2002 (ISBN 0-19-813148-8)
18. Beckensall, S., <u>Rock Carvings of Northern Britain,</u> Shire Archaeology, UK (1986) (ISBN 0-85263-760-8)
19. Peiser, B.J., Palmer, T., Bailey, M.E., <u>Natural Catastrophes during Bronze Age Civilizations,</u> BAR International Series 728, Oxford, 1998 (ISBN 0-86054-916-X): MacKie, E.W., "Can European Prehistory Detect Large-Scale Natural Disasters?", pgs.169-171.
20. Ref.19: Peiser, B.J. "Evidence for a Global Disaster in the Late 3rd Millennium BC", pgs.117-140.
21. Casson, L., <u>Ships and Seafaring in Ancient Times,</u> British Museum Press, 1994
22. Wachsmann, S., <u>Seagoing Ships and Seamanship in the Bronze Age Levant,</u> College Station, Texas, 1998
23. Heyerdahl, T., <u>The Ra Expeditions,</u> George Allen & Unwin, London, 1971
24. Haywood, J., <u>Historical Atlas of the Vikings,</u> Penguin Books, London (1995) (ISBN 0-14-051328-0)
25. Ordinance Survey Map, Pathfinder Series "Finstown" HY 21/31, 1:25,000
26. "Atlantic Ocean", National Geographic Magazine, 1968
27. Wallis Budge, E.A., <u>Osiris and the Egyptian Resurrection,</u> 2 Vol., Dover Pub., N.Y., 1973 (ISBN 0-486-22780-4)
28. Kemp, B.J., <u>Ancient Egypt, Anatomy of a Civilization,</u> London, Routledge, 1991
29. Siliotti, A., <u>Egypt, Temples, People and Gods,</u> Bergamo, Italy, 1997
30. De Jonge, R.M., and Wakefield, J.S., "The Passage Grave of Karleby, Encoding the Islands Discovered in the Ocean, c. 2950 BC", Migration & Diffusion, Vol.5, No.18, pgs.64-74 (2004)
31. Twohig, E. Shee, <u>The Megalithic Art of Western Europe,</u> Clarendon Press, Oxford, 1981
32. De Jonge, R.M., and Wakefield, J.S., "A Nautical Center for Crossing the Ocean, America's Stonehenge, New Hampshire, c.2200 BC", Migration & Diffusion, Vol.4, No.15, pgs.60-100 (2002)
33. De Jonge, R.M., and Wakefield, J.S., "Germany's Bronze Age Disc Reveals Transatlantic Seafaring, c.1600 BC", Ancient American, Vol.9, No.55, pgs.18-20 (2004)
34. De Jonge, R.M., and Wakefield, J.S., "The Three Rivers Petroglyph, A Guide-post for River Travel in America", Migration & Diffusion, Vol.3, No.12, pgs.74-100 (2002)
35. De Jonge, R.M., and Wakefield, J.S., "Ales Stenar, Sweden's Bronze Age 'Sunship' to the Americas, c.500 BC", Ancient American, Vol.9, No.56, pgs.16-21 (2004)
36. De Jonge, R.M., "Great Circle Mound: An Indiana Temple to the Egyptian SunGod?", Ancient American, Issue 60, Vol.9, pgs.31-32, 2004.
37. De Jonge, R.M., and Wakefield, J.S., "The Disc of Nebra, Important Sailing Routes of the Bronze Age Displayed in a Religious Context", Migration and Diffusion, Vol.5, No.17, pgs. 32-39, 2004
38. De Jonge, R.M., and Wakefield, J.S., "The Megalithic Megalithic Monument of Lagatjar, Brittany c.1600 BC", Ancient American, Vol.12, no.76, Pgs.32-37, 12/2007

Megalithic Wall, on the side of the Central Plaza, at Palenque, Mexico. All the buildings above this level are made of smaller blocks, with rubble fill. David Childress (Ref.21), when speaking of large blocks, walls, and arches at Monte Alba and Mitla, says "it is typical that the earliest phase of construction in these cities is megalithic".

THE PAINTINGS OF PORCELANO CAVE
The Discovery of Guadalupe, c.3000 BC
(Sierra de San Francisco, Baja California, Mexico)

R.M. de Jonge, drsrmdejonge@hotmail.com
J.S. Wakefield, jayswakefield@yahoo.com

Summary
Hundreds of remote caves in the mountainous arroyos of Baja are famous for thousands of enormous colorful "Great Mural" paintings of men and animals. Among these are some "abstract" paintings, but there is no explanation for their very different art style. In this article we interpret the "abstract" paintings of one cave, which explains the introduction of this style by prehistoric explorers of the West Coast of America, and establishes the parameters for dating these paintings.

Introduction
The Porcelano Cave, near the Arroyo de San Gregorio, is located in a very remote part of western Mexico, halfway down the Peninsula of Lower California, about 40km north of the town of San Ignacio **(Figs.1,2)**. This cave is the focus of a scientific paper by R. Vinas and others in the "International Newsletter on Rock Art", 2001 (Ref.1). The many Baja caves were explored and illustrated by the late H.W. Crosby, in his important book "The Cave Paintings of Baja California, Discovering the Great Murals of an Unknown People", 1997 (Ref.2). The Crosby book, with its beautiful color illustrations, is a popular "coffee table" book.

The mountainous area containing the Porcelano Cave is called the Sierra de San Francisco, a wilderness of volcanic outpourings from a shield volcano, rising from the surrounding desert to a height of 5,200 feet. From the uplands, there are views west to Scammon's Lagoon and the Vizcaino Desert, and to the east, to the abrupt eminences of La Tres Virgenes, taller, and more recent volcanos that tower in front of the Gulf of California. The Sierra embraces a world of rugged, extremely eroded canyons that would not be suspected from the low, barren lands outside.

"The arroyos vary considerably in the amount of art they exhibit. All evidence suggests that the beds of the arroyos were the avenues by which people made their way into the heart of the mountains, as they are today, though most of the caves are far from modern trails. The Arroyo de San Gregorio (and the Porcelano Cave) lie at about the geographic center of the area's rock art locations. In ancient times, this arroyo must have been the most direct route from any part of the highlands to the Gulf Coast. Shell mounds abound, and the entire sierra is littered with evidence of ancient marine harvests. Shells are found scattered profusely along every trail" (Ref.2).

The Baja Peninsula was the home of hunter-gatherer-fishermen of unknown origin, who are thought to be responsible for the pictorial style called the "Great Murals". Harry W. Crosby, whose book first documented the rock art of the Baja, visited 200 cave painting sites with thousands of figures over a period of years, with the help of the few local

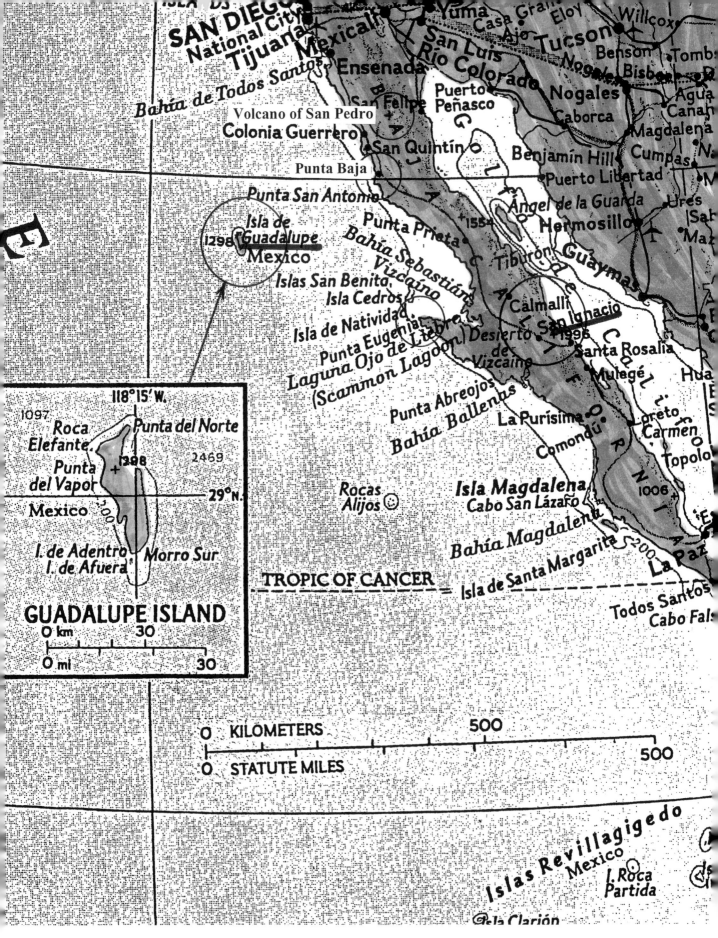

Fig.1a
Map of Baja California, with the island of Guadalupe enlarged.

inhabitants. He saw over 50 groupings of painted figures that could loosely be called "compositions", and reports that "it was obvious we had seen only a minor fraction of the total art". The author notes that the paintings in the area of the Sierra de San Francisco present the "most admirable expression of the Great Mural phenomenon ..., a style of naturalistic figures of people and animals, usually painted larger than life, and depicted in outline, with recognizable, classically realistic proportions." Largely because of his efforts, in 1993 large areas of the rockshelters were added to UNESCO's list of World Heritage Sites. Recent work, reported in 2002 and 2004, by Dr. Alan Watchman of Australian National University in Canberra, with National Geographic support, has identified a great many more sites. He carbon dated about 30 paint samples from caves in the Sierra de Guadalupe to the south, and found a wide range of dates, between 5500 and 3000 BC (Refs.18,19).

The Porcelano Cave **(Fig.2)** is a natural shelter of volcanic rock, situated in an arroyo about 750 meters above sea level, 25km from the east coast, near the Bay of Santa Ana. From the outside, the cave, which faces east, goes almost unnoticed due to fallen rock in the mouth **(Fig.2)**. Inside, the cave provides a vast shelter, with a wide horizontal entrance of 46 meters. The depth is at most 9 meters. In the back, where the long frieze of paintings are, it is almost dark, with a comfortable height of about 1.6 meters (Ref.1). Large realistic images of human figures and animals are painted in black. Though images of wildlife are the most common paintings in Baja rockshelters, these realistic images are only located on the ceiling in the northern part of the Porcelano Cave.

The Realistic Paintings: The Antelope and the Sea Turtles

In the cave are six important compositions, all having a size of about one square meter (Ref.1). The most remarkable painting (Fig.3, 170x75cm) shows a big, apparently pregnant antelope done in the Great Mural "Realistic" style. The head, the lighter tint of the belly, and the small tail show it is a Pronghorn Antelope. The front legs end in fingers, as though it were human. In its jump, it is chased by two small men with raised arms. The animal is being chased to the left, in the southern direction on the rockshelter roof. At the top of the painting are 5 horizontal strokes which may represent the 5 latitudes between the Cave, at about 28°N, and Cabo San Lucas, the southern end of the peninsula, at 28-5= 23°N.

Similar men accompany three sea turtles in the second composition **(Fig.4**, 95x100cm). The animals are probably crawling up a Pacific beach to lay their eggs, because they are painted crawling upwards, along the ceiling. The men are able to catch them by grabbing their front flippers. Both these animal paintings are on the ceiling of the mid-rear of the cave. They are executed in black paint and in a similar style, so it may be assumed both have been made by the same people at about the same time. They show the painters lived from hunting and "gathering". Note, that in both paintings the number of men equals twice the number of animals. So, they conquer the animals because they cooperate, and overwhelm the prey.

Crosby reports that pioneer Jesuits (1683-1720), intrepid travelers and explorers, knew the local Cochimi living on the land, as well as those who occupied the missions. The

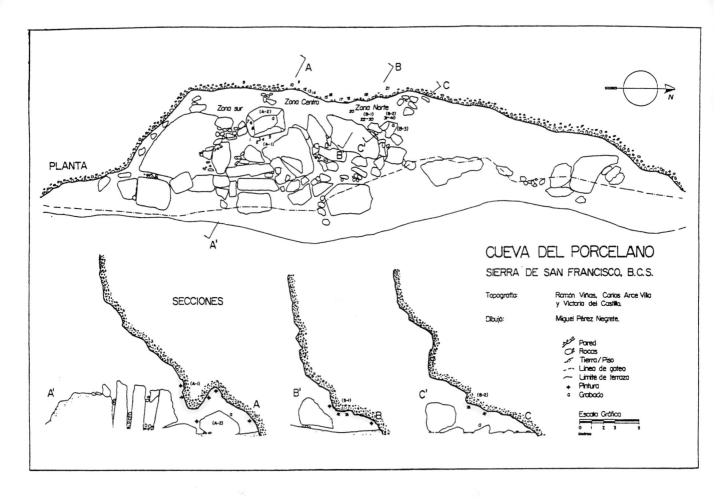

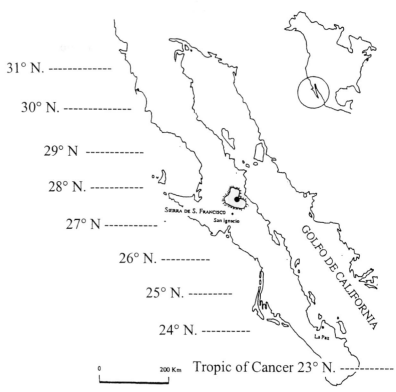

Fig.2
Groundplan of the Porcelano Cave (Ref.1), and its location on the Baja Peninsula. (San Ignatio, Baja California, Mexico)

Jesuits left several ethnographic documents of some depth, but none of these mentions rock painting as a contemporary activity. Nor does any rock art show evidence of the missionary presence, unlike the depictions of European people, or their animals, garb, or implements in many other parts of the world. Crosby recalls that two Jesuits (Rothea and Escalante) visited Great Mural sites and wrote that their Cochimi converts reported folkloric accounts of a giant people from the north who had painted in the Sierras, and each opined that the works were old (Ref.2).

Paintings in the Raton Cave near the north border of New Mexico, USA, 60 miles east of the Rio Grande, have been carbon dated to c.3000 BC. Although this cave is located 800 miles north-east of the Porcelano Cave, it contains "similar paintings" of a puma and a human of "great size". Due to the similar style, it has been presumed by Vinas and his associates (Ref.1) that these Realistic compositions in the Porcelano Cave have about the same age of c.3000 BC. This carbon date would fit the end of the 5500-3000 BC period provided by the carbon dating of Watchman (Refs.18,19).

The Abstract Paintings

The paintings from the Porcelano Cave have unusual, abstract-schematic images **(Figs.5-7)** that prevail over the realistic ones, and many of them are "atypical and foreign" to the themes of the Great Murals (Ref.1). There are reported to be seventeen abstract, schematic designs, in yellow, black, red and white in seven main compositions. R. Vinas and his associates say the other images include a "great sunlike form, and express some lunar and solar calendar system or registry", and that some of the schematic compositions "are a territorial or cosmogonic reference with the indication of the cardinal points". Crosby reports that a cave in Arroyo de San Gregorito, the next arroyo to the south of San Gregorio named "La Candelaria", has seven figures in the abstract checkerboard pattern. A three-foot figure "looks like nothing so much as a piece of Meso-American funerary pottery." Crosby says "Such breaks with convention are inexplicable" (Ref.2, pg.95). At a cave in Loma Alta, at the southern end of the Great Murals, in the Sierra de Guadalupe to the south, are another two abstract patterns of rectangles, one in red and black, and one in yellow and black. Crosby says that "attempts to locate the origin of this style outside the Great Mural area have failed" (Ref.2, pg.155).

However, note that in the abstract Porcelano paintings, one can quickly see a spiral **(Fig.5)**, spaced lines **(Figs.5-7)**, and patterns of squared circles **(Fig.6)**, features that are common with megalithic petroglyphs (Refs.3-5,17). In our research (Ref.3), we have found that many petroglyphs and cave paintings of the megalithic period are geographic in content. In America the megalithic period runs from 3000 BC to 500 BC, but evidence of degrees of latitude and distance lines can be seen in the monument of Barnenez in France, from c.4700 BC, so latitudes were in use earlier, and they were probably in use by sailors from the time of the discovery of the Canaries and the Shetlands, about 5500 BC (Ref.3). So as we examine these abstract paintings, we will look for geographic meanings, and encoded latitudes.

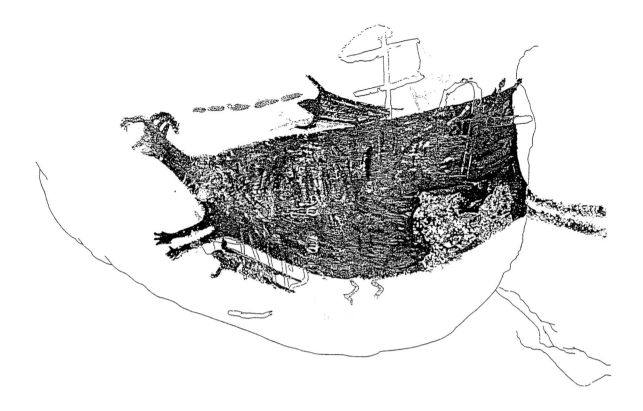

Fig.3 Realistic Art: Pregnant Pronghorn Antelope.
(Black painting, (Ref.1), Porcelano Cave, Baja California, c.3000 BC)

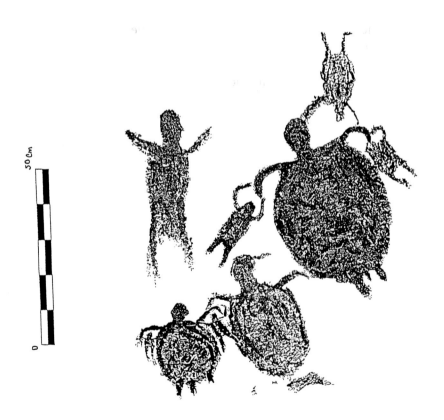

Fig.4 Realistic Art: Three Sea Turtles on the Pacific shore.
(Black painting (Ref.1), Porcelano Cave, Baja California, c.3000 BC)

The Column/Spiral and the Rib

These two yellow/black compositions are 10 meters south (to the left) of the animals, on the rear wall **(Fig.5)**. The left painting, 75cm wide and 165cm high, consists of a round spiral placed on top of a "column". The right painting, 75cm wide and 105cm high, resembles a rib of beef. They are separated from one another by a distance of only 10cm.

When studying the images we are looking in northwest direction. The lobe in the center of the spiral resembles the oblong island of Guadalupe, located northwest of this site at 29°N. This island is not on many of today's maps, because of its distance offshore and economic unimportance. It is very arid and volcanic in appearance, with tall seacliffs. It is said that the goats dropped off by whalers have had catastrophic impact, eroding 95% of the island. Nevertheless, a unique species of palm from the island, the Guadalupe Palm, is now grown all over the world. Today the island is an exotic destination for "not more than 100" scuba divers each year, for the cage viewing of white sharks and pinipeds (seals and sealions). The island has been designated as a piniped marine sanctuary by the Mexican Government.

The Porcelano Cave is situated at about 27.5°N. A possible sailing route to reach Guadalupe starts at Punta Eugenia in the west, at the western tip of Baja, west of Scammon's Lagoon **(Fig.1)**. The vertical column between the boxes below the spiral represents this sailing route. The 3 squares in this direction (left and right), correspond with the sailing distance from Punta Eugenia to Guadalupe, about 3dl= 3°= 333km, or 180 Nautical miles to the WNW. In our research (Ref.3), we have called lines on petroglyphs and paintings that are used to denote distances equal to one degree of latitude in directions other than north-south, as "distance lines" (dl). Of course, latitudes can only be taken, or measured, in the north-south direction, but one can certainly sail for similar lengths of time in other directions, and they indicated this with lines, circles and spirals. The length of one distance line is the same as the length of one degree of latitude.

Comparing the widths of the dark painted spacings between the circles of the spiral or the rib with the widths of the squares of the column, the widths are about half. Since the squares in this composition are equal to 1 dl (above paragraph), the spacings of the spiral and rib represent half distance lines (hdl). This unit of half a distance line (=1/2 dl) is commonly used in megalithic petroglyphs, and spirals are often used to give distance scales to a composition. In fact, the diameter of the center of the spiral (Guadalupe Island) equals about half the size of the squares, so the length of the oblong island of Guadalupe is about 1/2dl= ½°, or about 55km, which is correct **(Fig.1)**.

There are 4 dark circles in the spiral, encoding a distance between the edge and the center of 4hdl= 2dl= 2°= 120 NM. This distance equals the shortest sailing distance from Punta Baja to Guadalupe. Punta Baja is a west cape of Baja peninsula in the north, at 30°N (Fig.1). The width of the column consists of 2 squares, showing the distance of this route to Guadalupe, of 2dl= 2°= 120 NM offshore.

The column figure has a second meaning. The horizontal lines between the squares represent latitude lines. The Porcelano Cave is situated at about 27.5°N. So, the column

Fig.5 Abstract Art: The Column/Spiral and the Rib.
To the right and below, copies of the same figures, with notes used in the text.
Left: Discovery of the island of Guadalupe (the center of the spiral), at a sailing distance
of 3dl from Punta Eugenia (the column), and 4hdl from Punta Baja (the spiral rings).
Right: The Rib shows the distance from the Porcelano Cave to the volcano of San Pedro,
or Guadalupe: 9hdl. (Yellow/black paintings, Ref.1, Porcelano Cave, Baja California,
c.3000 BC)

shows the latitudes above this Cave, one after the other, 28, 29, and 30°N. The center of the spiral now symbolizes the enormous mountain of San Pedro, at 31°N. It is a huge volcano, 10,145 feet (3078 meters) high. The 3 squares of the column also correspond with the distance between the volcano and the island of Guadalupe, 3dl= 3°= 180 NM **(Fig.1)**.

The yellow/black spiral around the summit of the column indicates this volcano is thought to have a big influence. The yellow color is symbolic for the yellow, volcanic sulphur, and the black color is symbolic for the black, volcanic lava. The whole painting deals with the problem of the existence of the island of Guadalupe. America has an endless West Coast, where all the land ceases. But here a little, volcanic island is present in the vast Pacific Ocean. The painting is asking a question: does Guadalupe exist because of the mountains of the Sierra Pintada, west of the Porcelano Cave? This mountain range, up to 3,300 feet (1000 meters) high, points to Punta Eugenia, to the island of Cedros, and finally to Guadalupe **(Fig.1)**. Or does Guadalupe exist because of the volcano of San Pedro in the north, at the same distance from the island?

The right painting (the Rib), just beside it in **Fig.5**, resembles the spiral in style, and is painted in the same colors. We conclude that both paintings have been made by the same people at the same time. The spacings between the lines equal those of the spiral beside it. There are 9 spacings, encoding the distance from the Porcelano Cave to the volcano of San Pedro in the north, 9hdl= 4.5dl= 4.5°= 270 NM (500km). The rib also shows the correct distance from the Porcelano Cave to Guadalupe, about 270 NM.

At the right side of the Rib figure, connecting the horizontal lines, is a vertical line. This line represents the mountain range of Baja California to the north. The lengths of the horizontal lines correspond to the narrow width of the northern peninsula of Punta Baja, and the wider area near southern Punta Eugenia. This is the answer to the question about the existence of Guadalupe. The lower group of long lines points far beyond the mountain range of the Sierra Pintada and the island of Cedros to the sea. The second group of short lines points to the sea from the volcano of San Pedro. The makers believe the island of Guadalupe exists because of about equal influences of the Sierra Pintada mountains in the south and the volcano in the north!

The yellow/black paintings were made because of the discovery of the island of Guadalupe, not far offshore. Egyptians discovered America via the Bering Sea, c.2600 BC (Refs.3-5). However, earlier the West Coast was previously navigated by Japanese and Chinese sailors, c.3000 BC, at the start of the megalithic period in America (Ref.9). These sailors were probably the first to discover Guadalupe, c.3000 BC, and subsequently these paintings were drawn, probably by the local people, using the latitude methodology known by sailors worldwide. So the break in artistic style, from Realistic to Abstract, resulted from the discovery of North America by more civilized people from Japan and China. Note that the black antelope in **Fig.3**, discussed previously and also dated c.3000 BC, covers an abstract painting similar to the ones of **Fig.5**, and probably of similar date. The technique used is identical to these yellow/black paintings. It appears

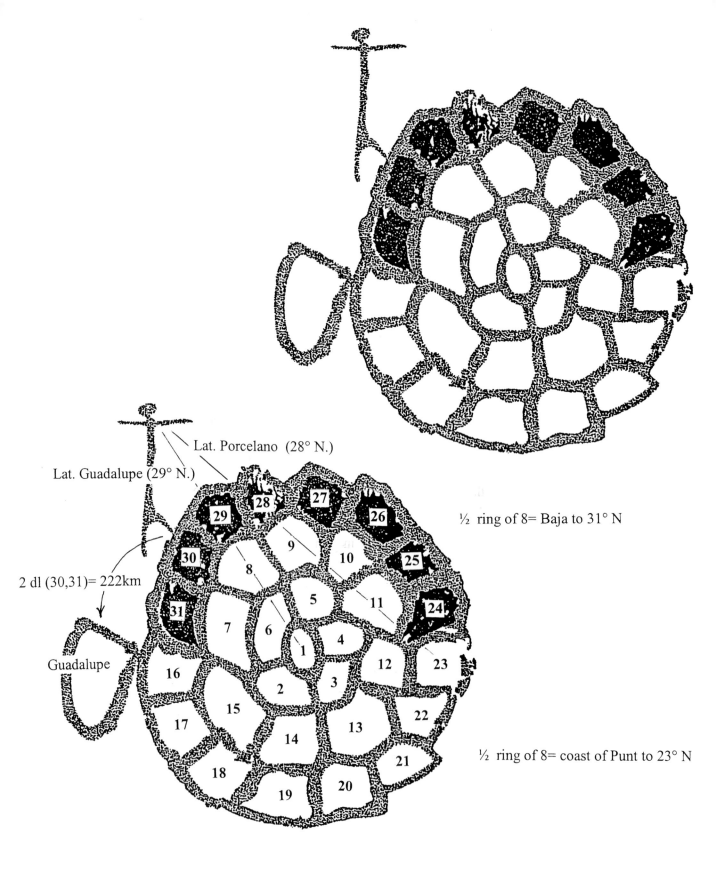

Fig.6 Abstract Art: The Ball. Below, the painting with the notations used in the text. The 8 latitudes of the peninsula of Baja California (the 8 closed segments), above the Tropic of Cancer, at 23°N (the 23 open segments). The man crosses from Punta Baja (#30, at 30°N), to Guadalupe (the loose segment), a sailing distance of 2dl= 120 NM, in the direction of the Realm of the Dead in the west. (Colored painting, Ref.1, Porcelano Cave, Baja California, 2000-500 BC)

that the makers of the antelope intentionally rejected a design which may have been misleading or inaccurate.

The Ball

At the rear end, in the center of the cave, is a big boulder having a diameter of 3m, and a height of 2m. On one of its eastern faces is an image of a ball **(Fig.6)**, probably the "sunlike form". It is composed of many segments, with a little man jumping off the ball, in the direction of a loose segment. The whole composition, 5 meters SE of the previous paintings, has a width of 80cm, and a height of 75cm. It is a design with most of the segments light (or open), but the upper ones painted dark (or closed). Information on the use of the colors, black, red, and white has not been provided in our reference materials. When looking at the painting, we are again looking in northwestern direction from the cave site.

Note that the segments of the ball are stylized squares. This is frequently seen in old European petroglyphs of the Atlantic Ocean (Ref.3). For thousands of years travelers determined their position on Earth in latitudes (Refs.3-5). The north-south dimension of each square is the distance of one degree of latitude, a unit called a "moira" in Egypt at the time. Each square has an east-west dimension of the same size, which was harder to measure, but clearly could be sailed, which we call a distance line (dl). So each segment also represents an area having a width of 1 dl, and an equal height.

The big ball represents the spherical Earth. To early peoples, the Porcelano Cave was situated in the extreme west. The offshore position and north-south orientation of the little man on the west side of the ball confirm the lower point of the ball is the South Pole, and the upper point is the North Pole. The innermost segment (#1) corresponds to a square area of land, from the equator to 1°N, along the West Coast of America. The shell of 5 segments around it represents the coast above it, to 1+5= 6°N. All these 6 segments are rather small, because the coast of South America is far away, and not what this painting is about. The next shell of 9 segments around it represents the coast above it, to 6+9= 15°N. These 9 segments are larger, because the corresponding coast of Central America is less far away. All these 15 segments form the inner part of the ball, meaning that those coastal lands are not very important in the meaning of the painting.

The last, and outer shell of 16 segments consists of 8 southern, light, or open segments, and 8 northern, dark, or closed segments. The 8 southern, open segments represent the West Coast of Central America, between 15°N and 15+8= 23°N. These segments are part of the surface of the ball, and the corresponding strip of coastal land is extremely important. It belongs to the civilization around the Gulf of Campeche (the Land of Punt), which has the same north-facing bowl shape as this series of segments (Refs.9-14).

The last open segment in the east is #23. It corresponds to the holy Tropic of Cancer, and the Southern Egyptian Empire, far in the east, at 23°N. This is the original center of the Sun religion (Refs.3-8). The 23 white segments of the ball also correspond to the place where the Tropic of Cancer leaves mainland Mexico, near the town of Mazatlan, at 23°N. They sailed out, and after crossing the gulf to the west, they reached the south point of

Fig.7 Abstract Art: The Royal Couple, embodying the peninsula of Baja California, protected against the Ocean by a shield (the Porcelano Cave), is looking beyond Guadalupe (the left loop), towards the setting Sun in the west. (Colored painting, Ref.1, Porcelano Cave, Baja California, 2000-500 BC)

the Peninsula of Baja California, near Cabo San Lucas, at 23°N. On midsummer day the Sun is above it at a right angle. The slow northern movement of the Sun then turns into a southern movement. Like the Egyptians, the creators of the painting must have also been believers in the Sunreligion, so finding that the Baja Peninsula terminates at the Holy Latitude must have held a special meaning to them.

The 8 closed segments on top of the ball represent the Peninsula of Baja California, from 23°N to 23+8= 31°N. The segments are part of the surface of the ball, and the corresponding strip of land is, of course, most important. The land has the approximate dimensions of the dark row of 8 segments, because the peninsula has an average width of about 1 distance line= 1 degree, and a height of 8 degrees. The 8 closed segments also correspond to the Egyptian Empire, far in the east, also from 23°N to 31°N. However, the culture in the Americas developed around the Gulf of Campeche, between 15°N and 23°N, as shown by the series of 8 open segments on the outside of the lower portion of the ball.

Left of the ball, in the west, off the continent of America, is the vast Pacific Ocean. However, left of the ball is a loose segment. Of all the segments of the ball, this loose one is the largest, showing it is the main subject of the painting. This segment is representing Guadalupe, the little island only 120 NM offshore in the west. By raised arms, the little man shows he was excited to "discover" this little island. Following its discovery, they explored the sea around the island for over 3 degrees of latitude north and south, and over 3 distance lines west, as shown by the 3 shells of the ball. The little oblong central segment of the ball (#1) represents the island of Guadalupe **(Fig.6)**, as did the oblong central segment of the spiral in the older painting **(Fig.5)**.

A line from the last white segment #23 on the right to the head of the man cuts the fifth closed segment #28, encoding the Porcelano Cave and Punta Eugenia, both at 28°N. Visitors touched this protruding part of the painting, confirming where they stood at the latitude of the cave site, so the image of this segment #28 is abraded the most. The ball has 3 layers around its center, corresponding to the sailing distance from Punta Eugenia to Guadalupe, 3dl= 3°= 180 NM. A line from the center to the head of the man cuts the sixth closed segment #29, encoding the island of Guadalupe, at 29°N.

The last closed segment #31 encodes the mighty volcano of San Pedro, at 31°N. This volcano is one of the reasons the island of Guadalupe exists. The ball has 3 shells around its center, also corresponding to the distance between the San Pedro and Guadalupe, 3dl= 3°= 180 NM. However, the man is standing on the last segment but one, #30, encoding Punta Baja at the coast, at 30°N. This is also the latitude of the Mississippi Delta, and the Nile Delta, far in the east. From closed segment #30, it is only 2 segments to the big, loose segment. So, from Punta Baja, at 30°N, the sailing distance to Guadalupe is only 2dl= 2°= 120 NM.

The island of Guadalupe is important to the Sunreligion. The Egyptian SunGod Ra, has said (Refs.2-4): "The Realm of the Dead is in the west, at the other side of the waters, in the land where the Sun sets." For that reason the loose segment, new land discovered in the west, has been placed due west of last open segment #23, corresponding to the holy Tropic of Cancer, and the Southern Egyptian Empire, at 23°N. This is the location of the center of the Sunreligion (Refs.3-5). It is in this tradition, that former President Ronald Regan was buried in 2004 on the West Coast at sunset, June 2, 2004.

Note that the loose segment is triangular, like the Nile Delta, at 30°N and 31°N. Here is another image of the "Realm of the Dead" (beyond Guadalupe), "at the other side of the waters, in the land where the Sun sets." The eight dark segments at the top of the ball represent the Peninsula of Baja California, and also the Egyptian Empire, both extending from 23°N to (23+8°=) 31°N. The long arms of the little stick man point to the distant west, and the distant east. Does this imply that the ball describes ocean sailing routes? This could be the case, because the ball symbolizes the whole earth. This helps explain why the Island of Guadalupe was such a focus of interest in these paintings.

The Royal Couple

Three meters above the ball on a vertical rock wall descending from the ceiling is a complicated painting we call the "Royal Couple" **(Fig.7)**. It has a width of 75cm, and a height of 85cm. A long vertical part in the center resembles a man on the right, facing left, who is hugging his shorter wife, her head below his chin. Her arms and legs reach to the right, with plaits or fronds of a skirt. They both appear to have a geographic meaning, embodying the Peninsula of Baja California. The eye of the man represents the volcano of San Pedro at 31°N with a line looking west toward Guadalupe, and the eye of his wife is probably Punta Baja at 30°N.

In front of the Royal Couple (to the left, **Fig.7**) we see a large triangle like a shield, representing the original groundplan of the Porcelano Cave. If we compare it with the real, present groundplan **(Fig.2)**, we recognize with some difficulty the two enormous rocks, and the three smaller boulders in the Cave as shown in the triangle figure. The 5 stones encode its latitude, 5 degrees above the Tropic of Cancer, at 23+5= 28°N. Of course, more rocks have fallen onto the cave floor over the intervening time, as shown in **Fig.2**. Inside the triangle left of the couple, the vertical line represents the outer border of the ceiling in the north. The Cave faces east. The shield, protecting the Royal Couple against the mighty ocean, may also represent the western mountain range of the Sierra Pintada, and the Sierra Santa Clara, in this wider part of Baja California. The couple looks beyond these to the far west, in the direction of the setting Sun.

In the west we see the coastal waters, with directly behind the shield a closed loop, with 6 half distance lines in it (6 white spaces between the lines). The loop represents the island of Guadalupe (at 29°N), 6hdl= 3dl= 3°= 180 NM from Punta Eugenia. In European megalithic petroglyphs of the Atlantic, the attached lines indicate the dl of explorations of adjacent waters. Here, they indicate the 3 coastal islands in the north, Santa Catalina Island, San Clemente Island, and San Nicolas Island, just beyond Baja California, at 33°N. The thin line below the loop may likewise point to the tiny and unimportant Rocas Alijos (at 25°N), some 2dl= 120 NM offshore.

Behind the back of the man, or the mountain range of Baja California, an oval is visible, representing the island of Angel de la Guarda in the Gulf of California (at 28+1= 29°N). The three lines indicate the route to the island, which shows, with two additional lines to the southeast, the easiest route to the other side of the Gulf, at the Island of Tiburon, which is not shown as it is considered a part of the mainland of Mexico. This part of the painting strongly indicates the ongoing connection with the culture of Central America (Refs.9-14).

Below the dark "heart" of the woman, probably the campsite near Porcelano Cave, is a small piece of line, indicating its latitude, at 28°N. Below it are two other lines, corresponding to the latitudes of 27°N and 26°N. Apparently, one crosses here the Gulf of California, too. The relatively short crossing at 26°N leads to the mouth of the River Fuerte, at the other side.

Below, a big dark, horizontal line is visible, representing the holy Tropic of Cancer, at 23°N. In the east, 2 lines run southwards, indicating the Maria Archipelago (left), below the present town of Mazatlan (right), only 1dl= 1°= 60 NM offshore. Left of these two dark lines are light lines, indicating the coastal waters. There is no indication of the islands to the SW, the Revillagigedo Islands, located at 19°N, 220 NM SSW of Cabo San Lucas. Apparently, these islands were considered part of Central America, like the Island of Tiburon, which is absent because it was considered part of mainland Mexico.

Dating

The composite ball **(Fig.6)** was made on a boulder, 5 meters in front of the yellow/black paintings on the rear wall, discussed earlier. In general, figures applied deepest in the cave, are oldest and holiest. Here, this rule seems to be confirmed. The maker of the ball painted his new creation less deep in the Cave, to pay respect to the old paintings, which deal with the discovery of Guadalupe. He also used other colors. The complex composition of **Fig.7**, three meters higher, has been made in the same style as the ball. So again, both these paintings **(Figs.6&7)** most likely were made by the same people at the same time.

The earliest signs of culture in Central America started c.2000 BC (Refs.9-16). Officially the so-called Early Formative Period started 1500 BC, while the Olmec civilization flourished from 1200 BC to 500 BC. The composite ball strongly refers to this developing culture. The 23 open segments of it point (by the complex associations of 23) to a date during the Egyptian civilization, confirming this. The Egyptian presence in the Olmec Civilization has been illustrated by Jairazbhoy (Ref.10) and others, as well as the huge stone heads with Nubian helmets and petroglyphs of upside-down skyboats and so on, that you can see for yourself in Mexico. If the 15 segments inside the Ball, ending with largest segment 15, were intended to encode the 15th Egyptian Dynasty, the encoding would give a date of about 1600 BC, during the Hyksos Dynasty. Is it possible that the creator has dated his painting, or might have wished to honor the Pharoah in this way? Guadalupe is a little island, only 120 NM offshore. It appears this island was of importance in a symbolic, religious way. There are no signs of intensive exploration of the Pacific. So we conclude that the last two paintings **(Figs.6&7)** were made contemporary with the Olmec civilization in Central America, between 2000 and 500 BC.

9

References

1. Vinas, R., Rubio, A., Castillo, V., Moran, C., Perez, M., Deciga, E., Mendoza, L., and Martinez, R., "Rock Art in the Mountain Range of San Francisco: The Porcelano Cave, B.C.S. (Mexico)", International Newsletter on Rock Art, No 29, 2001 (pg.20) (ISSN 1022-3282)
2. Crosby, H. W., The Cave Paintings of Baja California, Discovering the Great Murals of an Unknown People, Sunbelt Publications, San Diego, 1997 (ISBN 0-932653-23-5)
3. De Jonge, R.M., and Wakefield, J.S, How the Sungod Reached America c.2500 BC, A Guide to Megalithic Sites, 2002 (ISBN 0-917054-19-9). Available: MCS Inc., Box 3392, Kirk-land, Wa 98083-3392, also on CD
4. Jonge, R.M. de, and IJzereef, G.F., De Stenen Spreken, Kosmos Z & K, Utrecht / Antwerpen, 1996 (ISBN 90-215-2846-0) (Dutch)
5. Website: www.howthesungod.com, De Jonge, R.M., and Wakefield, J.S
6. Adams, B. and Cialowicz, K.., Protodynastic Egypt, Shire Egyptology, Princes Risborough, 1997
7. Kemp, B., Ancient Egypt, Anatomy of a Civilization, London, Routledge, 1991
8. Wallis Budge, E.A., Osiris and the Egyptian Resurrection, 2 Vol., Dover Pub., N.Y., 1973 (ISBN 0-486-22780-4)
9. Thompson, G., American Discovery, Misty Isles Press, Seattle, 1994
10. Jairazbhoy, R.A., Ancient Egyptians and Chinese in America, Rowman & Littlefield, Totowa, N.J., 1974 (ISBN 0-87-471-571--1)
11. Peterson, F.A., Ancient Mexico, 1959
12. Stuart, G.E.,"New Light on the Olmec", National Geographic, Nov. 1993
13. Bernal, I., The Olmec World, University of California Press,London, 1969 (ISBN 0-520-02891-0)
14. Gruener, J., The Olmec Riddle, An Inquiry into the Origin of Precolumbian Civilization, Vengreen Publications, 1987, Rancho Santa Fe, Cal. (ISBN 0-9421-85-56-0)
15. People of the Stone Age: Hunter-gatherers and Early Farmers,Weldon Owen Pty Lim., Australia, 1994
16. New World and Pacific Civilizations: The Illustrated History of Mankind, Weldon Owen Pty Lim., Australia, 1994
17. Twohig, E. Shee, The Megalithic Art of Western Europe, Clarendon Press, Oxford, 1981
18. Watchman, PhD, Alan, email 7/12/04, and http://news.national geographic.com/news/2003/07/0717_030717_bajarockart.html
19. Watchman, A., de la L. Gutierrez, M., and Hernandez Llosas, M., "Giant Murals of Baja California: new regional archaeological perspectives", Antiquity 76, 947-948, 2002.

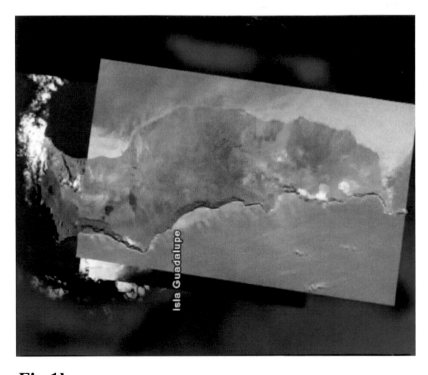

Fig.1b

Google Earth photo of the Island of Guadalupe, denuded by goats set ashore by whalers, now a Mexican piniped sanctuary.

THE PASSAGE GRAVE OF KARLEBY
Encoding the islands discovered in the Ocean
(Karleby, Falbygden, Sweden, c.2950 BC)

R.M. de Jonge, drsrmdejonge@hotmail.com
J.S. Wakefield, jayswakefield@yahoo.com

Summary

The Passage Grave of Karleby is a T-shaped Megalithic tomb with religious and geographic encodings, professionally dated to c.2950 BC. The encodings relate to the Sunreligion and islands discovered in the North Atlantic Ocean. The Island of Jan Mayen is particularly well encoded, showing its discovery at this early date. These numeric encodings commemorate the history of Megalithic discoveries. They are typical for all early Megalithic monuments, and clearly demonstrate that the old Swedish stone constructions are a part of the Megalithic heritage of Europe.

Introduction

The Falbygden area is situated in the south part of Sweden, between the two big lakes Vättern and Vänern, around the town of Falköping (Refs.1,2). In this early farming region there are about 270 passage graves, gathered within a triangular area covering 50x50x30 km, and constituting 3/4 of all known passage tombs in Sweden. The tombs are situated close to each other, mostly at distances of less then half a kilometer. The megalithic monuments are made of up to 40 big stones (uprights and coverstones, local rocks), having typical sizes of about 2x1x0.5 meters (m). The stone structures are T-shaped, most of them originally covered by a mound of stone and earth. The passages are 4-10 m long, about 1 m wide, and 1 m high. The chambers, at right angles, are 5-17 m long, 1-4 m wide, and about 2 m high, significantly higher than the passages. The mounds can be as much as 40 meters in diameter, and up to 2 m high, covering the chambers.

Passage Graves: General Interpretation

The megalithic monuments of Falköping are located near the west coast of Western Europe, about 100 km from the Ocean. All the passage graves point with their important burial chamber to the west, with entrances on the east side. These were monuments of the Sunreligion, and the people who built them were interested in following the SunGod across the Ocean, a kind of mission churches for spreading this religion to the other side of the planet. They were built at this location because of the fertile farming lands. However, also note that they are built at 58°N, the latitude of the north coast of Scotland. In that area are a lot of important megalithic monuments, like the enormous 60-stone Ring of Brodgar, also dated c.3000 BC, the Ring of Callanish, and numerous others. From this coast, important discoveries were made in the Ocean between c.3500 BC and 3000 BC. This was the time period of the great discoveries in the north of the Atlantic Ocean: the Faroes (c.3400 BC), Iceland (c.3400 BC), and Greenland (c.3300 BC) (Refs.3,4). It was during this time period that all these passage graves were built.

The tombs are typically T-shaped, like the Passage Grave of Karleby. When comparing them with a map **(Figs.1,2)**, the configuration of the passages resembles the crossing from Scotland via the

Photo: Overview of the north two of the four Karleby Passage Graves.

Faroes and Iceland to Greenland, and the burial chambers resemble the Island of Greenland, the westernmost land of the then known world. In general, the last coverstone of the passage (stone 15, **Fig.1**), locally known as the "keystone", was special, often made of granite or gneiss. This stone in these passage graves symbolizes Cape Holm, Greenland, where Greenland was first discovered, at the Arctic Circle. It has religious meaning in the religion of the SunGod, because the Arctic Circle is the northernmost line where the Sun still shines at midwinter day (winter solstice), when the Sun is at right angles above the Tropic of Capricorn. The slow southern movement of the Sun then turns northerly.

Therefore the burial chamber portions of these monuments represent Greenland, the western home of the SunGod. The southernmost portions of these chambers should be important, because they correspond to South Greenland. Here, at about 60°N, the megalith builders gave up their efforts to cross the Ocean, c.3200 BC **(Fig.2)**. In South Sweden, the belt of lands at the level of the north of Scotland (approx. 58°N) is a holy area, with numerous passage graves, Bronze Age petroglyphs, and references to the SunGod. Some of the artifacts found in Sweden are shown in **Fig.4**. This area runs from the Island of Gotland (passage graves) in the East Sea, via Östergötland (petroglyphs) and Västergötland (Falbygden, passage graves), to Bohuslän and Goteborgslän in the west, famous for its rock petroglyphs of the Bronze Age (Refs.5,6). In Jutland, Denmark, there are a lot of megalithic monuments at this latitude, too. Note, that the important names of these five areas contain the local word for "God".

The Passage Grave of Karleby

The four passage graves of Karleby are located 3 km ESE of the town of Falköping. The graves are built at the west side along a prehistoric NS road, about 100 m apart. Most of them have cup marks on the roofslabs. A groundplan exists of one of them **(Fig.1)** (Ref.1). It has a passage about 7 m long and 1.5 m wide. The chamber is also about 7 m long, but 3 m wide. The grave consists of a partly covered passage, with behind it at right angles an almost rectangular, higher, burial chamber. Note, that the third upright stone at the north side of the passage is clearly missing (stone 8, in dots).

Most of the passage graves in this area were originally covered with dirt, and some still are, so they look like mounds. At some sites, like Karleby, the dirt has washed away over the years (Photo 1). Most of the stones of the monument are set on edge, and then large "coverstones" are set over them, which held the dirt, as shown in **Fig.1**. In this monument, there are five stones (1,2, and 6,7,8) at the entrance, that did not have coverstones over them. So originally, when one entered this monument, one opened a small blocking stone, ducked under coverstone 12, and crawled over the large unnumbered "sill" stone in the floor of the entrance. All passage graves like this have an important religious meaning: when entering the passage, symbol of the Land of the Living, you are beginning the route to the west, which is to the chamber, which represents the Realm of the Dead.

Sunreligion/Egypt

The total number of big stones in the monument is 28 (1 to 28 in **Fig.1**), corresponding to the Nile Delta, the Northern Egyptian Empire, 28° below Karleby, at 58°-28= 30°N. As can be seen in the encodings of other megalithic sites, the latitude of the monument site itself is frequently used. In this case, the 58° latitude of the Karleby site, minus the total of 28 stones, leaves 30°, encoding Heliopolis, the holy city of the SunGod, where the pyramids of Giza would soon be built.

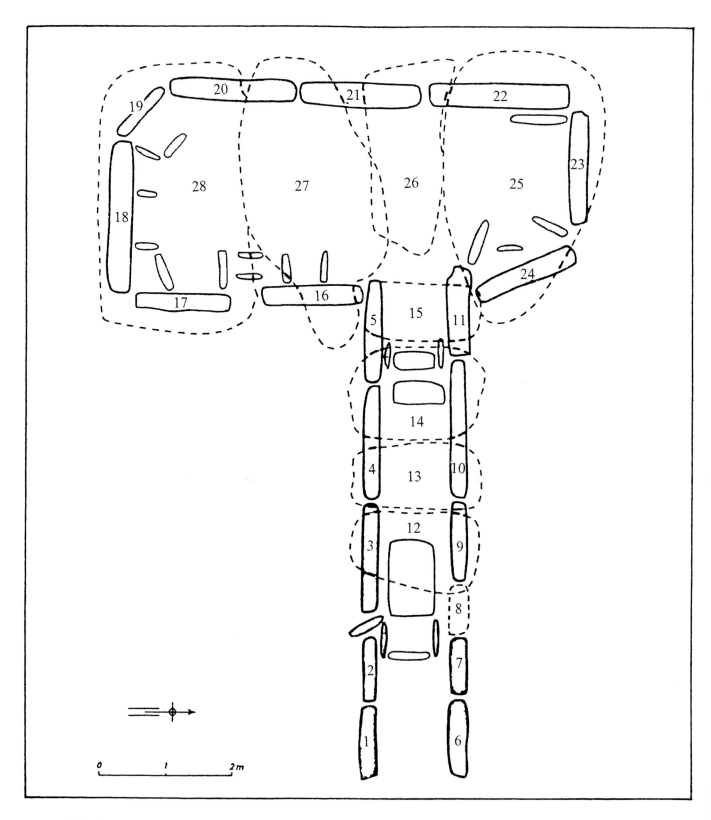

Fig.1 Groundplan of the passage tomb of Karleby (Ref.1), with uprights and coverstones numbered by the authors. The 28 stones show the geographical position of Karleby above the Nile Delta, at 30+28= 58 degrees N. The grave points with the important burial chamber exactly to the west, to the North Coast of Scotland. . The passage symbolizes the crossing from the Faroes to Cape Holm, Greenland, at the Arctic Circle. The grave chamber symbolizes the island of Greenland, the westernmost land of the then known world. (Karleby, Falbygden, Sweden, c.2950 BC)

The covered part of the passage grave has a total of 23 big stones (subtract the outside 5 entrance stones from the total of 28, see Fig.1), corresponding to the Southern Egyptian Empire at the holy Tropic of Cancer, at 23°N. This is the center of the SunGod religion. The 23 stones of the covered part of the grave also correspond to the latitude where the Tropic of Cancer crosses the west coast of Africa, at 23°N. In fact, at this latitude people wanted to cross the Atlantic Ocean in honor of the SunGod (Refs.3,4). One should not forget that this passage grave was built c.3000 BC, during the First Dynasty of Egypt, and the Pharaohs of Egypt were considered to be personifications of the SunGod Ra.

Explorations of the Upper North: The Faroes

The passage grave of Karleby contains 28 stones, encoding its own latitude, 28° above the Nile Delta, at 30°+28= 58°N. The burial chamber lies exactly to the west **(Fig.1)**. This is the direction to the important north coast of Scotland, also at 58°N. The passage has 4 coverstones, encoding the sailing distance from Scotland to the Faroes, 4dl= 4°= 240 NM (1dl= 1 distance line= 1 degree= 60 Nautical Miles. In ancient Egypt the distance of 1° was called the "moira" (Ref.10). Today, the international unit at sea is the nautical mile (NM), by definition one sixtieth of a degree.) The burial chamber has 4 large coverstones, pointing to the north, confirming the 4° distance from Scotland to the Faroes.

The Faroes Archipelago is situated at 58+4= 62°N. Megalithic sites also show the use of complementary latitudes in the old latitude encoding system. The reason for this is because handling large numbers of stones was difficult, so large numbers were easier to handle this way. The complementary number to the total number of stones in this monument is 90-28= 62, encoding these important Faroe Islands, at 62°N. Apparently, these islands were the first stop on the route of the voyage to the Realm of the Dead.

Iceland

The 4 coverstones of the passage (12 to 15 in **Fig.1**), also correspond to the sailing distance from the Faroes to the SE coast of Iceland, 4dl= 4°= 240 NM. The 2 entrance stones 1 and 6 encode the latitude of this coast, 2° above the Faroes, at 62+2= 64°N. The north side of the passage has 6 stones (6-11), confirming this latitude of Iceland, 6° above Scotland and Karleby, at 58+6= 64°N. The Faroes and Iceland were discovered c.3400 BC (Refs.3,4). Next, they sailed further up the passage, around Iceland to the west. The next pair of entrance stones, 2 & 7, encode the NW Peninsula of Iceland, 2° above the SE coast, at 64+2= 66°N. From here one enters the covered portion of the monument, into the holy portion, across to Greenland.

Greenland

The 5 uncovered entrance stones correspond to the sailing distance from Iceland to Cape Holm, Greenland, 5dl= 5°= 300 NM, situated at the holy Arctic Circle, 5° above the Faroes, at 62°+5= 67°N. The five southern uprights of the passage (up to the "keystone") confirm this. The first 3 coverstones of the passage (up to the "keystone") confirm the latitude of Cape Holm again, 3° above the SE coast of Iceland, at 64°+3= 67°N. The last coverstone, the "keystone", confirms the latitude of Cape Holm once more, 1° above the NW Peninsula of Iceland, at 66°+1= 67°N. Note that the "sill stones" (the unnumbered flat groundstones near the entrance of the chamber) are crossed just before the "Keystone", to emphasize its importance. The whole covered part of the passage grave has 23 stones, confirming the latitude of Cape Holm with the complementary latitude,

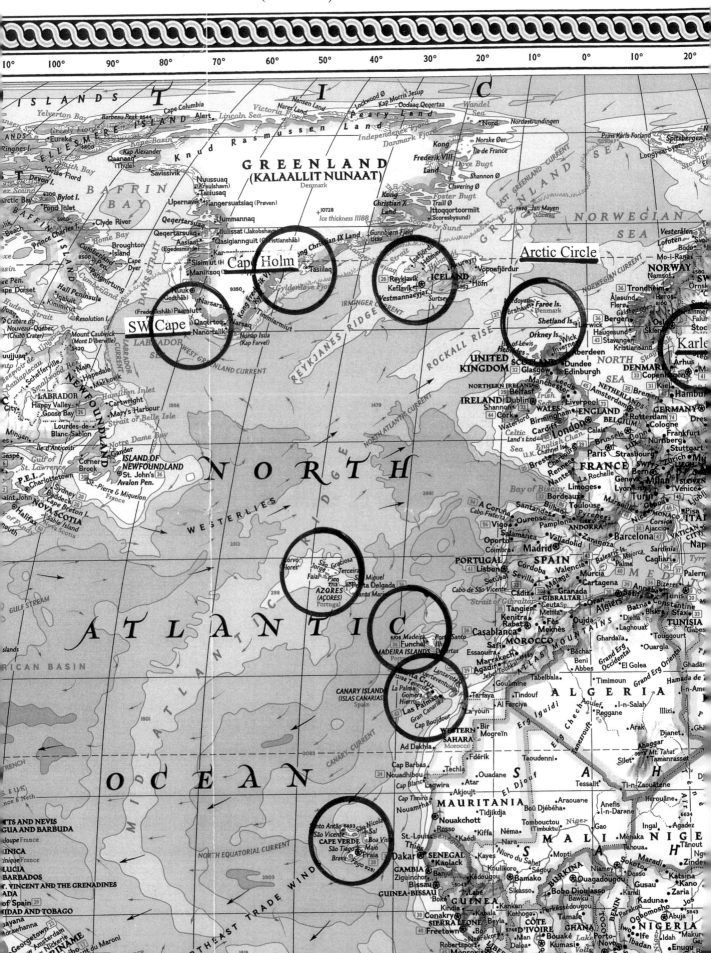

Fig.2 Chart of the eastern part of the North Atlantic Ocean (Ref.9). The circles indicate the islands discovered in the ocean (c.2950 BC).

90°-23°= 67°N. The holy Arctic Circle, running from Scandinavia to Cape Holm, Greenland, and beyond, is the northernmost line where the Sun still shines at midwinter day (winter solstice). So, thanks to the SunGod they reached this Cape of Greenland by sailing west at the Holy Latitude of 67°N. As memorialized in other monuments, including Stonehenge in South England, and Loughcrew in Ireland, Greenland had been discovered by c.3300 BC (Refs.3,4,7).

Jan Mayen

The uncovered part of the passage symbolizes the sailing route from the Faroes to Iceland. The large flat groundstone in the entry, as one enters the covered portion of the passage, shows that the next section of the voyage, beyond Iceland, is more important. The passage has 4 coverstones, corresponding to the sailing distance from the North Cape of Iceland, at the Arctic Circle, to the little island of Jan Mayen, 4dl= 4°= 240 NM, located 4° above Iceland, at 67°+4= 71°N.

Jan Mayen can also be reached from Cape Brewster, the east cape of Greenland. The covered part of the passage symbolizes the sailing route from Iceland to Greenland, and the burial chamber symbolizes the Island of Greenland itself. This burial chamber has 3 eastern uprights, stones 16, 17, and 24, corresponding to Cape Brewster, 3° above Cape Holm, at 67°+3= 70°N. The chamber has 4 large coverstones, corresponding to the sailing distance from Cape Brewster to Jan Mayen, again 4dl= 4°= 240 NM. The chamber has 9 upright stones, confirming the latitude of Jan Mayen, 9° above the Faroes (at the level of the North Cape of Scandinavia), at 62°+9= 71°N. In total, the burial chamber contains 9+4= 13 stones, again confirming the latitude of Jan Mayen, 13° above Scotland and Karleby, at 58°+13= 71°N. (The 10 stones of the covered passage and the 3 northern entrance stones also total 13.) Notice how clearly, and with big stones, this little island is encoded. Jan Mayen was the last discovery in the North Atlantic Ocean, c.2950 BC (Refs.1-4).

South Greenland

The whole passage symbolizes the sailing route from the Faroes to Greenland. The last coverstone, the "keystone", represents Cape Holm at the Arctic Circle. The burial chamber, representing Greenland, has 9 uprights, confirming the latitude of Cape Holm, 9° above Scotland and Karleby, at 58°+9= 67°N. The chamber has 4 coverstones, and 3 eastern uprights, together 4+3 stones, corresponding to Cape Farvel, the south cape of Greenland, 7° below the Arctic Circle, at 67°-7= 60°N. This cape is located at the latitude of the Shetland Islands. The southernmost upright stone 18 represents Cape Farvel, literally. Because of the huge cold icecap on Greenland, and the importance of its south cape, it is the biggest stone of the whole monument. Cape Farvel is situated at the complementary latitude of the southern Nile Delta, at 90°-30°= 60°N. This is where the Egyptian city of Heliopolis, dedicated to the SunGod, is located.

The next upright stone of the chamber, stone 19, represents the SW Cape, at 60°+1= 61°N. At Cape Farvel and the SW Cape of Greenland the megalith builders gave up their efforts to cross the Ocean, c.3200 BC, as shown by the petroglyphs of Loughcrew, Ireland, and the monument of Stonehenge I, South England (Refs.3,4). North America could have been reached most directly from this SW Cape. However, note that the small SW stone 19 confirms the early carbon date of the Karleby monument, of c.3000 BC (Refs.1,2). Stone 19 would not be so small if the monument were built after the discovery of America, 500 years later, in c.2500 BC.

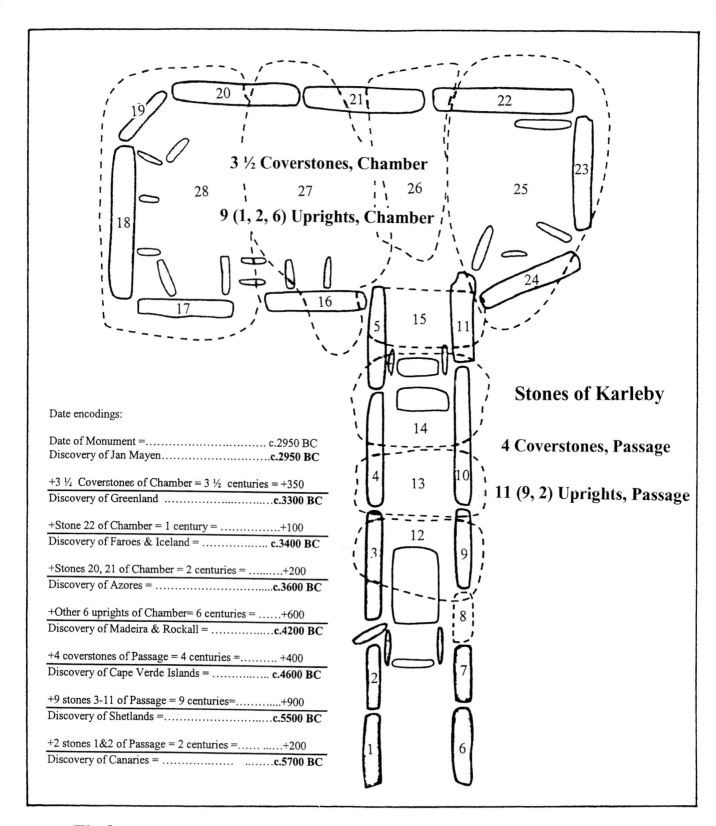

3 ½ Coverstones, Chamber

9 (1, 2, 6) Uprights, Chamber

Stones of Karleby

4 Coverstones, Passage

11 (9, 2) Uprights, Passage

Date encodings:

Date of Monument =……………...………… c.2950 BC
Discovery of Jan Mayen…………….……...**c.2950 BC**

+3 ½ Coverstones of Chamber = 3 ½ centuries = +350
Discovery of Greenland …………...………...**c.3300 BC**

+Stone 22 of Chamber = 1 century = ……………+100
Discovery of Faroes & Iceland = ……………... **c.3400 BC**

+Stones 20, 21 of Chamber = 2 centuries = ….........+200
Discovery of Azores = ……………………......**c.3600 BC**

+Other 6 uprights of Chamber= 6 centuries = ……+600
Discovery of Madeira & Rockall = …………...**c.4200 BC**

+4 coverstones of Passage = 4 centuries =………. +400
Discovery of Cape Verde Islands = ………..…. **c.4600 BC**

+9 stones 3-11 of Passage = 9 centuries=………...+900
Discovery of Shetlands =………………….…...**c.5500 BC**

+2 stones 1&2 of Passage = 2 centuries =…… ...…+200
Discovery of Canaries = ………………. …..…**c.5700 BC**

Fig.3 Groundplan of the Passage Grave of Karleby, illustrating the possible encoding of dates of discovery of islands in the Ocean, by century. (Falbygden, Sweden, c.2950 BC)

The 3 western uprights 20-22 symbolize the West Coast of Greenland. The last stone, 22, the biggest of these, indicates the highest latitude which could be reached, at 61°+3 stones= 64°N. The remaining stones 23 and 24 of the chamber point to "keystone" 15 of the passage, perhaps indicating the holy Arctic Circle at the West Coast, at 64°+3 stones= 67°N, however, its position at the east side of the chamber shows they could not reach this latitude. So, the sizes of the stones, and their arrangement in the chamber, confirm that the megalith builders of this monument were not aware of the continent of North America.

We just explained that the big southernmost stone 18 represents Cape Farvel, at 60°N, and that the little stone 19 represents the SW Cape of Greenland at 61°N. This means that the previous stone 17, at the east side of the chamber, symbolizes the Orkney Islands in the east, at 59°N, and that stone 16 represents the north coast of Scotland, at 58°N. However, in that case this first stone of the chamber also symbolizes Karleby in Sweden, at the same latitude, at 58°N. It implies this first stone 16 is much more important than previously thought. It represents the Passage Grave of Karleby, but also the start of the voyages of discovery around the continent of Greenland (see **Fig.1**), because stones 16 and 17 represent the narrow east coast south of Cape Holm, stones 18 and 19 the short south coast, and stones 20, 21,and 22, the important West Coast of Greenland. Details of slightly earlier explorations are recorded in the westernmost roofstone petroglyphs of the main passage grave in Loughcrew, Ireland (Ref.3).

The History of Discovery of Other Islands in the Ocean
Earlier explorations were perhaps also encoded in this monument. We have seen double meanings and double encodings in other megalithic sites. Especially at Dissignac, on the coast of Brittany, we have seen petroglyphic encodings sensibly added to, further regarding an ongoing story of discovery, over a period of thousands of years. This should not surprise us, since long spans of time were involved. So, earlier discoveries may be embedded in the design, and passed to posterity. We should be looking for mneumonic devices, which were used as the information storage devices of the time. Reverse-engineering mneumonic devices is a speculative proposition, but we will make some suggestions that are possible. We wonder whether it is common or unusual for mneumonic devices to be constructed in such a series of overlays as we propose below.

The Canary Islands
In total, the covered part of the passage grave contains 23 stones, encoding the place where the holy Tropic of Cancer leaves the continent of Africa, at 23°N. It had been an early focus for crossing the Atlantic Ocean in honor of the SunGod. Suppose important stone 16, the first upright of the chamber, were to represent the Tropic of Cancer, where it leaves Africa, at 23°N. Then the last western menhirs 21 & 22 (the 5th & 6th around the circle) would represent the Canary Islands, 5° & 6° above the Tropic, at their 28° and 29°N latitudes. The passage grave contains a total of 28 stones, confirming the southern Canary Islands (stone 21), at 28°N. The "keystone" symbolizes the sailing distance, 1dl= 1°= 60 NM. The 7 stones of the chamber (16-22) could represent these 7 islands, which had been discovered c.5500 BC (Refs.3,4).

The Shetland Islands
The first upright of the chamber, stone 16, represents Karleby and Scotland, at 58°N. Then the big stone 18, two spots over, symbolizes the Shetland Islands, 2° above the north coast of Scotland, at 58°+2= 60°N. These 3 stones, (16-18) represent the 3 islands, which also had been discovered

TABLE 1

PASSAGE GRAVE OF KARLEBY

Principal Meaning of the Passage: the Sailing Route from the Faroes, via Iceland, to Cape Holm, Greenland (also "Land of the Living")

- 2 uncovered southern stones.......... = 2 Islands of Madeira
- 3 uncovered northern stones...........= 3 Shetland Islands
- 10 covered passage stones............ = 10 Cape Verde Islands
- 11 upright stones of the passage...... = 11 islands of Madeira and the Azores
- 15 stones of the passage ....= Cape Verde and South Cape Verde Islands @ 15°N
- keystone ....= Cape Holm at Arctic Circle @ 67°N

Principal Meaning of the Chamber: the continent of Greenland (also "Realm of the Dead")

- 3 western stones........................ = 3 island groups of the Azores
- 9 upright stones of chamber........... = 9 islands of the Azores
- Large southern stone of chamber...... = Cape Farvel, Greenland @ 60°N
- SW stone of chamber.................... = SW Cape of Greenland @ 61°N
- Last western stone of chamber........ = West Coast of Greenland @ 64°N

Principal Latitude Encodings:

- 23 stones, covered portion ....= **Tropic of Cancer @ 23°N**
- 28 total stones..................................... = **Canary Islands @ 28°N**
- 28 total stones +30°N of Heliopolis, Egypt.... = **site latitude, Karleby @ 58°N**
- 90° -28 total stones............................... = **Faroes @ 62°N**
- 90° -23 stones, covered portion.................. = **Arctic Circle @ 67°N**

Latitude Encodings using Karleby, at 58°N:

- -20 uprights of monument ....+58 = Central Azores @ 38°N
- -1 keystone .... +58 = Rockall @ 57°N
- 2 entrance stones of S side of passage.............+58 =Shetlands @ 60° N
- 4 coverstones of passage .... +58 = Faroes @ 62°N
- 6 uprights of N side of passage .... +58 = SE Iceland @ 64°N
- 8 uprights of N side of monument .... + 58 = NW Iceland @ 66°N
- 9 uprights of the chamber .... +58 = Cape Holm & Arctic Circle @ 67°N
- 11 uprights of passage +keystone................. + 58 = Cape Brewster @ 70°N
- 13 stones of chamber..............................+58 = Jan Mayen @ 71°N
- 2 SE stones of chamber .... +58 = Cape Farvel @ 60°N
- 3 SW stones of chamber .... +58 = SW Cape of Greenland @ 61°N

c.5500 BC. The two entrance stones 1 & 2, before the "blocking stone", confirm the latitude, 2° above Karleby and Scotland. The 3 other entrance stones 6-8 confirm the 3 islands. Again, the "keystone" symbolizes the sailing distance, 1dl= 1°= 60 NM. The archipelago is located at the complementary latitude of the southern Nile Delta, at 90°-30°= 60°N, where the Egyptian city of Heliopolis is located.

The Cape Verde Islands

The passage contains 11 upright stones (1-11), corresponding to the Bissagos Islands, off the SW coast of Africa, at 11°N. Together with its 4 coverstones (12-15), it encodes Cape Verde, at 11°+4= 15°N. This is the westernmost point of all continental land. The covered part of the passage contains 10 stones, encoding the 10 Cape Verde Islands. The 5 entrance stones, and the 5 southern uprights of the passage, each encode the sailing distance to the islands, 5dl= 5°= 300 NM.

If we suppose stone 16, the first upright of the chamber, were to symbolize the Bissagos Islands, at 11°N, then the western menhirs 20-22 would represent the Cape Verde Islands, 4-6° above this latitude, at 15-17°N. The 5 stones 16-20 show the correct sailing distance to the Cape Verde Islands (stone 21) of 5dl= 5°= 300 NM. The Cape Verde Islands had been discovered c.4500 BC (Refs.3,4).

The Islands of Madeira

Karleby has 8 coverstones, corresponding to the northern Nile Delta, 8° above the Tropic of Cancer, at 23°+8= 31°N. The passage has 4 coverstones, encoding the center of the United Egyptian Empire, halfway to the Tropic of Cancer, at 23°+4= 27°N. If we suppose stone 16, the first upright in the chamber, to symbolize this then-important place, the big stone 18, two spots over, would represent the northern Canary Islands at 27°+2= 29°N, the small stone 19 would represent the small Selvagens Ilets at 29°+1= 30°N, and the last western menhir, 22, would symbolize Madeira, at 30°+3= 33°N. Finally, the small slab inside then represents the little island of Porto Santo, at the same latitude. (The other stones 23 and 24 could represent nearby seamounts, west of Gibraltar, that were formerly islands, at 31°N and 32°N.) The 4 western menhirs 19-22 provide the sailing distance from the northern Canaries to Madeira , 4dl= 4°= 240 NM. Madeira had been discovered c.4200 BC.

Rockall

Inside the passage grave are 23 smaller, less important stones (see **Fig.1**), including the groundstone at the entrance, again encoding the holy Tropic of Cancer, at 23°N, and the holy Arctic Circle, at 90-23= 67°N. Including these smaller stones, the monument possesses a total of 28+23= 51 stones, encoding Stonehenge I (c.3200 BC), the huge monument in South England, at 51°N, built to commemorate the discovery of Greenland about a hundred years earlier. If we suppose stone 16, the first upright of the chamber, to symbolize Stonehenge, at 51°N, then big stone 18 would represent the west coast of Ireland, at 53°N, the westernmost coast of Europe. The last western menhir 22 would then symbolize the island of Rockall, 4° higher, at 53°+4= 57°N. The 4 western menhirs 19-22 provide the sailing distance from NW Ireland to Rockall, 4dl= 4°= 240 NM. The 4 coverstones 12-15 of the passage provide the other sailing distance, from the west coast of Scotland to Rockall, also 4dl. The "keystone" symbolizes Rockall, 1° below the north coast of Scotland and Karleby (stone 16), at 58°-1= 57°N. Rockall, located at the complementary latitude of Madeira, at 90-33= 57°N, was discovered c.4100 BC (Ref.3). The petroglyphs of Paredes, NW

Fig.4 Samples of much later Bronze Age encoded Swedish objects, that still show geographic latitudes and holy numbers of the Sunreligion (c.1500-500 BC, Montelius, Ref.8)

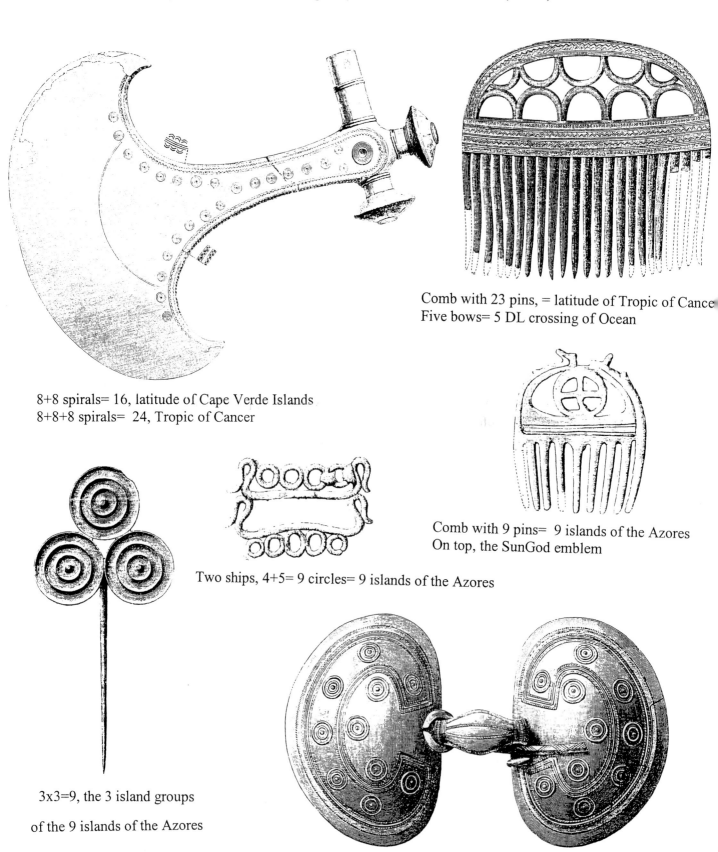

Comb with 23 pins, = latitude of Tropic of Cance
Five bows= 5 DL crossing of Ocean

8+8 spirals= 16, latitude of Cape Verde Islands
8+8+8 spirals= 24, Tropic of Cancer

Comb with 9 pins= 9 islands of the Azores
On top, the SunGod emblem

Two ships, 4+5= 9 circles= 9 islands of the Azores

3x3=9, the 3 island groups

of the 9 islands of the Azores

10+10= 20 circles, + center 3= 23= latitude of Tropic of Cancer

Spain, and of Dissignac, Brittany, show Madeira and Rockall were discovered more or less at the same time.

The Azores

Madeira was used as a point of departure for the Azores (**Fig.2**). If we suppose stone 16 were to symbolize Madeira, at 33°N, the 3 western stones of the chamber would represent the 3 island groups of the Azores, 4-6° above Madeira, at 37, 38, and 39°N. The 8 coverstones of the passage grave provide the sailing distance from Madeira to the Azores, 8dl= 480 NM, and the latitude of the Central Azores, 8° above Heliopolis, at 30°+8= 38°N. The 9 upright stones of the chamber represent the 9 islands of the Azores. The chamber has 2 northern stones (23, 24), corresponding to the 2 northern islands of the Azores, called the West Azores. In total the chamber has 9 upright stones, also corresponding to the latitude of the West Azores, 9° above Heliopolis, at 30°+9= 39°N.

The passage contains 2+9= 11 upright stones, encoding the 2+9= 11 islands of Madeira and the Azores. The whole monument possesses 28 stones, corresponding to all 28 islands discovered in the south. The Azores had been discovered c.3600 BC, as clearly and dramatically documented by the Passage Grave of Gavrinis, near Carnac in Brittany. The West Azores were the westernmost islands of the Ocean for about 300 years, until Greenland was found, c.3300 BC (Refs.3,4,7).

Dating

Most of the dates mentioned so far are based on Carbon-14 determinations of monuments elsewhere in Europe (Refs.3,4). However, we have the impression that dates may be encoded in this grave, in a way not seen before (follow this in **Fig.3**).

The passage grave of Karleby was erected at the discovery of the Islet of Jan Mayen, c.2950 BC (Refs.1,2), because Jan Mayen is so prominently encoded, not seen before in these monuments. The 3.5 huge coverstones of the burial chamber suggest that Greenland was discovered 3.5 centuries earlier, in c.3300 BC, which is firmly established (Refs.3,4). Stone 22, with the parallel slab inside, is the last one of the three westernmost stones. So, the discovery of Iceland and the Faroes was 1 century earlier, in c.3400 BC. The other 2 stones (20 and 21) determine the discovery of the Azores, 2 centuries earlier, in c.3600 BC. The other 6 uprights at both sides of the chamber might encode the discoveries of Madeira and Rockall, 6 centuries earlier, in c.4200 BC. The 4 coverstones of the passage show the discovery of the Cape Verde Islands, 4 centuries earlier, in c.4600 BC. The remaining 11 uprights of the passage carry the discovery of the Canaries, 11 centuries earlier, at the early date of c.5700 BC. Finally, the two entrance stones 1 & 2, before the "blocking stone", reveal the discovery of the Shetland Islands, only 2 centuries later, c.5500 BC.

These results are simply amazing. For the first time the estimated date of the discovery of the Canary Islands, and the Shetland Islands, c.5500 BC, has been confirmed (Refs.3,4). Coastal sailing started in the Mediterranean, so the Canaries were discovered first. The "blocking stone" points NW, so the Shetlands in the NW of Europe were discovered slightly later. It also implies the "century" was an important unit of time at the end of the Neolithicum. We have not seen dating encoded in this way before, but probably, it was intended here. We draw this conclusion because these dates are very close to similar carbon-dates established from monuments elsewhere in Europe (Refs.3,4).

Discussion

Table 1 gives an overview of the geographic meanings of Karleby. The last part shows latitude encodings using the site location of Karleby, at 58°N. It illustrates the beauty of the methodology they used to encode large numbers. Rather than building a huge, laborious monument, as was done in Carnac, Brittany, they used the latitude of the site to make the construction labor easier. Many of the numeric encodings of Karleby are based upon the 58° latitude of the site itself, as shown in the Table.

We have studied all the megalithic monuments and petroglyphs of Western Europe (see www.howthesungod.com). Almost all the monuments have religious and geographic meanings. Most of the petroglyphs are primitive coastal maps. We have written two books about this subject (Refs.3,4). The passage grave of Karleby in Falbygden, Sweden, fits in this megalithic tradition. The numbers and layouts of the huge stones in these monuments, which were set in place by hand, are not happenstance, but carefully designed by the human mind.

Perhaps some people are dismayed by the complexity of this monument. The encodings are complicated because the efforts to cross the Atlantic Ocean had been going on for 3000 years. The early stone constructions, such as Barnenez and Kercado in Brittany, dating from c.4500 BC, are much more simple, though both already demonstrate the use of encoded latitudes. What we see here is the result of an enormous effort of the whole community, to commemorate their religion and their achievements in a monument for the glorification of the interred individuals for generations to come.

One should realize that Neolithic men had no opportunity to express themselves in writing. Recording their story was accomplished by creating numerical encodings, as described in this article. This was only done until the end of the Bronze Age, in Scandinavia c.500 BC (see **Fig.4**). With this article, added to our other work, we hope to demonstrate that Swedish monuments and petroglyphs are clearly a part of the megalithic heritage of Europe.

References

1. Ekornavallen, the Prehistoric Enclosure of, B. Hjohlman, Svenska Fornminnesplatser 52, 1977 (ISBN 91-7192-376-4)
2. Silent Messengers from a Distant Epoch: Falbygden area passage tombs, Hugin & Munin Kulturinformation AB, Länsstyrelsen, Västra Götaland, Sweden
3. De Jonge, R.M., and Wakefield, J.S, How the Sungod Reached America c.2500 BC, A Guide to Megalithic Sites, 2002 (ISBN 0-917054-19-9). Available: MCS Inc., Box 3392, Kirkland, Wa 98083-3392, also on CD
4. Jonge, R.M. de, and IJzereef, G.F., De Stenen Spreken, Kosmos Z & K, Utrecht/Antwerpen, 1996 (ISBN 90-215-2846-0) (Dutch)
5. Coles, J., Images of the Past, A Guide to the Rock Carvings of Northern Bohuslän, Bohusläns Museum, 1990 (ISBN 91-7686-110-4)
6. Evers, D., Felsbilder, Botschaften der Vorzeit, 1991 (ISBN 3-332-00482-4)(German)
7. Casson, L., Ships and Seafaring in Ancient Times, British Museum Press, 1994
8. Montelius, O., "Minnen Fran Var Frontid", ARCKEO-Forlaget, Gamleby, 1994
9. Portion of map "The World, Physical", by National Geographic Society, 2003
10. Tompkins, P., Secrets of the Great Pyramid, Harper Colophon Books, Harper & Row, New York, 1971 (ISBN 0-06-09-0631-6)

The "Beaker People" who discovered America

(Fourknocks Passage Grave, Ireland, and beakers of the Devises, Salisbury/South Wiltshire, and Poverty Point Museums, c. 2500 BC)

J.S. Wakefield, jayswakefield@yahoo.com

Since prehistory has been researched by digging tombs, groups of people around the world have been categorized by their pottery. At the end of the third millennium BC a distinctive pottery style known as "beakers" became widespread in Western Europe. They had a tall and narrow form, and decoration consisting of organized zones of incised geometric designs. This pottery has been found over a wide area, stretching from Hungary to Ireland, and from Norway to Morocco, with greatest concentration along the Atlantic coasts of Europe. Beaker graves differed from the communal Neolithic graves of the earlier period, having grave goods for the deceased, and the first evidence of widespread metallurgy. "Certainly beaker-users were responsible for the introduction of metallurgy into the British Isles" (Ref.5).

In our previous published work, we have shown that these people were exploring the huge ocean to their west, trying to discover what was on the backside of the Earth. By studying the number of big stones in their monuments, the orientations of the stones, the surveyed ground plans of the monuments, and other features of monument design, we have shown that the intentions of the builders can be determined.

One of the most decorated passage graves in Europe is the little-known Irish monument, just a half hour drive south of the Newgrange Complex, called "Fourknocks". **Photo 1** shows the road sign for it, taken during our visit in the summer of 1999. **Photo 2** shows the mound itself. **Photo 3** shows Dr. de Jonge explaining the water motif to Suzy Wakefield. This is the motif for water in Egyptian hieroglyphs, and is used worldwide in petroglyphs to represent water. In the Fourknocks photo there are many repeated waves, characterizing the nearby North Atlantic Ocean.

Photo 4 is a Beaker pot, a photo taken in the Devises Museum (in Devises, just south of Avebury) during our trip in May 2008. The upper portion of the pot has the same water motif, here decorated waves, while the lower portion shows the waves undecorated, with the decoration on the triangles between. Both patterns are common in megalithic petroglyphs. **Photos 5 & 6** show Dr. de Jonge lighting important chamber entry stones with his flashlight. These patterns are called "lozenges". They are the diamond-shaped figures, usually with associated latitude lines; these are units of measure of distances on the ocean. These symbols are also very common in megalithic "art". The lozenge motif is well illustrated by the next two beaker pots. The pot **(Photo 7)** with the #3 tag is in the Devises Museum, while the "Cherhill" labeled pot **(Photo 8)** is in the Salisbury and South Wiltshire Museum in Salisbury. These pots tie the "Beaker People" to the huge stone monuments of Europe that encode the sailing discoveries across the oceans to the

Photo. 1   Roadsign to "Fourknocks Passage Grave", Ireland (Photo by authors, May, 1998)

Photo. 2   Fourknocks Passage Grave (Photo by authors, May 1998)

west. Photo Group 10 shows at the top a pot excavated at the trading center of Poverty Point, Louisiana, with a smaller photo, left, of a pot on exhibit in the Devises Museum, Devises, England, and right, a smaller photo of a pot in the Salisbury Museum. These pots were made in the same styles, by the same cultural group, probably at about the same time. The clay should be studied in an attempt to learn where it was made.

References

1. De Jonge, R.M., and Wakefield, J.S., How the SunGod Reached America c.2500 BC, A Guide to Megalithic Sites, MCS, 2002 (ISBN 0-917054-19-9)
2. O'brien, W., Bronze Age Copper Mining in Britain & Ireland, Shire Pub.., 1996, pg 36, ISBN 0-7478-0321-8
3. De Jonge, R.M., and Wakefield, "The Discovery of the Islands in the Atlantic", Stone C-8, Cairn T, Loughcrew, Ireland, c.3200 BC, Ancient American, Vol.13, No.81, January, 2009
4. La Musee de la Prehistorie Finisterienne, Station scientifique de L'Universite de Rennes, Penmarc'h, Brittany, France (contains finds of Cairn of Barnenez, including beaker pots).
5. Salisbury & South Wiltshire Museum, The King's House, 65 The Close, Salisbury SP1 2EN, www. Salisburymuseum.org.uk
6. Devises Museum, Devises, England (just south of Avebury)
7. Malone, C., Avebury, English Heritage, Bratsford, London, 1994 (ISBN 0-7134-5960-3)
8. Atkinson, R.J.C., Stonehenge and Neighboring Monuments, English Heritage, London, 1993 (ISBN 185074-172-7)
9. Richards, J., Stonehenge, English Heritage, London, 1992 (ISBN 0-7134-6142-X)
10. Balfour, M., Megalithic Mysteries – An Illustrated Guide to Europe's Ancient Sites, Collins Brown, 1992 (ISBN 1-85-585-3558)
11. Burl, A., From Carnac to Callanish, Yale University Press, New Haven and London, 1993 (ISBN 0-300-05575-7)
12. Grinsell, L.V., Barrows in England and Wales, Shire Archaeology, 1990 (ISBN 0-7478-0052-9)
13. Burl, A., The Stone Circles of the British Isles, Yale University Press, London, 1989 (ISBN 0-300-02398-7)
14. Butler, J., Dartmoor, Atlas of Antiquities, Vol.2, The North, Devon Books, Exeter, 1991 (ISBN 0-86114-870-3)
15. Mitchell, J., De Geheimen van Glastonbury, Kosmos-Z&K Uitgevers, Utrecht/Antwerpen, 1993 (ISBN 90-215-2075-3) Dutch
16. Molyneaux, B.L., Vitebsky, P., Gewijde Aarde/Heilige Stenen, Atrium, 2000 (ISBN 90-6113-942-2) Dutch
17. Devereux, P., Ancient Earth Mysteries, Cassell & Co., London, 2000 (ISBN 0-7137-2764-0)
18. Twohig, E. Shee, The Megalithic Art of Western Europe, Clarendon Press, Oxford, 1981
19. Beckinsall, S., Rock Carvings of Northern Britain, Shire Archaeology, 1986 (ISBN 0-85263-760-8)

Photo. 3 Dr. de Jonge explaining the "water motif" to Suzy Wakefield in Fourknocks (Photo by authors, May, 1998)

Photo. 4 Beaker Pot in the Devises Museum, Devises, England. This is a
beautiful "water" or "wave" pattern pot. (Photo by authors, May, 2008)

Photo. 5 Dr. de Jonge lighting a chamber entry stone that has "lozenge" symbols in Fourknocks Passage Grave (Photo by authors, May, 1998)

Photo. 6 Dr. de Jonge lighting another stone with "lozenge" symbols in Fourknocks (Photo by authors, May, 1998)

Photo. 7 Beaker Pot"#3" in the Devises Museum, Devises, England. This is one of the best "lozenge" motif pots. (Photo by authors, May, 2008)

Photo. 8 Beaker Pot "Cherhill" in the Salisbury and South Wiltshire Museum, England. This is a beautiful "lozenge" motif pot.
(Photos by authors, May, 2008)

Comb-stamped Beaker.
Cherhill.

Photo. 9   Beaker Pot in the Devises Museum, Devises, England. This is a
beautiful "lozenge" motif pot. These motifs were used to encode
distances in megalithic petroglyphs. (Photo by authors, May 2008)

Photo. group 10   Above, a pot on display in the Museum of Poverty Point, Louisiana, which shows similarities with European Beaker Pots (photo by authors, Oct. 2006). These pots are always "one-offs", unique in their own designs. The smaller photo on the left is of a beaker pot on exhibit in the Devises Museum, Devises, England, while the pot on the right is in the collection of the Salisbury & South Wiltshire Museum, England (photos by authors, May, 2008).

Punt Circle
(Boscawen-un Circle, c. 2400-2300 BC, Cornwall, England)

J.S. Wakefield, jayswakefield@yahoo.com

Summary
Study of the relatively undisturbed site of Boscawen-un Circle reveals an explanation of its meaning, which celebrates the new lands of Punt discovered in the Gulf of Campeche, (Mexico) in the western Ocean.

Overview: Stone Circles
There are said to be approximately a thousand megalithic stone circle monuments in the British Isles. These are more thickly sited along the western coasts, from Cornwall, to Ireland and the Orkney Islands. The books by Aubrey Burl and the Circle catalogue (Burnham & Bullock) on two CD discs available through the Megalithic Portal on the Web, illustrate most of these. All of these intriguing circular monuments are thought to date from between 2500 BC to 1200 BC, within the Bronze Age. Often they are built on hilltops, in beautiful locations, with grand views. Aubrey Burl, who has surely written and published more about them than anyone, thinks that stone circles represent a paradigm shift in thinking. It would surely be nice to gain some understanding of what these monuments are about.

Megalithic Culture
The megalithic culture of Europe lasted from 6500 BC to 1200 BC, a little later in some places.Their petroglyphs and pottery show that they originated in the western Mediterranean, and shared a Sun Religion with other Mediterranean cultures.Unlike today, mysteries of geography were a part of their religious/political world view. Evidence has shown us that they knew they lived on a landmass that was surrounded by water that covered only part of the Earth, and they did not know if there was more land on the backside. Monuments like Stonehenge I, built in 3200 BC, have a ring (land) surrounded by a big ditch (the surrounding ocean). Monuments and petroglyphs in Europe show that these people discovered in 2600 BC that fur trade routes to Alaska and beyond had shown that there was land on the Backside. Having learned this, in 2500 BC they pushed west again, to Baffin Island onthe Arctic Circle ("Route of the Upper North"), and west with the trade winds beyond the Cape Verde Islands (the "Southern Crossing"), and discovered that roundtrip travel to these new lands was possible by returning on the Gulfstream to the Azores. We feel it was this new conception of the Earth's geography that brought the paradigm shift that is seen in the stone circle monuments. Now, after 2500 BC, ring-ditch monuments were built with the ring (the lands) surrounding the ditch (the seas), and like churches replicated in many small towns today, stone circle monuments were replicated throughout the populated areas of the culture.

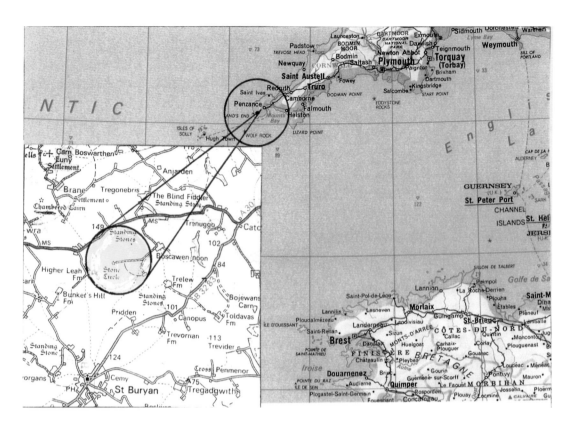

Map 1 The location of Boscawen-un on Ordinance Survey map Landranger #203 (English) "Land's End & Isles of Scilly"

Photo 1 Aerial photo of Boscawen-un, internet photo

Punt, new lands in Central America

King Sahura was Pharaoh of Egypt in the 5th Dynasty of the Old Kingdom. His hieroglyphic inscriptions proclaim that he was the first to visit the Holy Land of Punt, in 2497 BC. Other voyages followed. Pharaoh Asa (Isesi) followed this example, sending out his fleet to Punt in 2400 BC. The tombstone of a ship pilot named Knemhopet from Elephantine Island, reports he had been on eleven voyages to the Land of Punt. The facts known about Pwnt ("Holy Land") cloud its actual location, which is much disputed. Archaeologists are convinced it was Somalia, or Nubia, or somewhere on the East African Coast. Further clouding matters is "Bas-Punt", which is not known either, and a long list of probable synonyms. The fleet later sent to Punt by 18th Dynasty Queen Hatsheput consisted of 210 men in 5 seventy-foot ships, illustrated in great detail in the reliefs of her temple, Del el-Bahari. The unloading of the ships is shown in Thebes, port city on the Nile, upriver from the Mediterranean. The saplings, logs, apes, giraffe, ingots, panther skins, and elephant tusks unloaded, show the vessels traded in Africa during its reported "three year" voyage to Punt. The Punt people are recorded as asking, "How have you arrived? Have you flown here through the sky, or have you sailed across the Great Ocean (the sea of Ta-Nuter)? You must have followed the path of the Sun." The inscriptions say they sailed across the "Great Sea of Mou-Qued, where the water runs back", perhaps refering to the Gulfstream, which may have brought them back home from the "Ends of the Earth".

In our book, <u>How the SunGod Reached America</u>, we have a chapter on Barry Fell's interpretation of the Orient Stone. The stone, found in Orient, New York, is inscribed with a sailing story in Egyptian heiroglyphics. When the Micmac Indians of Arcadia, Canada, were being taught Christian stories by French priests, the Indians were found to be writing down the stories using Egyptian hieroglyphics. The study of the movement of plants and biologicals, and the use of American tobacco and Cocaine in Egyptian mummification helped settle the issue of diffusion. The Olmec civilization developed in the hot river flooding plain in the Gulf of Campeche, Mexico, ("Egyptian Gulf") at 18°N, where the priests dressed in leopard skins with tails, just like Egyptian priests, built pyramids, and carried their kings in sedan chairs. This sudden infusion of culture led to rapid development of a series of civilizations in Central America.

Boscawen-un Circle

The site of Boscawen-un is well signed on the small road off the A-30 highway, halfway between Penzance and Land's End (**Map 1 & Photo 2**). Cornwall is very dense with megalithic ruins, and was not far from the cultural centers of England and the coast of Brittany, today's France. The attached photos show the details of the site. Cooke reports that three stones were re-erected (probably stones 5, 9 and 12), and cleared of undergrowth in c.1864 **(Fig. 1)**.You will note a menhir near the center of the circle that is tilting to the ENE (see aerial **Photo 1**). There is a very bright quartz boulder (#18 in **Fig.1 & Photo 6**) among the 19 stones of the circle. At the time we were taking our photos, there were some folks trying to measure "energies" given off by the stones (**Photos 4&5**). Straffon notes that the site was checked for radiation, ultrasound and compass deflections, and no significant variations were found. There are reported to be 7 Ley Lines, passing through Boscawen-un, aligning with other sites, according to John Mitchell.

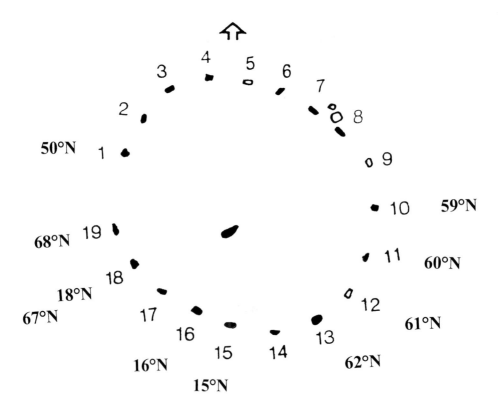

Fig.1 Groundplan of Boscawen-un from Cooke, with numbers and latitudes added by the authors.

Photo 2 The signage of the site, on the side road off highway A-30. (Photo by authors, May, 2008)

The Circle is at the latitude of 50° North **(Fig.1)**. There are 19 stones in the circle, as there are in quite a surprising number of other circles, such as Merry Maidens, Tregeseal in Cornwall, and Torhouse Circle, in Dumfries. (Burl adds that the number of stones, entrance width, cardinal point position, are similar to Merry Maidens (Ref.3). If you add the standing stone at the center, to the ring stones, you have 20 stones. If you subtract these 20 stones from the latitude of the site, 50, you find a possible encoding of the latitude of the Nile Delta, the center of the SunReligion at Heliopolis, at 30°N, or the possible encoding of the Mississippi Delta, entry point to North America. If you add the three other stones lying around (two can be seen in the foreground of **Photo 3**), the stones total 23, a number often found in Megalithic sites, encoding 23°N, which is known today as the Tropic of Cancer. This is the latitude that is as far north as the Sun goes(overhead) in the summertime, before turning south again, changing the seasons. The appearance of the number 23 is a clue that the thinking of the monument builders was influenced by the Sun Religion.

There is a gap of 6m in the western side of the circle, as shown on the groundplan of Cooke, between stones labeled #19 and #1. We think the count should begin at this gap, so we have numbered the circle starting with this stone as #1. The counting should go clockwise, as the sun goes, when looking south in the northern hemisphere. Usually we find that megalithic monuments have their site latitude encoded. Since the Ring is at 50°N, we think stone one represents the site location at 50°N. Counting each stone as one degree of latitude, tall stone #10 is then at 59°N, the site of the huge three rings in the Orkneys, the jump-off point for voyages to the west. Stone #11 has a latitude of 60°N, Cape Farvell, the southern cape of Greenland. Stones #12 and #13 have latitudes of 61 °N and 62°N, the habitable Capes of West Greenland, the jump-off point for voyages to the west by the Northern Crossing. Stones #15 and #16 are numbers that encode the latitudes of landfall of 15°N and 16°N in Central America (Honduras) the western end of the Southern Crossing from the Cape Verde Islands. Stone #18, the Quartz stone that "glows with the full moon", is the latitude of the new Olmec Civilization in the Gulf of Campeche, Mexico, at 18°N, called "Punt" by the Egyptians. Stone #18 bears the latitude of 67°N, the latitude (by providing the reciprocal of 23) of the Arctic Circle, where the SunGod had correctly indicated successful crossings from Iceland to Cape Holm, Greenland, and later, from Greenland to Baffin Island. The last and largest stone, #19, then represents the newly discovered continent of North America. At this point in time, the land was thought to extend from 15°N to 68°N.

There were formerly outliers (outlying stones) around the Ring, so there probably were astronomic encodings in the site, as at most megalithic sites. Cooke notes that special stone #18 with the big quartz veins is in the direction of midsummer full moonset from the center menhir. The only site that might help us understand the tall central menhir is the American Stonehenge site in New Hampshire, where a stone circle had a tall central menhir. That menhir, now broken, is carved up the side with "39" in huge roman numerals. We think the "39" menhir indicates, by its shadow, the proper calendar date to safely set sail for the Azores, at the latitude of 39°N. So we presume here, an

Photo 3 The site of Boscawen-un, looking SW between stones 7&8. On the far side of the circle, Reinoud is standing in front of the Quartz stone. The big stone 19 is to his left. (Photo by authors, May, 2008)

Photo 4 The Quartz stone of Boacawen-un, looking south, with a visitor visitor trying to sense its "energy field". (Photo by authors, May, 2008)

astronomical or calendrical meaning to the central menhir. Astronomic focus on stone #18 reinforces the special identity of the quartz stone.

Conclusion

This stone circle appears to possess both geographic and astronomic encoded information in its design. Since the focus of the circle is the special quartz stone #18, the location of Punt at 18°N, we call this a "Punt Circle". We think this Circle, located on the very Southwest tip of England, is celebrating the new lands found in Central America.

Most stone circles are small, and many of them have been disturbed, with missing stones. Often there are not clearly highlighted stones, like this quartz stone. So it has been difficult to discern their meaning. Frustrated by this difficulty, people are looking for magical "power" of "earth energies" as an explanation. This ring is small, and the explanation we provide of the meaning of the Ring, which is based upon simple math, reading of latitudes, sailing skills, and astronomy, can be seen as simplistic or speculative. Even this site has a few odd stones lying about. But this explanation is consistent with the timeline of megalithic sailing exploration, and consistent with information learned at many other megalithic sites. We hope that further study of other ring sites will lead to a better understanding of these interesting sites.

References
1. Cooke, Ian, Mermaid to Merrymaid, Journey to the Stones, BAS Printers Ltd., Hampshire, 1987, reprinted 2004 (ISBN 0-9512371-7-9)
2. Straffon, Cheryl, The Earth Mysteries Guide to Ancient Sites in West Penwith, Meyn Mamvro Publications, Penzance, 1992, reprinted in 2006 (ISBN 0-9518859-0-1)
3. Burl, Aubrey, From Carnac to Callanish, The Prehistoric Stone Rows and Avenues of Britain, Ireland, and Brittany, Yale University Press, London, 1993 (ISBN 0-300-05575-7
3. Bord, Janet & Colin,and Jason Hawkes, Prehistoric Britain From the Air, Weidenfeld & Nicholson Ltd, 1997, Leicestershire, reprinted 2004 (ISBN 1-84509-125-6)
4. De Jonge, R.M., and Ijzereef, G.F., De Stenen Sprecken, Kosmos Z&K, Utrecht/Antwerpen, 1996 (ISBN 90-215-2846-0) (Dutch)
5. De Jonge, R.M., and Wakefield, J.S., How the SunGod Reached America c.2500 BC, A Guide to Megalithic Sites, 2002 (ISBN 0-917054-19-9). Also on CD
6. De Jonge, R.M., and Wakefield, J.S., "A Nautical Center for Crossing the Ocean, America's Stonehenge, New Hampshire, c.2200 BC", Migration and Diffusion, Vol.4, No. 15, pgs.60-100 (2002).
7. De Jonge, R.M., and Wakefield, J.S., "The Rings of Stenness, Brodgar and Bookan, Celebrating the Discovery of South Greenland", Migration and Diffusion, Vol.6, No.24, 2005.
8. De Jonge, R.M., and Wakefield, J.S., "Crossing the Labrador Sea, The Stone Rows of Lagatjar, Brittany, c.1600 BC", Ancient American, Vol. 12, No.76, pgs.32-37, 12/2007
9. Burnham, Andy, and Bullock, Tony, Stone Circles and Rows Greatly Updated Second Eddition (V2.1), A Photographic Tour on CD Rom (Two discs), 10 English Pounds +p&p, www.megalithic.co.uk, "the Megalithic Portal"
10. Burl, A.., A Guide to Stone Circles of Britain, Ireland, and Brittany, Yale University Press, London, 1995 (ISBN 0-300-06331-8)
11. Fabre, D., Seafaring in Ancient Egypt, Periplus, London, 2004/2005, (ISBN 1-902699-33-5)
12. www.maat-ka-ra.de/english/bauwerke/djeser/dj_portico_2hall_punt.htm
13. www.digital.library.upenn.edu/women/edwards/pharaohs/pharaohs-8.html
14 www.cristobalcolondeibiza.com/2eng/2eng15.htm

Photo 5 The center menhir, viewed ESE, with the visitor feeling its "energy". (Photo by authors, May, 2008)

Photo 6 Closeup of the Quartz stone #18, showing its quartz veins. (Photo by authors, May, 2008)

The Comet Graves and Comet Petroglyphs of Brittany
(The Comet Catastrophe of c.2345 BC)

J. S. Wakefield, jayswakefield@yahoo.com

Summary
A new type of passage grave and new-style petroglyphs dated c.2345 BC in Brittany, France, are shown to record known cometary events. These findings, when combined with scientific data, mythology, and early writings, increase our understanding of events in prehistory.

Introduction: Passage Graves
The megalithic culture of Western Europe lasted for four thousand years, from 5500 to 1500 BC. The greatest concentration of monuments from these people are found in Brittany, along the western coast of France, though this culture left stone monuments from the coast of North Africa to the Orkneys. Passage graves, often made of huge stones, were almost all located along the west coast, close to the Atlantic Ocean, with their burial chambers pointed to the west, often the northwest (examples, **Fig.1**). In these traditional passage graves, a passage leads to a burial chamber in the end, facing west. Going through the passage, one makes a symbolic transition from the "Land of the Living", to the "Realm of the Dead"- making entry to Paradise in the West where you would meet your deceased relatives and friends (Ref.8). The petroglyphs found in these structures have geographic meanings: coastlines, seas, rivers, islands, or sailing routes (Ref.8). These passage graves and petroglyphs show that the people were trying to explore the Earth's unknown backside. Their monuments reveal a series of discoveries of islands in the Atlantic Ocean (Refs.8-12). Due to the enormous size of the Atlantic Ocean, and the limited capabilities of these early explorers, these efforts at exploration went on for more than two thousand years before finding the backside, and probably continued throughout the megalithic period.

Gallery Graves
However, in addition to the passage graves, a modified design suddenly appeared, called "gallery graves" (or covered alleys - "allees couvertes") though they have not been given any special meaning in the literature (Ref.13). These have a fundamentally different architecture compared with the traditional passage graves (**Fig.2**). They face any direction. The chambers are small, and incomplete. They have a huge Blocking Stone between the passage and the incomplete chamber. The petroglyphs inside gallery graves look completely different from those in passage graves, because unlike those in passage graves, these have no geographic meanings. While the passage graves of Brittany are situated along the coast, the new gallery graves are spread over the entire peninsula. The question is: what are they?

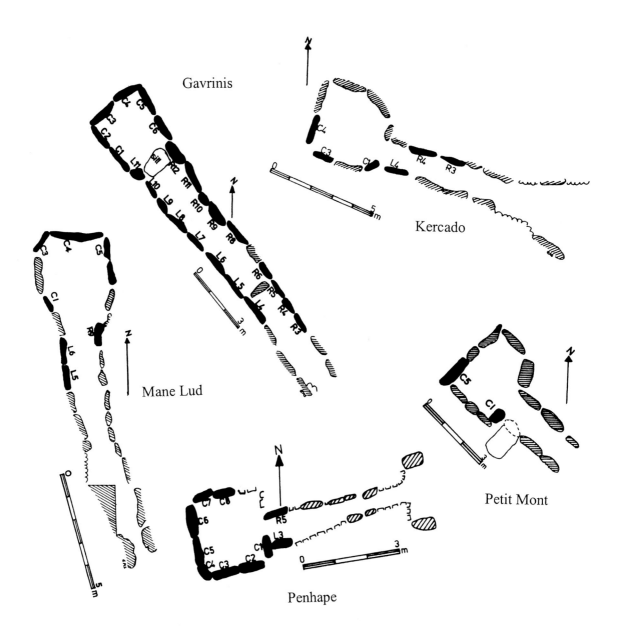

Fig.1 Passage Grave groundplan examples, aligned with true north: Kercado, Mane Lud, Gavrinis, Penhape, Petit Mont. The chambers are often an enlarged area, and their endstones face west (or SW or NW). The endstones usually bear the most important petroglyphs (the darkened stones). Note, there may be a "sill" stone in the passage floor at the entry to the chamber, but there is never a Blocking Stone in the passage (groundplans from Twohig, Ref.13).

About Comets

The planet Earth is still accreting mass from impacts of comets and asteroids, and we know these impacts have shaped the emergence, evolution, and extinctions of life on Earth. The most dramatic of these events are comets, sometimes called "tail stars". They are thought to be dirty ice balls with diameters of 0.1 to 20km, which move in huge elliptical orbits around the sun. In exceptional cases they can be much larger. There are estimated to be more than 2,000 of these orbit-crossing objects that are larger than half a kilometer. When close to the sun a part of the material evaporates, so a long thin transparent luminescent tail develops, which sometimes can be visible from Earth. However, in general the back of the tail usually has a thin and transparent character, as seen in a telescope. Sometimes the head can be clearly seen, sometimes not. Usually large comets can be seen with the naked eye for only a few months, at most. Comet Encke is today just below naked-eye detectability.

A comet is thought to lose about 2% of its mass during one revolution past the sun. As a consequence, the lifetime of a comet often does not exceed 10,000 years, and their progressive breakup and demise is somewhat predictable. This material, mostly ice, turns into a vapor trail that often is a filmy (transparent) tail. Often, these tails are pointed away from the Sun, not directly behind the trajectory of the comet.

A known cosmic catastrophe of this approximate date is the "Rio Cuarto Impact Event" (Ref. 42.) This was an explosion estimated in an article in *Nature* (1992) to have been 350 megatons, equal to 28,000 Hiroshimas. The craters are at Matawil, in the center of Argentina, caused by objects or a broken object which came in at a low angle over the Atlantic Ocean. Legends in South America indicate that its heat set most of South America on fire.

The Gallery Grave of Mougau-Bihan

The gallery grave of Mougau-Bihan **(Photo 1)** is located near Commana in West Brittany, close to the source of the Élorn River, which empties into the sea in the west, near the town of Brest. The grave is 14 meters long, 1.5 to 2m wide, and about 2m high, with 5 large coverstones **(Photo 1)**. Notice that the Gallery grave is very long, with a small room at the head, though there is no chamber endstone, and it may never have had one (Fig.3). This new design is shaped like a comet.

Petroglyphs found on stones inside Mougau-Bihan are shown in **Fig.3**. In the literature, these are called "daggers", but we will explain them as representations of a comet. Notice in the groundplan (**Fig.3**, lower right; the Blocking Stone can be seen (dark). In **Photo 2**, you can see that the "end stone" is missing, and there is a "blocking stone" in the passage. Two more examples of big "blocking stones" are shown in **Photo 3**. We visited 96 megalithic tomb sites in Brittany in May of 2005, and saw far more of these "gallery graves" than we expected. Most of the Blocking Stones were larger than the surrounding stones, as though an important point was being emphasized by the builders. They seem to be saying that the route to the chambers, the "Realm of the Dead" was blocked. There was a big catastrophe, so we surmise that people could not make it to the Realm of the Dead, or could not be properly buried.

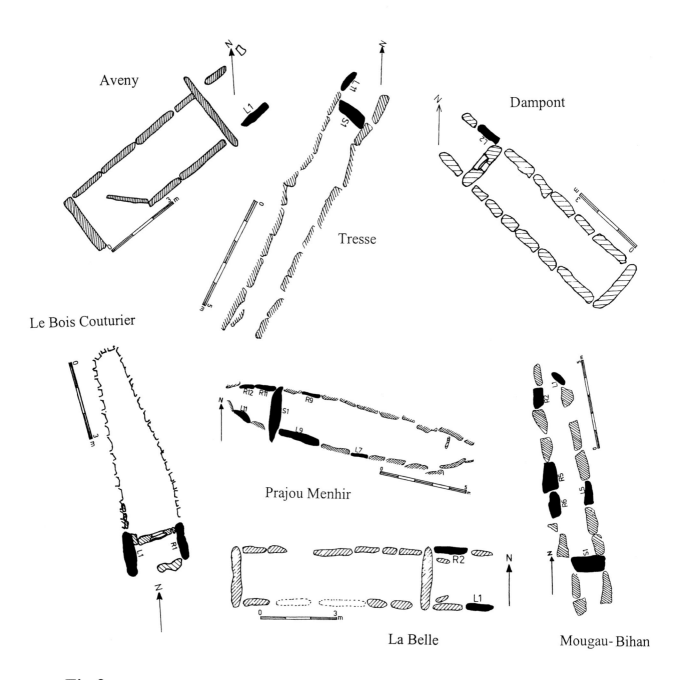

Fig.2 Gallery Grave groundplan examples, aligned to true north: Mogau-Bian, Tresse, Prajou Menhir, Aveny, La Belle, Dampont, Le Bois Couturier.
(groundplans from Twohig, Ref.13).

The Gallery Grave of Tressé

The gallery grave of Tressé is located near Combourg, Ile-et-Vilaine, in the northeast of Brittany **(Fig.4)** (Ref.13). It is situated at exactly the same latitude as the menhir of Kermorvan and Mougau-Bihan, 160km due east of this grave. The groundplan of the gallery grave of Tresse (see **Fig.4**) is interesting, and quite similar. On top of its gallery part are 8 coverstones. Just like Mougau-Bihan, Tressé was built because of the catastrophe, and the grave has the shape of a comet, consisting of a small head portion, and a long tail portion. It also has a "passage" which represented a movement from the "Land of the Living", to the chamber at the west end, the "Realm of the Dead" (Ref.8). On this groundplan in **Fig.4**, which is also missing its endstone, a chamber-blocking stone (S1) is shown. It is on this important stone, and one in the incomplete end chamber, that the two bas-relief petroglyphs are carved, known as two sets of breasts, one set with a necklace. This can also be called a comet grave, with its head chamber, and long tail passage. These blocking stones, not seen in passage graves, are perhaps indicating a major catastrophe that prevented a lot of people from reaching paradise, by not being properly buried in the end chamber of a passage grave.

Comet Impacts

It is now understood, through dendrochronology (tree ring dating), site abandonment, civilization collapse, movement of people, water level and vegetation changes, glacier and desert expansions, earthquakes, floods , and extinctions, as well as studies of mythology, that in late neolithic times, the earth experienced a series of cometary events, experienced as "disasters" (dis-evil, asters-stars) by prehistoric man. The dates of these were 3,113 BC, 2,345 BC, 1,628 BC, and 1,198 BC. The last of these dates coincides with the unexplained burning of all the cities of the eastern Mediterranean, and the end of the Bronze Age. Some of these were multi-year events, perhaps spread over even hundreds of years, especially the second and the last. Evidence of volcanic activity is found in Greenland and Antarctic ice cores, showing acid tephra (volcanic dust) during these periods.

It is believed that these relatively recent events (last 10,000 years), were close encounters with the comet "proto-Encke". This was a larger, not-yet reduced version of the Encke comet, and the Taurid meteor stream, from associated now-dark comets. The Taurid Stream is seen every Fall, and Encke returns in the early days of November, a date associated with Festivals of the Dead in cultures worldwide. The progressive breakup of this large comet, over the last 15,000 years or more, has produced phenomena which have greatly influenced human belief systems.

Mythology

The mythologies of early man confirm these repeated world-scale cataclysmic events. There has been a lot of research by Donnelly, Velikovsky, Joseph, Kobres, Baillie, and others (Refs.3,15-17,21-24,40). There are stories of protracted impact-induced winter in summer in the aftermath of spectacular "celestial battles" when the sky was ablaze with celestial fireworks. In Scandanavian Ragnarok, there are wolves devouring the sun. The sun had apparently been slain by an evil thing. The myth of Athena being born from the

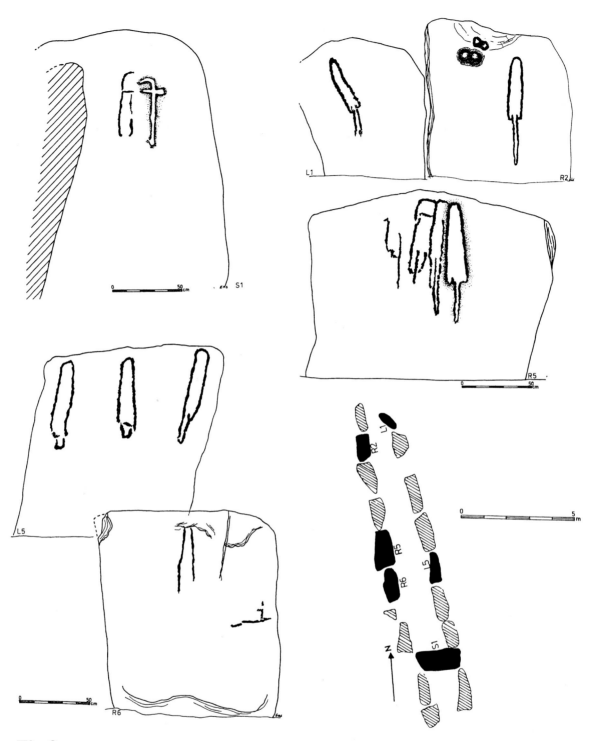

Fig.3 Lower right, groundplan of the comet grave of Mougau-Bihan, facing SSE. Stone S1 blocks the entrance to "Paradise", the chamber at the left, which has no endstone. On stone S1 is a Mediterranean Sign, indicating the comet, drawn to its left, traveled from south to north over the Ocean. On stone R5, four images of the same comet. At the left, only the head is shown. In the middle two, a channel is shown, in the thin material. At the right a figure that becomes the image-convention. Notice the comet on stone L1, which has a curved tail. Upper right, on stone R2, a periodic comet returns to earth, and shown in shown in haut relief, two double moons of the synodic calendar. Below left, notice the comet disappearing behind clouds (the natural edge of the stone) (Mougau-Bihan, Commana, Finistere, Brittany, c.2330 BC, Ref.13).

head of Zeus, and other stories of weakening gods and fantastic births are perhaps a description of comet fragmentation. Another aspect of comets which is evident in ancient lore involves shape-shifting. A comet is three-dimensional, and might appear a quite different animal when viewed from a different angle. Both east and west of the Atlantic, the traditions of mankind refer to a series of deluges (tsunamis) and catastrophes occurring at times far apart. Donnelly suggests that it was these dread events, and the reappearance or "resurrection" of the sun, that led to the world-wide worship of the Sun in many forms. In their book, The Cosmic Winter (Ref.7), Clube and Napier summarize the principal motifs of the worldwide pattern of mythic conflict: that the "world" became peopled with giants in the sky, when there was a combat between these giants, gods, dragons, in the sky, with fire and flood following on the earth below. Sometimes there were hordes of lesser creatures, noisy, winged, serpent-like, in recurrent battles in the sky, and sometimes they crashed to the ground in flames. Kobres (Ref.15) has summarized this well: "human belief systems have been greatly influenced by the progressive break-up, over thousands of years, of this large comet. The ideas of a wrathful sky god or star positions influencing events on Earth are legacies of this influence".

The Catastrophe of 2345 BC

At some time around 2345 BC, a large number of the major civilizations of the world collapsed. These included the Old Kingdom in Egypt, the Akkadian Empire in Mesopotamia, the Early Bronze Age societies in Anatolia, Greece, and Israel, as well as the Indus Valley civilization, the Hilmand civilization in Afghanistan, and the Hongshan culture in China. The reasons for these widespread and apparently simultaneous disasters which coincided with major social and climatic changes elsewhere have long been a fascinating mystery. During the last two decades, however, scientists have found widespread and unambiguous evidence for abrupt climate change, sudden sea level changes, catastrophic inundations, widespread seismic and tectonic activity, and evidence for a dramatic drop in lake levels at around 2345 BC. Areas such as the Sahara and the Dead Sea region, which were once settled or farmed, became deserts. Tree rings show disastrous growth conditions at c.2300 BC, while sediment cores from lakes and rivers in Europe, America, Asia and Africa show a catastrophic drop in water levels at the same time. In Mesopotamia, vast areas of land appear to have been devastated, inundated, or totally burned (Ref.34). The work of Moe Mandelkehr has produced strong evidence for the global destruction levels and climatological changes (Refs.29-31). Further investigations of glacial oscillations during the Holocene have identified a distinct climatic downturn and glacier resurgence at c.2345 BC.

Egypt suffered draught, famine, dust storms, plagues, and subsequent splitting into feudal states. The Ipuwer Papyrus, believed to be a Middle Kingdom document (describing the conditions at the end of the Old Kingdom), says: "It is inconceivable what happened to the land – its whole extent confusion and terrible noise … nine days there was no exit from the palace and no one could see the face of his fellow …towns were destroyed by mighty tides … Egypt suffered devastation … blood everywhere… pestilence throughout the country … The Sun is covered and does not shine to the sight of men. Life is no longer possible when the Sun is concealed behind the clouds … Ra has turned his face

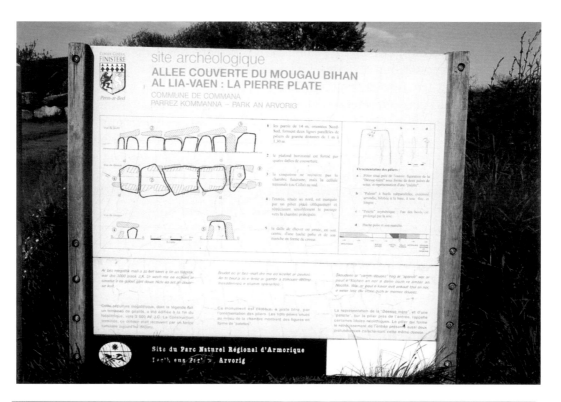

Photo 1 The "Gallery Grave" or "Allee Couverte" (covered alley) of Mougau Bihan. Dr. Reinoud de Jonge sits at the west side, where only a broken part of a stone remains. The second stone to his right is a narrow-looking stone, actually the big Blocking Stone S1 seen in side view. (Mougau Bihan, Commana, Brittany, May 2005).

from mankind. If only it would shine even for one hour! No one knows when it is midday. One's shadow is not discernible. The Sun in the heavens resembles the moon" (Ref.39).

The Gallery Grave of Mougau Bihan

The petroglyphs of the Gallery Grave of Mougau Bihan of **Figure 3**, on the darkened stones in the drawing **(Photos 4&5)** show heads and tails that look like comets. Clearly, these were carved from larger events than have been experienced in modern times. On stone L5 **(Photo 4)** are three equally sized petroglyphs of probably the same comet. In the archaeologic literature, these are called "daggers". Maybe because of the distance, or its brightness, or maybe because it appeared to change over time, the artist could not tell exactly what the comet looked like, so it was carved repeatedly. They saw that the tail at the end was transparent, so rendered that part more narrowly. In the two central petroglyphs the artist engraved the bottom of the glyph with a channel in the transparent portions. With this detail, they are trying to show that the tail is thin and transparent. Sometimes, a comet has a bent tail, since they are formed by streaming away from the sun, and we sometimes get side views of the tail. An angled tail is seen in the glyph on stone L1 **(Photo 5)**. On stone R6 **(Fig.3)** is a similar image. The comet was disappearing behind the clouds, represented by the natural relief near the upper edge of the stone.

On Blocking Stone S1 in the Mougau-Bian passage, part of a "Mediterranean sign" in haut relief is visible (Fig.3 top left). It is a symbol commonly seen in megalithic petroglyphs about and around the Mediterranean Sea (Refs.8,9,13). The long handle of the figure represents the Mediterranean "seen from above". Crossing the "handle", are side-branch sailing routes outside Gibraltar, to the north and south. This glyph bends left, pointing toward an incomplete comet glyph. With this glyph, we are being told that the comet was seen out over the ocean, beyond Gibraltar.

"Breast", and "necklace" petroglyphs, as they are called in the literature, are shown in **Figure 4**, and **Photos 6-13**. **Photo 9** shows Dr. de Jonge at the site of Tresse, a passage grave of 23 upright standing stones, looking at a double set of these breast glyphs, the right two joined by a necklace. There are two sets on the blocking stone under his right hand in the upper photo, which have been greatly damaged within the past 4-5 years. Typically, these appear in pairs, as in **Photo 2** (with chalk), or **Photo 6** (without chalk), or as in **Photos 7 or 8**. Note that the "breasts" are raised (the stone is pecked out around them), in "Haut-Relief".

The "necklaces" link or emphasize particular pairs. We think the breasts are full moons, and the coupling may show the time period between two successive full moons, the so-called synodic month, of 29.5 days. We think a likely scenario is that the earth was darkened for 2 months (two moons linked by the necklace), and the climate was disrupted for a total of 4 months.

A chain of "breasts and necklaces" at Kerguntuil is shown in **Photo 10**. In the upper photo, without chalk, you can see that the necklace of the 3rd of six pairs is deeply grooved, emphasizing it. This is showing which months of the year that the event occurred. When chalked, in the lower photo, you can see that the comet tail indicates that

Photo 2 The upper photo, the small end chamber of Mougau Bihan, with no endstone. The lower photo, the entry, with the two stones leaning in a bit, over the years. Note the two haut-relief bumps, or Double-Moon set on the entry stone, which we chalked for emphasis (not reported in the literature).

it came in late May, the 5th of 12 full moons of the year. **Photo 11** shows another glyph at Kerguntil, and again shows the double moon motif, this time beside a boat, and again the necklace has 8 "beads" in it. The "beads" are additional days added to the month (s), to make them more accurate. The boat probably indicates there was associated flooding.

The Prajou Menhir glyphs show "dot boxes" between two comet images **(Photos 12 & 13)**. The 33 and 40 dots on stone S1 may show the days of darkness at two different latitudes. These petroglyphs indicate a catastrophe had occurred with very serious consequences or they would not have been carved onto the Blocking Stone. Box R12 at the upper left has 36 dots, with two inside, giving (36x2=) 72. If these dots are months, like the larger "breast" reliefs, then the 72 months would agrees with the 6 year periods of the "Jupiter Family" of about 60 short-periodicity comets. The two boxes of S1 total (33+40=) 73 months, again agreeing with a periodicity of 6 years.

After the cataclysm, in Brittany the gallery graves were built. Usually, it appears that important people were given rites and burial in the chambers of passage graves. Suddenly there had been a catastrophic event, probably with fearsome extended darkness, frightful storms, and perhaps electrical events in the atmosphere, and simultaneous volcanic eruptions. Many people probably perished in these difficult times, which may have seemed like the proverbial "end of the earth". We speculate that these "comet graves" show that this calamity brought a new conception in tomb design, which took into account the catastrophic event, by blocking the way to paradise, or proper burial in an end chamber, because so many people had been unable to be sent to the underworld in the usual manner.

Photo 13, lower, shows a connected moon-set at the comet grave called Creche-Quille. **Photo 14** shows another connected moon-set on a stone in the Penmarch Museum (famous as a Mother Goddess), and a bowl with a similar motif. In the literature these bosses are sometimes interpreted as breasts, as though this was a culture based on a Mother-goddess. However, this suggestion may be wrong. Each boss may represent the full Moon, and the time period between two full Moons, the so-called Synodical Month, lasting 29.5 days. Since both inscriptions are done in haut relief (haut relief was not done prior to c.2500 BC), this confirms the disaster happened after c.2500 BC.

The gigantic comet petroglyph of Kermorvan

Originally, this menhir (a single standing stone) was situated at the coast near Le Conquet, at the westernmost tip of Brittany. At the start of the 20th century this stone was found projecting from the side of a small elliptical mound on the Kermorvan peninsula. In the center of this mound a rectangular cavity lined with dry stone walling was found. However, no burials or grave goods were excavated. Now, there are remains of a Nazi fortification at the site, and the menhir is on exhibit in the Prehistoric Museum of Penmarch **(Photo15)**.

The menhir has a completely unique petroglyph, which can provide insight into the nature of the comet catastrophe. The carving represents the huge comet (see **Fig.5**). At the top the head is shown, in accord with the head-up convention of the other

Photo 3 Examples of Blocking Stones. At the top, Dr. de Jonge is inspecting one at Pors Poulhan, and below, he is photographing one at Kernic. Both gallery graves are on the Brittany coast. (Photos by authors, May, 2005.)

petroglyphs we have seen. The top of the stone was carefully picked and dressed. Below it the tail of the comet was engraved, and further below, the tail narrowed down, because this part of the comet must have been thin or narrow. The upper part of the menhir was beveled and smoothened over a large surface area. In this manner this upper part of the standing stone itself resembled the upper part of the comet. These details strengthen the astronomic interpretation of the petroglyph. This must have been a very huge comet, unlike anything modern man has seen.

At both sides an encircled dot is visible, each representing the planet Earth. In the east (right) the Earth enters the tail, and in the west (left) our planet left it, again. This view is in agreement with the Sun Religion, because in the east lies the Land of the Living, and in the west lies the Realm of the Dead. The deeper circle on the left side may be indicating that they thought the most severe damage probably occurred in the west, across the Ocean. The suggested path through the tail shows the Earth passed just below the head of the comet, as seen from Brittany. Below on the stone, a horizontal line shows this path. The natural reliefs at both sides are the "edges" of the tail, again. Experts feel that a passage through a tail would produce not only a meteor storm, but also many atmospheric explosions of the kiloton-megaton class, with a lesser number of the Tunguska (10-100 megaton) class.

Up to the time of the carving of this petroglyph, most megalithic petroglyphs had geographic meanings (Ref.8). This petroglyph has a geographic meaning as well as an astronomic meaning (see **Fig.6**). The whole figure also represents the North Atlantic Ocean. At the top is an accurate image of the whole island of Greenland (the "dressed", or pecked area). Before the discovery of America, from 3200 to 2500 BC, Greenland was the westernmost area of the known world (Ref.8). The SE Coast of Greenland is clearly shown, with Cape Brewster in the east, and Cape Farvel in the south. At the left side below we see, beside Cape Farvel, the SW Cape.

Below the dressed part of the petroglyph is a curved line, representing the sailing route around South Greenland (Ref.8). Perhaps the sailing route portion of the glyph is recording a voyage that was going on during the event. The route starts at Iceland (the dot), proceeds around Cape Farvel and the SW Cape, and finishes at the west coast of Greenland. There the line ends, which is at 66°N, the latitude of the shortest crossing to Baffin Island. This crossing to America has not been engraved beyond the coast of Greenland, because that is not what the petroglyph is about.

The little round dot in the east represents Brittany, where the menhir of Kermorvan is located. The little round circle and dot in the west is the island of Newfoundland, at the same latitude, the East Cape of North America. Below the inscription we see a horizontal line. The natural reliefs in the stone are used here at both sides represent the shores of Europe and North America. The horizontal line is the latitude line of Brittany and Newfoundland, at 48°N. This is at the latitude of Le Conquet, where the menhir of Kermorvan is located. Below the eastern circle (Brittany), the coastline of South Europe was engraved. Beneath it, at the level of the narrowed part, runs the sailing route from Madeira, via the Canaries, to the Cape Verde Islands. At the bottom of the carved glyph

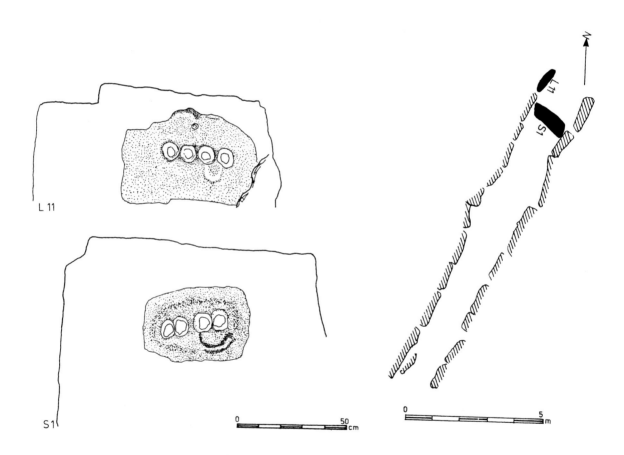

Fig.4 The Comet Grave of Tresse, facing NNE. Notice an endstone is lacking in the groundplan. Below, of petroglyphs of synodic double moons, one set joined. (Tressé, Bois du Mesnil, Combourg, Ile-et-Vilaine, Brittany, c.2300 BC) (Ref.13).

is the Southern Crossing of the Ocean, at the level of the equator. The petroglyph indicates the comet had almost the length of the North Atlantic Ocean!

Menhirs of Kerhouezel and Tremblas

The comet graves of Tressé, Mougau-Bian, and the Kermorvan menhir are located at exactly the same latitude line, at 48°N **(Fig.7)**. This latitude is illustrated on the menhir of Kermorvan, between the two little circles in the large comet petroglyph, and is illustrated a second time, by the line lower on the stone **(Fig.6)**. This concentration of sites at 48°N could be due to population differences, cultural or leadership differences, different observational conditions, or something related to the event itself.

The Kerhouezel Menhir (located near Porspoder a bit north of Kermorvan at 48°30'), with a petroglyph in haut relief, is shown in **Photo 16**. This monument on the northwest tip of Brittany also suggests that the event occurred over the North Atlantic Ocean. Since the haut relief process laboriously removes all the surrounding rock, leaving the glyph raised above the surface, we conclude this glyph was very intentional. This menhir was very carefully shaped into tapered square symmetry by pecking. The Tremblas Menhir (located near Lannion further east on the north coast) **(Photo 17)** shows the same "dagger" style glyph as in the Comet Graves, and it is also viewed toward the northwest.

Dating

The comet graves of Brittany were built after the catastrophe of 2345 BC. We know this because of two confirming radiocarbon results from the comet grave of Liscuis II in Laniscat, in the center of Brittany, 2500 BC and 2220 BC. The nearby grave of Liscuis III provided a similar value of 2250 BC (Ref.13). This dating was also determined by Baillie with dendrochronology, the study of tree rings (Ref.17).

Conclusion

The megalith builders of Brittany preserved the story about a comet catastrophe for posterity in their stone monuments. They recorded the important facts over and over again. These petroglyphs show that observations by people in the distant past are far more interesting and accurate than we have thought, and can make a contribution to our knowledge today.

References

1. Peiser, B.J., Palmer, T., Bailey, M.E., Ed. Natural Catastrophes during Bronze Age Civilizations; Archaeological, geological, astronomical and cultural perspectives, BAR International Series 728, Oxford, 1998 (ISBN 0-86054-916-X)
2. Bruce Masse, W., Earth, Air, Fire, and Water, The Archaeology of Bronze Age Cosmic Catastrophes, Ref.1, pgs.53-92
3. Baillie, M.G.L., Hints that Cometary Debris played some Role in several Tree-Ring Dated Environmental Downturns in the Bronze Age, Ref.1, pgs.109-117.
4. Peiser, B.J., Evidence for a Global Disaster in the Late 3rd Millennium BC, Ref.1, pgs.117-140.
5. Courty, M.-A., The Soil Record of an Exceptional Event at 4000 BP in the Middle East, Ref.1, pgs.93-109.
6. Clube, S.V.M., and Napier, W.M., The Cosmic Serpent, Faber and Faber, London, 1982
7. Clube, S.V.M., and Napier, W.M., The Cosmic Winter, Blackwell, Oxford, 1990
8. Jonge, R.M. de, and Wakefield, J.S, How the Sungod Reached America, A Guide to Megalithic Sites, MCS Inc., 2002 (ISBN 0-917054-19-9)
9. Jonge, R.M. de, and IJzereef, G.F., De Stenen Spreken, Kosmos Z&K, Utrecht/Antwerpen, 1996 (ISBN 90-215-2-

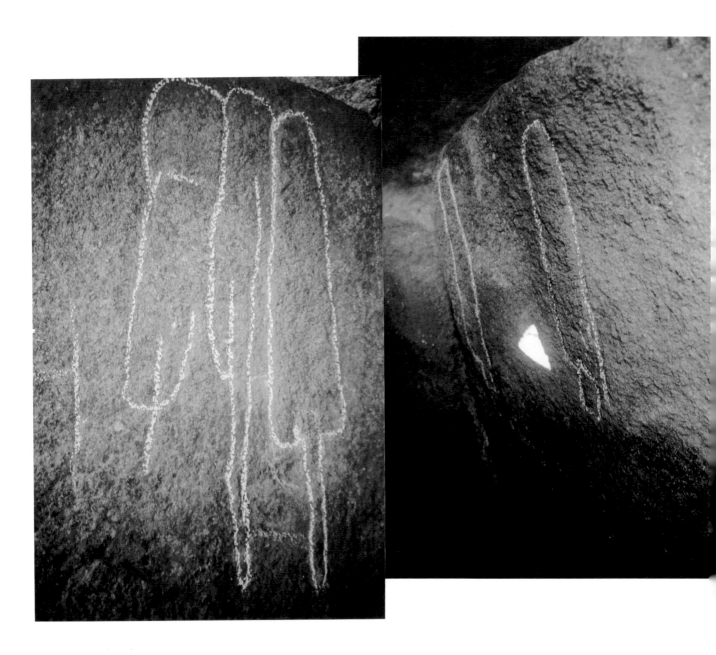

Photo 4 On the left, photo of glyphs on stone R5, and right, two glyphs on stone L5, chalked by authors. (Mougau Bihan, Commana, Brittany, May 2005)

846-0) (Dutch)

10. Jonge, R.M. de, and Wakefield J.S., "The Discovery of the Atlantic Islands", Migration & Diffusion, Vol.3, No.11, pgs.69-109 (2002)
11. Jonge, R.M. de, and Wakefield J.S., "A Nautical Center for Crossing the Ocean", America's Stonehenge, New Hampshire, c.2200 BC, Migration & Diffusion,Vol.4, No.15, pgs.60-100 (2002)
12. Jonge, R.M. de, and Wakefield, J.S., "Ales Stenar, Sweden's Bronze Age Sunship to the Americas", Ancient American Vol.9, No.56, pgs.16-21 (2004)
13. Twohig, E. Shee, The Megalithic Art of Western Europe, Clarendon Press, Oxford, 1981 (ISBN 0-19-813193-3)
14. Pankenier, D.W., Heaven-Sent: Understanding Cosmic Disaster in Chinese Myth and History, Ref.1, pgs.187-197
15. Kobres, B., "Comets and the Bronze Age Collapse", Society for Interdisciplinary Studies in the Chronology and Catastrophism Workshop 1992, number 1, pp.6-10, (ISSN 0951-5984)
16. Joseph, F., Survivors of Atlantis, Their Impact on World Culture, Bear &Co.,Vt. 2004 (ISBN 1-59143-0-040-2)
17. Baillie, M., Exodus to Arthur, Catastrophic Encounters with Comets, BT Batsford Ltd., London, 1999 (ISBN 0-7134-8681-3)
18. Fields, N., Mycenaean Citadels c.1350-1200 BC, Osprey, Oxford, 2004 (ISBN 1-84176-762-X)
19. Drews, R., The End of the Bronze Age, Changes in Warfare and the Catastrophe C.1200 BC, Princeton University Press, Princeton, N.J., 1993 (ISBN 0-691 02591)\
20. Joseph, F., The Destruction of Atlantis, Compelling Evidence of the Sudden Fall of the Legendary Civilization, Bear & Co., Rochester, Vt., 2002 (ISBN 0-89281-851)
21. Donnelly, I., Atlantis, The Antediluvian World, Harper & Row, San Francisco, 1882, 1971 edition (ISBN 0-06-061960-0)
22. Donnelly, I., The Destruction of Atlantis, Ragnarok: The Age of Fire and Gravel, Rudolf Steiner Publications, New York, 1971 edition (ISBN 0-8334-1718)
23. Velikovsky, I., Worlds in Collision, Pocket Books, New York, 1950 (ISBN 0-671-55464-6)
24. Velikovsky, I., Earth in Upheaval, Pocket Books, New York, 1955 (ISBN 0-671-52465-8)
25. Associated Press, "On a Mission to Catch a Comet, NASA's Deep Impact Spacecraft will Smash into the Center of a Comet", King County Journal, Jan.13, 2005, pg A6.
26. Joseph, F., "Celestial Catastrophe", Atlantis Rising, #35, Sept/Oct.
27. Eyton, J.R., Parkhurst, J.I., "A Re-Evaluation of the Extraterrestrial Origin of the Carolina Bays", Paper #9, April 1975, http://abob.libs.uga.edu/bobk/cbayint.html
28. Randall, F.E., "Did a Half Million Meteors Fall on the Carolinas?", Science Frontiers Online, No.82, July-Aug 1992, www:science-frontiers.com/sfo82/sfo82g12.htm
29. Mandelkehr, M.M., 1983, "An Integrated Model for an Earth-wide event at 2300 BC. Part 1: The Archaeological Evidence", SIS Review V, 77-95.
30. Mandelkehr, M.M., 1987, "An Integrated model for an Earth-wide Event at 2300 BC. Part II, Climatology", Chronology and Catastrophism Review IX, 34-44.
31. Mandelkehr, M.M., 1988, "An Integrated model for a Earth-wide event at 2300 BC, Part III, The Geological Evidence", Chronology and Catastrophism Review X, 11-22.
32. Steel, D., "Before the Stones: Stonehenge I as a Cometary Catastrophe Predictor", Ref.1, pg.33
33. Napier, W.M., "Cometary Catastrophes, Cosmic Dust and Ecological Disasters in Historical Times: The Astronomical Framework", Ref.1, pg.21.
34. Peiser, B.J., "Comparative Analysis of Late Holocene Environmental and Social Upheaval: Evidence for a Global Disaster around 4000 BP", Ref.1, Pg 177.
35. Pankenier, D.W., "Heaven-Sent: Understanding Cosmic Disaster in Chinese Myth and History", Ref.1, pg.187
36. Fiorucci, D., "Earthquake – Volcano link jolts Alaska scientists", @/25/2005, Channel 2 Broadcasting Inc, Anchorage, www.ktuu.com/CMS/templates/master.asp?articleid=11985&zoneid=4
37. Howe, L.M., "NASA 'Deep Space' Craft Will Hit Comet On July 4, 2005", 2/27/2005, http://earthfiles.com/news/news.cfm?ID=845&category=Science
38. The First Bird's Eye View of Carolina Bays, 2/20/2005 HTTP//ABOB.libs.uga.edu/bobk/cbaybsc.html
39. Burroughs, W.J., Climate Change In Prehistory, The End of the Reign of Chaos, Cambridge University Press, New York, 2005 ISBN: 13978-0-521-82409-5
40. Joseph, F., "New Find Identifies Great Serpent Mound with Meteor Strike", Ancient American, Issue #63, pg.25.
41. Cope, J., The Megalithic European, Harper Collins, London, 2004 (ISBN: 0-00-713802-4)
42. Grondine, E., Man and Impact in the Americas, 1998,(ISBN: 0-9776152-0-0)
43. Firestone, R., West, A., Warwick-Smith, S., The Cycle of Cosmic Catastrophes; Flood, Fire, and Famine in the History of Civilization, Bear & Co., Vermont, 2006 (ISBN: 159143061-5)

Photo 5 Beautiful comet glyph on stone L1, Mougau Bihan. (Mougau Bihan, Commana, Brittany, May 2005).

Photo 6 Two double moon sets on stone R2, Mougau Bihan, without chalk, clearly showing the haut-relief style. (Mougau Bihan, Commana, Brittany, May 2005)

Photo 7 Dr. de Jonge indicates a joined double moon set in Haut-Relief, with a chalked background. (Kerantiec Allee Couverte, Belon, Brittany, May 2005)

Photo 8 a The most beautiful example of the haut-relief double-month motif. (Prajou Menhir, Treburden, Brittany, May 2005)

Photo 8 b A single double moon glyph in haut-relief, with necklace and 3 details, a

Photo 9 Dr. de Jonge in the incomplete end chamber of the Comet Grave of Tresse. His left hand is near the double moon sets on stone L11, shown closer up in the photo below. His right hand is on the backing stone, just above another (damaged) double moon set on the Blocking Stone. (Tresse, France, May 2005)

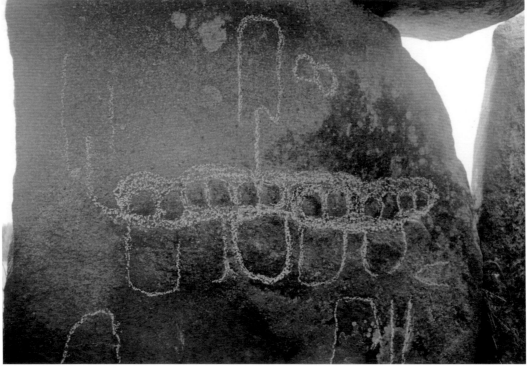

Photo 10 Top, the twelve full moons of Snyodic year, showing with connected emphasis, the months when the celestial event occurred. The photo below of the same stone is chalked, so it reveals the comet glyphs and double month glyph, that tie all these images into an interdependent and consistent story. (Kerguntuil, Tregastel, Brittany , May 2005).

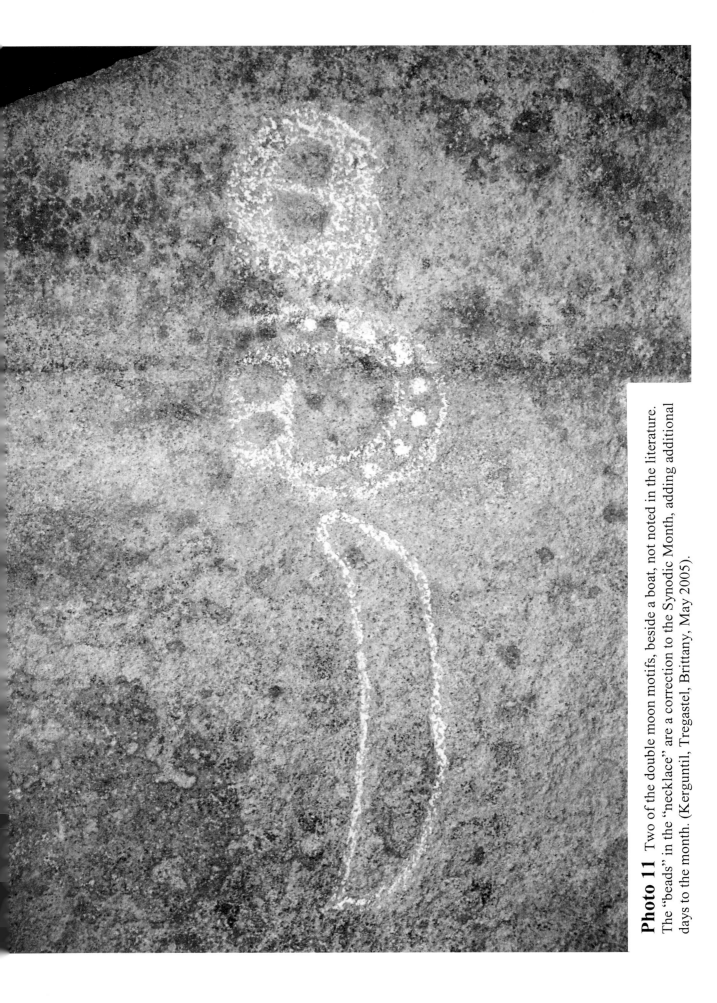

Photo 11 Two of the double moon motifs, beside a boat, not noted in the literature. The "beads" in the "necklace" are a correction to the Synodic Month, adding additional days to the month. (Kerguntil, Tregastel, Brittany, May 2005).

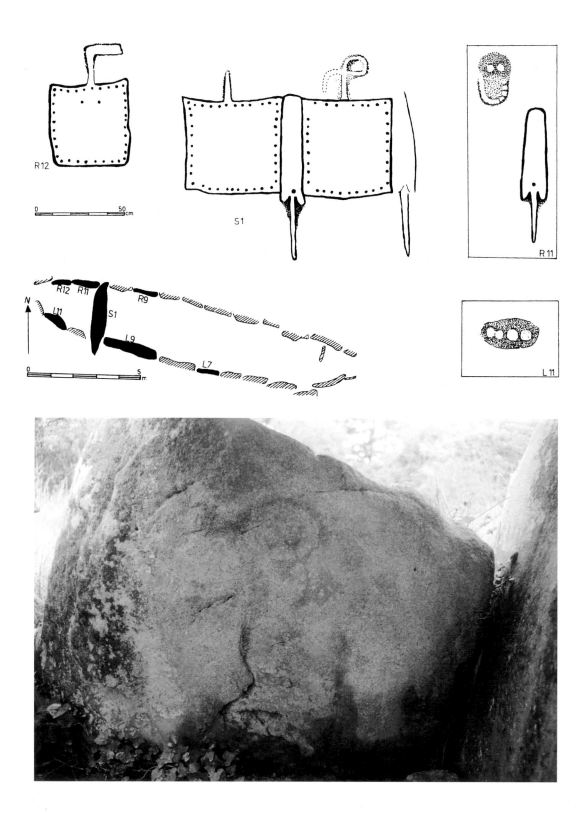

Photo 12 Groundplan of Prajou Menhir, with some of the petroglyphs found in the Comet Grave. The photo below is a double moon set in Haut-Relief in the passage. (Prajou Menhir, Treburden, Brittany, May 2005)

Photo 13 Top, the boxes with dots, integral with two comet glyphs, at Prajou Menhir Comet Grave. Below, a connected double moon glyph at Creche-Quille. (Prajou Menhir, Treburden, and Creche-Quille, St. Quay Perros, both in Brittany, France, May 2005).

Photo 14 Above, a joined double moon motif on a stone called a "mother figure". (Penmarch Museum, Brittany, May 2005). Below, the Vase of Le Moustoir, Carna, from the Tumulus of St. Michel, with similar motif, showing that these glyphs had an important cultural meaning, appearing on a variety of objects (Ref.41).

Photo 15 Photo of Dr. de Jonge looking at the petroglyph of Kermorvan. We chalked the carving in its grooves for the photo with the permission of the Museum Director. In the circle, on the map is the now destroyed site where the stone was removed. This petroglyph is the best written record by man of a celestial catastrophe in prehistory. (Prehistoric Museum of Penmarch, Brittany, May, 2005)

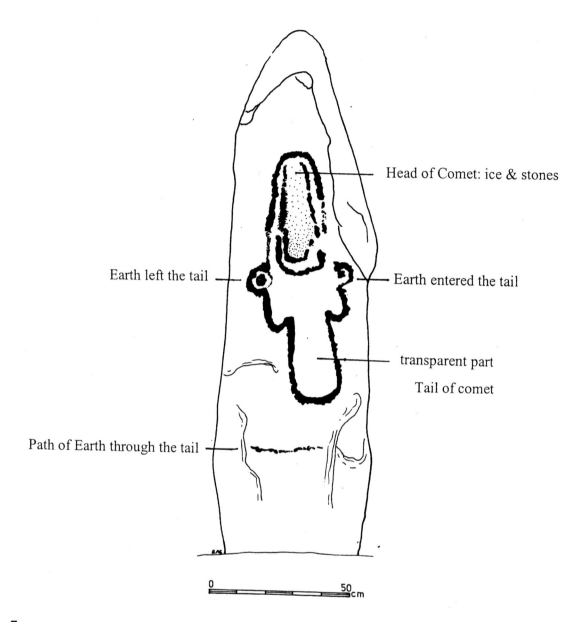

Head of Comet: ice & stones

Earth left the tail

Earth entered the tail

transparent part

Tail of comet

Path of Earth through the tail

0   50 cm

Fig.5 The menhir of Kermorvan (Ref.13), **astronomic interpretation**. On top, the head of the comet (dressed), consisting of ice and stones, and below the tail, containing a lot of water. The tail is narrowed, because it is thin and transparent. At the right side the Earth (the little circle) entering the tail, and at the left side the Earth, (the other circle) leaving it. The horizontal line below on the stone is the path of the Earth through the tail of the comet. (Le Conquet, St. Renan, Finistère, now in Prehistoric Museum of Penmarch, Brittany, c.2330 BC).

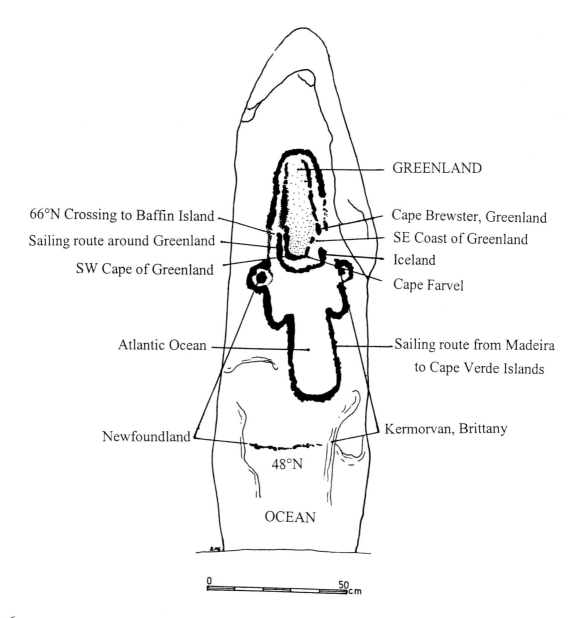

GREENLAND

66°N Crossing to Baffin Island

Cape Brewster, Greenland

Sailing route around Greenland

SE Coast of Greenland

SW Cape of Greenland

Iceland

Cape Farvel

Atlantic Ocean

Sailing route from Madeira
to Cape Verde Islands

Newfoundland

Kermorvan, Brittany

48°N

OCEAN

0   50
                       cm

Fig.6 The menhir of Kermorvan, **geographic interpretation**. The whole petroglyph
also represents the North Atlantic Ocean, from the North Pole to the equator. On top, the
island of Greenland (dressed). Below it, the sailing route from Iceland (the dot), around
South Greenland, to the West Coast. The little round in the east represents Kermorvan,
Brittany, and the little round at the left side is Newfoundland. The horizontal line below
on the stone is the latitude line between these locations, at 48°N. (Le Conquet, St. Renan,
Finistère, now in the Prehistoric Museum of Penmarch , Brittany, c.2330 BC).

Photo 16 The comet as seen from the ground in Brittany, pecked in haut-relief on a menhir, not noted in the literature. There is a blue water tower to the right of this photo, which is directly north of the menhir. Therefore, this view is toward the NW, over the Ocean. (Kerhouezel, near Persponder, Brittany, May 2005).

Photo 17 Looking NW at comet petroglyph on east side of Menhir of Tremblas .
(Saint Samson – Sur Rance, Brittany, May 2005)

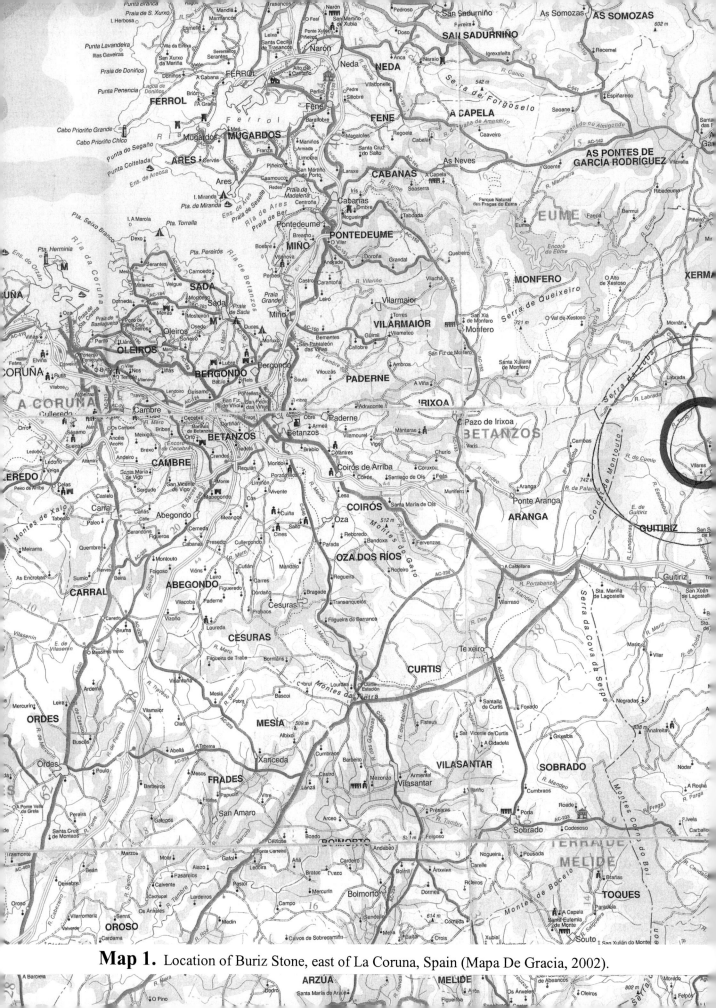

Map 1. Location of Buriz Stone, east of La Coruna, Spain (Mapa De Gracia, 2002).

The Northern Explorations
(Buriz Petroglyph, c.2300 BC, Buriz, Galicia, NW Spain)

J.S. Wakefield, jayswakefield@yahoo.com

Summary
The Buriz Petroglyph is located in Galicia, NW Spain is a large megalithic petroglyph. At the right side is a horseshoe figure, representing continental land in the east, and at the left side is a grid pattern, describing a part of the Atlantic Ocean in the west, including a record of explorations in the Canadian North.

Introduction
Galicia is the name of the very northwestern region of Spain, where the little town of Buriz is located, about halfway between the cities of Lugo and La Coruña. La Coruna is the NW Spanish port from which the Armada was launched for the invasion of England, with a terrific museum in its harbor fort. Recently, this large megalithic petroglyph was discovered near the village of Ventisca, close to Buriz, 35km north-west of Lugo at 43.5°N. We are calling it the "Buriz Petroglyph". We believe it has not yet been described in the literature. The inscription is carved into a rounded, oblong rock on the edge of a farmer's field. The site can be reached by foot via a small dirt road or track, about half a mile from the paved public road, the LU-170. There is a small white sign at the start of the track, indicating the site. The **Google 1** sattelite photo should be helpful in finding the site.

The rock is about 8 meters long, 3 meters wide, and 2 meters high **(Photo 1)**. It consists of a white granular granite, with its surface covered by mosses and lichens. The carvings are primarily on the south side of the stone, which has been cleaned of mosses, but not the thinner lichens. The inscription is large: 2.5 meters long and 1 meter high. To make the carvings more visible for photographs, the carved grooves were carefully chalked. These grooves are about 0.5cm deep and 1cm wide. At the right side of Photo 1 is seen a "horseshoe" figure, and left of it is a large rectangular grid pattern. Grid patterns like this have been seen at other megalithic sites, such as the passage grave of Kercado, in Carnac, Brittany, Butten-er-Hah on the Island of Groix, and the Serrazes Stone in Portugal (these can be seen in our books, this one, and Ref.2). Since Buriz is located close to the Ocean, in the NW corner of the Iberian Peninsula, we suspect this petroglyph is a primitive chart of the North Atlantic Ocean. The shortest distance from Buriz to the sea is 30km to the northwest. The grid petroglyph is on the south side of the stone, so our photographs were taken looking northward toward the glyphs, and also the northward direction toward the sea.

Scaling the Petroglyph
The upper row of boxes is the most detailed portion of the petroglyph, and runs furthest west. So it appears the petroglyph deals with the Northern Crossing of the Ocean. This Crossing takes place at both sides of Greenland, at about 65°N

Google 1. The Buriz Stone is located in the center of the black circle, with the grid petroglyph on its south side. The village of Ventisca is on the small paved road at the right. (Google Earth, in Galicia, NW Spain).

(probably the upper line). This is close to the holy Arctic Circle at 67°N, important in the Sunreligion, and the latitude where both Greenland and Baffin Island were first discovered. If the lower line is close to the holy Tropic of Cancer at 23.5°N, then the 8 boxes of the glyph chart would be at 5° intervals, for a total of 40° of latitude for the petroglyph. The Buriz site then would be near the centerline, with its 43.5°N latitude. From other sites, especially the Serrazes site, we have found that 2.5° intervals appear to have been in common use in navigation at sea. The boxes that are subdivided are then clearly at 2.5° intervals.

Since many of the boxes are not square, but appear stretched to rectangles, perhaps the short vertical dimension of these is only the 2.5° interval, giving the petroglyph a total of only 20° of latitude from top to bottom. This would place the Buriz site close to the lower line. If the petroglyph has several overlapping meanings, the Grid Glyph could run from 65 to 45 degrees of latitude, then from 45 to 25, and then from 25 to 5. This may be the case. For this article, we are going to give a simple interpretation (**Fig.1**, 23° to 67°), which focuses upon the most important and most clear encodings, which are in the north.

The Horseshoe
The horseshoe shaped glyph on the right represents the lands of Western Europe. The vertical left edge coincides with the west coasts of Galicia and Ireland. These are the westernmost coasts of Western Europe. The top of the horseshoe symbolizes the West Coast of Norway, at 65°N. In principle, the horizontal grooves are lines of latitude, and the vertical grooves are parallel distance lines, which are similar to longitude lines. However, meridians, which come together in the north Pole were not used in prehistoric times. The width of the horseshoe equals 3 boxes, or 3 x 5°= 15 moira= 15 x 60 Nautical Miles/degree = 900 NM. The second inner line, all around the horseshoe, was made to emphasize the shape of the figure, and probably also to show the coastal sailing route around the northern land of Europe.

The whole petroglyph indicates the other side of the Ocean had been reached before this petroglyph was carved. As we will show, using the 2 ½° interval, the distances across the grid are correct, and Canadian lands and their latitudes are correctly indicated. To study and illustrate the petroglyph, we will apply today's latitude lines, which are easy to compare with today's maps. The ancients knew that sailing a given time west would cover the same distance as that time sailing north, so they drew boxes (often curved for the curvature of the earth) to represent these longitude distances. They may have used a different "zero point" for their distance lines, but the spacing and number of their lines show that they understood the correct distances. From studying the site of Barnenez, on the coast of northern Brittany, we know they could read latitudes from before its construction date of c.4800 BC. So they knew that Buriz was located at 43.5°N, and they knew that the huge megalithic monument of American Stonehenge they had recently built on the coast of New Hampshire was at this latitude also. The hundreds of slate Ocean Plaques found in Iberian Passage Graves, usually inscribed with four waves across the ocean, confirm that they knew that the shortest distance between Iberia and the Canadian coast was 4 Big Egyptian Moira = 40° (=40 moira). In this petroglyph, note there are 8 half Moira of 5°, or 40° (=2400 NM), between Newfoundland and the Iberian Coast. It is

Photo 1 The Petroglyph of Buriz, chalked for easier visibility of the carvings. At the right side, note the horseshoe (continental land), and at the left side the grid pattern (the Ocean). The grids describe the North Part of the Ocean. On top of the stone Dr. De Jonge inspects some other petroglyphs. (May 1996, Galicia, NW Spain)

clear they knew (or very close to) the correct 2580 NM distance. By this time, people knew that Cape Race, Newfoundland, was the east cape of North America.

Western Europe

The horseshoe represents the Atlantic parts of Western Europe. The vertical left edge coincides with the West Coasts of Iberia and Ireland, and shows the coastal sailing route from Buriz (Iberia) to Scotland, the Orkneys, and even the Norwegian coast. These are the westernmost coasts of Western Europe. The top of the horseshoe symbolizes the the jump-off point in the Orkneys at 59°N, and the West Coast of Norway, at 65°N. The central boxes, inside the horseshoe, are the British Isles, which are 5° wide (the box sizes are correct). Usually the latitude of a megalithic site can be found within the site itself. It is reasonable to suppose that the tiny box at the terminus of the 45°N horizontal line at the horseshoe, represents the site of the Buriz Petroglyph itself at 43.5°N

The Northern Crossing

The minimal western land features of the petroglyph show that the petroglyph is an older one, from shortly after the discovery of America, c.2500 BC, so we have dated it to c.2300 BC. In this early period, the nice plank ships of Pharoah Sahura were carved in his funerary temple, celebrating a 3-year voyage that the hieroglyphs say discovered the land of Punt in 2497 BC . Most routes illustrated in petroglyphs and monuments of this date are focused on short crossings. These multiple short crossings, combined with waiting for the safest sailing seasons, are why the voyages too so long. The two upper rows of this Stone of Buriz represent a step-by-step Northern Crossing, between 60 and 65°N. Each box encodes a sailing distance of about one half Moira, or 5°, or 300 NM.

Departures on voyages start from coastal waters at Northern Scotland or the Orkney Islands, at 59°N, as shown on the edge of the horseshoe. Box 1 represents the crossing to the Faroe Islands, which are at 62°N. Box 2 is the crossing to the SE coast of Iceland, at 64°N. The next box 3 is the southern sailing route to the NW Peninsula of Iceland, at 66°N. Finally, box 4 is the crossing along the holy Arctic Circle to Cape Holm, Greenland at 67°N. These are all sailing distances of about 300 NM, or 5°, or 5 moira, so the box symbolism is actually a reasonable conception of distances for an actual sailing trip. Box 5 is the sailing voyage along the east coast of Greenland, at 62°N, and box 6 is the route around Cape Farvel (the South Cape) to the SW Cape of Greenland at 61°N. This famous route was already known at c.3200 BC, as shown by many monuments. There is a small cupmark in the box immediately SW of it, which may show a preferred sailing direction of the Direct Crossing to Labrador, of 30°SW. This route is the focus of the Monument of Lagatjar, near Brest, in Brittany, and dates from c.1600 BC, so this cupmark was probably added at the later date of c1600 BC.

Next there are two split boxes in the upper row, 7a and 7b, the voyage along the West Coast of Greenland to the north to 66°N. People knew they were making a detour north before turning south, but it was felt to be a safer course, than through the icebergs and fogs of the Labrador Sea in July. The next box 8a is the shortest crossing of Davis Strait (c.150 NM), and the half boxes 8b and 9a are the final journey to Cape Chidley, the NE

Fig 1. Buriz petroglyph, with in the east the horseshoe of Western Europe, and in the west the grid pattern, which describes the North Atlantic Ocean. The upper rows of boxes provide the Northern Crossing of the Ocean. The grids in the northwest show the attempts to find a Northwest Passage to the Bering Sea (c.2300 BC, Buriz, Galicia, NW Spain). (photos by authors, May 2006)

Cape of mainland North America at 60°N, at the top of the Labrador Coast. This completed the Northern Crossing of the Ocean.

The Northwestern Explorations

Now we arrive at the surprise of the petroglyph. At the left side is a group of boxes going up, where we might expect them going down, showing a coastal sailing route to Central America. However, this whole petroglyph does not deal with that. It appears to deal with a search for a Northwestern Passage around the American land mass on the north.

Box 10 is the sailing voyage through Hudson Strait, and Boxes 11 and 12 may describe the Foxe Basin and Hudson Bay. Finally, a last, half box 13 is indicated. It may describe the narrow passage through Chesterfield Inlet, at 64°N, or the Gulf of Boothia at 70°N. Above that in the moss appears to be at least a partial box 14 of a voyage up Prince Regent Inlet toward Lancaster Sound. The three box widths west indicate 5+5+5=15°, or 900 NM (1665 km) of exploration past Newfoundland at 55°W. This distance sailed would take them to these remote places, ice permitting. Our uncertainty here is because the latitudes and distance lines of these places are stretching far beyond the modern chart, though the distance lines of these folks did not pinch toward the pole at these latitudes, like the modern chart.

Ice core studies in the Greenland ice sheet are now showing that the North Atlantic was as warm in the winter c.2500 BC as it now is in the summer. So summertime explorations in these laitudes at this date are not unreasonable, though they are surprising. No continuation of the Ocean to the west was found, as nothing is shown, though cleaning the moss & lichens off the stone might reveal something interesting. Note that Hudson Bay was explored, as a box is spaced to represent James Bay. A deeply inscribed wide line at the bottom of the last box on the western end of the line marked 50° (below box 11) represents Cape Race, Newfoundland, the easternmost land of North America at 47°N and 55°W. The deep tee in the top box above it represents the waterway connections of Hudson Bay.

Dating

From study of the megalithic wall groundplan at America's Stonehenge (c.2200 BC) (Ref.2) we know that attempts to find a Northwestern Passage occurred in the centuries immediately after the discovery of America, c.2500 BC. There are walls in the site that show northern explorations to Lancaster Sound, Jones Sound, and Smith Sound. For this reason, we date this petroglyph of Buriza little after this, c.2300 BC. These are the only two sites in the world that we know of that illustrate megalithic explorations in the arctic regions of Canada. Probably more sites remain to be found.

Other Glyphs

Above the first two boxes of the upper row of the grid pattern are two interlocking semicircles (look above boxes 1&2 in **Fig.1**). The whole glyph has a size of about one box, so about 300 x 300 NM. The left half circle resembles a coast map of the Gulf of St. Laurence, emphasizing its south coast. The right half circle is a coast map of the

Map 2. Map with the Northern Crossing and the Arctic Explorations of the 15 top row boxes of the Buriz Stone added by the authors. (portion of "The Top of the World", National Geographic Magazine, 1949) (Spain, May, 2006)

Box 1
Box 2
Box 3
Box4
Box 5
Box 6
Box 7 ab
Box 8ab
Box 9a
Box 10
Box 11
Box 12
Box 13
Box 14

Orkney
ORKNEY ISLANDS
SHETLAND ISLANDS
FAEROE ISLANDS (FØROYAR)
NW Peninsula
Cape Holm
SW Cape
Foxe Basin
Hudson Strait
Lancaster Sound
Gulf of Boothia

neighboring island of Newfoundland, emphasizing its north coast. This is a graffiti, revealing a lasting impression of sailors recently returned from this area of Canada. They had been impressed by this unusual layout of land and sea which they found at the other side of the Ocean.

At the right side of the horseshoe, a series of circular depressions called "cupmarks" are made visible with chalk. These round depressions have diameters ranging from 3 to 10cm, and about half as deep. They are large and deep, and beautifully formed, though if there were only one, it might difficult to judge whether the cavity was natural or not. According to us, this series consists of 11 large and intentional cupmarks. Probably, these represent the 9+2= 11 islands of the Azores and Madeira. These islands were important for the retun route across the Ocean. There is one very large cup over the horseshoe, and then more to the right (2 western Azores), then 5 more (5 Central Azores), then 2 more (2 Eastern Azores), and then 2 more (Madeira). The first big cupmark above the horseshoe probably represents Flores, the main island of the West Azores. The next-to-last cupmark is probably the island of Madeira. The direction of the cupmarks on the stone roughly correspond with the sailing direction from the Azores to Madeira. Their precise positions probably deal with the directions and distances between the individual islands.

Why the Azores and Madeira are not placed on the "chart" is odd. The Return Route via the Azores was part of the discovery of an ability to do round-trip voyages across the Ocean c.2500 BC. Perhaps the carver was unsure just where to put them yet. These cupmarks could have been on the stone before the bigger carving, because their discovery c.3600 BC is clearly celebrated in the megalithic monument of Gavrinis on the coast of Brittany. Maybe they were so well known, that they wanted to show them at this much larger scale. Or maybe they were added later, since we know that some megalithic monuments were "updated" to include later knowledge and later discoveries. Nevertheless, it remains odd that there is no indication of Greenland or the Azores in the big graphic petroglyph.

The Glyphs on the Top
On the top of the stone are more cups and lines, spread across the top. There are cups across the middle, probably with geographic meanings, which may represent the Azores. Until the moss is carefully removed, the surface cannot be thoroughly examined. We look forward to seeing the results of others who study this site. With the importance of this beautiful petroglyph, which dates so far back in time, we hope this cleaning will be properly done, and that the site is given care by the local people.

References
1. De Jonge, R.M., and IJzereef, G.F., De Stenen Spreken, Kosmos Z&K, Utrecht/Antwerpen, 1996 (ISBN 90-215-2846-0) (Dutch)
2. De Jonge, R.M., and Wakefield, J.S., How the SunGod Reached America c.2500 BC, A Guide to Megalithic Sites, 2002 (ISBN 0-917054-19-9), also on CD
3. Website: www.howthesungod.com, De Jonge, R.M., and Wakefield, J.S.
4. De Jonge, R.M., and Wakefield, J.S., "The Discovery of the Atlantic Islands", Migration & Diffusion, Vol.3, No.11, pgs.69-109 (2002)
5. De Jonge, R.M., and Wakefield, J.S., "The Passage Grave of Karleby, Encoding the Islands Discovered in the Ocean,

c. 2950 BC", Migration & Diffusion, Vol.5, No.18, pgs.64-74 (2004)

6. De Jonge, R.M., and Wakefield, J.S., "A Nautical Center for Crossing the Ocean, America's Stonehenge, New Hampshire, c.2200 BC", Migration & Diffusion, Vol.4, No.15, pgs.60-100 (2002)

7. De Jonge, R.M., and Wakefield, J.S., "Germany's Bronze Age Disc Reveals Transatlantic Seafaring, c.1600 BC", Ancient American, Vol.9, No.55, pgs.18-20 (2004)

8. De Jonge, R.M., and Wakefield, J.S., "The Three Rivers Petroglyph, A Guide-post for River Travel in America", Migration & Diffusion, Vol.3, No.12, pgs.74-100 (2002)

9. De Jonge, R.M., and Wakefield, J.S., "Ales Stenar, Sweden's Bronze Age 'Sunship' to the Americas, c.500 BC", Ancient American, Vol.9, No.56, pgs.16-21 (2004)

10. De Jonge, R.M., "Great Circle Mound: An Indiana Temple to the Egyptian SunGod?", Ancient American, Issue 60, Vol.9, pgs.31-32, 2004.

11. De Jonge, R.M., and Wakefield, J.S., "The Disc of Nebra, Important Sailing Routes of the Bronze Age Displayed in a Religious Context", Migration and Diffusion, Vol.5, No.17, pgs. 32-39, 2004

12. De Jonge, R.M., and Wakefield, J.S., "The Monument of Ales Stenar, A Sunship to the Realm of the Dead", Migration and Diffusion, Vol.5, No. 19, pgs. 94-106, 2004

13. De Jonge, R.M., and Wakefield, J.S., "The Rings of Stenness, Brodgar, and Bookan, Celebrating the Discovery of South Greenland", Migration and Diffusion, Vol 6, No.24, 2005

14. De Jonge, R.M., and Wakefield, J.S., "The Paintings of Porcellano Cave, The Discovery of Guadelupe, c.3000 BC", Migration and Diffusion, Vol. 6, No. 22, 2005

15. De Jonge, R.M., and Wakefield, J.S., "Mexican Cave Artists, 3000 BC", Ancient American, Vol. 10, No. 62, 2005

16. De Jonge, R.M., and Wakefield, J.S., "Greenland: Bridge between the Old and New Worlds", Ancient American, Vol. 11, No. 67, 2006

17. De Jonge, R.M., and Wakefield, J.S., "The Passage Grave of Karlesby: Encoding the Islands Discovered in the Ocean c.2950 BC", submitted to Ancient American, and accepted for publication

18. De Jonge, R.M., and Wakefield, J.S., "The Discovery of the Islands in the Atlantic, Stone C-8, Cairn T, Loughcrew, Ireland, c.3200 BC", Ancient American, Vol.13, No.81, January, 2009

19. De Jonge, R.M., and Wakefield, J.S., "The Stone Rows of Tormsdale: A Voyage to Central America, The Realm of the Dead; Caithness, NE Scotland, c.1600 BC, Ancient American 10/06.

20. De Jonge, R.M., and Wakfield, J.S., "A Return Route across the Ocean, encoded in the Tormsdale Rows; Caithness, NE Scotland, c.1600 BC", Ancient American Vol.12, No.74, pgs 8-12, 8/2006

21. De Jonge, R.M., and Wakefield, J.S., "The Megalithic Megalithic Monument of Lagatjar, The Crossing of the Labrador Sea; Camaret-sur-Mer, Crozon Peninsula, Finistere, Brittany c.1600 BC", Ancient American, Vol.12, No.76, Pgs. 32-37, 12/2007

22. De Jonge, R.M., and Wakefield, J.S., "Germany's Bronze Age Disc: A Transatlantic Device?", <u>Discovering the Mysteries of Ancient America, Lost History and Legends, Unearthed and Explored</u>, edited by Frank Joseph, New Page Books, 2006, pgs 84-87, ISBN: 1-56414-842-4

23. De Jonge, R.M., and Wakefield, J.S., "A Sunship to the Realm of the Dead", <u>Unearthing Ancient America</u>, Ed, Frank Joseph, New Page Books, N.J., 2009 ISBN: 978-60163-031-5

A Date for the Arrival of Michigan Copper in Europe
(Los Millares, Andalucia, Spain, c.3,200-2,200 BC)

J.S. Wakefield, jayswakefield@ yahoo.com

Los Millares is a ruin of a Chalcolithic (Copper Age) town and smelting center, 12 miles from the coastal city Almeria on the SE corner of Spain. The site sits on a flat point of land, with dramatic cliffs down to now-dry rivers on both sides. Obviously the climate has dried up, from when the town was functioning. In back, the land rises to hilltops, with 13 trenched and walled ancient forts on them. An archaeologist with the nearby University of Grenada reportedly spent his career convincing the profession that this was a huge megalithic copper smelting center, occupied for a millennium. (The town was occupied five times as long as the United States since the American Revolution). We could see no green rock in the surrounding area, so we think rock for smelting must have been brought down the rivers from mine sites in the Sierra Nevada Mountains. On the hillside above the walls of the settlement, the site is famous for "over 100" megalithic circular, chambered corbel-roofed tombs, called tholoi, some of which still had some paint on the walls. They say there was a pottery factory. There are quite a few pot shards scattered about.

The attached photos we took in 2007 show site signs, the remains of a town wall, and a smelting center. The site signs advise that the site was abandoned in c.2,200 BC. Our work on megalithic sites for the last 15 years has taught us that round-trip routes to and from America were found possible in 2500 BC (Ref.: How the SunGod Reached America, c.2500 BC). It is reasonable to suppose that by 200 or 300 years after the discovery, that the slabs of "float copper" flushed from their lava beds by the huge glaciers in Michigan could have been discovered, mined, and shipped. Michigan float copper is 99.9% pure crystallized copper, but has some lumps of silver crystallized in it, called "halfbreed" copper. Roger Jewel, the author of excellent books on Michigan copper, said, in a Laura Lee radio interview available on the Internet, that "I heard an Egyptologist ask on TV, "why is there all this silver in Egyptian copper?" They have no answer." The vast quantity of float copper was unique in the world, and of extreme value. When the old miners' pits were deeply mined in the late1800's, the copper was used to run wire across America. Shiploads of Michigan float copper in the nearby harbor of Almeria would have ruined the copper market, which we guess caused the closing of this smelting center. When you are in the British Museum, read the placards on their beautiful Bronze Age axhead collection. One of them says, "the use of Bronze, previously found around the Mediterranean, suddenly exploded all over Europe after c.2500 BC."

Photo 1 The signage at LosMillares (Photo taken by authors, May, 2008)

Photo 2 What remains of one line of the defensive walls of the town. (Photo taken looking south, town to the left, tombs to the right. May, 2008)

Photo 3 Remains of copper Smelting building at Los Millares (Photo by authors, May, 2008)

anillo de barro cocido, con una depresión en su parte central para situar las vasijas-hornos donde se calentaba el mineral de cobre y una pequeña estructura de lajas de pizarra en su esquina nordeste. La falta de agujeros de poste en el suelo interior hacen presumible que una parte de la edificación no estuvo techada. La distribución de escorias y restos de mineral sobre el suelo delata el desarrollo de actividades relacionadas con la fundición y manufactura de objetos de cobre.

This is the best preserved metallurgical workshop at Los Millares. It is 8 metres long and 6.5 metres wide and its stone foundations are more solid than those normally found in the dwelling huts. There is an entrance in its eastern wall. Inside three main features stand out: a 1.2-metre-deep pit furnace, a furnace surrounded by a ring of baked clay, with a hollow in the centre to locate the furnace-vessels in which the copper ore was reduced, and, in the north-eastern corner, a small structure of slate slabs. The absence of post holes in the floor suggest that at least part of the building was unroofed. The abundance of mineral residues and waste scattered on the floor leave no doubt that this building was a workshop for the smelting of copper and the manufacture of metal tools.

Photo 4 Close-up of the smelting sign (Photo by authors, May, 2008)

Santa Fe de
ógico de la
as datacio-
nplejo está
ificación y
as circula-
o de coli-
ambla de
ambla de
orio más

le Alme-
ierra de
de una
tempo-
siones.
nocida
Siret,
cava-
sores
es el
onti-

The area known as Los Millares, at Santa Fe de Mondújar, is the site of a very important Copper-Age settlement, which, according to calibrated carbon-14 dating, was occupied from 3,200 to 2,200 B.C. The site comprises a village protected by several fortified walls and a necropolis of megalithic passage tombs containing round chambers. The plateau of Los Millares is overlooked to the south by a line of hills flanking the Rambla de Huéchar. The tops of these hills are crowned by 13 small forts, which would have held sway over the immediately surrounding territory and guarded the entrance to the settlement itself.

Farther south still, beyond the line of hill forts, in the municipalities of Gádor and Alhama de Almería, there are several groups of dolmen grave sites scattered across the slopes and terraces of the foothills of the Sierra de Gádor, associated with smaller settlements which have been dated to the same period as that at Los Millares.

The extraordinary importance of the site was immediately recognised when it was first discovered in 1891 by the Belgian civil engineer Louis Siret, who undertook the initial excavations with the help of his foreman Pedro Flores. After this the site was abandoned until the 1950's, when work was restarted by Professors Almagro and Arribas. The current excavations have been going on since 1978 supervised by Professors Arribas and Molina of the Department of Prehistory and Archaeology of the University of Granada.

tral
by
olic
ore
ain
ner
et-
as
ch
or-
ret
gs
ng

structures that were clearly devoted to communal use, such as the large square building and the metallurgical workshops inside the third wall and the cistern in the citadel. Siret also records a water conduit, which crossed the plateau through the necropolis, passed under the walls and arrived at the innermost areas of the settlement.

The stratigraphic sequence of the site shows that the settlement went through various phases of occupation, firstly during the early Copper Age (3,200 to 2,800 B.C.), when the three interior walls were constructed, then the Middle Copper Age (2,800 to 2,450 B.C.), when the thrid wall was demolished and the outer wall constructed, together with most of the small forts outside the settlement itself. Finally, in the Late Copper Age (2,450 to 2,250 B.C.) the first bell beakers appeared, a form of pottery that was produced henceforth on a large scale in the setllement. The site appears to have been finally abandoned around 2,200 B.C., much at the same time as new settlements belonging to the Argar Culture were appearing in the region.

comes

Photos 5 & 6 Enlargements of the english sections of the site sign in Photo 1. Red notes by authors. (Photos by authors, May, 2008)

Ocean Pendants
(Portugal, Spain, Ireland, and America, c. 2200 BC)

J.S. Wakefield, jayswakefield@yahoo.com

Summary

In quite a few of the megalithic "anta" or "burial dolmen" of Iberia, small inscribed tablets (pendants) of slate have been found. At least one or two of them are now to be seen in most of the archaeological museums in the cities and towns of Portugal and Spain. Photos of them will be seen in tourist brochures and in archaeological publications. They are each unique, but they have common characteristics. Considered anthropomorphic artistic objects, or idols, we show they also have geographic meaning. They represent a crossing of the ocean to the backside of the world, on the other side of the ocean. The pendant accompanied the wearer in burial, to show he/she had made the risky journey to Paradise, and deserved a special place in the Realm of the Dead. Related examples show that they were admired and copied in Denmark, Ireland, Greece, and America during the Bronze Age.

Introduction

The Megalithic Culture of Western Europe lasted from 5500 BC to 1200 BC. The characteristic and well-known features of that culture are visible in the big stone monuments: the passage graves, the dolmens, the stone circles, and the stone rows. The megalithic petroglyphs are less known, but these are very interesting. Several thousands of carvings are identified, and most of these have geographic meanings. They often represent coastlines, islands, and sailing routes. Usually, they are carved rather roughly on the inside faces of upright passage stones or the endstones of passage graves.

An unusual type of petroglyph are to be seen upon the small engraved tablets found in southwest Iberia. Since they have been excavated from passage graves, it is certain they belong to the Megalithic Culture. **Figures 1 and 2** show many of them, reduced from their original sizes of about 3 ½ inches long (10cm). They are almost always about 3/8 of an inch thick, and usually are slate rock. Their surfaces are polished, and usually have inscriptions only on one side. Usually they have a hole or two at the somewhat tapered top, so are considered pendants. In the limited existing literature, they are referred to as religious idols. They are all unique, but they all share design characteristics. Understanding these objects will contribute to a better understanding of this Culture and its achievements.

It is not known how many of these engraved pendants have been found, but probably there are hundreds. More than 60 are reported to have been found in one passage grave, the Anta 1 do Olival de Pega. We have collected images of quite a few, from archaeologic literature, museum exhibits, and tourist brochures. Many tablets have come from the area surrounding the town of Evora, 100 km east of Lisbon, Portugal. They have also been excavated in the tombs of the tholos type at Los Millares, in southeastern Spain, and numerous other places in SW Iberia.

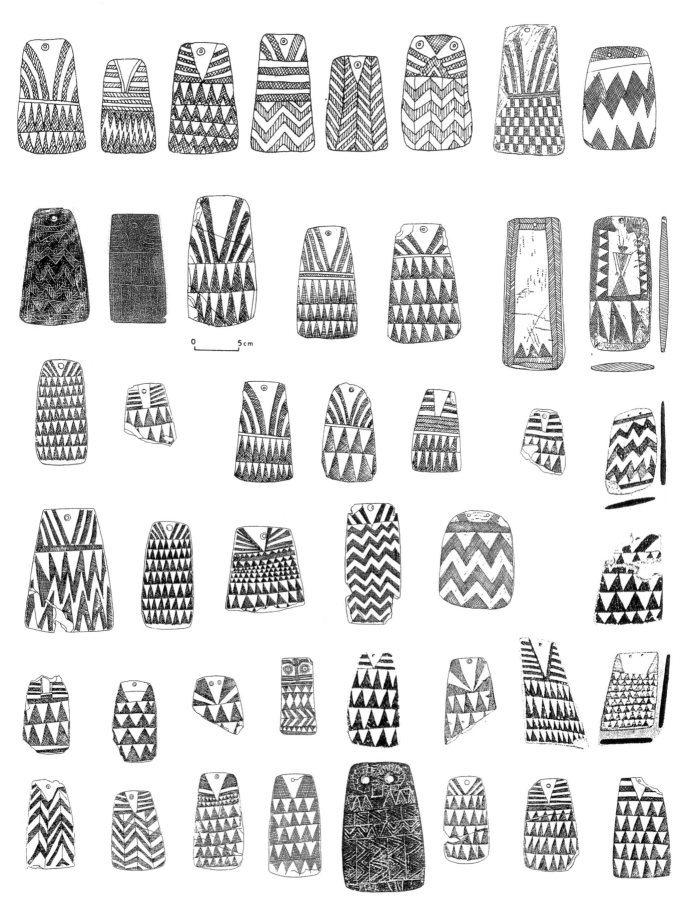

Fig.1 Ocean Pendants from various sites and sources in Iberia
(see References).

Background

The Megalithic Culture, starting from 5,500 BC, two thousand years before the first Pharoahs of Egypt, had developed a SunGod religion, and had developed a tradition of building SunGod temples, facing the western ocean, along the coasts of western Europe. Today, these churches are called "passage graves", because burials have been found in them, like Winchester Cathedral, which also has a long passage, and graves in it. Their political and spiritual leaders told them the Earth was a big sphere, just like the sun and the moon. They said that all the known land was surrounded by a sea, and that in the west there was the Empire of the Dead, at the other side of the earth. (As the Sunreligion was later developed in Egypt, Osiris was called the God of this Underworld in the West.)

Impressed by this story, people tried to cross the Ocean. At first, they tried to cross at the Tropic of Cancer, at 23°N, in honor of the Sungod, who came north to that latitude each year, before turning south for the winter. Unfortunately, at that latitude, the courageous sailors died, because that is the latitude of the windless doldrums of the "horse latitudes", where later sailing ship crews ate their horses. Some early "Culture Bringers", as they are called in myth in the Americas, apparently made it across, but they were not heard from again, because the tradewind patterns of the Ocean were not yet understood. Some boats were blown north out of the Doldrums, and, following the birds, discovered the Azores Islands. This discovery was commemorated at the highly decorated megalithic tomb of Gavrinis in c.3600 BC, as explained in our book, How the SunGod Reached America. Interestingly, most of the pendants have been found in Iberia around the latitude of 38°N, the latitude of the Azores Islands, considered the western home of the SunGod after their discovery.

The Pendants: distances

All the Ocean Pendant tablets of Iberia show inscribed crosshatching, triangles, or zig-zag lines. The up-down waveform is a universal symbol for water, and is, in fact, the Egyptian hieroglyph for water. Thus many of the pendants are clearly depicting water. We have learned, from our study of megalithic petroglyphs, that the up/down lines are used to encode units of distance that are based upon the distance on the surface of the Earth of one degree of latitude. In Egypt, this unit of one degree was called the moira. The moira was applied to curving distances in the west, as well as the latitudes easily measured with a simple "Jacob's Staff", when moving to the north or south. Today, we use Nautical Miles for navigation, where 1°= 60NM, so one Egyptian moira = 60NM.

The number of zig-zags on many of the pendants is four, so we see they often show the correct size of the Ocean, which is four multiples of ten degrees, or 40°, or 2400 NM, from Iberia to Newfoundland, or Africa to South America. Usually there are 3 or 4 Big Moira (30 or 40 degrees of latitude) or 6 or 8 half Big Moira, which are correct distances at the different latitudes sailed after the discovery of America. Like the pendants, the Ocean is tapered. The triangles are a stylized modification of the wave/distance motif, and the cross-hatchings are the distance lines laid out, like a fishnet on a globe. After confirmation of land in the west, following Asian explorations in c.2600 BC, and the

Fig.2 More Ocean Pendants, with below, ceremonial crooks, inscribed with Ocean motifs. (see References).

confirmation of a return route via the known Azores in c.2500 BC, sailors were again venturing to the west, via previously explored southern and northern routes.

The Pendants: religion

Most of the tablets have a centered hole, for hanging the objects around the neck of the hero who went on the dangerous journey across the Ocean. Sometimes there are two holes, like "eyes". The "vee" at the upper portion represents the huge land of Greenland, which had been revered as the westernmost known land in the world for about 600 years. The latitude line at the bottom of the vee is the 60°N latitude line of Cape Farvel, and usually the lines below are inscribed to represent Big Moiras, or 10° intervals.

Clearly these pendants are meant to be anthropomorphic representations of the SunGod, also the God of the Ocean. These plaques certify that the person wearing it, and buried with it, had taken the Journey across the western Ocean to Paradise. These plaques , accompanying the dead, help the dead return to Paradise in the West. The cocaine later put into in Egyptian mummies, which had been obtained in the West, also meant to help the deceased reach Paradise. The obtaining of these drugs was one of the purposes of later voyages to the west, as first suggested by Perry. In some of the pendants, the eye-holes have little rays around them, like little suns, so these may be SunGod images. Note that one pendant has a stick figure (**Figure 3, right**) of the SunGod crossing the Ocean. The eyed plaques are seen by some reasearchers as the Owl Goddess, a representation of the Mother Goddess, in the very old tradition. Such simultaneous meanings of symbols is not unusual, such as the Christian cross, which is both a symbol of torture and resurrection.

The Pendants: dating

From the petroglyphs it can be concluded that these people knew the size of the North Atlantic Ocean, so we call these artifacts "Ocean Pendants". From this information their approximate date can be determined. By study of other megalithic sites, we learned that America was discovered via the Bering Sea, c.2600 BC. A century later the continents were reached via the Southern Crossing of the Atlantic, between Africa and South America, for the first time (c.2500 BC). In the same century, America was also reached via the Upper North, via Greenland. Since all these pendants relate to the effort of this culture to explore the backside of the Earth, they are all roughly contemporary with one another.

The Pendant of Crato

Figure 3 (left) shows a photo we took, showing a very simple design, so we think it is one of the older pendants. It was excavated by Portuguese archaeologist A. Isidoro in one of the dolmen in the District of Crato, near the town of Portalegre (Alto Alentejo). This town is located 80km NNE of Evora, close to the Spannish border. The site is at the latitude of 39°N, the latitude of the West Azores, also at 39°N. Now it is on display in the Museum of Mendes Correa in Porto, in the north of Portugal.

The petroglyph represents the North Atlantic Ocean, in a stylized way. It is divided into 4 strips of triangles, each corresponding to 15° of latitude. One after the other, the horizontal lines are situated at 0°N (the equator on the bottom edge), 15°N (the latitude of

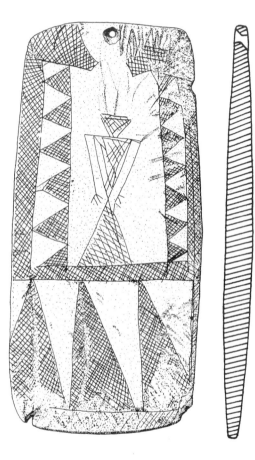

Fig.3 Left: **Ocean Pendant of Crato**, c.12-14 cm long, found near the town of Portalegre (Alto Alentejo) in South Portugal at the latitude of the West Azores, 39°N. by archaeologist August Isidoro (Museum of Mendes Correa, Porto, photo by the authors, May, 2007) . Right**: Pendant of Sesimbra**, an Ocean Pendant from Sepultura 9 e Sepultura 11 (Ossario), Estampa 19, in Setubal Arqueologica, Vol 1X-X. (see References)

the southern Cape Verde Islands), 30°N (the Nile Delta and the northern Canaries), 45°N (halfway to the pole), and 60°N (the south point of Greenland, no horizontal line). The hole itself perhaps represents Cape Farvel, the south tip of Greenland, known since c.3200 BC.

The upright, shaded triangles each have a width of one Big Moira = 10°= 600 NM. The lowest strip has 4 triangles, corresponding to a total width of 4 Moiras = 40°= 2,400 NM. Above it are 4 ½ triangles, then 5, corresponding to a width of 5 Moira = 50° = 3,000 NM. At the top, there is a strip of 4 triangles again. More important than the exact distances, is the fact that the order of magnitude is correct, and that the middle of the Ocean is its broadest part. Note that each triangle has a width of 1 Moira, and a height of 1.5 Moira, so the shapes are proportionate to distance. The shading of the triangles are done with horizontal lines, showing they are stylized small latitude lines. In total there are 18 triangles, possibly encoding the destination in the west, the Civilization developing in the Gulf of Campeche at 18°N. At the top of the pendant are 4 horizontal lines on the left, 5 on the right. Possibly these encode the discovery of America by the 5th pharaoh of Egypt, of the 4th Dynasty c.2580-2562 BC.

The Pendant of Pavia

Figure 4 shows an Ocean tablet found in the Dolmen of Pavia, 40 km north of Evora, again at 39°N, the latitude of the West Azores. This big dolmen, which was later reused as a chapel, was declared as a National Monument in 1910. The unusual design of the pendant shows the edges engraved all around, showing that at this time, they thought there was land all around the Ocean. The double edge is probably covering coastal Ocean over a width of 1 Big Moira, or 10° (=600 NM). At the bottom, three triangles have the same width, so they show the length of the Southern Crossing from Africa to South America, with the wind and current, to be 3 Big Moira, or 30° (= 1,800 NM), which is correct. From this length, it appears they probably landed at the latitude of about 5°N, French Guyana. The fishbone shading on the right edge points upwards, as they are living in the Northern Hemisphere, oriented to the north, but the left side points downward, because the goal of the crossing, Central America, is in the southwest. The edging across the top suggests they know the Upper North route around Cape Farvel, Greenland. The dotted lines, if not accidental scratches, would be showing the holy 23°N line of the Tropic of Cancer, crossed by a line going south, showing that one must sail southwest from Iberia to accomplish the Southern Crossing, with its length and southern location given by the three triangles.

The Pendant of Sesimbra

Figure 3 (right) also shows a pendant excavated in one of the dolmen near the town of Sesimbra, 30 km south of Lisbon, at the latitude of the West Azores, at 39°N. It is on display in the Archaeological Museum of Setubal. This petroglyph has the same Southern Crossing shown at the bottom, with 3 triangles showing a distance of 3 Big Moira (1,800 NM). The edge at the right is the coast of the Old World, with 6.5 or 7 triangles encoding the Arctic Circle at the holy 67°N (reciprocal of 23°N), where they had to go for the Northern Crossing via Greenland. The thicker edge on the left side is the coast of the New World, with the larger triangles showing that is the important location of he Realm

4

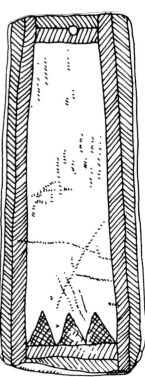

Fig.4 Ocean Pendant, from Anta Capela de S. Dionisio ou Anta de Pavia, Monumento Nacional, Portugal (see References). Below, photos front and rear, of the Anta de Pavia (photo by authors, May, 2007)

of the Dead (America). The 5.5 or 6 triangles in the west correspond with Cape Chidley, Labrador, at 60°N, entry to the American Coast in the west.

In the middle of the Ocean is a stick-figure person, the SunGod or Ocean God, which consists of 3 triangles, also representing the 3 island groups of the Azores. The large triangles point with great emphasis upward, to this figure. The thick horizontal line the figure stands on is the Return Route, with the wind and the current, from Newfoundland via the Azores back to the Old World. The tablet can mean that "our king, who crosses the Ocean is highly esteemed", or it could be more religious, "the SunGod who crosses the waters and visits the Realm of the Dead, and returns to the Land of the Living, is our highest God".

Pendants in Porto

Figure 5 shows an Ocean Pendant that is c.12-14 cm long, in a collection of 15 of similar appearance, but somewhat varying designs. They are in the Museu de Historica Natural, Faculdade de Ciencias do Porto, Portugal, formerly a collection at the University of Porto, now in the Natural History Museum in Porto. You can see how thin these slate tablets are, by looking at the holes at the top. Many of the stones are hung by nylon fishing line in the exhibit, as it appears they are designed to be worn hanging from the neck. Note the "vee" at the top of the stone, a representation of the big land that had been discovered in the north, Greenland, which comes to a point at Cape Farvel at 60°N. The discovery of Greenland had been commemorated by the construction of the huge megalithic Ring complex of Brodgar, Stenness, and Bookan in the Orkney Islands. The three shaded "vee" patterns illustrate that the seas extend in open water for an extended distance on both sides of Cape Farvel, which indeed it does. The checkerboard squares on this pendant are a symbolic chart of the ocean, eleven squares across, and five rows down.

The pendant beside it, also from the Natural History Museum, has an anthropomorphic appearance, now also representing the Ocean God or SunGod. In the center is a three-sided triangle, representing the highly revered three island groups of the Azores. These Islands had been revered as the western home of the Sungod, from their discovery c.3,600 BC until the discovery of further land to the west, as explained in our book, How the SunGod Reached America, c.2500 BC, A Guide to Megalithic Sites. The megalithic tomb most decorated with petroglyphs in the world is the Tumulus of Gavrinis, in the Gulf of Morbihan, Brittany, built in celebration and commemoration of the discovery of the Azores Islands, in the middle of the Ocean.

Many interesting details can be found while looking at the many pendants. For example, the last small reduced pendant image on **Fig.2** does not calibrate distances, but has a hole incised on the right side of the stone (the edge of it is broken away), and a hole on the left. These might represent either Iberia on the right, and Newfoundland on the left, or the Mediterranean Sea on the right, and the Carribbean, on the left, like the carved circles on both sides of the Ocean in the huge petroglyph of Serrazes, also found in mid-Portugal.

Related finds

Figure 2 shows some "crooks" below the pendants. All the images have been greatly reduced, to show the interesting variety, and yet common characteristics of these objects.

Fig.5 Two **Ocean Pendants of Porto**, the left one is in the collection of 15 pendants
exhibited at the Museu de Historica Natural, Faculdade de Ciencias do Porto, Portugal.
The "vee" at the top of these pendants is the known land, Greenland, and the squares are
a chart of the ocean in latitude lines and distance lines. The 3 center triangles of the right
pendant are the 3 island groups of the Azores, in the middle of the Ocean (photos by
authors, May, 2007).

It is thought the large stone crooks had a ceremonial function. Note they all are inscribed with similar ocean motifs, so the ocean voyages were important.

The **top left object of Figure 6** is also a Bronze Age pendant, reported by Archaeology Magazine, found in a 2008 dig in the megaron (Palace area) of Mycenae, in Greece. It bears a petroglyph of a sundisc, so is a SunGod pendant of a probable similar date to these others, perhaps inspired by them. The bronze axehead found in Denmark, in the **center of Fig.6**, from the book by Cooke, carries the same Ocean motifs. It also surely has a similar Bronze Age date, both by the axehead design, and the motifs. On the **right of Fig.6** is a pendant found in County Antrim, Ireland, from the referenced book by Dames. It appears to be an Ocean Pendant,carrying an ogham inscription, which needs decipherment. Like the Iberic pendants, it has continental edges, a 60°N latitude line through Cape Farvel, at the top, and the important 40°N latitude line which runs through the West Azores. This appears to be an Irish version, inspired by the Iberic pendants.

Below, on Figure 6 is an American Indian "gorget", or pendant, reproduced with the photo legend. It has a guaranteed authenticity, as it is reproduced from the 1917 work of the great American archaeologist, Warren K. Moorehead. His book does not discuss the object,except in this note, where he calls the mesh triangles "wigwams". The "snowshoe" is probably a land mass, depending upon the orientation of the stone, and the experience of the sailor. Note the classical appearance of the two fluted columns, each with stone capitals. To the right are photos of fluted columns found off Bimini (Ref.37). Clearly, a classical building is being remembered somewhere. The rectangular pendant shape with two holes in this position is common among American Indian gorgets. Somehow, this one, found in New Jersey, has been inscribed with Old World motifs, so this can be called an American Ocean Pendant, confirming the Trans-Atlantic crossings in the Bronze Age.

Conclusion

It was a daring thing to cross the Ocean to the west. We think early attempts at the Tropic of Cancer probably cost many lives, in the course of learning the tradewind patterns of the Atlantic Ocean. These slate pendants honor persons who successfully made trips across the Atlantic Ocean, some of the greatest sailing adventurers in prehistory.

References

1. Dos Santos, A. P., Megalith Sites in Alto Alentejo, Guias Archeologicos de Portugal, Fenda EdicoesLDA,1994 (Portugese)
2. Da Silva, C. T., Setubal Arqueologica Vols IX-X, Museu De Arqueologia Ethngrafia Do Distrito De Setubal, 1992 (ISSN 0872-3451) (Portugese)
3. Dias, A., and Albergaria, J., Antas de Elvas, Archaeological Circuits, Roteiros Da Arqeologia Portuguesa, Instituto Portugues, Sept. 2000 (ISBN 972-8087-74-8) (English)
4. Museum exhibit, Rio Tinto, Andalucia, Spain
5. Museu Nacional de Arquelogia, Lisbon, Portugal
6. Museu de Arqueloga E Etnografia Do Distrito De Setubal
7. Escoural Archaeological Guide, IPPR, 2000
8. Museo Arquelogico Nacional, Madrid, Mysteries of the Ancient World, National Geographic Society, 1985
9. Museum of Guimares, Portugal
10. Natural History Museum, Porto, Portugal
11. Archaeological Museum of Largo do Carmo, Lisbon, Portugal
12. Archaeological Museum, Silves, Portugal

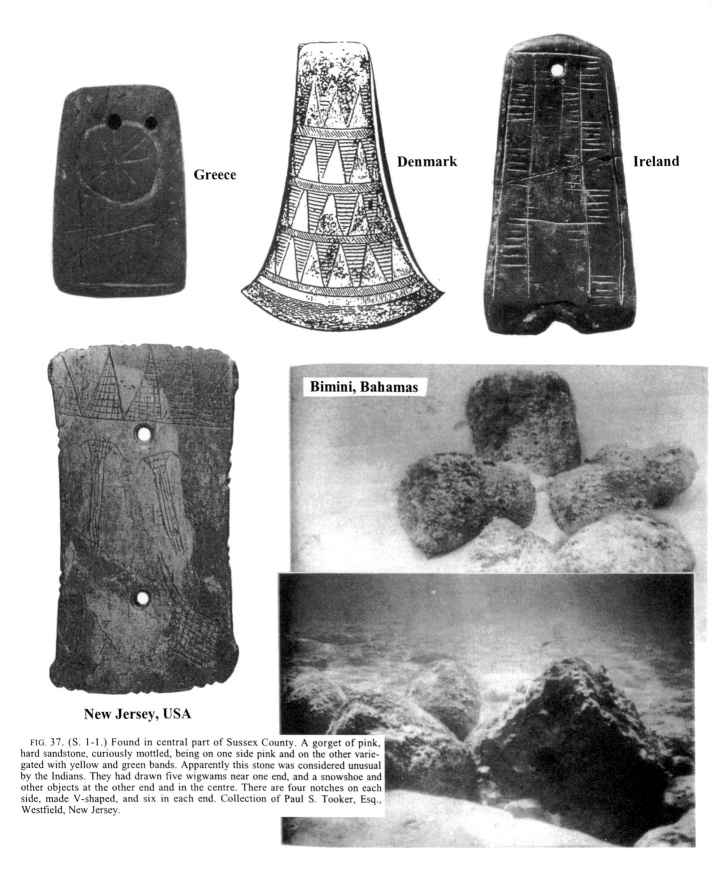

Greece

Denmark

Ireland

New Jersey, USA

Bimini, Bahamas

FIG. 37. (S. 1-1.) Found in central part of Sussex County. A gorget of pink, hard sandstone, curiously mottled, being on one side pink and on the other variegated with yellow and green bands. Apparently this stone was considered unusual by the Indians. They had drawn five wigwams near one end, and a snowshoe and other objects at the other end and in the centre. There are four notches on each side, made V-shaped, and six in each end. Collection of Paul S. Tooker, Esq., Westfield, New Jersey.

Fig.6 Related Finds: Upper left, Bronze Age SunGod pendant from Mycenae; Center, an axehead from Denmark; and right, Ocean Pendant with ogham from Ireland. Below, American Ocean Pendant/Gorget from Moorehead, and classical fluted column sections off Bimini, 11/29/69 by C.P. Turolla (Ref.37).

13. Cooke, I., Mermaid to Merrymaid, Journey to the Stones, BAS Printers Ltd., Hampshire, 1993, pg.26, (ISBN: 0-9512371-7-9)
14. Dames, M., The Avebury Cycle, Thames and Hudson, 1997, London, pg.25, (ISBN 0-5000-27886-5)
15. Joussaume, R., Dolmens for the Dead, Megalith Building Throughout the World, Guild Publishing, London, 1985, no ISBN
16. Moorehead, W.K., Stone Ornaments Used by Indians in the United States and Canada, Being a Description of Certain Charm Stones, Gorgets, Tubes, Bird Stones and Problematical Forms, Gustavs Library, Iowa, 2005 (original, 1917), page 62 (ISBN: 0-9758914-9-9)
17. North, J., Stonehenge, A New Interpretation of Prehistoric Man and the Cosmos, The Free Press, New York, 1996 (ISBN: 0-684-84512-1)
18. De Jonge, R.M., and IJzereef, G.F., De Stenen Spreken, Kosmos Z&K, Utrecht/Antwerpen, 1996 (ISBN 90-215-2846-0) (Dutch)
19. De Jonge, R.M., and Wakefield, J.S., How the SunGod Reached America c.2500 BC, A Guide to Megalithic Sites, MCS, 2002 (ISBN 0-917054-19-9). also on CD
20. Website: www.howthesungod.com, De Jonge, R.M., and Wakefield, J.S.
21. De Jonge, R.M., and Wakefield, J.S., "The Discovery of the Atlantic Islands", Migration & Diffusion, Vol.3, No.11, pgs.69-109 (2002)
22. De Jonge, R.M., and Wakefield, J.S., "The Passage Grave of Karleby, Encoding the Islands Discovered in the Ocean, c. 2950 BC", Migration & Diffusion, Vol.5, No.18, pgs.64-74 (2004)
23. De Jonge, R.M., and Wakefield, J.S., "A Nautical Center for Crossing the Ocean, America's Stonehenge, New Hampshire, c.2200 BC", Migration & Diffusion, Vol.4, No.15, pgs.60-100 (2002)
24. De Jonge, R.M., and Wakefield, J.S., "Germany's Bronze Age Disc Reveals Transatlantic Seafaring, c.1600 BC", Ancient American, Vol.9, No.55, pgs.18-20 (2004)
25. De Jonge, R.M., and Wakefield, J.S., "Ales Stenar, Sweden's Bronze Age 'Sunship' to the Americas, c.500 BC", Ancient American, Vol.9, No.56, pgs.16-21 (2004)
26. De Jonge, R.M., and Wakefield, J.S., "The Monument of Ales Stenar, A Sunship to the Realm of the Dead", Migration and Diffusion, Vol.5, No. 19, pgs. 94- 106, 2004
27. De Jonge, R.M., and Wakefield, J.S., "The Rings of Stenness, Brodgar, and Bookan, Celebrating the Discovery of South Greenland", Migration and Diffusion, Vol 6, No.24, 2005
28. De Jonge, R.M., and Wakefield, J.S., "Greenland: Bridge between the Old and New Worlds", Ancient American, Vol. 11, No. 67, 2006
29. De Jonge, R.M., and Wakefield, J.S., "The Discovery of the Islands in the Atlantic, Stone C-8, Cairn T, Loughcrew, Ireland, c.3200 BC", submitted to Ancient American, for 1/1/2009
30. De Jonge, R.M., and Wakefield, J.S., "The Stone Rows of Tormsdale: A Voyage to Central America, The Realm of the Dead; Caithness, NE Scotland, c.1600 BC, submitted to Ancient American, Vol.11, No.70, pgs 28-34, 10/2006
31. De Jonge, R.M., and Wakfield, J.S., "A Return Route across the Ocean, encoded in the Tormsdale Rows; Caithness, NE Scotland, c.1600 BC", submitted to Ancient American, Vol.12, Number 74, pgs.8-12, 8/2007
32. De Jonge, R.M., and Wakefield, J.S., "The Megalithic Megalithic Monument of Lagatjar, The Crossing of the Labrador Sea"; Camaret-sur-Mer, Crozon Peninsula, Finistere, Brittany c.1600 BC", Ancient American, Vol.12, no.76, pgs.32-37, 12/2/2007
33. De Jonge, R.M., and Wakefield, J.S., "Germany's Bronze Age Disc: A Transatlantic Device?", Discovering the Mysteries of Ancient America, Lost History and Legends, Unearthed and Explored, edited by Frank Joseph, New Page Books, 2006, pgs 84-87, (ISBN: 1-56414-842-4)
34. Perry, W.J., The Children of the Sun, Adventures Unlimited Press, Illinois, 2004, originally published in 1923 (ISBN: 1-931882-27-4)
35. Lobell, J.A., "Search for the Mycenaeans", Archaeology, Jan/Feb 2008, Vol.61, No.1
36. Cope, J., The Megalithic European, Harper Collins, London, 2004 (ISBN 0-00-713802-4)
37. Childress, D. H., Lost Cities of North and Central America, 1992, Adventures Unlimited Press, Illinois, p.431, (ISBN 0- 932813-09-7)
38. Peabody, C., and Moorhead, W.K., "The So-called Gorgets", Bulletin 2, Department of Archaeology, Phillips Academy, Andover, Mass. 1906.

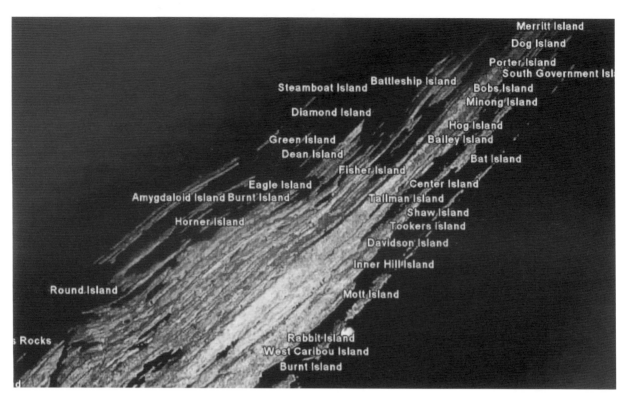

Upper photo: Sattelite photo of the north end of the island of Isle Royale, in Lake Michigan. The ancient lava beds are shown on edge, the softer rocks scoured out by repeated glaciation, now lakes, valleys and harbors.

Lower photo: Alex Fagotti shows me what remains of 3,000 year old miner's pits in the woods behind his rock shop, in the Keweenaw. Starting in the 1840's mines went down as far as 9,000 feet in some of these pits.

Michigan Copper in the Mediterranean
(Isle Royale and Keweenaw Peninsula, c. 2400BC-1200 BC)

J.S. Wakefield, jayswakefield@yahoo.com

Summary

Recent scientific literature has come to the conclusion that the major source of the copper that swept through the European Bronze Age after 2500 BC is unknown. However, these studies claim that the 10 tons of copper oxhide ingots recovered from the late Bronze Age (1300 BC) Uluburun shipwreck off the coast of Turkey was "extraordinarily pure" (more than 99.5% pure), and that it was not the product of smelting from ore. The oxhides are all brittle "blister copper", with voids, slag bits, and oxides, created when the oxhides were made in multiple pourings outdoors over wood fires. Only Michigan Copper is of this purity, and it is known to have been mined in enormous quantities during the Bronze Age.

The Geology of Copper

Copper is said to be the most common metal on the face of the Earth with the exception of iron. However, most of it is in the form of low-grade ores that require a sequence of concentration mechanisms to upgrade it to exploitable ore through a series of proto-ores. Copper ores of the **"oxidized type"**, including the oxide cuprite, and carbonates (malachite) are generally green or blue, and reducible to copper metal by simple heating with charcoal. Ores of the **"reduced type"** are sulfides or sulfosalts (chalcocite, chalcopyrite, tetrahedrite), and are not readily identified in outcrops as ores; they require roasting to convert them to oxides, then reduction of the oxides to produce metal. There are a number of places in the world where copper can be found in small deposits in the **pure state**, but it is usually embedded in a rock matrix, from which it must be freed by intensive labor, or, today, crushed in huge volumes, and treated to obtain the metal.

The Unique Geology of Michigan Copper

Early in Earth's history, there were huge volcanic outflows over the Great Lakes area. As new sediments overlaid these flows, copper solutions were crystallizing in the Precambrian flood basalts of the lava layers. The copper had been crystallized in nodules and irregular masses along fracture zones a few inches, to many feet wide. After a billion years, about a quarter of the age of the Earth, four major glaciations ground upon the edges of the old layered basalt lava beds, and exposed some of the embedded copper (**Fig.2**, top drawing). Isle Royale and the Keweenaw Peninsula remained high ridges of volcanic basalt. The scraping and digging by the glaciers, followed by surface exposure of the hardest material, the metal, was followed by sluicing of the land by glacial meltwaters. This left many mineral nodules of all sizes on the surface, in the huge pine forests. This was called **"float copper",** as it appeared that it had "floated" to the surface. Nodules of copper were discovered shining in the surf along the shores of Isle Royale. The prolonged crystallization, followed by glacial exposure, was a unique sequence of events. When exploited, it took man from the stone age to an industrial world. The half billion pounds mined in prehistory were followed by six and a half billion pounds mined in the "industrial age" in America, starting in the late 1800s

"In the old works on the "Minnesotah" location near the forks of the Ontonagon River, there was found, at a depth of 18 feet, a mass of copper weighing 11,588 pounds which had been taken out of the vein by the ancients. It had been raised a few feet along the slope of the vein by means of wedges and cobwork made of logs ... showing distinctly the marks of a narrow axe, 1 ¾ inches wide, and very sharp ... Although the timber ... was very soft and tender, by reason of its age, it had not rotted from exposure to the atmosphere, having been always covered by water." (Ref.1, pg 50).

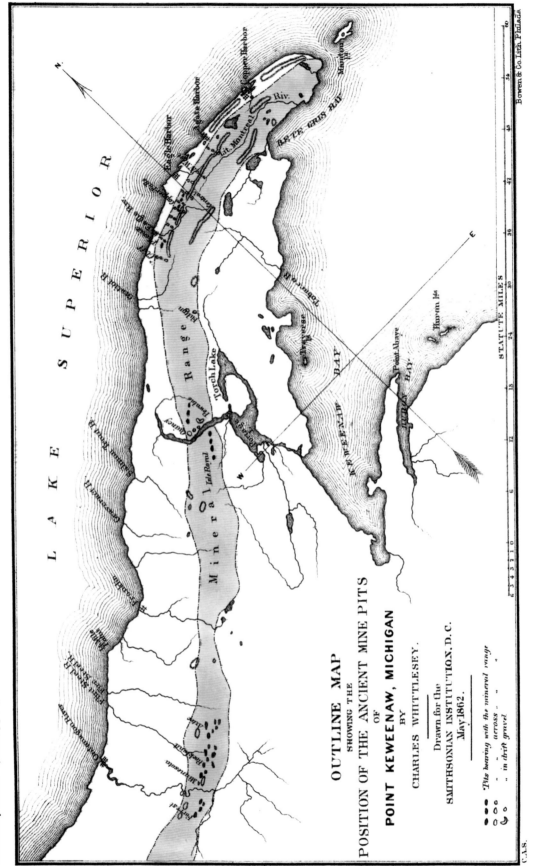

Fig.1 The ancient mining region of the Keweenaw, from Whittlesey, 1862 (Ref.18). The technique of mining with firesetting, and stone hammers was used during the Bronze Age, both in Michigan and Europe. The highly recommended classic book by Drier and Du Temple has been recently reprinted, so is no longer a rare book (Ref.1).

Old World Copper

Most European copper was **smelted** out of copper ores starting about 4460 BC. These ores often had only a concentration of 15% copper in them, and had many trace element contaminants, such as lead (Ref.19). Buried hoards of bronze are usually composed of broken axeheads, miscellaneous broken pieces, and lumps, recycling the valuable metal. Henderson's book (Ref.19) reports a German study that did 12,000 [!] chemical analyses of copper-containing artifacts, with the aim of identifying "workshops". They were not able to do this, but noted that "hoards which often contain low impurity metal in South-Eastern England and Northern France may be linked to the occurrence of copper ingots, which also had low impurities." Barber (Ref.28) says that "ingot (or 'cake') fragments are a common feature of founder's hoards of the late Bronze Age, and often comprise pure, unalloyed copper." Barber (Ref.25) says only one mining site in the British Isles (Great Orme) shows evidence of activity after the early Bronze Age. Burgess (Ref.16) says of the British Isles Bronze Age, "the remarkable thing is that metallurgy seems to have started in the south-east, apparently as early as anywhere in Britain, [though] the southeast has no local ores".

The Miners of Michigan Copper

It is estimated that half a billion pounds (Ref.1) of copper were mined in tens of thousands of pits on Isle Royale and the Keweenaw Peninsula of Michigan by ancient miners over a period of a thousand years. Carbon dating of wood timbers in the pits has dated the mining to start about 2450 BC and end abruptly at 1200 BC. Officially, no one knows where the Michigan copper went. All the **"ancient copper culture"** tools that have been found could have been manufactured from just one of the large boulders. A placard in London's British Museum Bronze Age axe exhibit says: "from about 2500 BC, the use of copper, formerly limited to parts of Southern Europe, suddenly swept through the rest of the Continent". No one seems to know where the copper in Europe came from.

Indian legends tell the mining was done by fair-haired "marine men". Along with wooden tools, and stone hammers, a walrus-skin bag has been found (Ref.1). A huge copper boulder was found in the bottom of a deep pit raised up on solid oak timbers, still preserved in the anaerobic conditions for more than 3,000 years. Some habitation sites and garden beds have been found and studied (various ref.). It is thought that most of the miners retired to Aztalan (near Madison, Wisconsin) and other locations to the south at the onset of the hard winters on Lake Superior. The mining appears to have ended overnight, as though they had left for the day, and never came back. A petroglyph of one of their sailing ships has been found (**Fig.7**).

During this thousand-year period of mining, some of the miners must have explored the continent to the west, as evidenced by strangely large skeletons in a lot of places, such as the red-haired giants who came by boat to Lovelock Cave on Lake Lahontan (Nevada), that were found in 1924 with fishnets and duck decoys (Ref.77). There is "biological tracer" evidence for foot traffic back and forth across the continent, more that three thousand years before the Lewis and Clark Expedition. Huber (Ref.27) describes the "remarkable" presence of the shrub Devil's Club on Blake Point, the northern tip of Isle

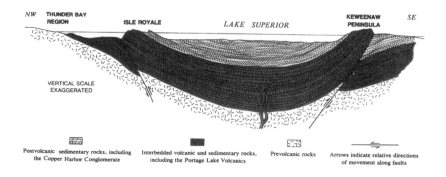

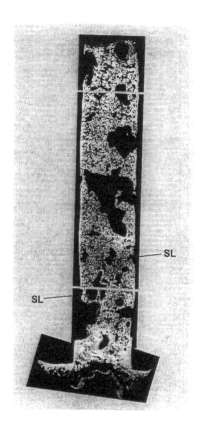

Fig.2 **Above**, a drawing of the geology of Michigan Copper. Early in Earth's history copper crystallized in the lava bed, which now lies mostly deep under Lake Superior, but is exposed between the lava layers at the ends of the bed.

Below, left, a 4.2 cm core drilling showing the porosity and voids of "blister copper", found to be the typical structure of all the Uluburun Ingots studied by Hauptmann et.al. There are a few slag inclusions, labeled SL (Ref.54).

Below, right, a copper nugget weighing 5,720 pounds, found at a depth of 16 ½ feet in a pit dug by prehistoric miners at the site of the Minong Mine. The surface shows working to remove some of the copper, probably made easier by heating the nugget with fires beneath it (Detroit Public Library, Ref.24).

Royale, and on Passage Island, offshore, and also on small islands around Rock Harbor, on Isle Royale. Its usual habitat is the rainforest gullies of the conifer forests of the Pacific Northwest. Huber claims it appears nowhere else east of the Rocky Mountains. This plant has giant leaves, with spines underneath, and frightfully spiny woody stems. It has a history of traditional use as a medicine, to treat diabetes, tumors, and tuberculosis, with its effectiveness confirmed by modern studies. It appears likely it was carried in a medicine bag to this remote island in Lake Superior in ancient times, and the places where the Devil's Club are found are showing us where the miners were using medicines.

Silver in the Copper

Pieces of the "native" Michigan copper sometimes have crystals of silver inclusions, mechanically enclosed but not alloyed; this is called **"halfbreed copper"**. In the commercial mines, the miners are said to have cut these silver nodules off with knives, and take them home. The presence of silver nodules in "Old Copper Culture" tools shows they were made by hammering, called **"cold working"**. These hammered weapons and tools found in Hopewell mounds sometimes "show specks of silver, found only in copper of Lake Superior" (Ref. 69). Apparently, one instance of identification by silver inclusion has occurred overseas: In this letter of December 1st, 1995, Palden Jenkins, a historian from Glastonbury, writes, "I met the farmer who owns the land on which a megalithic stone circle is, called Merry Maidens, in far west Cornwall. While clearing hedges, he discovered an arrowhead, which was sent to the British Museum for identification. The answer returned: '5,000 years old; source, Michigan, USA'." (Ref.76).

Trace Element Analysis

The temperature of a wood fire is 900°C, and with charcoal above 1000°C, but forced air fires are hotter, and met the need to obtain the 1084°C melting point of copper. The **melting** of crystallized copper, and pouring it into oxhide molds (the shape of the skin of a flayed ox) for shipping, wherever it was done, is the first step in its contamination. Re-melting, for pouring into tool molds, can involve the use of fluxes, fuel contamination, the addition of used/broken tools, and the addition of arsenic or tin.

Since metals always contain small portions of trace elements, it was thought we could follow the copper, by looking at trace elements in copper elsewhere, to see if it matched. The six early studies reported by Griffin (Ref.25), all report native copper at **99.92%** copper. Rapp and others (Ref.8,53) report that using trace element "fingerprints", using mostly Lake Superior copper samples, probable geographic/geologic source identification can be done. The work of Hancock et al. (Ref.47) showed again that native copper, including Michigan copper, showed lower levels of tin, arsenic, gold, and especially cobalt, than "European copper" manufactured artifacts. The British Museum reported "generally low trace element content [in] our Egyptian artifacts" (Ref.2). Years ago, the author collected some European copper and bronze axes, thinking that he might do some sampling of them for some commercially-available trace element analysis. Unfortunately, sample testing is only useful for hammered copper tools, not melted/cast ones. Looking at artifacts, full of mixed contaminants in their manufacturing, has for the most part, not been helpful. We need to look at the least-disturbed samples, the ingot form in which copper was shipped.

Fig.3 This ancient ship's prow, made of 3 tons of copper, was photographed by the author in the French Maritime Museum, in Paris. We read that there were at least a thousand of these, one of the many military uses of copper.

The Uluburun Ingots

In the excellent 30-page 2002 study by Hauptmann et al, on the "Structure and Composition of Ingots from the 1300 BC Uluburun Wreck" (Ref.54) the authors say "the cargo represents the 'world market' of bulk metal in the Mediterranean. The wreck contained **354 oxhide-shaped ingots** and 121 discoid, or bun ingots, altogether 10 tons of copper (see **Fig.4**). Additionally a ton of tin ingots were recovered, in 120 ingots and fragments, a ratio which roughly corresponds to the ratio of copper to tin in 'classical' bronzes." The cedar hull was badly damaged by a collision with the shore, but some of the wood was preserved by the corrosion products of the copper ingots. These ingots are all now in the Museum of Underwater Archaeology, in Bodrum, Turkey, with the ingots also found in the later date Cape Gelidonya shipwreck. These are more ingots than the total in all other museums and private collections put together. Some oxhide ingots have been excavated in the Minoan ruins of Hagia Triadha in Crete (dated to 1550-1500 BC), and others have been found in Sardinia, Cyprus, the Nile Delta, Turkey and Bulgaria. Researcher Zena Halpern, (Ref.71), reports "I saw heaps of copper ingots in the Maritime Museum in Haifa, Israel". "Metal bars in the oxhide shape dating from c.1700 BC have been found at Falmouth in Cornwall", England (Ref.78). Egyptian New Kingdom tomb paintings and temple reliefs depict a great number of copper ingots, but only one has been found in Egypt, as they were consumed there. (Ref.23).

For many years, the archaeological community has thought that lead isotope studies by an Oxford group, Gale et.al.(Ref.23,35,44,56) have proved that the ingots all came from Cyprus. In 1998 the Gale group (Ref.56) reports performing "approximately one thousand [!] lead isotope analyses of ores and ingots, including about 60 Uluburun ingots". (They did not test a single sample of Michigan copper.) The study reports that the "Uluburun ingots are **greater than 99.5% pure copper**".

In the Hauptmann study, a steel chisel was used to cut pieces for surface sampling of 151 of the Uluburun ingots, and three oxhides and one bun were drill cored all the way through (see **Fig.2**). Their report states that he samples showed porous volume typical of **"blister copper"**, that "exceeds by far our previous ideas on their inner structure, with void volume reaching 20% or higher, especially in the upper portions of the ingots. In general, cavities like these, called "spratzen", are caused by the effervescence of gases, such as oxygen, carbon monoxide, and carbon dioxide, by water from burning charcoal. This is in contrast with copper from other periods and other localities... All the ingots contain angular-shaped inclusions of **iron-silicate slags**, features compatible with natural rocks affected by the impact of high temperatures in the solid state. These can be removed by repeated melting, but, while these were regular steps ... at many metallurgical sites all over the middle and southern part of Africa, the Uluburun ingots were not processed in this way. The angular shape of the slag inclusions, the structure, and the existence of iscorite point to a pouring of copper into a mold when the slag was already solidified... Interfaces in the crystalline structure of the ingots points to different batches during casting. Almost all the samples contained **cuprite** (Cu_2O) distributed in changing amounts throughout the ingots, associated with large voids. The cuprite formed by corrosion in the sea does not penetrate for more than 5mm or so. An oxygen-rich atmosphere necessary to produce cuprite in an amount observed does not prevail during

Fig.4 Above, the National Geographic sketch of the Uluburun ship, a trading vessel of 1300 BC, discovered wrecked off the Turkey coast. In its hold was found 10 tons of oxhide-shaped copper ingots, with half a ton of tin ingots, and other trading goods.

Below the ship, left, one of the ingots from the wreck (Ref.65); in the middle, an ingot in the British Museum (Ref.7), and to the right, some of the Uluburun ingots in the seabed.

Bottom row, right, an ingot from Hagia Trihadha, Crete (Ref.14). Taylor adds that 3 were found near Cagliari, Sardinia, inscribed with a trident, a double axe, and an angular P. The trident was the symbol for Poseidon, god of the Atlanteans, who Plato says ran the metal trade in the Ocean named for them. The 3 supervised men are carrying an oxhide and baskets of bun ingots, on the tomb walls of Rekh-Mi-Re at Thebes (Ref.10). The bearded Phoenician-looking man is carrying an ingot on the wall of the Tomb of Huyat, also at Thebes (Ref.3). Left and right of this note, two ingots found in Egypt (Ref.3).

the smelting of (roasted) ores. We therefore can eliminate the conclusion that the ingots consist of as-smelted raw copper from a smelting furnace. Most of the ore available on Cyprus is of chalcopyritic composition, and relics of sulfides are quite difficult to completely remove, yet this mixed sulfide does not occur in the copper ingots."

The Hauptman study concludes that "from a chemical point of view, the purity of the ingots is extraordinary in comparison with other sorts of copper from Wadi Arabah (high lead), from the Caucasus (high arsenic), from Oman (high arsenic and nickel). The ingots are made of **pure copper**, and all the ingots show a homogeneous composition. From our metallographic investigations, we are able to exclude a conscious purification or even a refining process to produce the ingots. We see few indications that bronze scrap could have been added, due to the very low tin concentration, and would not include gas bubbles and slag inclusions. The ingots provide an explanation for the previously vexing question of how an ingot of a metal as ductile as copper could have been broken up into **small pieces** such as those excavated by the hundreds in Sardinia. Two characteristics of the Uluburun ingots stand out – the presence of a substantial degree of porosity, and a high concentration of copper oxide inclusions, which made it **brittle**. Simply dropping the ingots onto a hard surface would easily shatter the ingots."

A 32 page 1995 study by Budd et al (Ref.55), reviewed all the work to date, and says "all the oxhide ingots are composed of essentially **pure copper**… No meaningful conclusions on provenance can currently be drawn from a consideration of trace element data for oxhide ingots, ores, and artifacts on Cyprus or Sardinia… It is no surprise that the only oxhide **ingot mold** ever found, at Ras Ibn Hani, Syria, in 1983 was surrounded by droplets bearing the same isotope signature as the vast majority of the oxhide ingots. The 1989 (Ref.35) Gale report concludes that the Aghia Triadha ingots on Crete "are certainly not made of Cypriot copper", and the copper source could not be identified. Dickinson, author of the <u>Aegean Bronze Age</u> (Ref.1) "From outside the Aegean came …oxhide ingots. These have all, when tested, proved to be non-Aegean metal."

Where did the copper go?
Enormous orders for bronze weapons are recorded on excavated Bronze Age clay tablets, for swords in the tens of thousands. The Roman soldier is said to have worn up to 48 pounds of bronze in his uniform. Armies throughout the ancient world were equipped with bronze weapons. Statues and musical instruments, chariots, furniture and vases were made of copper and bronze. Even rooms were lined with copper and bronze. After the bronze **Colossus of Rhodes** was destroyed in an earthquake in 226 B.C., it was sold to a merchant, who used almost 1,000 camels to ship the pieces to Syria (Ref.13). "From only 5% of the Karum Kanesh tablets, we already know of 110 donkey loads carrying 15 tons of tin into Anatolia, enough to produce (at 5-7% tin content) 200 to 300 tons of bronze."(Ref.23).

Minoan Traders
A variety of cultural groups were involved in the mining, shipping, and trading of copper, among them the Egyptians, the Megalithic peoples of the western coast of Europe, the Atlanteans, and the Minoans. The Minoans have the reputation of controlling the copper

Fig.5 Grave Goods of a rich burial at the hillside site of discovery, near the salt mines above Hallstatt, Austria. Twelve hundred rich graves were excavated, but are thought to be only half the necropolis. The salt was valuable as a food preservative in prehistory. It could be traded to the copper merchants for copper cauldrons, tools, and even a Minoan red pot. Similar 4-sided circular pottery patterns are common among American Caddoan pottery. The author believes you are looking at Michigan Copper,

trade in the Eastern Mediterranean. "It is in the New Palace period in **Bronze Age Minoan Crete**, that we find a large increase in population, particularly in settlements along the coasts, the growth of towns, which in some cases surround mini-palaces, luxurious separate town houses at palatial and other sites, and fine country villas…Villas and houses at Ayia Triadha and Tylissos contained not only weights and loom weights, but also copper oxhide ingots and Linear A tablets, and both are rich in luxury products and bronze objects. Minoan prowess in metal weapon production was not limited to the long sword, but included the short sword, the solid long dagger and the shoe-socketed and tube-socketed spearhead and arrowhead, all of which may have made their first Aegean appearance in Crete"… Neopalatial Crete is extremely rich in bronze, but very poor in sources of copper and of course totally lacking in sources of tin" (Ref.23). The **Newberry Tablet** of Newberry, Michigan (**Fig.6**) is in a Cypriot/Cretan sylabary. Cretan script may have been the basis of the Cree sylabary (Ref.7), and Mayan writing (Ref.3). The "Cavern of Glyphs" on the Ohio River had images of clothed figures that "singularly recall the dress of the Minoans, as seen on the frescoes at Knossos in Crete" (Ref.79). A Minoan pot has been unearthed in Louisiana. The Olmecs laid mosaic tiles at La Venta, (Mexico) upon asphalt, the same technique used in Crete (Ref.3). The excavation of the wealthy grave goods at **Hallstatt** (see **Fig.5**) show that traders brought Minoan pots as well as copper/bronze pots to trade for salt. It appears that the ruling elite of Hallstatt were among the end customers of Michigan copper, as well as the Egyptians.

References

1. Drier, R.W., Du Temple, O.J., Prehistoric Mining in the Lake Superior region, A Collection of Reference Articles, reprinted privately January 2005, #367
2. Davies, W.V., Catalogue of Egyptian Antiquities in the British Museum, VII, Tools and Weapons, Axes, British Museum Publications, London, 1987 (ISBN 0 7141 0934 7)
3. Bailey, J., Sailing to Paradise, The Discovery of the Americas by 7000 BC, Simon & Schuster, New York, 1994, (ISBN 0-684-81297-5)
4. Rydholm, C.F., Michigan Copper, The Untold Story, A History of Rediscovery, Winter Cabin Books, Marquette, 2006 (ISBN 0-9744679-2-8)
5. "Michigan's Copper Country, The History of Copper Mining in Michigan's Upper Peninsula, featuring cooperating sites of the Kaweenaw National Historical Park", The History Channel, DVD, www.keweenawvideo.com
6. TerHaar, C., "Isle Royale Impressions, Video DVD of the Wildlife, Moods, and Scenery of Isle Royale National Park, set to Music", Mackinac Scenics, 803 Islington Rd., Cedarville, Mi 49719, 2004
7. Jewell, R.J., Ancient Mines of Kitchi-Gumi, Cypriot/Minoan Traders in North America, Jewell Histories, Fairfield Pa., 2nd Ed, 2004 (ISBN 0-9678413-3-X)
8. Scott, D.A., and Meyers, P., Archeometry of Pre-Columbian Sites and Artifacts, The Getty Conservation Institute, Los Angeles, 1994, (ISBN 0-89236-249-9)
9. O'Brien, W., Bronze Age Copper Mining in Britain and Ireland, Shire Publications Ltd., Buckinghamshire, 1996 (ISBN 07478 0321 8)
10. Scheel, B., Egyptian Metalworking and Tools, Shire Publications Ltd., Aylesbury, 1989 (ISBN 0 7478 0001 4)
11. Martin, S.R., Wonderful Power, The Story of Ancient Copper Working in the Lake Superior Basin, Wayne State Univ. Press, Detroit, 1999 (ISBN 0-8143-2843-1)
12. Trevelyan, A.M., Miskwabik, Metal of Ritual, Metallurgy in Precontact Eastern North America, U. Press of Kentucky, Louisville, 2004 (ISBN 0-8131-2272-4)
13. Childress, D.H., Lost Cities of Atlantis, Ancient Europe & the Mediterranean, Adventures Unlimited Press, Stelle, Ill., 1996 (ISBN 0-932813-25-9)
14. Taylour, L.W., The Mycenaeans, Thames & Hudson, 1964 and 1983, New York (ISBN 0-500-27586-6)
15. Milner, G.R., The Moundbuilders, Ancient Peoples of Eastern North America, Thames and Hudson, London, 2004, (ISBN 0-500-28468-7)
16. Burgess, C., The Age of Stonehenge, Castle Books, Edison, N.J.,1980-2003 (ISBN 0-7858-1593-7)
17. De Jonge, R.M., and Wakefield, J.S., How the SunGod Reached America c.2500 BC, A Guide to Megalithic Sites, MCS., Kirkland, Wa. 2002 (ISBN 0-917054-19-9)
18. Whittlesey, C., Ancient Mining on the Shores of Lake Superior, Smithsonian Contributions to Knowledge, 1862, reprinted 2007 Gustavs Library, Davenport Iowa, no ISBN

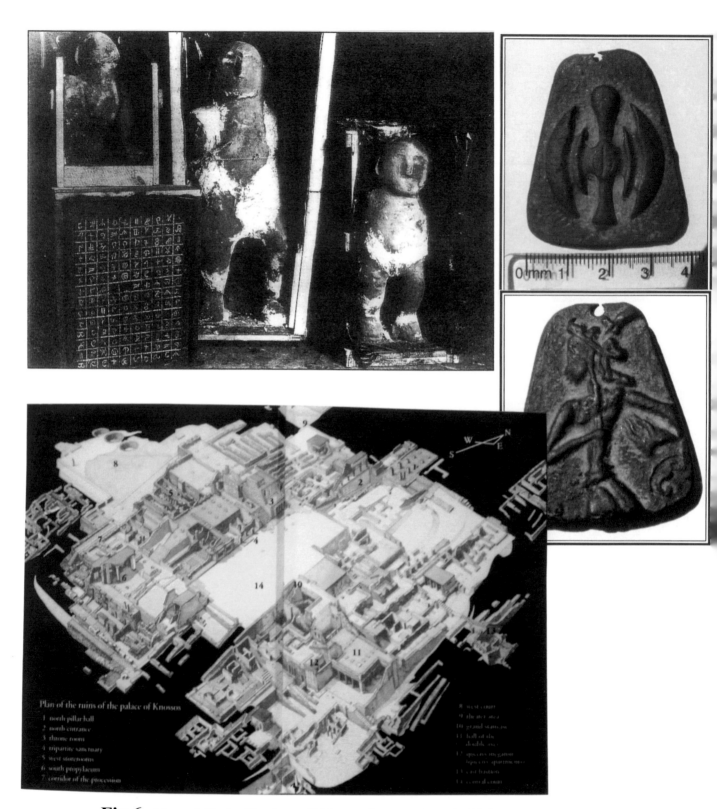

Fig.6 Above left, the Newberry Tablet, and statues found with it in Newberry, Michigan was found by Barry Fell in 1980 to be written in a "crolinized form of Minoan, having a vocabulary similat to that of Hittite, but lacking in the formal declensions and conjugations of Hittite, a Cypro/Minoan script, comprising an omens text" (Ref.4).
Above right, Minoan pendant found in Ohio riverbed fill dirt by Daniel Byers in October, 2006, dated by glyphs to 1700 BC to 1550 BC. (From Ancient American, Vol.13, #83).
Below, Knossos, capital of the Minoan copper traders (Ref. 80).

19. Henderson, J., <u>The Science and Archaeology of Materials, An Investigation of</u> Inorganic Materials, Routledge, New York, 2000, (ISBN 0-415-19934-4)
20. Halsey, J.R., <u>Miskwabik – Red Metal, The Roles Played by Michigan's Copper in Prehistoric North America</u>, Michigan Dept of State, no date, publisher, or ISBN
21. Dickinson, O., <u>The Aegean Bronze Age</u>, Cambridge University Press, New York, 1994 (ISBN 0-521-456649)
22. Schertz, J.P., <u>Old Water Levels and Waterways During the Ancient Copper Mining</u> Era (about 3000 BC to 1000 BC), 1999, no ISBN
23. Gale, N.H., <u>Bronze Age Trade in the Mediterranean</u>, Papers Presented at the Conference held at Rewley House, Oxford, 1989, /Studies in Mediterranean Archaeology Vol.XC, Paul Astroms Forlag, 1991, no ISBN, Weiner, M.H., "The Nature and Control of Minoan Foreign Trade"
24. Isle Royale National Park, National Geographic Trails Illustrated Map, www.nationalgeographic.com/maps
25. Griffin, J.B., <u>Lake Superior Copper and the Indians: Miscellaneous Studies of Great</u> Lakes Prehistory, Anthropological Papers, Museum of Anthropology, University of Michigan No.17, Ann Arbor, 1961
26. Rothenburg B., Tylecote, R.F., Boydell, P.J., <u>Chalcolithic Copper Smelting</u>, Excavations and Experiments, Archaeo-Metallurgy/ Number One, Institute for Archaeo-Metallurgical Studies, London, 1978,(ISBN 0 906183 00 6)
27. Huber, N.K., <u>The Geologic Story of Isle Royale National Park</u>, Formerly U.S. Geologic Survey Bulletin 1309, 1983-1996, Isle Royale Natural History Association, Houghton, Mi (ISBN 0 932212-89-1)
28. Barber, M., <u>Bronze and the Bronze Age, Metalworking and Society in Britain</u> c.2500-800 BC, Tempus, Gloustershire, 2003 (ISBN 0-7524 2507 2)
29. Moore, C.N., <u>Bronze Age Metalwork in Salisbury Museum</u>, Salisbury and South Wiltshire Museum Occasional Publication, 1972, no ISBN
30. Gore, R., "Men of the Sea, A Lost History, Who were the Phoenicians?, National Geographic, October 2004, nationalgeographic.com/magazine
31. Wood, D.J., "Bronze Age Michigan" a final of 3 parts, Ancient American, Vol.8, no.51, pg.21
32. Rydholm, F., "Old World Copper Miners of Ancient Michigan", The Barnes Review, July/Aug, 2002 Vol.VIII, No.4, pg.37
33. "Missing Link Discovered", Ancient American, Issue #12, pg.14
34. Carter, G.F., and Razi, H., "Chemical Composition of Copper-Based Coins of the Roman Republic, 217-31 BC", American Chemical Soc, Advances in Chemistry Series 220, Archaeological Chemistry IV, 1989, pg. 213
35. Gale, N.H., and Stos-Gale, Z.A., "Bronze Age Archaeometallurgy of the Mediterranean: The Impact of Lead Isotope Studies", American Chemical Society, advances in Chemistry Series 220, Archaeological Chemistry IV, 1989, pg.160
36. Great Lakes, National Geographic Society, 1987
37. Ozment,K., "Journey to the Copper Age", National Geographic, Vol. 195, No.4., April 1999 pg.70
38. Marquis, A.L., "Fighting Gravity, Saving What Remains of Michigan's 19th Century Copper Industry", National Parks, winter 2009, pg. 14
39. Carter, L.D., and Cheesman, P.R., "Michigan's Mound Builders, Historical Background of the Soper-Savage Collection of Inscriptions and Photographs", Ancient American, Issue #53, pg.2
40. Avery, R., Copper Country –God's Country, Avery Color Studios, 1973, no ISBN
41. Pleger, T.C., "The Old Copper Complex of the Western Great Lakes", 2000, www.fox.uwc.edu/depts/tpleger/oldcopper.html
42. Viegas, J., "Ancient Metalworking Recreated", April 2005, www.disc.discovery.com/news/briefs/2005050425/metalworking.html
43. Wagner, H., "Wiconsin's Ancient Copper Miners", From Wisconsin Outdoor Journal, Ancient American, No. 75
44. Stos-Gale, Z.A., Maliotis,G., Gale, N.H., and Annetts, N., "Lead Isotope Characteristics of the Cyprus Copper Ore Deposits Applied to Provenance Studies of Copper Oxhide Ingots", Archaeometry, Vol.39, Issue 1 Feb 1997, Pg.83-123
45. Ackley, J., Strauss Center for Conservation, Harvard Univ. Art Museums, personal email re: Knapp, S., "Mystery in Bronze", Dartmouth Life, Pg.4, April 2003
46. Freeman, A.M., "Copper Artifacts: Correlation with Source Types of Copper Ores", Science, Vol. 152, 1996, pg 1504
47. Hancock, R.G.V., Pavlish, L.A., Salloum, R.M., Fox, W.A., Wilson, G.C., "Distinguishing European Trade Copper and North-Eastern North American Native Copper", Archaeometry 33, 1991 69-86
48. Fitzgerald, W.R., Ramsden, P.G., "Copper Based Metal Testing as an Aid to Understanding Early European-Amerindian Interaction: Scratching the Surface", Canadian Journal of Archaeology, Vol.12, 1988
49. Martin, S.R., "The State of Our Knowledge about Ancient Copper Mining in Michigan", The Michigan Archaeologist, 31 (2-3):119-138
50. Guerra, M.F., "Analysis of Archaeological Metals. The Place of XRF and PIXE in the Determination of Technology and Provenance", X-Ray Spectrometry, Vol.27, 73-80, 1998
51. Budd, P., "Seeking the Origins of Bronze Tools", British Archaeology, No.36, July, 1998: Features
52. "Uluburun Shipwreck", http://uluburun-shipwreck.area51.ipupdater.com/

Figs.7,8,9 Copper Harbor (Keweenaw) Petroglyphs: Bronze-Age Bird Ship which probably transported miners and copper. It was carved upon a glacier-smoothed small island in the eastern end of Copper Harbor when the water level in Lake Superior was higher. The carver was probably guarding the ship, waiting for it to be loaded. On the following page is the hand of a giant beside the hand of the author. Many giant skeletons (7-8 feet) have been found in early mound burials in the Midwest. Above is a Tanit figure has a bird head. The circle with cross in it, some call a "SunGod" symbol, has been seen on a copper Oxhide ingot. Note also the deeply carved eye, and the bear (white sand in it). The greenish-colored Bronze Age maze petroglyph, one of a pair behind an old mill in Rocky Valley, in the tin mine cliffs between Tintagel and Boscastle in Cornwall, England, is drawn with single lines, like the ship petroglyph and the bear. (Soskin, R., <u>Standing with Stones</u>, Thames & Hudson, New York, 2009).

53. Rapp, G. Jr., Allert, J., Hendrickson, E., "Trace Element Discrimination of Discrete Sources of Native Copper", American Chemical Society, 14, pg.270-293, 1984

54. Hauptmann, A., Maddin, R., Prange, M., "On the structure and Composition of Copper and Tin Ingots Excavated from the Shipwreck of Uluburun", American Schools of Oriental Research, Bulletin No.328, pgs.1-30, Nov.2002

55. Budd, P., Pollard, A.M., Scaife, B., Thomas, R.G., "Oxhide Ingots, Recycling and the Mediterranean Metals Trade", Journal of Mediterranean Archaeology, Vol.8, Issue 1, 1995 pgs.1-32, ISSN: 0952-7648

56. Stos-Gale, Z.A., Gale, N.H., Bass, G., Pulak, C., Galili, E., Sharvit, J., "The Copper and Tin Ingots of the Late Bronze Age Mediterranean: New Scientific Evidence", Proceedings of the Fourth International Conference on the Beginning of the Use of Metals and Alloys (BUMA-IV), The Japan Institute of Metals – Aoba, Japan, 1998, pp. 115-126.

57. Salter, C.J., Northover, J.P., Jones, S., "Study of possible Bronze Age copper smelting debris from the Great Orme, Gwynedd, Wales", Gwynedd Archaeological Trust, Current Research Projects, Oxford Material Science-Based Archaeology Group Index (abstract)

58. Ixer, R.A., "The Role of Ore Geology and Ores in the Archaeological Provenancing of Metals", http://www.rosiehardman.com/harvard.htm

59. Joel, E.C., Sayre, E., Vocke, R., "Statistical Evaluation of the Lead Isotope Data on Geological Ore Samples from Western and Central Europe", Smithsonian Center for Materials Research and Education, SCMRE Research Report FY 1993: Historical Archaeology, http://www.si.edu/scmre/about/93histarch.htm

60. Srinivasan, S., "The Use of Tin and Bronze in Prehistoric Southern Indian Metallurgy", JOM, July, 1998

61. Ancient Cyprus Web Project, Bibliographies: Metallurgy 1990s, http://www.ancientcyprus.ac.uk/bibliographies/metal90.asp

62. Cherry, J.F., "Economy & Trade in the Later Bronze Age Aegean and East Mediterranean, Graduate Seminar, http://proteus.brown.edu/bronzeageeconomy/Home

63. Goodway, M., "Metals in Antiquity", Smithsonian Center for Materials Research and Education, http://www.socarchsci.org/bulletin/9809/9809q.htm

64. Arch-Metals Archaeo-Metallurgical Bibliography, http://usersox.ac.uk/~salter/arch-metals/met-bib-ak.htm

65. Bass, G.F., and Pulak ,C., "Bronze Age Shipwreck Excavation at Uluburun", http://ina.tamu.edu/ub_main.htm

66. Budd, P., "Seeking the origins of bronze tools", British Archaeology, No.36, July 1998 Features

67. Viegas, J., "Ancient Metalworking Recreated, Ancient Metalworkers Burned Out of History", Discovery News, http://dsc.discovery,.com/news/briefs/20050425/metalworking.html

68. Friedman, A.M., Conway, M., Kastner, M., Milsted, J., Metta, D., Fields, P.R., Olsen, E., "Copper Artifacts: Correlation with source Types of Copper Ores", Science, Vol 152, 10 June 1966, pg 1504-06.

69. Cornell, M.F., Prehistoric Relics of the Mound Builders, Battle Creek, Michigan, 1892

70. Rapp, G., Copper Project Database, Archaeometry Laboratory, 214 RLB, University of Minnesota, Duluth, 55812

71. Halpern, Z., personal email 10/16/2007

72. Glascock, M.D., Archaeometry Laboratory, University of Missouri Research Reactor, Columbia, Mo. 65211, GlasscockM@missouri.edu

73. Analytical Chemistry, Tukwila, Wa. 206-622-8353, www.ancheminc.com

74. http://www.museum.mtu.edu, www.mg.mtu.edu/district4.gif, www.mg.mtu.edu/hist.htm

75. Roach, J., "Bronze Age Factory Discovered in Jordan", National Geographic News 6/25/2002, http://news.nationalgeographic.com/news/2002/06/0620_020625_metalfactory.html

76. May, W., "Missing Link Discovered", Ancient American, Issue #12, pg.14

77. Childress, D.H., Lost Cities of North and Central America, Adventures Unlimited Press, Illinois, 1992, (ISBN 0-932813-09-7)

78. Herrmann, P., Conquest by Man, Harper & Brthers., N.Y., 1954

79. Wilkins, H., Secret Cities of South America, 1952, Adventures Unlimited Press, Kempton, Ill, p.291-292.

80. Farnoux, A., Knossos, Abrams Inc., (ISBN 0-8109-2819-1)

A Chart of the Southern Crossing of the Ocean
Pedra Escrita de Serrazes
(near Sao Pedro do Sul, Viseu, Portugal, c.2000 B.C.)

J.S. Wakefield, jayswakefield@yahoo.com

Summary A remarkable granite monolith called "Pedra Escrita de Serrazes" (the carved stone of Serrazes) has one of its sides covered with geometric petroglyphs. The site is near Viseu, Portugal, not far from a town named "Sao Pedro do Sul" ("The Holy Stone of the South"). It appears to be one of the largest geograhic petroglyphs in the world. We suggest a decipherment of the stone that is supported by its internal consistency, and is consistent with other megalithic petroglyphs. Study of the stone shows that the grid pattern makes sense when it represents the Atlantic Ocean, and the carved circles symbolize important places in the sailing routes across the Ocean. Some glyphs are suggested by the authors in the damaged sections. The sailing route called "Southern Crossing" appears to be the primary focus of the petroglyph.

Introduction: The Site   The town Sao Pedro do Sul (the "Holy Stone of the South") is located 17 km northwest of the town of Viseu, Portugal. The site of the stone is in the hills, on the paved road from the village of Serrazes to the next village of Penso, west of Oliveira de Frades. The site is indicated by a small sign in a new parking lot **(Photo 1)**. A forest path leads about 100m to the site, where the stone is under a small metal roof **(Photo 2)**. The stone is yellow-brown granite.The petroglyph is about five feet by eight feet square. Unfortunately it is damaged toward the bottom on both sides **(Photos 3&4).** There are remains of a small quarry in the area behind the stone. Quarrying activity is likely related to the damage visible on the petroglyph.

When the petroglyph is looked at in the woods, it is seen in the northern direction, which is the usual orientation for stone charts like this. The latitude of the site is 41.7°N. The distance to either the north or south coasts of Iberia are about the same from here, so the location is geographically central. This suggests that the map on the stone might show an overall view of the whole ocean. The stone is situated on a hillside above the river Vouga, so boats probably could have reached the ocean easily from here. The Vouga mouth is near the town of Aviero in the west, a distance of 40-50 km, or about half an Egyptian moira, perhaps a clue that half moira distances may play a role in the petroglyph.

Introduction: The Petroglyphs   Until Portugal joined the European Union, it was less developed in some respects, and archaeological sites were often undeveloped. One of the things that make travel fun, we accidentally discovered this site. We noticed a small photo of it in a new tourist brochure in the small museum of Olivera de Frades, when we had to go there to obtain the gate key to the nearby famous Antelas "painted dolmen" (Ref.1). As far as we know, the remarkable petroglyph on this huge monolith has not yet appeared in the archaeologic literature. The carvings consist of a large grid pattern with a number of concentric circles and cupmarks **(Photos 3&4)**. These elements are frequent symbols in megalithic art. To improve the visibility of the glyphs for our photographs, we chalked the grooves, which are about 0.5 to 1.0 cm deep, and 1-2 cm wide. The grid pattern is similar to other megalithic-period ocean charts we have seen, such as the petroglyphs in the passage grave of Kercado, in Carnac, Brittany, and the huge petroglyph of Buriz, in Galicia, Spain. These other grid-pattern petroglyphs have turned out to be primitive charts of the North Atlantic Ocean, dating after 2500 BC (Refs.2-4).

The Decipherment   The grid pattern extends over the entire surface of the front side of the stone. These carvings are framed by a deep and wide groove around the edge of the stone, encircling the petroglyph. Only at the bottom, where the petroglyph is damaged, is the groove discontinuous. It appears that the carver wanted to indicate that the whole subject was being contained in the petroglyph. So if this is an ocean representation, as we suspect, the carver has made it clear that the entire ocean is being depicted. The interpretation of the carving is difficult, because the concentric circles cannot be directly linked with known geographic locations by size or position alone. The damaged portions and the changes in the sizes of the grid patterns make the interpretation difficult, and leave us with questions at the end.

Getting started, we notice the double concentric circles **A&M** in the upper corners (see **Photo 4** and **Map 1**). These appear to set the parameters of the chart. Between these circles is a very straight line, with regular grid lines crossing between them. These patterns do not continue to the edges of the circles. The grid pattern below the line appears more regular than above, and divides into 16 equal boxes (labeled in **Photo 4**). We would not expect to see detailed carvings on both sides of the ocean unless the ocean had been crossed and explored earlier than the carvings were made. Since there are circular carvings at both sides, we can see they had crossed the ocean, and had knowledge of the size of it.

Time and Distance Methodology   Vertical longitude lines as we know them, meeting at the poles, were not in use yet. Vertical distance lines were used instead, which look like longitude lines, but do not converge at the poles. We have called these "distance lines", dl and DL (ten dl= one DL). They frequently look like the sides of curved-sided boxes. The unit of measure used was the ancient Egyptian moira, the unit of distance of one degree (10 moira= one big Moira). (For a more lengthy discussion of this subject, see our book, How the SunGod Reached America, c.2500 B.C., A Guide to Megalithic Sites.)

This is an Iberian chart, so we would expect an important location for Iberia on the chart, in keeping with the usual practice we have seen before in megalithic petroglyphs. So we think the upper right circles (**Photo 4**, **Map 1**) represent Iberia, the peninsula of Spain and Portugal. The shortest distance between Cape Finisterre, the NW Cape of Iberia (at today's longitude of 9°W), and the most Eastern Cape of America, Cape Race (at today's longitude of 53°W), is approximately 40° of latitude. This is equal to 4 Moira, which is quite close to correct. This knowledge that the North Atlantic Ocean is about 40° across is seen in quite a few megalithic petroglyphs. For example, the little Ocean Pendants of Iberia, small necklace plaques so often seen in museums in Iberia, usually have rows of four triangles inscribed across them, showing this distance. (see **Fig.6**), (Ref.22).

Photo 1. New Parking lot at roadside on road from Serrazes to Penso, and new site sign (near Viseu, Portugal, May, 2006)

Photo 2. Dr. de Jonge beside the Pedra Escrita de Serrazes, and its roof (Near Viseu, Portugal, May, 2006)

Since this distance across the Ocean is shown on this stone of Serrazes as 16 boxes, each small box must be a distance measure of 2 ½° (40°/16), or 2 ½ moira, or ¼ big Moira. Two and a half degrees is a distance of 150 Nautical Miles (60 Nautical Miles are defined as the distance of 1°). Sailing with the usual steady tradewind of 20-25 knots in the Southern Crossing route, a 50 foot boat would cover his distance in 24 hours, a speed of 6.25 NM/hour. Longer vessels would have faster hull speeds, and would average this speed more easily. So it appears they were using a "box", or chart spacing that would be sailed in one day's time, and using this measure in both north/south and east/west directions. So given favorable winds, this is a "time chart" of the days required at sea. The other huge ocean petroglyph we found on this trip, the Buriz Stone, in Galicia, Northern Spain, also appears to have grid dimensions of 2 1/2°, so this dimension must have been commonly used when sailing.

The double circles in the upper corners of the petroglyph, and the deeply carved ringing border, frame the sides and width of the Ocean for the whole petroglyph. On each side are the double rings at the corners. Possibly, the distance between them is indicated in the two rings (2+2= 4), showing the 4 Moira, or 40° distance. The carefully proportioned and straight connecting line (labeled 43°N) is high on the stone. This was done because most of the story to be illustrated was in the southern portion of the ocean to be carved below. This most famous sailing route to the western world was explained in the lower part of this stone. This is why the stone was probably called "The Holy Stone of the South".

The Southern Crossing The center of the "Iberia" double circle **A** at the upper right side of the stone is most likely Cape Finisterre, at 43°N because this is the northwest tip of the Iberian Peninsula. The Stone of Serrazes, being 2° more to the south at 41°N, is indicated on the outer edge of the double circle **(Photo 4)**. The village of Serrazes is situated on the River Vouga, half a moira (1/2°) from the sea. Continuing to use the methodology of one ring donut= 1°, the distance from Cape Finisterere to the Stone is 2 rings +1/2 moira = 2/12 moira, the distance of the grid pattern.

The large, triple circle **B** below it should then represent the SW Cape of Iberia, where ships would depart for the south, Cape Sao Vicente. Between both centers are 5 rings and a space between them, a total of six spaces = 6°. Cape Sao Vicente has a latitude of 37°N, or 6° south of Cape Finisterre, encoding the latitude of this cape, 6° lower, at 43-6= 37°N, which is correct. So the rings and spaces, also interpreted as 1° distances, support the interpretation.

At its lower end, this big triple circle **B** touches a small single ring **C (Photo 4)**. From Sao Vicente (37°N) one would set out to sea, and so we use a new methodology, where we apply 2 ½ moira to each ring and space (chart box). So the first point of contact with the Canaries would be the Eastern Islands (Lanzarote) at 29.5°N where the rings touch (Sao Vicente at 37° minus 3 rings x 2.5 moira/ring = 29.5°N). The center of the small ring corresponds with the Central Canary Islands, 1° lower, at 29.5-1= 28.5°N.

Photo 3.   A side-view, showing the depth of the carvings
(Near Viseu, Portugal, May, 2006)

Below it is a circle **D** with a big cupmark in the center, with a large ring around it. The two circles do not touch. A bent connecting line runs between the rings. Here they are sailing at sea, on a curving route around the west coast of Africa. The center of the lower circle corresponds to the west coast of Africa, at 23.5°N (28.5°-[2 rings x 2.5 moira/ring] = 23.5°N). This is the latitude of the holy Tropic of Cancer. Identification of this latitude in the petroglyph shows involvement in the Sunreligion by the persons carving the petroglyph. These two circles (for the Canaries, and the Tropic of Cancer), are situated along the edge of the right side, outside the grid pattern. It is obvious that neither of them are the goal of the voyage. So let us look at the big triple circle **E** beside them.

When sailing from the Canary Islands, the 3 rings of the large circle **E** indicate that the center of this ring is Cape Blanco, the important West Cape of North Africa, at 21°N (28.5° Canaries – [3 rings x 2.5 moira/ring] = 21°N). The vertical line within this circle, not a part of the grid system, probably is indicating that that Cape Blanco is located due south of the Canary Islands. It appears Cape Blanco is very important, because this was where the boats left the coast of Africa.

To the left, is the largest ring **F**. The center of it is at the level of the second inner circle of the previous glyph. It represents the island of Boa Vista, of the Central Cape Verde Islands, at 16°N (21° Cape Blanco- [2 rings x 2.5 moira/ring]= 16°N). The triple circle around Cape Blanco may indicate the sailing distance from Cape Blanco to Boa Vista, a sailing distance of 450 Nautical Miles (3 rings x 2.5 moira/ring= 7.5 moiras = 450 NM), which is correct.

At the lower left side of the circle of Cape Blanco, is a box with a cupmark. In view of the 3+1= 4 spacings, this cupmark could represent the Bissagos Islands, at 11°N (21° Cape Blanco –[4 spacings x 2.5 moira/ring)] = 11°N). We think this may have been an alternative departure point for shorter crossings to South America.

Note that the two large triple circles **E&F** have a space between them. Apparently, 2.5 more moiras have to be sailed before reaching the Cape Verde Islands. It can be exlained in a different way. The inner ring of the last circle contains two cupmarks. The upper dot now represents Boa Vista, of the Central Cape Verde Islands, at 16°N, where submerged architectural remains have been reported (Ref.21). The central dot is the southwestern island of Brava, at 16-1= 15°N. So the inner ring shows that we have to go 1° to the south. The sailing distance along this archipelago is 2.5 moira= 2.5°= 150 NM, as shown by the one ring.

So the center of the last triple circle **F** represents Brava, the southwestern Cape Verde Island, at 15°N. Around this center are 3 rings, corresponding to the length of the Southern Crossing Sailing Route, with the wind and the current, 3 Moiras = 30°= 1,800 NM. This is correct for the Crossing to French Guyana, at 5°N. It is known that this was a popular landing point for a long time (Ref.4).

We suggest that the landing point may be represented by the simple round donut **G** just below the damaged area. This circle is simple, because the specific landing point along the coast was not of crucial importance. When comparing the scale of the 16 box

4

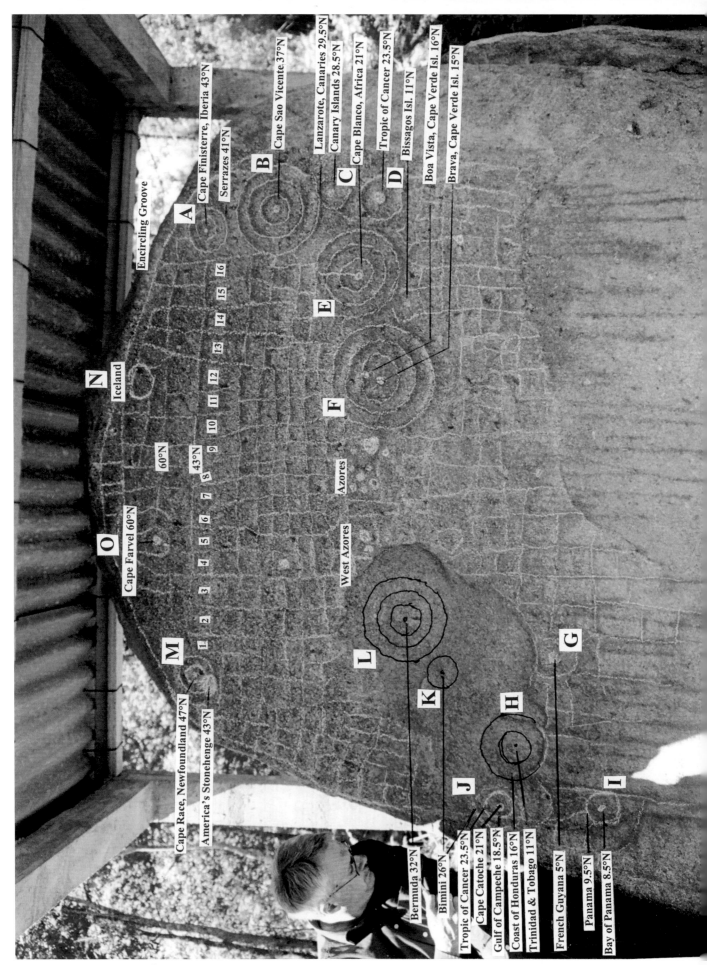

Photo 4   Pedra Escrita de Serrazes, with author's labels and reconstructed area.

horizontal line between the two upper corner figures, the length of the Southern Crossing is roughly ¾, or 3 Moira,= 30°= 1,800 NM, which is encouraging that we have a correct interpretation. The 3 rings of the first circle and the single ring of the second one show the correct latitude of French Guyana, at 5°N (15° Brava – [3 rings of big circle x 2.5 moira/ring] – [1 ring of small circle x 2.5 moira/ring]= 5°N).

Central America   Probably, a double circle **H** was engraved in the deep, damaged part of the left side of the stone depicting the landing point in French Guyana. The diameter of the lost layer roughly corresponds with a double missing circle, where the lower groove is still present on the stone. The outer edge of the simple, first round corresponds with the coastal waters above French Guyana, at 6°N (5° + (space=1°) = 6°N). The 2 rings of the lost circle provide the latitude of its center, the islands of Trinidad and Tobago, at 11°N (6° French Guyana + [2 rings x 2.5 moira/ring] = 11°N). Here a route starts to the north, sailing a reach across the tradewinds, up the Antilles Islands chain, though a coastal route toward Central America was preferred in the petroglyphs we have studied (Ref.4). This route past Aruba is a downwind run, and being along the coast, was probably considered safer.

The lost circle **H** had 2 rings, also corresponding to the important culture along the North Coast of Honduras at 16°N (11° Trinidad + [2 rings x 2.5 moira/ring] = 16°N). This coast was a favorite goal for trading. The eight circles of the route used so far contain 16 rings, perhaps intentionally showing the 16° latitude. Including the circle of the Bissagos Islands, we think the petroglyph of Serrazes had a total of 16 circles, confirming this important 16° latitude again.

The lower edge of the lost inner circle **H** provides the latitude of the Bay of Panama, at 8.5°N (11° - [1 ring x 2.5 moira/ring] = 8.5°N). At the left side below on the stone is a simple round donut. The center of it represents the Bay of Panama. The upper edge encodes the start of the land crossing of Panama, at 8.5° (Bay of Panama) + space of 1° = 9.5°N. This strip of land apparently was important for reaching the Pacific Ocean. The carving is isolated, because this land crossing was not part of the usual route. Note that later on, the easy upriver route to Lake Nicaragua and the Pacific may have been the popular route, as indicated by the many huge Atlantean statues on the island in the lake.

At the left side of the stone is another double circle **J**. Due to the damage, the quality of this glyph is quite reduced. It is even possible that this circle was at one point completely lost, and some "restoration" has been done, perhaps in prehistory. In any case, this is a nice figure, because it provides information. The 2 rings of the circle provide the latitude of its center, Cape Catoche, the NE Cape of the Yucatan, at 21°N (16° coast of Honduras +[2 rings) x 2.5 moira/ring] = 21°N). This Cape Catoche, where the sailors enter the land of Punt, and is at the same latitude as Cape Blanco, where the vessels left Africa.

The lower edge of the deep inner circle of this figure provides the latitude of the Civilization around the Gulf of Campeche, Mexico, at 18.5°N (21° Catoche – 1 ring x 2.5 moira/ring = 18.5°N). This was the most important goal of the journey. It had a special religious meaning, the Land of Punt. It was the center of the oldest Civilization that developed in America, that of the Olmecs. The lower half of this circle has the shape of

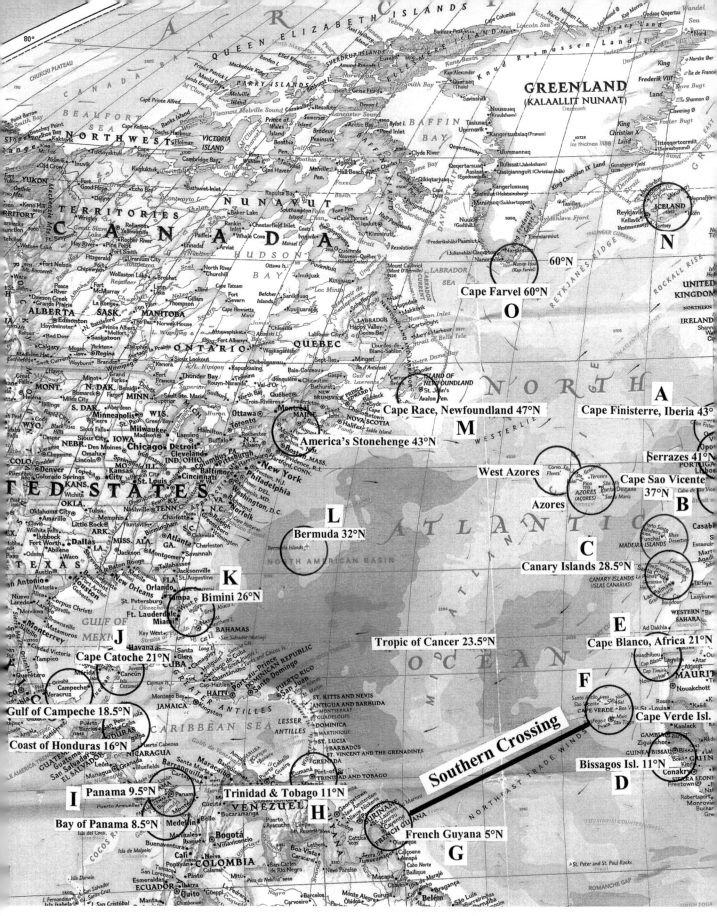

Map 5   A map of the Atlantic Ocean, showing the labels we put on the petroglyph.

the South Coast of the Gulf of Campeche. The nine circles used so far have 18 rings, confirming the 18° latitude of the south point of the Gulf of Campeche.

Probable Return Route Via Bermuda   The upper side of the inner circle **J**, at the left edge of the stone, encodes the holy Tropic of Cancer and the North Coast of Cuba, both 2.5° above Cape Catoche, at 23.5°N (21° Catoche +[1 ring x 2.5 moira/ring] = 23.5°N). The Tropic of Cancer has important religious meanings. It is the latitude of the center of the Sunreligion, and of the Southern Egyptian Empire. Note, that the Pedra Escrita de Serrazes site is situated 18° above the holy Tropic of Cancer, at 23° + 18° holy Punt= 41° the latitude of Serrazes! The upper side of the outer circle corresponds with the island of Bimini, on the Gulfstream offshore Florida, 2.5° above the north coast of Cuba, at 26°N (23.5° Tropic +[1 ring x 2.5 moira/ring] = 26°N). This island was a well-known way station on the Return Route of the Ocean (Ref.4).

Now a problem occurs. At the left side of the stone, a large piece of the petroglyph has disappeared. Unless the pieces turn up somewhere, or are dug up nearby, we will not know what was engraved. (Someone ought to dig and look for the pieces in case they simply broke off if the stone was recently set upright by a contractor with a backhoe.) However, to complete the story of the Enscripted Stone of Serrazes, we have reconstructed what we feel is the most likely scenario. This scenario is a personal vision - a speculation by the authors. We think that in the damaged area, a large triple circle was engraved., with at its left side, a small simple circle. Following the methodology we have been using, the small circle is Abaco in the Bahamas, and the large circle would represent Bermuda at 32°N (27° Abaco) + [2 rings x 2.5 moira/ring] = 32°N). This island had already been discovered by c.2400 BC (Ref.4). The rings of this big circle would give the latitude of the West Azores at 39 1/2°N, and the sailing distance of 3 Moira, or 1800 NM. The return route via Bermuda can also be seen in this chart, if one uses double meanings for two of the glyphs, the first center of the big triple circle **F** being the West Azores, and the center of the second triple circle **E** being Madeira. It is not unreasonable to expect double symbolism, as we have seen it before in petroglyphs.

The Northern Return Route   The easternmost land of North America is Cape Race, Newfoundland, at 47°N. Note in the bottom of the upper left double circle **M** is a huge cupmark. We think it represents America's Stonehenge, on the New Hampshire coast, at 43°N (47° Cape Race – [1 ½ rings x 2.5 moira/ring] = 43°N). It is the greatest megalithic monument in North America, a nautical center for teaching how to cross the Ocean (Ref.4). The double circle has 2 rings, giving the latitude of the West Azores, at 47° (Newfoundland) –[2 rings x 2.5 moira/ring] – [1 ring W. Azores x 2.5 moira/ring]= 39.5°N. The double circle of Newfoundland shows that the sailing distance from Cape Race to the West Azores is about 2 Moiras = 20° =1,200 NM, which is correct.

The Northern Crossing   This Crossing is only roughly indicated on the Enscripted Stone of Serrazes. The first circle N at the upper right side symbolizes Iceland. The circle **O** on its left, near the top, represents the south point of Greenland. As is well-known, this south point, Cape Farvel, is situated at 60°N. This Cape had been discovered c.3200 BC (Refs.3,4). So the horizontal line to this point is the 60°N latitude line. This implies that

Fig. 6 Some Iberian Ocean "I sailed to Paradise" Pendants, all reduced from 4-5" sizes. The top left example shows that some have chart grids like the Pedra Escrita de Serrazes. The top right two show the 4 Moira (40°) width of the North Atlantic, while the lower three show the 3 Moira (30°) width of the Southern Crossing at their bottoms.

the important line connecting the double circles below it now is the 50th latitude line, not the 43°N line. So the scale of the grid pattern in the northern area is complicated by being on a different scale, apparently compressed, but using these circles a sensible explanation of this route can be seen.

The Cupmarks   In the center of the stone are a number of cupmarks, that are different from the other carvings of the petroglyph. There are 9, with one especially large one, in the middle of the Ocean. The eastern two would be the islands of Madeira. It appears that someone other than the original carver added these, in later generations, because of the different style. Note the two more cupmarks to the west, probably the West Azores. Certainly the nine islands of the Azores and the two islands of Madeira continued to be a rest stop of survival importance to returning sailors for thousands of years, so one can understand how someone who no longer fully understood the double symbolisms of the original petroglyph might feel compelled to add them to the old Enscripted Stone when he returned.

 One might argue that this accounts for the depth of the cupmark for America's Stonehenge, for which people might have felt especially thankful, for the safe return passage. Finally, note the cupmark four boxes north of the West Azores. This probably represent a boat crew's experience and the reporting of something like Sable Island, seen in the fog, or something seen when they were lost or blown off course, in their passage between the American coast and the West Azores. The two cupmarks near the damaged area on the right, probably represent St. Peter & St. Paul Rocks, Ascension, or St. Helena, since these places have been noted in other petroglyphs (Ref.4).

The Damaged Areas   It appears that only some of the grid pattern was lost in the damaged area at the right side. The most serious damage was probably on the left. Our examination shows that the grid pattern plays a subordinate role in the story told on the Stone. The grid shows that the petroglyph deals with the North Atlantic Ocean, and it illustrates that the unit of length of a Quarter Moira of 150 NM was important during the crossings of it.

Dating   It is striking that the sailing route of the Southern Crossing is indicated so prominently. Of course, this site of Escrita Serrazes is in Iberia, closer to the Southern Crossing than sites in Brittany. The petroglyph probably dates from after the comet catastrophe of c.2345 BC, when the climate became colder, making the northern route more difficult. As far as the Return Route is considered, we think the Crossing Via Bermuda is more likely to have been indicated than a route off Cape Race, though this depends, of course upon our reconstruction of the damaged area of the stone. We think people favored the long crossing via Bermuda, which points to a late date for the carving, since Bermuda was not discovered until c.2200 BC (Ref.4). Therefore we give the petroglyph a date of c.2000 BC. If the missing pieces are found in the ground nearby, or in a nearby house, and there are no ring carvings on them, the date is probably earlier than the discovery of Bermuda, so should be dated earlier than 2200 BC.

Significance   This is one of the largest megalithic period petroglyphs yet found in the world. Looking at it, one is viewing a human story being told deep in the past. It was carved more than a thousand years before "history" started with the invention of written language. This stone tells a story of sailing on the Ocean that is similar to other megalithic Stones of a similar date. This stone is very valuable evidence of man's heroic explorations of the seas in prehistory.

References

1. "Archaeological Tours: Dao Lafoes Tourist Region", Viseu, Portugal, 2005 (free booklet in Museum of Olivera de Frades, and Viseu tourist Offices)
2. Twohig, E. Shee, The Megalithic Art of Western Europe, Clarendon Press, Oxford, 1981
3. De Jonge, R.M., and IJzereef, G.F., De Stenen Spreken, Kosmos Z&K, Utrecht/Antwerpen, 1996 (ISBN 90-215-2846-0) (Dutch)
4. De Jonge, R.M., and Wakefield, J.S., How the SunGod Reached America c.2500 BC, A Guide to Megalithic Sites, 2002 (ISBN 0-917054-19-9) also on CD
5. Website: www.howthesungod.com, De Jonge, R.M., and Wakefield, J.S.
6. De Jonge, R.M., and Wakefield, J.S., "The Discovery of the Atlantic Islands", Migration & Diffusion, Vol.3, No.11, pgs.69-109 (2002)
7. De Jonge, R.M., and Wakefield, J.S., "The Passage Grave of Karleby, Encoding the Islands Discovered in the Ocean, c. 2950 BC", Migration & Diffusion, Vol.5, No.18, pgs.64-74 (2004)
8. De Jonge, R.M., and Wakefield, J.S., "A Nautical Center for Crossing the Ocean, America's Stonehenge, New Hampshire, c.2200 BC", Migration & Diffusion, Vol.4, No.15, pgs.60-100 (2002)
9. De Jonge, R.M., and Wakefield, J.S., "Germany's Bronze Age Disc Reveals Transatlantic Seafaring, c.1600 BC", Ancient American, Vol.9, No.55, pgs.18-20 (2004)
10. De Jonge, R.M., and Wakefield, J.S., "The Three Rivers Petroglyph, A Guide-post for River Travel in America", Migration & Diffusion, Vol.3, No.12, pgs.74-100 (2002)
11. De Jonge, R.M., and Wakefield, J.S., "Ales Stenar, Sweden's Bronze Age 'Sunship' to the Americas, c.500 BC", Ancient American, Vol.9, No.56, pgs.16-21 (2004)
12. De Jonge, R.M., and Wakefield, J.S., "The Monument of Ales Stenar, A Sunship to the Realm of the Dead", Migration and Diffusion, Vol.5, No. 19, pgs. 94-106, 2004
13. De Jonge, R.M., and Wakefield, J.S., "The Rings of Stenness, Brodgar, and Bookan, Celebrating the Discovery of South Greenland", Migration and Diffusion, Vol 6, No.24, 2005
14. De Jonge, R.M., and Wakefield, J.S., "The Paintings of Porcellano Cave, The Discovery of Guadelupe, c.3000 BC", Migration and Diffusion, Vol. 6, No. 22, 2005
15. De Jonge, R.M., and Wakefield, J.S., "Mexican Cave Artists, 3000 BC", Ancient American, Vol. 10, No. 62, 2005
16. De Jonge, R.M., and Wakefield, J.S., "Greenland: Bridge between the Old and New Worlds", Ancient American, Vol. 11, No. 67, 2006
17. De Jonge, R.M., and Wakefield, J.S., "The Discovery of the Islands in the Atlantic, Stone C-8, Cairn T, Loughcrew, Ireland, c.3200 BC Vol.13, No.81, January 2009
18. De Jonge, R.M., and Wakefield, J.S., "The Stone Rows of Tormsdale: A Voyage to Central America across the Atlantic, Ancient American Vol. 11, No. 70, (2006)
19. De Jonge, R.M., and Wakfield, J.S., "A Return Route across the Ocean, encoded in the Tormsdale Rows; Caithness, NE Scotland, c.1600 BC", Ancient American, Vol12, Number 74, pgs. 8-12
20. De Jonge, R.M., and Wakefield, J.S., "The Megalithic Megalithic Monument of Lagatjar, The Crossing of the Labrador Sea; Camaret-sur-Mer, Crozon Peninsula, Finistere, Brittany c.1600 BC", Ancient American, Vol.12, no.76, Pgs.32-37, 12/2007
21. Berlitz, C., The Mystery of Atlantis, Grosset & Dunlap, New York, 1969
22. De Jonge, R.M., and Wakefield, J.S., "Ocean Pendants, Portugal, Spain, Ireland and America, c.2200 BC", unpublished, or published with this article

Megalithic Stone Rows and Petropots in Iberia
(Barbanza Peninsula, Galicia, Spain c.2000 BC)

J.S. Wakefield, jayswakefield@yahoo.com

Introduction

On a May 2006 trip to Iberia to study megalithic paintings and petroglyphs (Ref.9), the authors discovered megalithic stone rows in Galicia (NW Spain), which do not exist in this part of Europe according to the official literature. We also observed a new feature of the megalithic landscape, we call "petropots". These appear to be vessels for signal fires at prominent points along the coast, near entrances, and on ceremonial pathways. Many photos in this article show these petropots. We hope both items will help to deepen our understanding of megalithic culture, and encourage others to look for them elsewhere.

Stone Rows

Megalithic stone rows can be distinguished from more recent farmer's walls by a number of characteristics. Megalithic rows often use very large stones, often deeply set into the ground. Sometimes though, they can consist of smaller stones, as in Caithness, Scotland, and in Cornwall, England. Megalithic rows always have the flat sides of the stones parallel with the line of the row, not across it, as farmer's walls often have, and the stones in megalithic rows are usually not contiguous, but spaced, more or less evenly apart. Of course, deciding what you are looking at can get dicey, since farmers have often been making stone walls in the same areas for subsequent thousands of years. They have sometimes re-used the megalithic stones, in-filled old rows, and have cris-crossed the countryside and mountainsides with arrays of stone walls. What remains of these stone walls can be difficult to understand. The confusion is so challenging that even authority figures in archaeology are cautious about declaring any but the most huge stones megalithic. Surely an early authority figure is responsible for the statement that there are no megalithic rows in Iberia, and the statement has been copied by other authors ever since.

Photo 1 shows Dr. de Jonge standing on one of the stones of a large, south-facing semi-circle, typically belonging to the Megalithic Culture. It is located near the town of Boiro, on the Barbanza Peninsula, Galicia, at a distance of c.10km from the Ocean **(Map)**. He is standing about in the middle of the semi-circle, and the eastern end of the row is in the left of the photo, running down close to the road. **Photo 2** shows the other, western end of the row, which is below the road, with our rental car in the background.

Photo 3 shows a more or less straight row in the vicinity. The view is east, from a high plateau in the mountain range of the Serra do Barbanza, at an altitude of c.650 meters. Note that the stones are all lined up with their faces along the row, and spaced equal distances apart. It is obvious, that this row does not serve any purpose for a farmer. **Photo 4** shows the same row leading to a tomb site on the mountaintop in the distance (view

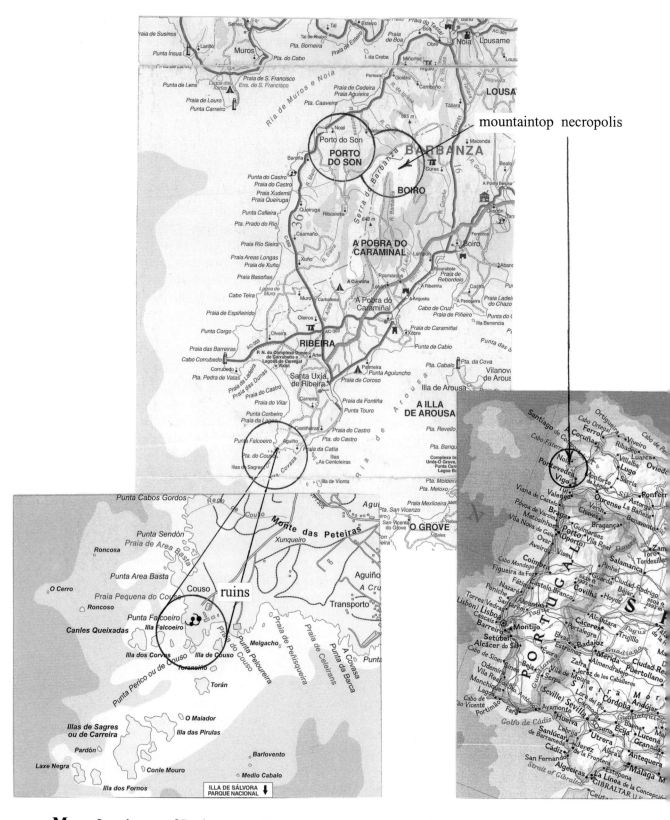

Map Local map of Barbanza Peninsula, Galicia, at the Atlantic Coast of NW Spain (at 43°N).

southeast). The association of this row with a megalithic tomb, or dolmen, increases the likelihood that the row is megalithic.

These rows are part of the megalithic necropolis on this peninsula, at 43°N. Note, that this is the latitude of America's Stonehenge and the south point of Nova Scotia, also at 43°N. After the discovery of America, c.2500 BC, these were the departure points for crossing the Ocean, with the wind and the current, to the archipelago of the Azores, and finally back to the Old World. So the location of this necropolis and its ceremonial features may be due to the importance of these latitudes to the megalithic maritime culture.

Photo 5 shows Dr. de Jonge taking a photo of another row, which is coming up the mountainside toward the megalithic necropolis called "San Cibrao", located in the Lebroeiro Mountains, south of Ourense, in Galicia. This row can also be considered a processional walkway.

Petropots

Photo 6 shows a pothole at San Cibrao found in the top of a prominent boulder at the end of the long stone row shown in Photo 5. Another pothole in a boulder on a high point near another row is shown in **Photo 7**. This row is coming up the slope from the west toward the necropolis on the heights of the Barbanza Peninsula. As you can see in **Photo 8**, these "holes" are always about 18 inches in diameter, and about 4-6 inches deep. These petropots may have started out as a natural feature or natural weathering, but it appears they have been intentionally enlarged and rounded to this consistent size and depth by man. They are usually prominently located on the top of prominent boulders, so apparently the sites have been purposefully chosen and worked by man. As can be seen in the photos, few other holes occur in the rest of the boulder surfaces, and usually they do not occur in the other boulders in the surroundings.

We are calling these features "petropots". They repeatedly occur only in prominent places. The next photo is the most dramatic one (**Photos 8 & 16**). To the right in Photo 16 is a town on the coast, called "Port of the Sun" (see Map). The name of it still relates to the megalithic Sunreligion. The valley behind the petropot leads directly from this harbour up to the mountaintop necropolis. **Photo 10** shows Dr. de Jonge looking at another petropot in a location overlooking a large portion of the plateau, where more than a dozen megalithic tombs have been found. **Photo 11** shows another petropot near the stone row, and **Photo 13** shows still another petropot, located beside a communications tower, on a high point nearby on the plateau.

The petropot in **Photo 12** is a closeup of the Petropot in Photo 6. It is located in the megalithic necropolis named San Cibrao, south of Ourense, near the River Laboreiro. This site is located c.100km SE of Barbanza Peninsula, so the petropots are not a local phenomenon. Petropots are also found at sea level. **Photo 14** shows several on a "gateway stone" at Punta Falcoeiro, the south cape of Barbanza Peninsula. The site is protected by a natural wall of huge boulders across the narrow neck. **Photo 15** shows a

Photo 1. Dr. de Jonge, standing on a stone of a south-facing Stone Semi-Circle of the Megalithic Culture. (2500-1500 BC, Boiro, Barbanza Peninsula, Galicia, NW Spain, Spring 2006)

Photo 2. Dr. de Jonge on the top of the Serra do Barbanza. His hand is on one of the larger stones of a long Stone Row. (2500-1500 BC, view east, Boiro, Brabanza Peninsula, Galicia, NW Spain, Spring 2006)

overlooking the fishing grounds to the west. It is a great spot for what appears to have been a megalithic era "lighthouse".

Conclusions

We think the explanation for them is that signal fires were needed or desired at these particular places. Fires require fuel, oxygen, and heat. To maintain heat at the bottom of a fire on a round boulder, one needs a slight bowl to hold the hot coals, or they roll away, and your fire goes out. Usually these pots have a low side, to empty ash. The petropots may have deepened themselves over time, due to repeated heating and freezing of the bottoms of the pots, which were usually of granite at these sites. What is striking is the consistent size and the prominent locations of these petropots. If they are a natural phenomenon, it is remarkable how they are all almost the same convienient size, and on the ends of stones at prominent overlooks. We became almost able to reliably predict the sites where they could be found. Below the Sallas Dam south of Ourense is a prominent balanced pointed rock, which may be another site, but a ladder is needed to reach the top.

The petropots are always located on the outward side of a projecting point of a high prominent boulder overlooking an important pathway. The photos show them at an access pathway to a fortified site, and on the pathways to high-altitude ceremonial sites. We will leave the dramatization of flaming pathways and full-moon night ceremonies to others. We hope other researchers will be able to find and study petropots in other locations. Jenkinson (Ref.16) has reported finding pots in Dartmoor Park, though we did not notice any there while exploring the stone rows of the Park for nearly a week. Probably the Petropots belong to the megalithic culture and are not be unique to Galicia.

References

1. De Jonge, R.M., and IJzereef, G.F., De Stenen Spreken, Kosmos Z&K, Utrecht/Antwerpen, 1996 (ISBN 90-215-28-0) (Dutch)
2. De Jonge, R.M., and Wakefield, J.S., How the SunGod Reached America c.2500 BC, A Guide to Megalithic Sites, 2002, (ISBN 0-917054-19-9), also on CD
3. Website: www.howthesungod.com, De Jonge, R.M., and Wakefield, J.S.
4. De Jonge, R.M., and Wakefield, J.S., "The Discovery of the Atlantic Islands", Migration & Diffusion, Vol.3, No.11, pgs.69-109 (2002)
5. De Jonge, R.M., and Wakefield, J.S., "Greenland: Bridge between the Old and New Worlds", Ancient American, Vol. 11, No. 67, 2006
6. De Jonge, R.M., and Wakefield, J.S, "The Stone Rows of Tormsdale: A Voyage to Central America across the Atlantic", Ancient American, Vol. 11, No. 70 (2006)
7. De Jonge, R.M., and Wakefield, J.S., "A Nautical Center for Crossing the Ocean, America's Stonehenge, New Hampshire, c.2200 BC", Migration & Diffusion, Vol.4, No.15, pgs.60-100 (2002)
8. Jairazbhoy, R.A., Ancient Egyptians and Chinese in America, Rowman & Littlefield, Totowa, N.J., 1974 (ISBN 0-87471-571-1
9. Twohig, E. Shee, The Megalithic Art of Western Europe, Clarendon Press, Oxford, 1981
10. Twohig, E. Shee, Irish Megalithic Tombs, Shire Archaeology, 1990 (ISBN 0-7478- 0094-4)
11. Balfour, M., Megalithic Mysteries - An Illustrated Guide to Europe's Ancient Sites, Collins & Brown, 1992 (ISBN 1-85-585-3558)
12. Burl, A., From Carnac to Callanish, Yale University Press, New Haven and London, 1993 (ISBN 0-300-05575-7)
13. People of the Stone Age: Hunter-gatherers and Early Farmers, Weldon Owen Pty Limited, McMahons Point, Australia (1995)
14. Fell, B., America BC, Pocket Books, Simon & Schuster, 1994
15. Bailey, J., Sailing to Paradise, Simon & Schuster, 1994
16. Jenkinson, T., "Discovering Rock Basins On Dartmoor", Dartmoor Magazine, No.87, Pg.22, (ISSN 0268-5027)

Photo 3. The western end of the same circle as Photo 1. It is located on the highlands of the Serra do Barbanza, at 43°N, c.10km from the Ocean.

Photo 4. The same Stone Row as in Photo 3, leading to a stone tomb covered with an earthen mound (site is labeled "Dolmen #14") on the mountaintop at an altitude of c.650 meters (view east).

Photo 5. Dr. de Jonge photographing the lower, uphill portion of another Megalithic Row approaching the mountaintop necropolis of San Cibrao in the Lebroreiro mountains. It may be considered a processional walkway (near A Bola, south of Ourense, Galicia).

Photo 6. The "petropot" in the necropolis of San Cibrao that is shown in Photo 12, here showing how it is overlooking a processional walkway (2500-1500 BC, near A Bola, south of Ourense, Galicia).

Photo 7. A view of the long stone row on the Serra Do Barbanza, with a petropot in the overlooking rock.

Photo 8. A closeup photo of a petropot, showing its roundness, and the consistent size of about eighteen inches (Barbanza Peninsula).

Photo 9. A nice view across the heather on the mountaintop necropolis, with several collapsed/looted tombs in the foreground (Sierra do Barbanza, Galicia, Spain; May 2007)

Photo 10. Dr. de Jonge looks at a petropot overlooking the Stone Semicircle of Photo 1. (Serra do Barbanza, Galicia).

Photo 11. Petropot overlooking the processional walkway of Photos 4 and 5 (Serra do Barbanza, Galicia).

Photo 12. Petropot at the megalithic necropolis of San Cibrao, 50km south of Ourense, near the River Laboreiro. It is another mountaintop megalithic necropolis of about 130 tombs, 30 in Spain and 100 in Portugal. (2500-1500 BC, A Bola, Pardavedra, Ourense, Galicia)

Photo 13. Petropot near the mountaintop signal tower shown in Photo 2 (Barbanza Peninsula, Galicia).

Photo 14. Petropots at entrance to Punta Falcoeiro, at the southernmost tip of Barbanza Peninsula. This "gateway" stone, today overlooking a fish processing plant, was part of a wall of huge boulders across the neck of the point. (2500-1500 BC, Galicia, NW Spain, Spring 2006).

Photo 15. A petropot above the western shore, overlooking fishing grounds, inside the site of Punta Falcoeiro, at the southern end of the Barbanza Peninsula (see dark symbol of Arqueoloxia -"castro/dolmen" on the enlarged lower portion of the map).

Photo 16. The site of the petropot of Photo.8, showing its location above the valley leading from the town on the coast, "Port of the Sun", to the necropolis on the mountaintop. (2500-1500 BC, Boiro, Barbanza Peninsula, Galicia).

Sailing Routes used in the Discovery of America found carved into Stonehenge

(Stonehenge, Salisbury Plain, Wiltshire, England, c.2000 BC)

J.S. Wakefield, jayswakefield@yahoo.com

Introduction

Figures 1 & 2 are reproduced from the Introduction chapter of our book, How the SunGod Reached America c.2500 BC, A Guide to Megalithic Sites. **Figure 1** shows 36 examples of the megalithic petroglyph called the "Buckler", reproduced from the important work of E. Shee Twohig, The Megalithic Art of Western Europe. Ms.Twohig is now a Senior Lecturer in Archaeology at University College, Cork, Ireland. **Figure 2** is an example of one of the 36 glyphs, this one of late date, with notes explaining the features of the figure. The detailed features of the coastlines are increasingly depicted in the petroglyphs,as you move from left to right, and down the page. All these "bucklers" are symbols of the North Atlantic Ocean, and they show a continued use and development of the symbol over several thousand years of sailing exploration.

The new petroglyph: Stonehenge

In May, 2008, we tried to take photos of the reported Stone 57 petroglyph at Stonehenge, but could not get entry to do so, even after paying admission fees. All visitors are monitored on a raised wooden walkway that circles the site at a considerable distance from the stones (approximately on the former site of the Ring). To enter the site center, one must complete an application form to join a special tour group, and you must indicate which future years you are available for, since they are so booked up. Even then, photos are not permitted in the tour group without an application process, permission depending upon your purpose, proposed use, fees, and so on. "Even if you get in one of the special groups, the group may not go to the stone you want to go to, so you might be out of luck." With a million dollars a year being generated here in admission fees, a dozen coach busses in the parking lot coming and going all day amid the cars, the crammed guestshop, the food, and the tape rentals, there is no interest in accommodating anything else.

Figure 3 shows two photos of Stone 57 of Stonehenge hanging on the wall in the Devises Museum, a half an hour to the south by car, from Avebury. This terrific little Bronze Age museum is the collection of an archaeologist who was the brother of Lawrence of Arabia. This "Sarcen Stone" or big-stone inner "horseshoe" phase of Stonehenge is called "Phase III", the last construction phase of Stonehenge. We have marked Stone 57 with a circle on the small copy of the official groundplan. Archaeologists, based on radiocarbon dating, agree that the construction date for this phase of the monument was 2000 BC. The petroglyph, though obviously weathered, can not be carbon-dated.

You can read in the Museum photos of **Figure 3** that the exhibit explanation in calls the petroglyph a "Breton Mother Goddess", a "Torso of a Cult Figure". Remarkably, the

Megalithic petroglyphs of the North Atlantic Ocean from various locations in Brittany (Ref.5). The top left one is very old (c.5000 BC), the bottom right one is more recent (c.2000 BC).

Fig.1 "Buckler" page reprinted from Introduction to <u>How the SunGod Reached America, c.2500 BC, A Guide to Megalithic Sites</u>, 1992

Museum compares the petroglyph not only with "buckler" petroglyphs in chambered tombs and on menhirs, but also with decorated Iberian Plaques, which we agree are similar in some ways! At the right, are two examples of these four inch long plaques, or pendants. Like the Stonehenge petroglyph, they are a box-like shape. The pendants have horizontal lines, and triangular or wave patterns. In another article, we have dated the Iberian Plaques to be "Ocean Pendants" to be about 2200 BC. All these box-shaped carvings portray the North Atlantic Ocean, which was being explored at the time.

In these photos, you cannot feel the depth of the carving with your fingers. Often, with careful use of white aquarium sand to fill depressions in a horizontal stone, you can find patterns not readily visible. What you "see" in a photograph like these depends on the side lighting and angle of the camera to the subject. Early take-offs from petroglyphs that were taken directly from the stone are important, and the careful work by Twohig is absolutely invaluable. Often we have seen that a petroglyph no longer shows the level of detail formerly recorded. While we were at the Tresse site in Brittany, several locals remarked that big haut-relief carvings there had been knocked off by vandalism since they had last been there, a couple of years before.

The drawing in **Figure 4** is reproduced from page 232 of Burl's book on Stonehenge. Since he reports this drawing to have come from "Castleden in 1993" (author of 1993 book "The Making of Stonehenge"), we think this drawing is probably a more accurate representation of the original carving than what we can see in the museum photographs. Back then, Castleden would probably have had full access to the site. Note on the drawing, the two lines below the box, that you cannot see in the photographs. It is clear they were not seen, or not considered part of the petroglyph. However, these lines make sense, when compared with other ocean petroglyphs, such as the maps on stones at Kercado, the Kermorvan petroglyph, or the unprovenanced painting now in Porto University, Portugal which also have these lines, as shown in the small copies of them on the right side. The Stonehenge "Box" is illustrating the North Atlantic Ocean above the 20°N line of latitude.

Greenland is well illustrated at the top of the Stonehenge Petroglyph as a large semicircle, so this is a relatively late petroglyph. The most interesting features of this petroglyph are the two curved lines west of Greenland. These show the sailing routes across the Labrador Sea to Baffin Island, and their turn to the south. The upper route is at 67°N, the route given by the SunGod (reciprocal of the 23° Tropic of Cancer –as far north as the SunGod travels). The lower route is the shortcut at 65°N, shown on many other megalithic petroglyphs. For a lengthy explanation of these routes, see our recent publication "Crossing the Labrador Sea, The Stone Rows of Lagatjar, Brittany, c.1600 BC", published in Ancient American, Vol.12, No.76, 12/2007.

Another new petroglyph: Menhir of Kermaillard
Figures 5 and 6 show another North Atlantic "buckler" box. This petroglyph was unknown until recently, because it was carved on the underside of the Menhir de Kermaillard. The petroglyph was found after heavy equipment was used to lift and straighten up the menhir, causing a stir in the local news. It is located near the end of the

Cult Figure Carvings

On STONE 57, R.S. Newall identified a SUB–RECTANGULAR CARVING. The symbol is comparable to carvings on STANDING STONES and in CHAMBERED TOMBS in Brittany.

A waisted shape, 41cm in length carved on STONE 29 may represent a stylised human TORSO, comparable to decorated IBERIAN PLAQUES.

Breton "Mother Goddess" Symbols

The shallow angular figure carved on Stone 57, one of the upright sirens of the trilithons forming the "horseshoe" at STONEHENGE has been equated with a symbol found frequently among carvings upon megalithic tombs in Brittany. The carving may be a very stylised representation of a goddess. There is, however, no clear evidence to suggest if she was a fertility or a funerary deity or if she had perhaps another function.

The "Mother Goddess" symbol on Stone 57 at Stonehenge

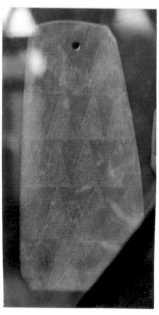

Fig.3 "Cult Figure Carvings" about two feet square, on Stone 57, Devises Museum, Devises, England. At right side, Ocean Pendants from Iberia that are each about 4 inches long, of thin slate. Note the horizontal latitude lines in these Pendants.

peninsula on the south side of the Gulf of Morbihan, west of the town of Sarzeau. Unlike the other "bucklers", this one has a boat attached, illustrating that this is a sailing route on a map. The boat points to the route of the Northern Crossing, which ran from the Orkneys, to the Faroes, to Iceland, to Greenland, to Baffin Island, and down the Labrador Coast to Belle Isle. In the second photo, on the left side of the box, is a short line indicating the crossing to Baffin Island. This petroglyph is clearly showing that boats were using the Northern Crossing, and reaching lands in the west. The menhir is not dated, but this Kermaillard Petroglyph, also showing the detail of a crossing to Baffin Island, probably dates near the same time as the Stonehenge petroglyph.

Conclusion

The bottom line here is that Stonehenge Phase III, has carved in it a petroglyph of the northern sailing routes used in the discovery of America. We did not know of this petroglyph when we wrote our book, published in 2002. The petroglyph also shows the shortcut route at 65°N subsequently discovered and used during the construction of these large stones of Stonehenge, at 2000 BC, 500 years after the discovery. The new petroglyph on the Menhir of Kermaillard tells a similar story, with a boat.

References

1. Burl, A., Stonehenge, A New History of the World's Greatest Stone Circle, Constable, London, 2006. ISBN -13- 978-1-84119-964-1
2. De Jonge, R.M., and Wakefield, J.S., "Crossing the Labrador Sea, The Rows of Lagatjar, Brittany, c.1600 BC", Ancient American, Vol.12, No.76, pgs.32-37, 12/2007
3. De Jonge, R.M., and Wakefield, J.S., How the SunGod Reached America c.2500 BC, A Guide to Megalithic Sites, MCS, 2002 (ISBN 0-917054-19-9)
4. Devises Museum, Devises, England, photos by authors, May 2008.
5. Twohig, E. Shee, The Megalithic Art of Western Europe, Clarendon Press, Oxford, 1981
6. De Jonge, R.M., and Wakefield, J.S., "Ocean Pendants, Portugal, Spain, Ireland, and America, c.2200 BC", to be published.
7. Ocean Pendant, Photo taken by authors, May, 2007. It is in the corner of an unopened case in the upstairs Archaeological Museum of Guimaraes, Portugal.

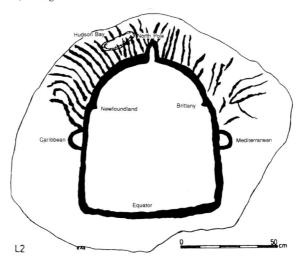

Megalithic inscription on one of the upright stones (L2) of the passage grave of Isle Longue, Locmariaquer, Brittany (Ref.1, after the discovery of America, c.2200 BC).

Fig.2 Reprinted from How the SunGod Reached America, C.2500 BC, a Guide to Megalithic Sites

STONEHENGE

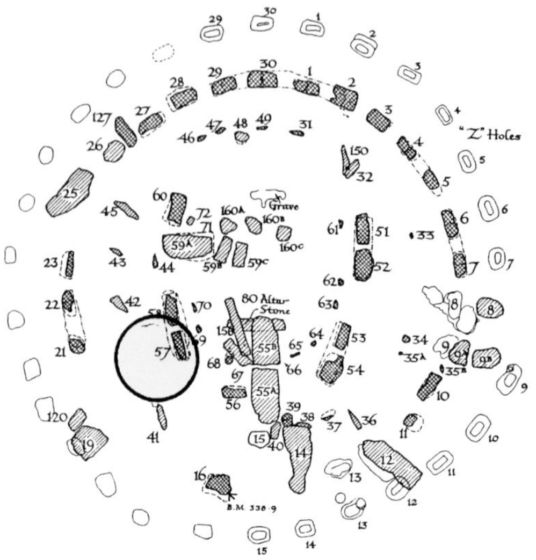

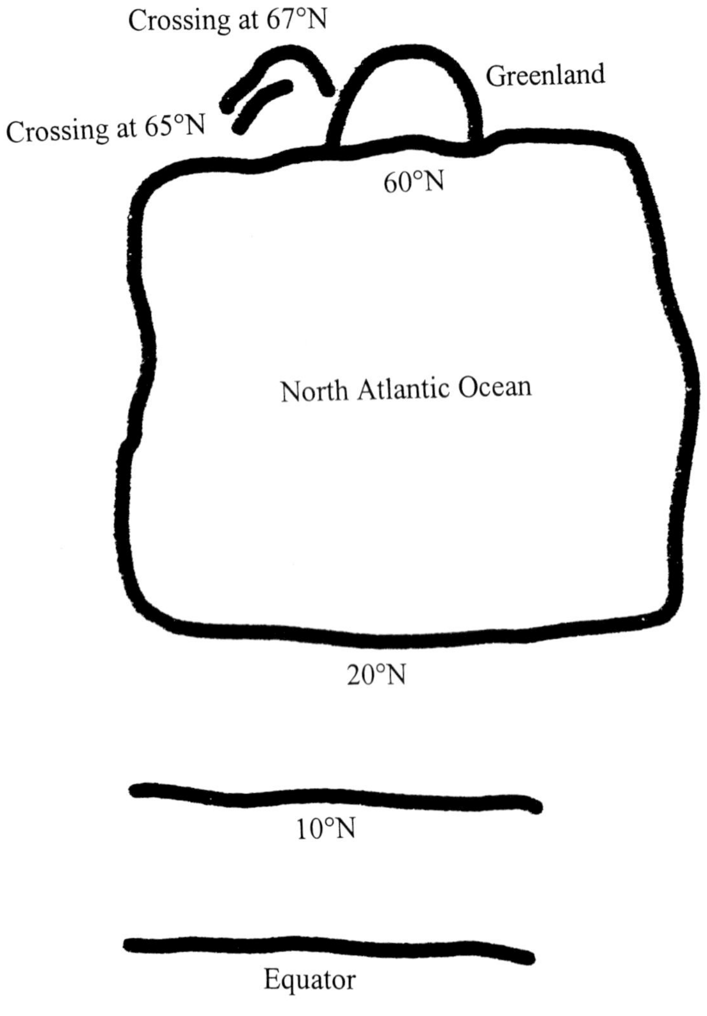

Crossing at 67°N

Crossing at 65°N

Greenland

60°N

North Atlantic Ocean

20°N

10°N

Equator

Fig.4 A petroglyph of the North Atlantic Ocean, stone 57, Stonehenge. "Drawing from Castleden, 1993", reprinted from Burl, with our labels of explanation. At the right, the location of Stone 57, and below, small images of other petroglyphs with latitude lines at the bottom of each of them. (Burl, Stonehenge)

Fig.5 "Buckler" petroglyph of the North Atlantic Ocean, with a boat connected to the Northern Crossing. Above, small photo of the menhir and a map of its location. (Photo taken by authors, Menhir de Kermaillard, Arzon, Brittany, May, 2005)

Fig.6 Left corner detail of petroglyph, showing the Northern Crossing detail of the crossing to Baffin Island. (Photo taken by authors, Menhir de Kermaillard, Arzon, Brittany, May, 2005)

The Rows of Kermario
The Royal Crossing of the Ocean
(The Rows of Kermario,Carnac, Brittany, c.2000 BC)

R.M. de Jonge, drsrmdejonge@hotmail.com
J.S. Wakefield, jayswakefield@yahoo.com
www.howthesungod.com

Introduction

This is the middle set of Alignment Rows at Carnac, on the coast of Brittany, France. Carnac, in the area of the Gulf of Morbihan, is considered the center of the Megalithic Culture, which stretched along the coast and along coastal rivers, from the Orkney Islands north of Scotland, to Lixus, on the coast of Africa. These rows are a major world tourist site, and among the world's largest megalithic ruins. To date, there are no scientific explanations of the purpose or meaning of these monuments in the scientific or lay literature.

The first report of scientific study, is reported to be the early work of Dryden and Lukis, done in 1864-1872. The Bodleian Library at Oxford University claims not to have it. The next study was the work done by James Miln in 1881, a book we obtained on microfilm from the Bodleian. We have preferred to use the careful survey of Alexander Thom, done 1970-1974, and have used his figures 1-4 unaltered. However, while the angles mentioned on the figures are excellent, we found the north-south arrows on his figures 1&2 to be slightly off (approx 1°), so there was a slight error in the drafting of his first two figures. We did not use some of the labels in his figures, such as the Sections 1-7, but we think it better to reproduce them without removing these.

Description

The monument of Kermario is located in the town of Carnac, Morbihan, at the SW coast of the peninsula of Britanny. It has a length of more than one kilometer, and an average width of c.90 meters. It contains 7 parallel rows, and at the south side some extra rows, with all together 1181 menhirs. There is a bend in the rows, in about the center of the monument. The height of the menhirs slowly increases from about 0.5 meter in the east, to more than 3 meters in the west. Especially in the most western 100 meters the sizes of the menhirs are quite big. The eastern rows have a total of 409 menhirs, and the western rows have 772 menhirs. About halfway in the eastern rows there is short break of 37 meters, the Ravin de Keroquet, without a single menhir. East of the break are only 152 stones, but west of it are 1029 menhirs.

The monument begins in the extreme east with big menhir E, shown in the first figure, now out behind some buildings. The stones of the first eastern group (East-1, **Figs.1,2**) do not start until 134 meters further west. In this group, 152 menhirs are laid out in 14 almost parallel rows, over a distance of 288 meters. The width of the rows of East-1 is 61 meters. The average distance between the rows is just a bit less than 5 meters.

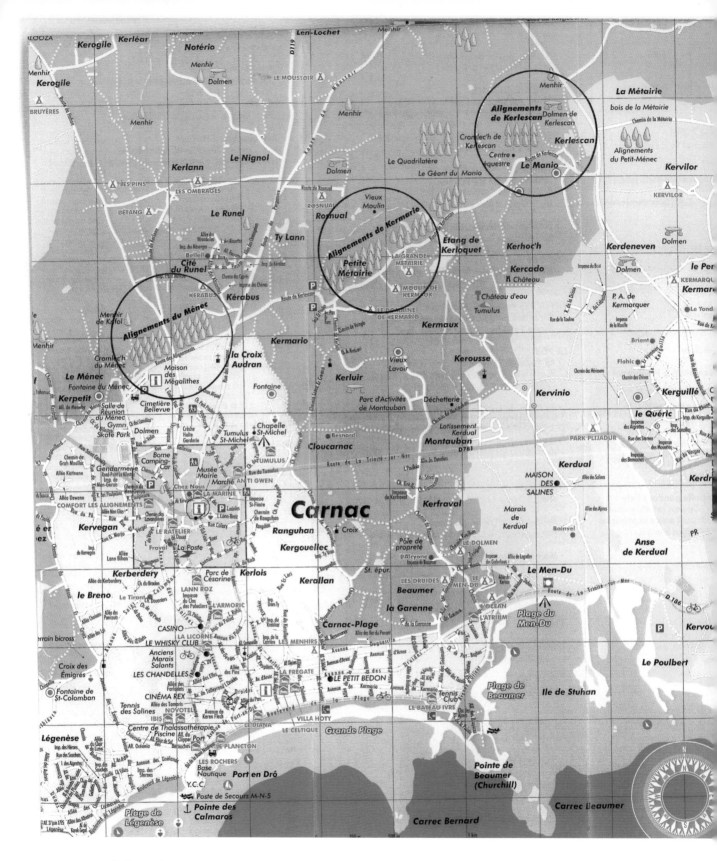

Map 1 The 3 sets of Alignment Rows in Carnac, France (from Carnac tourist brochure)

After this group is the Ravin de Keroquet, a shallow valley of 37 meters without menhirs, currently flooded in the center with a pond. Behind it is the second eastern group (East-2), having a length of 153 meters (measured along the center row), a width of 78 meters, and a total of 199 menhirs. Here 7 parallel rows start, which all run to the west end of the monument. The eastern part discussed so far has a total length of 612 meters, or 478 meters when the eastern menhir E is neglected, and possesses a total of 151+199= 350 menhirs. The original presence of 8 menhirs not accounted for is suspected, so the total amount is 350(+8).

The 7 main rows bend to the right in an area which is called Central-1 (**Figs.1,3**). The width of the rows here is 42.meters. The equal distances between the alignments is increased to about 7 meters. A separate row below the others is included in Central-1 (Table 2). So, the group has 58 menhirs, while the total width reaches 57 meters.

The 7 alignments again bend to the right in an area known as Central-2. The width of the rows is 50meters, with the distance between the rows increasesed to about 8 meters. Central-2 with 77(+4) menhirs, has a width of 91 meters. The total Central group of Kermario has 58+77 = 135 menhirs, and has a length of 177 meters.

Next, the 7 rows bend to the left in an area which is called West-1 (**Figs.1,4**). The width of these rows is 60 meters, and distance between the rows is about 10 meters. Below the 7 alignments are 2 (to 3) new rows. West-1, with 286 menhirs in total, has a length of 204 meters and a width of 98 meters.

So far, the 7 main alignments in all sections were straight lines. However, in the last area, West-2, these rows curve gradually to the right. The width of these rows, and their mutual distances, remain the same. Below the 7 rows are now 3 more or less new rows. West-2, with 409 menhirs in total, has a length of 280 metres and a width of 99 meters. The West part just discussed has a total length of 204+280= 484 meters, and possesses 286+409= 695 menhirs.

When the monument is divided into an eastern and a western part, with the slanted line in the Central section, the whole monument has a length of 666+607= 1273 meters, having 409+772= 1181 menhirs. If the eastern menhir E is not included, the rows have a length of 532+607= 1139 meters. After the Ravin de Keroquet, the rows have a length of 207+607= 814 meters, having 257+772= 1029 menhirs in total. In the course of time, many of the stones of Kermario have fallen over. The re-erected menhirs are indicated with a bit of red plaster at their base.

Meaning

The megalithic monument of Kermario is located at the west coast of Western Europe, at a distance of 2 km from the Ocean. The width of the rows of menhirs increases from 70 meters in the NE, to 100 meters in the SW. The average height of the menhirs increases in the same direction from 0.5 meter until more than 3 meters. In the last 100 meters, near the SW end of the monument, really gigantic menhirs are placed,

Photo 2 Aerial photo of the western Rows of Kermario (www.megalithic.co.uk)

emphasizing again the south-western direction. Kermario is just an enormous arrow pointing to the southwest, toward the Ocean.

The 7 alignments of the Central-2 part of Kermario all point 28°WSW, toward Santa Maria, the eastern island of the East Azores. When looking at a globe, this symbolism is apparent: Menhir E symbolises Lanzarote, the eastern Canary island, the East-1 group represents the Islands of Madeira, the East-2 group is the East Azores, the Central group is the Central Azores, and the West groups are the important West Azores. But even more becomes visible. The long monument of Kermario also represents the sailing route from Lanzarote, via Madeira and the Azores, to Cape Race, Newfoundland! The height profile of the rows confirms this image. From the East-1 group the rows run downward to the flooded valley. Then the rows raise to the Central part, after which a wide valley appears. At the West-2 group the alignments raise again, after which huge menhirs finish the rows of Kermario.

Lanzarote and Madeira

 The 7 rows of the Central-2 part (**Fig.3**) all point 28°WSW, also corresponding to the 7 Canary islands, at 28°N. Below this section an extra row starts, pointing 29°WSW, twice corresponding to Lanzarote (menhir E), the eastern Canary island, at 28°+1= 29°N. The important NE alignment through menhir E also represents Lanzarote, the NE Canary island. In part East-1 7 rows of menhirs point 33°WSW (Figs.1,2), corresponding to the complementary sailing direction from Lanzarote to Madeira, 90°-33= 57°NW. The group has 4 important rows of more than twenty menhirs, encoding the sailing distance of 4dl= 4°=240NM.

7 Rows point 33°WSW (**Figs.1,2**), also corresponding to Madeira (menhir S), at 33°N. Menhir S has an height of c.3 meters, and its base bears several zig/zag-shaped petroglyphs, showing numbers of distance lines of a crossing of the Ocean. In total there are 14 rows, confirming the latitude, seen from of Kermario at 47°N, at 47°-14= 33°N. In East-2 the alignments I-VII point 35°WSW (**Fig.1**), corresponding to the initial sailing direction from Madeira to Santa Maria, East Azores, 35°NW. The 7 rows also determine the terminal sailing direction in the neighborhood of Santa Maria, 35°-7= 28°WSW. The 7 rows of Central-2 point 28°WSW, confirming this sailing direction. The difference between both directions is caused by the curvature of the surface of the Earth. In East-2 are 8 important rows with more than ten menhirs, encoding the sailing distance of 8dl= 8°= 480 NM. The lowest row X has 8 menhirs in the west, confirming this sailing distance. The East-1 group has 4 important rows of more than twenty menhirs, also corresponding to Santa Maria, 4° above Madeira, at 33°+4= 37°N. In the west of the whole eastern group are 7+3= 10 rows I-X (**Fig.1**), confirming the latitude seen from Kermario, at 47°-10= 37°N. Row IX points 38°WSW, corresponding to Sao Miguel and the Central Azores, at 38°N.

Cape Finisterre

However, menhirs E and S (both shown on eastside of **Fig.1**) also have other meanings. From Kermario (menhir E) we can also sail via Cape Finisterre (menhir S) to the Azores. The East-1 group (**Figs.1,2**) contains 4 important rows with more than twenty menhirs,

Photo 3   Dr. de Jonge in the Rows of Kermario, looking west toward the viewing tower. (Kermario, Carnac, Brittany, France, 2002).

Photo 4 The western end of the middle Kermario Rows, looking east, at midday in May. (Kermario, Carnac, Brittany, France, 2002)

also corresponding to Cape Finisterre (menhir S), as seen from Kermario, at 47°-4= 43°N. This is the NW cape of the Iberian Peninsula. Apart from rows I-X this group has 4 extra rows 1'-4', confirming the latitude. In the eastern groups row IV has by far the highest number of menhirs, confirming this again. The East-1 group possesses 14 rows in total, confirming the latitude as seen from Lanzarote, at 29°+14= 43°N.

On the average the 14 rows point 34°WSW, corresponding to the initial sailing direction from Cape Finisterre to Sao Miguel, the main island of the East Azores, 34°-14= 20°WSW. On the average the 8 rows of Central-2 point 28°WSW, confirming this sailing direction at 28°-8= 20°WSW. The 7 main rows of East-2 determine the sailing distance, 20-7= 13dl= 780 NM. Row IX does not have any menhirs in East-1. The 14-1= 13 remaining rows in this group confirm the sailing distance. The 7 rows of Central-2 point 28°WSW, all equal to the terminal sailing direction in the neighborhood of Sao Miguel. Row IX points 38°WSW, corresponding to the latitude of Sao Miguel, at 38°N. So, the East-1 group does not only represent the Islands of Madeira, but also Cape Finisterre.

Egypt and the Azores
The 7 rows of Central-1 (**Fig.3**) all point 31°WSW, corresponding to the Nile Delta, at 31°N. This is the center of the Northern Egyptian Empire. The row below has 31 menhirs confirming the latitude. The 7+1= 8 rows encode the holy Tropic of Cancer, and the center of the Southern Egyptian Empire, at 31°-8= 23°N. This latitude is also the center of the Sunreligion in Egypt, and the latitude where the Tropic of Cancer leaves the continent of Africa. Originally, this was the departure place, where people tried to cross the Ocean, in honor of the SunGod.

The 7 main rows now symbolize the 2+5= 7 islands of the East and Central Azores. These 7 rows all make an angle of 31°, and the row below it has 31 menhirs, both corresponding to the Central Azores, at 31°+7= 38°N. The 7 rows also symbolize the 5+2= 7 islands of the Central and West Azores. At the bottom of Central-2 is an extra row of 31 menhirs, at the west side pointing 32°WSW. So, the 7 to 8 rows of the group correspond twice to Flores, the main island of the West Azores, at 32+7= 31+8= 39°N. The 8 rows confirm Flores from Kermario (47°N), at 47°-8= 39°N.

Cape Race, Newfoundland
The 7 main rows of the West-1 group (**Fig.1**) all point 33°WSW, corresponding to the other island of the West Azores, Corvo, 7° above Madeira (33°N), at 33°+7= 40°N. The 7 rows confirm Corvo from Kermario, at 47-7= 40°N. The 7 rows all make an angle of 33°, corresponding to the initial sailing direction from Corvo to Cape Race, Newfoundland, 33°WNW. The west part of Kermario consists of 7 straight and 7 curved rows (**Fig.4**). These 7+7= 14 rows correspond to the terminal sailing direction in the neighborhood of Cape Race, 33-14= 19°WNW, and with the sailing distance, 19dl= 19°= 19 Egyptian moira= 1140 NM. The West-1 group possesses a total of 7+2= 9 rows, and the West-2 group has a total of 7+3= 10 rows, together 9+10= 19 rows, confirming this. The curved alignments of West-2 clearly show, the sailing direction has to be adjusted during the crossing continiously. The difference between initial and terminal sailing direction is due to the curvature of the surface of the Earth. The 7 rows of the last group correspond to

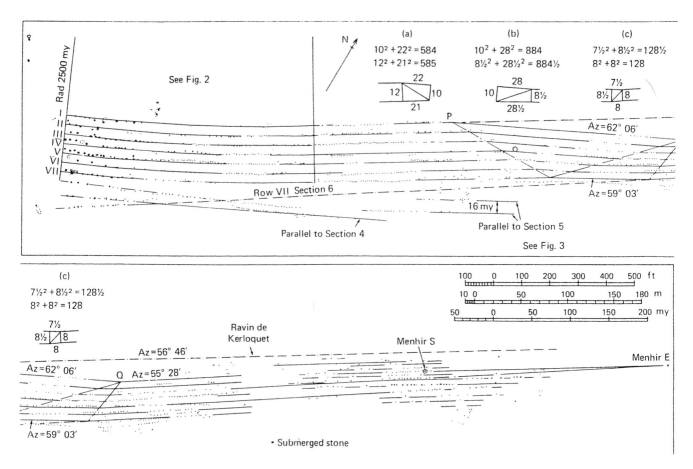

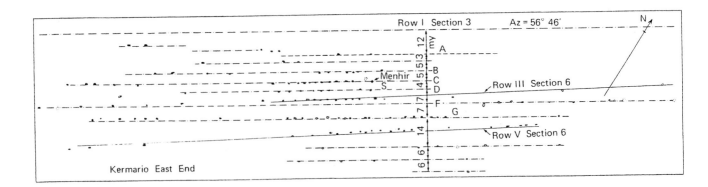

Fig.1 Groundplan of the menhir rows of Kermario (from Thom). Below the East side, and above the West side of the monument. The long rows(1.3 km) represent the sailing route across the Ocean, from the eastern Canary island of Lanzarote (E), via Madeira (S), and the Azores (the bend), to Cape Race, Newfoundland. (Kermario, Carnac, Brittany, c.2000 BC)

Fig.2 Groundplan of the menhir rows of the East-1 group (from Thom; note this is his Figure 4). The group contains 4 important rows of more than twenty menhirs, corresponding to Cape Finisterre (menhir S), seen from Kermario (E), at 47°-4= 43°N. The 14 rows of the group encode the eastern Canary island of Lanzarote (also E), seen from Cape Finisterre, at 43-14= 29°N. Seven rows of menhirs point 33°WSW, corresponding to Madeira (also S), at 33°N. (Kermario, Carnac, Brittany, c.2000 BC)

CapeRace, Newfoundland, 7° above Corvo, at 40°+7= 47°N. The latitude of the monument of Kermario, at 47°N, confirms this. The 7 alignments with the high menhirs at the west end show this is the important subject of the alignments.

Bermuda and Cape Hatteras

Below the start of the West-1 group (**Fig.1**) are 2 rows of menhirs parallel to the 7 alignments of Central-1. The 7+2= 9 rows correspond to the 9 islands of the Azores. The rows point 31°WSW again, corresponding to the Nile Delta, the Northern Egyptian Empire, at 31°N. Below the center of West-1 is only 1 row. The 7+1= 8 rows now correspond to the holy Tropic of Cancer, and the Southern Egyptian Empire, at 31°-8= 23°N.

These 7+2= 9 rows also correspond to the Central Azores, seen from Lanzarote at 29°+9= 38°N, and seen from Kermario at 47°-9= 38°N. So there is another, southern route of importance in the Central Azores. The 2 lowest rows show the Central Azores, 2° below Corvo, at 40°-2= 38°N. The center of section West-1has 7+1= 8 rows, corresponding to Flores, the main island of the West Azores, seen from the Nile Delta at 31°+8= 39°N, and seen from Kermario at 47°-8= 39°N. The lowest row X confirms Flores, 1° below Corvo, at 40°-1= 39°N.

The 7 main alignments of West-1 correspond with the initial sailing direction, 7°WSW, from Flores to Bermuda, at 39°-7= 32°N. Row IX runs parallel to the 7 rows of Central-2. They point 28°WSW, encoding the long sailing distance involved, of 28dl= 28°= 1680 NM. The last part of row VIII points 25°WSW, equal to the terminal sailing direction in the neighborhood of Bermuda. Bermuda is shown 7+1 = 8° below Corvo, at 40°-8= 32°N.

Down in West-2 row VIII makes an angle of 25°, also corresponding to the initial sailing direction from Bermuda to southern Cape Hatteras, 25°WNW. The ends of the 7 alignments above it also make an angle of 25°, confirming this. These 7+1= 8 rows, encode the sailing distance of 8dl= 8°= 480 NM. The 7 main rows also provide the terminal sailing direction in the neighborhood of southern Cape Hatteras, 25°-7= 18°WNW. Row X is part of the remote row VII of East-2 (**Fig.1**). This row points 35°NW, corresponding to southern Cape Hatteras, at 35°N. The angle of 35° also encodes the direct sailing distance from southern Cape Hatteras to the West Azores, 35dl= 35°= 2100 NM. Row IX above it points 28°WSW. Together with the 7 main alignments it forms 28°+7= 35 units, confirming southern Cape Hatteras and the direct sailing distance to the Azores, 35°N, and 35dl.

Discussion

In the Bronze Age, the sailing routes via Bermuda and from Cape Race, Newfoundland, were only used with the wind and the current to return to the Old World. Yet on purpose, the colossal monument of Kermario indicates these routes the other way around! Kermario is a huge representation of the "Royal Crossing to the Realm of the Dead", against the wind and the current. "Kermario" literally means "Place of the Dead". The end of Kermario contains huge menhirs. This is because people believed that if the King were not able to reach the other side, the people of Brittany would be lost. However, they

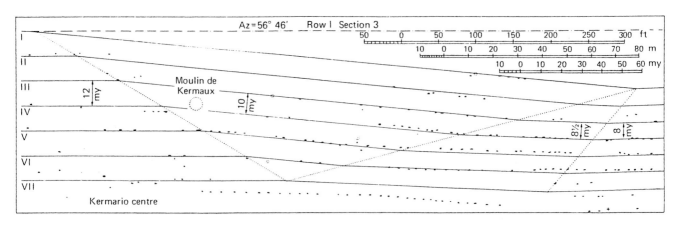

Fig.3 Groundplan of the menhir rows of the Central groups (from Thom). The 7 rows of Central 1 all point 31°WSW, corresponding to the Nile Delta, the Northern Egyptian Empire, at 31°N. The 7 rows of Central-2 all point 28°WSW, corresponding to the 7 Canary islands, at 28°N, and directly pointing from Kermario to Santa Maria, the eastern island of the East Azores. (Kermario, Carnac, Brittany, c.2000 BC)

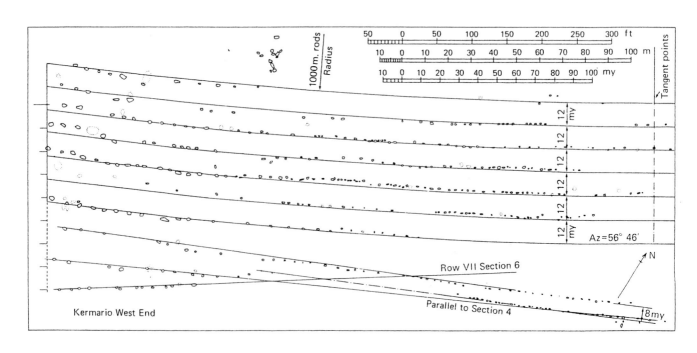

Fig.4 Groundplan of the alignments of the West groups (from Thom). The 7 main rows of West-1 all point 33°WSW, corresponding to the island of Corvo of theWest Azores, 7° above Madeira, at 33°+7= 40°N, and corresponding to the initial sailing direction from Corvo to Cape Race, Newfoundland, 33°WNW, at the latitude of Kermario, at 47°N. (Kermario, Carnac, Brittany, c.2000 BC)

saw that that nobody could accomplish this tough crossing, except the King, when he traveled to the Realm of the Dead (Central America, the Land of Punt, the Underworld). It is recorded in hieroglyphics in an Egyptian temple, that the Sun-God Ra has said: "The Realm of the Dead is in the west, at the other side of the waters, in the land where the Sun sets."

Dating

When comparing Kermario with nearby Le Menec, it turns out that in Kermario the cromlechs (stone circles) at both ends are lacking, and that south of the alignments they made use of extra rows at different angles. In its design and in its interpretation Kermario is more primitive and less subtle than Le Menec. We think the reports by Burl and 3rd Stone Magazine, of a missing "colossal horseshoe" where the car park is located at the west end, based upon the Miln work is in error. The Miln book says "the primitive constructions near the head of the alignments of Kermario gave us the impression of having been made in haste and in the rudest manner (pg 83)…consisting of two or three layers of undressed stones, rudely built, without mortar… considered as Celtic". Miln says (pg 93) that "in the head of the alignments of Menec and Kerlescant the large menhirs form a cromlech..." We find in the Miln work, no mention of or evidence for a Kermario cromlech.

We conclude that the more complicated rows of Menec and Kerlescan were constructed with Kermario as a model. We give them both dates of c.1900 BC. Kermario is older than these, and surely the monument was built after the discovery of America via the Atlantic, c.2500 BC. So probably, Kermario is contemporary with Stonehenge III in South England, and so dates from c.2000 BC.

References

1. De Jonge, R.M., and IJzereef, G.F., De Stenen Spreken, Kosmos Z&K, Utrecht/Antwerpen, 1996 (ISBN 90-215-2846-0) (Dutch)
2. De Jonge, R.M., and Wakefield, J.S., How the SunGod Reached America c.2500 BC, A Guide to Megalithic Sites, 2002 (ISBN 0-917054-19-9). also on CD
3. Website: www.howthesungod.com, De Jonge, R.M., and Wakefield, J.S.
4. De Jonge, R.M., and Wakefield, J.S., "The Discovery of the Atlantic Islands", Migration & Diffusion, Vol.3, No.11, pgs.69-109 (2002)
5. De Jonge, R.M., and Wakefield, J.S., "The Passage Grave of Karleby, Encoding the Islands Discovered in the Ocean, c. 2950 BC", Migration & Diffusion, Vol.5, No.18, pgs.64-74 (2004)
6. De Jonge, R.M., and Wakefield, J.S., "A Nautical Center for Crossing the Ocean, America's Stonehenge, New Hampshire, c.2200 BC", Migration & Diffusion, Vol.4, No.15, pgs.60-100 (2002)
7. De Jonge, R.M., and Wakefield, J.S., "Germany's Bronze Age Disc Reveals Transatlantic Seafaring, c.1600 BC", Ancient American, Vol.9, No.55, pgs.18-20 (2004)
8. De Jonge, R.M., and Wakefield, J.S., "The Three Rivers Petroglyph, A Guide-post for River Travel in America", Migration & Diffusion, Vol.3, No.12, pgs.74-100 (2002)
9. De Jonge, R.M., and Wakefield, J.S., "Ales Stenar, Sweden's Bronze Age 'Sunship' to the Americas, c.500 BC", Ancient American, Vol.9, No.56, pgs.16-21 (2004)
10. De Jonge, R.M., "Great Circle Mound: An Indiana Temple to the Egyptian SunGod?", Ancient American, Issue 60, Vol.9, pgs.31-32, 2004.
11. De Jonge, R.M., and Wakefield, J.S., "The Disc of Nebra, Important Sailing Routes of the Bronze Age Displayed in a Religious Context", Migration and Diffusion, Vol.5, No.17, pgs. 32-39, 2004
12. De Jonge, R.M., and Wakefield, J.S., "The Monument of Ales Stenar, A Sunship to the Realm of the Dead", Migration and Diffusion, Vol.5, No. 19, pgs. 94-106, 2004
13. De Jonge, R.M., and Wakefield, J.S., "The Rings of Stenness, Brodgar, and Bookan, Celebrating the Discovery of South Greenland", Migration and Diffusion, Vol 6, No.24, 2005

14. De Jonge, R.M., and Wakefield, J.S., "The Paintings of Porcellano Cave, The Discovery of Guadelupe, c.3000 BC", Migration and Diffusion, Vol. 6, No. 22, 2005

15. De Jonge, R.M., and Wakefield, J.S., "Mexican Cave Artists, 3000 BC", Ancient American, Vol. 10, No. 62, 2005

16. De Jonge, R.M., and Wakefield, J.S., "Greenland: Bridge between the Old and New Worlds", Ancient American, Vol. 11, No. 67, 2006

17. De Jonge, R.M., and Wakefield, J.S., "The Passage Grave of Karlesby: Encoding the Islands Discovered in the Ocean c.2950 BC", submitted to Ancient American, and accepted for publication

18. De Jonge, R.M., and Wakefield, J.S., "The Discovery of the Islands in the Atlantic, Stone C-8, Cairn T, Loughcrew, Ireland, c.3200 BC", submitted to Ancient American, Vol.13, No.81, January 2009

19. De Jonge, R.M., and Wakefield, J.S., "The Stone Rows of Tormsdale: A Voyage to Central America, The Realm of the Dead; Caithness, NE Scotland, c.1600 BC, Ancient American, Vol.11, Number 70, pgs 28-34, 10/2006

20. De Jonge, R.M., and Wakfield, J.S., "A Return Route across the Ocean, encoded in the Tormsdale Rows; Caithness, NE Scotland, c.1600 BC", Ancient American, Vol.12, Number 74, pgs.8-12, 8/2007

21. De Jonge, R.M., and Wakefield, J.S., "The Megalithic Megalithic Monument of Lagatjar, The Crossing of the Labrador Sea", Camaret-sur-Mer, Crozon Peninsula, Finistere, Brittany c.1600 BC", Ancient American, Vol.12, No.76, pgs 32-37, 12/2007

22. Thom, A., and Thom, A.S., "The Kermario Alignments", J. of the History of Astronomy (1974), pgs 30-47 (in Bodleian's Radcliffe Science Library, Oxford University, under HISTPER 29,1974; it is listed in their Sackler Library, but missing)

23. Thom, A., "Megalithic Geometry in Standing Stones", New Scientist, Mar. 12, 1964.

24. Batt, M., and others, Au Pays des Megalithes, Carnac-Loc-mariaquer, Jos, 1991 (French)

25. Briard, J., The Megaliths of Brittany, Gisserot, 1991

26. Giot, P.R., Prehistory in Brittany, Ed JOS (ISBN 2-85543--123-9)

27. Bailloud, G., et.al., Carnac, Les Premieres Architectures de Pierre, CNRS Edition, 1995 (ISBN 2-85822-139-1) French)

28. Giot, P.R., La Bretagne. des Megalithes, Ed. Ouest France, 1995 (ISBN 2-7373-1388-0) (French)

29. Balfour, M., Megalithic Mysteries, Dragon's World (1992) (ISBN 1-85028-163-7)

30. Burl, A., From Carnac to Callanish, The Prehistoric Stone Rows and Avenues of Britain, Ireland and Brittany, Yale University Press, 1993 (ISBN 0-300-05575-7)

31. Fell, B., America BC, Pocket Books, Simon & Schuster, 1994

32. Bailey, J., Sailing to Paradise, Simon & Schuster, 1994

33. Thompson, G., American Discovery, Misty Isles Press, Seattle, 1994

34. Jairazbhoy, R.A., Ancient Egyptians and Chinese in America, Rowman & Littlefield, Totowa, N.J., 1974 (ISBN 0-87471--571-1)

35. Miln, James, Excavations at Carnac, a Record of Archaeological Researches in the Alignments of Kermario, David Douglas, Edinburgh, 1881. Obtained on microfilm, from the Photographic Studio of the Bodleian Library, Oxford, OX1, 3BG

The Rows of Kerlescan

The Royal Crossing of the Ocean
(The Rows of Kerlescan, Carnac, Brittany, c.1900 BC)

R.M. de Jonge, drsrmdejonge@hotmail.com
J.S. Wakefield, jayswakefield@yahoo.com
website: www.howthesungod.com

Introduction

The 13 rows of the menhirs of Kerlescan are on the northeast edge of the town of Carnac in Brittany. The Kerlescan rows are east of the larger, but disturbed, but similar alignment of Kermario. The Menec rows are west of Kermario. The three stone row sets at Carnac are the largest megalithic monuments in the world, constructed of approximately 3,000 large stones. To date, there have no reasonable explanations of these sites. They have not even been studied much, despite being major French tourist sites since the 19th century. The sites are on a large hilltop just north of the Gulf of Morbihan, in an area with the largest number of megalithic monuments in the world, probably the center and homeland of the megalithic culture. The highly decorated Tumulus of Gavrinis, located on a nearby island in the Gulf of Morbihan has been shown in our previous work (How the SunGod Reached America, 2002) to clearly commemorate the discovery of the Azores Islands in c.3600 BC. During the time of the megalithic culture, people were curious about what was on the other side of the Earth, at the other side of the big Ocean. It took them 5,000 years to discover and understand the tradewind patterns of the Oceans. In this article, we will show that the Rows of Kerlescan encode sailing directions to the Azores Islands, and the latitudes and sailing directions for the Royal Crossing of the Atlantic.

Site Description

Kerlescan consists of 352 standing stones (in French: "menhirs"), standing in13 rows, and a U-shaped stone "circle" in the west with 46 menhirs (see **Photos**, and **Fig.l**). In **Figure 2**, built upon the work of previous investigators, lines have been added by others and the authors. Most of the menhirs have a diameter of about a meter, and a height of about two meters. The stones are smaller in the eastern section, larger in the west.

A description of this site in the literature written by Aubrey Burl (From Carnac to Callanish, 1993) notes that "…the ranks of stones to the east, optimistically considered a 'fan', are megalithic chaos. Rows swerve, intersect and collide in 'alignments' lacking both symmetry and focus…. Wrecked or unwrecked, what all these rows of Carnac have in common is their association with a (ring)… It is the (ring) that stands at the top of a slope, with rows leading uphill to it, increasing in height as they near the ring, in the same manner as avenues in England. From this, it is likely that the (ring) was the focus."

As we shall show, Burl is correct that the "ring", which actually is a "U" shape, is a very important focus of the monument. While the rows appear chaotic, that is only because the monument is complicated. Actually, this is a straightforward monument, because its numeric encodings are stored in single digits, a stone for each digit. The rows are huge

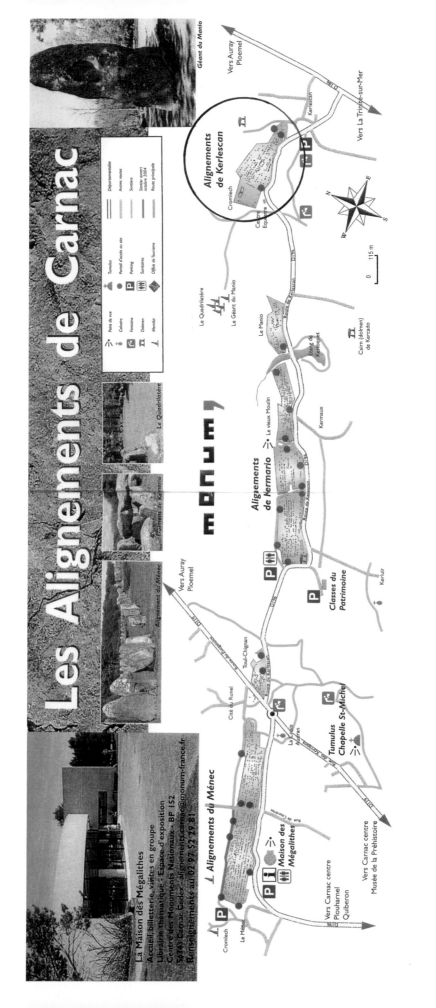

Map 1 The Rows of Carnac, from a tourist brochure.

mneumonic devices, used before the invention of writing, to commemorate and record their explorations and discoveries. It was laborious to set up this many stones, but it was carefully designed by the human mind.

The rows of Kerlescan have a length of 450 meters, and a width of about 150 meters. The menhirs in the rows are arranged in 13 straight lines, which, when extended, run to the east to point 0 (**Fig.6**), where houses are now located, as can be seen in the photos. You will see that some of these rows have bent sections, which we will discuss below. The menhirs of all rows can be placed within the geometrical figure of two back-to-back triangles as shown in **Fig. 2**. At the western end of the rows, a perpendicular laine can be run to the axis (dashed line) of the monument at point C. Similarly, below the axis, a perpendicular line from row XIII at D also runs (via the last menhir of Row XI) to point C. Almost all the menhirs are now situated within the big figure OACD, which can be seen as a big arrow, pointing to the U-shaped stone "circle" in the west. The east side of the U-shape is a vertical row of menhirs at right angles to the axis, while the south and west sides are curved (the rows are enlarged and numbered in Figure 6, and the U-shape is enlarged and numbered in **Fig.7**).

Sun religion features encoded

Aubrey Burl (Ref.8) says that "Kerlescan" means "place of burning". He reports that "as late as the 19th century, a midsummer bonfire was lit on the nearby gigantic Tumulus of Mont St. Michel, and that its Breton name was "tan heol", "the fire of the sun". This was probably a Celtic holdover from the megalithic sunreligion in the deep past. Reinoud thinks "ker" means "place", while "scan" means to recite, or to disclaim. This would mean that this monument is intended to teach, record, or memorialize, which we think is correct.

The angle AOD of the outer menhir rows on the east side of the figure, is 23° (**Fig. 2**). This corresponds with the latitude of the Tropic of Cancer, at 23°N. The number of menhirs on the two rows that are the legs of this triangle (the 8 menhirs of row 1 plus the 15 menhirs of row XIII, **Fig.2**) total 23, confirming this latitude. This repeatedly confirms the use of the 360° circle system, as well as the repeated importance of 23°, encoded in all the large megalithic sites we have studied.

On midsummer day, the sun is at right angles above the Tropic of Cancer at 23°N. This is as far north as the sun goes. At this point, the slow northern movement of the sun stops, and slowly turns into a southern movement. For this reason 23°N is a holy latitude of the Sun Religion. The prominence of the 23° angle in this monument shows that this is a monument of the Sun religion. According to the Kingship Theory of the Sun religion, the King (or pharoah) is the living representative of the god on earth, in Egypt, called the "Living Horus". It is recorded in Egyptian heiroglyphs that the SunGod Ra has said: "The New King will come from the Realm of the Dead in the west, at the other side of the waters, in the land where the Sun sets." We will explain how this tenet of the Sun Religion is important in the design of this monument of Kerlescan.

Fig.1 Groundplan of the monument of Kerlescan (Carnac, Brittany, France, c.1900 BC, Ref.30)

The big arrow: sailing to the West Azores

Kerlescan is located on the coast of Brittany at 47°N (**Fig. 8**). The headaxis along the line OC is the East-West axis of the monument. One might vizualize this monument OACD as an arrow, pointing along the 47° latitude line to the west to Cape Race, Newfoundland, the easternmost point of North America, also at 47°N (**Fig. 8**). Because of the opposing winds and current of the Gulfstream, no one could sail this route directly to Newfoundland. They had been able, however, to reach the Azores (**Fig.3**), as commemorated in the nearby monument of Gavrinis c.3600 BC. Until the discovery of the Americas, eleven hundred years later, (c.2500 BC), these mid-ocean islands were the most westerly known islands in the ocean to the west, and had been revered as the western home of the SunGod. After the discovery of the Americas, however (Ref.2) these islands became the focus of the return route back to the Old World.

Angle COE encodes the angle of 15° (**Fig.2**), and the fifteen menhirs on the baseline OD (Row XIII in **Fig.6**) encode the initial sailing direction (ISD) from Kerlescan to the West Azores, 15°WSW (**Fig.8**). The number of menhirs of Row I is 8, encoding the latitude of these islands of the West Azores 8° south of Kerlescan, at 47°-8= 39°N.

The rows encode the Islands of the Azores

Below Row I on **Fig.2** are 9 rows of menhirs, II through X, which run parallel in their eastern segments (see **Fig.4**). These 9 rows represent the nine islands of the Azores. The 9 rows can be divided into 3 groups, representing the 3 island groups of the Azores. As we shall demonstrate below. Rows II and III correspond with the 'two islands of the East Azores, while Rows IV, V, VI, VIII, and X correspond with the five islands of the Central Azores, and Rows VII and IX correspond with the two islands of the West Azores. As shown on **Fig.4**, the eastern segments all make an angle of 15° with the line of Row XIII, which confirms the important initial sailing direction (ISD) from Kerlescan to the West Azores of 15° WSW.

Row I: Cape Finisterre

Let us explain each of the stone rows, starting with Row I , which is connected with Row II by a line of 8 menhirs, the eastern upturned end of Row II (see **Fig.6**). The two segments of Row II contain 20 menhirs (12+8), which combined with the top Row 1 (8) and the bottom RowXIII (15), encode the latitude of Cape Finisterre, the NW cape of Iberia, at 43°N (20+8+15=43). Cape Finisterre is located north of the Azores, so the uppermost Row I represents Cape Finisterre, literally. From Cape Finisterre, people would sail to the Azores, and hoped to welcome their New King arrive from the "other side of the waters".

Row II: Sailing to Sao Miguel, East Azores

Row II has 20 menhirs (12+8=20), encoding the initial sailing direction (ISD) from Cape Finistere to Sao Miguel, the main island of the East Azores, at 20° WSW. The western segments of these island Rows II to VIII make an angle of 20° with the baseline OD (= angle BOD), confirming this ISD to the East Azores seven times (**Figs.5&8**). Row II represents the island of Sao Miguel, literally (**Fig.7**).

3

Photo 1. The tail ends of the stone rows of the "Royal Avenue" in the east, near the house. (Kerlescan, Brittany, taken in May, 2005)

Photo 2. The true N-S row of the U (representing Europe and Africa), view south. (Kerlescan, Brittany, taken in May, 2005, Reinoud de jonge in the photo)

The next seven rows represent the (2+5=7) islands of the East and Central Azores. Looking westward toward the Azores from point 0 (**Fig.2**), all these rows bend to the right, because after Sao Miguel, their ships have to change course to the north, on a new heading. The second segment of Row II is extrapolated via a single menhir (#13) to starting point 0 at the right (**Fig.6**). This line BO has 13 (12+1=13) menhirs, corresponding to the sailing distance from Cape Finisterre to Sao Miguel, 13dl= 780 nautical miles (NM), which is correct (1 dl= 1 Egyptian moira= 1° of latitude= 60NM). The 13 total rows of the Kerlescan monument also encode this important distance of 13dl (13 moira) to the Azores.

The legs of angle BOD contain 28 (12+1+15= 28) menhirs, corresponding to the terminal sailing direction (TSD) in the neighborhood of Sao Miguel, 28°WSW. The difference between the TSD and the ISD on a straight sailing course is caused by the curvature of the earth over long distances. These angles were created using the polar star at each end of the course. You can place a protractor on each end of the course, line up the protractor with true north, and see the ISD and TSD sailing angles as seen by Neolithic man, and as encoded in these monuments. The big angle EOA of 28° (**Fig. 2**) confirms this once more, and the eastern segments of Rows II to VIII make an angle of 28° with the line CK, from the tall menhir K (**Photos 6&7**), as shown in **Fig.5**, confirming this important TSD seven more times.

The three menhirs of Line OE, plus the 15 menhirs of Row XIII, and the 20 menhirs of Row II, provide the 38 menhirs that encode the latitude of Sao Miguel at 38°N. Note that the headaxis also bisects the smaller arrow OBCD. So, after reaching the island of Sao Miguel (Row II), the most difficult part of the voyage to the West Azores has been accomplished (the route of the smaller arrow has been sailed). The line from point C to the big menhir K makes an angle of 38° (**Fig. 2**), confirming the latitude of Sao Miguel, 38°N. So now we start to see why the outlying large menhir K was added to this site! Menhir K unequivocally identifies the location of the important Central Azores.

Row III: Santa Maria

Row III represents the other island of the East Azores, Santa Maria. The row has a lower number of stones (11, not 20), because observed from Kerlescan, this smaller, southern island is less important. Row II and the east end of Row III have 23 menhirs (20+3=23), showing the ISD from Cape Finisterre to Santa Maria, 23°WSW (**Fig.8**).. Adding the western segment of Row III gives (23+8=31) 31 menhirs, the TSD in the neighborhood of Santa Maria, 31°WSW. Note that these angles also correspond to the centers of the Southern and Northern Egyptian Empire, at 23°N and 31°N. Egypt was the greatest civilization on earth, and also the center of the Sun religion. Also, Santa Maria, the most southeast of the Azores Islands, was important for people heading to the Azores from the Mediterranean, so the double meanings of the angles were probably intended by the creators of the monument.

The 11 menhirs of Row III (and the menhirs of the big angle AOE (8+3= 11) (**Fig.6**), corespond to the 11 islands of Madeira and the Azores. Rows II (20) and III (11) have

4

Photo 3. The 11 western stones of the U, representing the coast of North America, looking south. The big squarish stone on the right, represents Cape Race. (Kerlescan, Brittany, May, 2005)

Photo 4. The menhir K, and what remains of the tumulus behind Dr. de Jonge. Stone 1 (Cape Race) of the western row is in the background on the right side of the photo. (Kerlescan, Brittany, May, 2005)

together with the common menhir on Row I (#8) and the single menhir on OB (#13), a total of 33 menhirs (20+11+1+1=33), corresponding to the islands of Madeira at 33°N (**Fig.8**). Rows I (8) and II (20) have, together with the single menhir on OB (#13) and the west segment of Row III (8), 37 menhirs (8+20+1+8=37), corresponding to the latitude of Santa Maria, at 37°N. The east segment of Row III has 3 menhirs, because, coming from the Mediterranean, Santa Maria is the third island, after Madeira and Porto Santo.

What we are doing here is the decoding of a complex mneumonic device, used in prehistoric times. With this device, geographic knowledge was successfully passed to many subsequent generations. At this point, we cannot tell if all these findings are intended, or whether some are coincidental. We are sure that at least some multiple meanings were intended, perhaps even considered lucky or holy, because we have seen multiple meanings frequently used in other megalithic monuments.

Row IV: Terciera
When extending the west segment of Row III straight to the east (**Fig.3**), the extension of this line runs to stone 19 of Row IV. Row IV represents the next island in the westerly direction, Terciera. This "projected connection" indicates it is possible next to sail from Santa Maria to Terciera. It is the first island of the Central Azores.

Rows II and III each consist of two segments, corresponding to the approximate distance from Sao Miguel or Santa Maria (East Azores) to Terciera (Central Azores), about 2dl= 120 NM, which is correct. Rows II (20), III (11), and the east segment of IV (7) have together 38 menhirs (20+11+7=38), and the east segment of Row II (8), with Row III (11) and Row IV (19) have together 38 menhirs (8+11+19=38), both corresponding to the sailing direction from Sao Miguel to Terciera, 38°NW, and to the latitude of Terciera and the Central Azores, at 38°N.

When you add the extra menhir on line OB (stone #13), the total now moves to 39 menhirs (38+1=39), twice corresponding to the West Azores at 39°N. Rows II and IV contain 20+19=39 menhirs, confirming this latitude. Together with the 8 menhirs of Row I, this adds up to 39+8=47 menhirs, referring twice to Kerlescan and Cape Race, both at 47°N (and to the sailing direction from Santa Maria to Terciera, 47°NW (**Fig.9**).

The east and west segments of Row IV have 12 menhirs (7+5=12), which indicate the initial sailing direction from Cape Finisterre to Terciera, 12° WSW. Together with Row III, the menhirs total 23 (12+11=23), in agreement with the terminal sailing direction in the neighborhood of Tierciera, 23° WSW. The east and west segments of Row IV have together 14 menhirs (7+7=14), corresponding to the sailing distance from Cape finisterre to Terciera, 14dl= 840 NM, which is correct. Note that the third segment of Row IV bends to the left, to show that on the usual route via Sao Miguel, after Terciera one has to change course to the left to reach the next island of Sao Jorge. The purpose of this is to disuade folks from sailing to the northern island of Graciosa.

Note that Row III and the eastern two segments of Row IV possess 23 menhirs (11+7+5=23), and together with the western segment (7), 30 menhirs, again encoding the

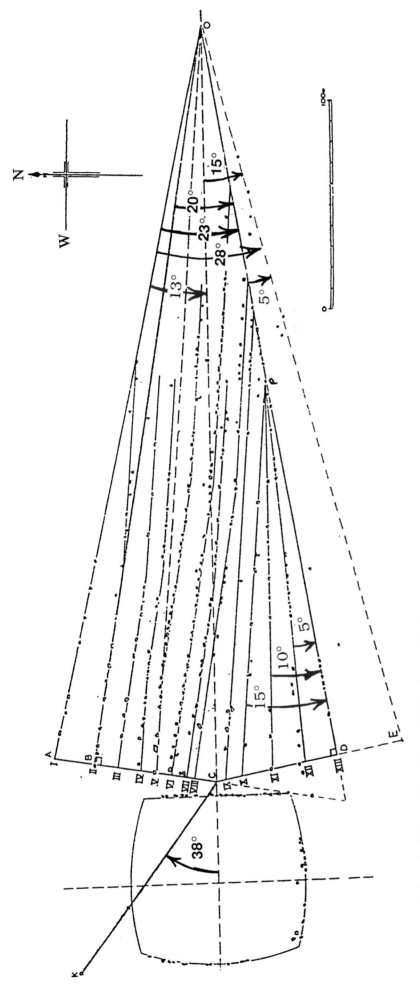

15° = COE = direction (ISD) from Kerlescan to W. Azores, 15° WSW

20° = BOD = direction (ISD) from Cape Finisterre to Sao Miguel, 20° WSW

23° = AOD = latitude of Tropic of Cancer at 23°N

23° = also = direction (ISD) from Cape Finisterre to Sta. Maria, 23° WSW

28° = AOE = direction (TSD) of E. Azores, 28° WSW

38° = latitude of Sao Miguel (E. Azores) at 38°N

Fig.2 The Rows of Kerlescan: Angles from O and C, with author's lines

centers of the Southern and Northern Egyptian Empire, at 23°N and 30°N, the center of the Sun religion, and the greatest civilization on earth.

Row V: Sao Jorge

When extending the middle segment of Row IV to the east (**Fig.3**), we arrive at the east end (stone #39) of Row V, representing the next island in the western direction, Sao Jorge. Thus it is indicated that one can sail from Terciera to Sao Jorge. This elongated central island is considered to be very important, because the long row contains a great number of menhirs. The first (easterly) menhir (#39) lies close to the axis, which indicates that we are approching an important goal. The total number of menhirs on the easern segment of Row V is 14, in agreement with the sailing direction from Terciera to Sao Jorge, 14°WSW (**Fig.9**). The western segment of Row V also bends toward the axis (left, viewed to the west from point 0), showing that, on the usual route to Sao Miguel, after Terciera and Sao Jorge, the ships have to change course to the left to reach the next island of Pico. The total number of menhirs on Row V is 39, encoding the latitude of the West Azores, at 39°N. This has been the main goal since the beginning: to welcome the new King at the West Azores. The western segment of Row IV has 8 menhirs, confirming this goal, 8° south of Kerlescan, at 47-8= 39°N.

As stated before, the seven western segments of Rows II to VIII are symbolic for the 7 islands of the Central (5) and the West (2) Azores. The mid segments of Rows IV and V are now symbolic for the 2 islands of the West Azores. The western segment of Row V can be extended toward the east to point 0 (indicated by the dashed line, in **Fig.6**), giving a 15° angle with line OD. this is also true of the western segment of Row V, twice again showing the sailing direction from Kerlescan to the West Azores, 15°WSW. The easterly segments of Rows II to X (as previously illustrated in **Fig.4**), also give the 15° angle (**Fig.8**), which was obviously very important to them. It may have taken many trial-and-error voyages, over a long period, to establish this figure.

The total number of stones on the legs of angle VOD (western leg of V and OD) is to 8+15= 23, corresponding to the holy Tropic of Cancer at 23°N, again referring to the Sun religion, and the latitude of the Southern Egyptian Empire. The number of menhirs on the easterly segments of Row V correspond to the Northern Egyptian Empire, at 31°N (14+17= 31).

The angle of the westerly segments of Rows IV and V with line OD is 20°, as shown in the right side of **Fig.5**. This 20° angle twice corresponds to the direction from Kerlescan to Pico, the main island of the Central Azores, 20°WSW. Together with the other eastern segments of Rows II through VIII (**Fig.5**), this 20° angle has been indicated 2+7= 9 times. The total number of menhirs on the legs of angle VOE (western leg of V, and OE) is 11 (8+3= 11), these lines encoding the eleven islands of Madeira and the Azores.

Row VI: Pico

If we extend the middle section of Row V via the single menhir (#34) on the axis to the east (**Fig.3**), to the start of the next Row VI (at stone #47), one can see that it is recommended to sail from Sao Jorge to Pico. Row VI represents the next island in the

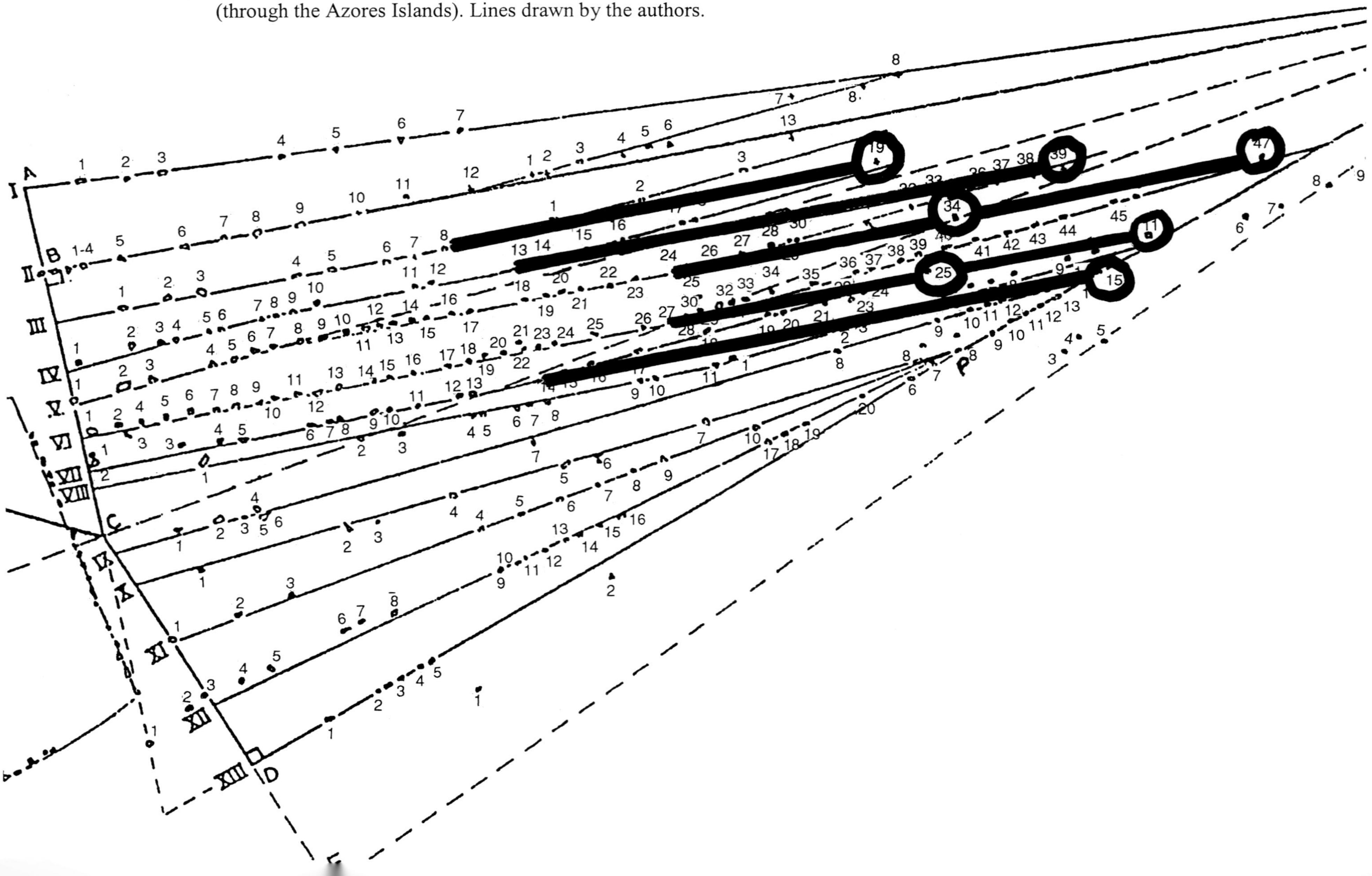

Fig.3 The Rows of Kerlescan: The methodology for sailing west through the rows (through the Azores Islands). Lines drawn by the authors.

western direction, Pico, the highest volcanic island of the Central Azores. The east segment of Row VI contains 20 menhirs (#27 to #47), in agreement with the sailing direction from Sao Jorge to Pico (**Fig.9**), and also with the TSD direction from Kerlescan to Pico, both 20°WSW (**Fig.8**). This main island is considered to be very important, because VI is the longest row, with the most menhirs. Having now crossed the axis, we have now reached an important goal, the prominent cone volcano of the Central Azores.

The total number of menhirs of row VI is 47 (20+27), corresponding to the latitude of Kerlescan in Brittany, and of Cape Race, Newfoundland, the east cape of North America, at 47°N. The western segment of Row VI has 27 stones, showing the sailing direction from Pico and Fayal to the West Azores, 27°WNW. This number also corresponds to the center of the United Egyptian Empire, at 27°N, halfway between the Southern (31°N) and Northern (23°N) Egyptian empires.

Row VII: Fayal

Extending the western segment of Row VI straight to the east (**Fig.3**), we arrive at the start of Row VII (stone 25 of row VII, **Fig.6**). Row VII represents the island of Fayal, so it is indicated to sail from Pico to Fayal. The eastern segment of Row VI is situated closely below the previous row, so it is clear that this row deals with a neighboring island of Pico. Also, Rows VI and VII both bend on the axis in the direction of point C, which means both islands are located on the usual route for the West Azores. Line CK makes an angle of 38° with this axis, corresponding to the latitude of Pico and Fayal, at 38°N (**Fig.2**). Fayal is also the westernmost island of the Central Azores. The eastern segment of Row VII has 12 menhirs, and the western segment has 13 menhirs. The average of these segments is 12.5 menhirs. Combined with the western segment of of Row VI, this adds up to 39.5 menhirs (12.5+27=39.5), the precise latitude of the West Azores, at 39.5°N. Row VII has 25 menhirs, encoding the (12+13= 25) sailing direction from Fayal to Flores, the main island of the West Azores, at 25°WNW (**Fig.9**). The western segments of Rows II to VIII make an angle of 25° with line OE, confirming this important sailing direction 7 times (**Fig.5**). On the West Azores the new King will arrive after the long crossing from Newfoundland, as do nearly all the returning ships from the New World. The two segments of Row VII indicate the approximate distance from Fayal (Central Azores) to Flores (West Azores), about 2dl, =120 NM.

Row VIII: Graciosa

Extending the western segment (**Fig.3**) of Row VI (the main island of Pico) further to the east, we pass row VII (Fayal) (at stone #25), and we arrive at the start of Row VIII (at stone #11), representing the northern island of Graciosa. The island is indicated after Fayal (Row VII) and it has less menhirs, because it is less important. The bend between its two segments is not on the axis (C-O), indicating Graciosa is not on the usual route to the West Azores.

Graciosa can be reached from Terciera (Row IV), by steering the ships to the right, instead of to the left, to Sao Jorge. The western segments of Row IV (Terciera-7 stones) and Row VIII (Graciosa-22 stones) have 29 stones, encoding the sailing direction from Terciera to Graciosa, 29° WNW (**Fig.9**). Both segments of Row VIII have 11 stones,

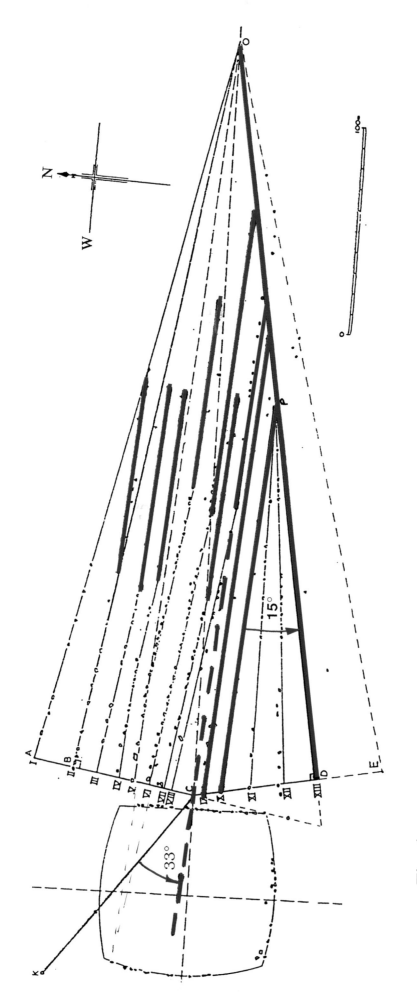

Fig. 4 The nine rows of Kerlescan (including the bent eastern segments), showing their angles of 15°, the sailing direction (ISD) to the West Azores, and the 33° sailing direction (TSD) from Cape Race (menhir K) to the West Azores. (Lines drawn by the authors.)

showing the sailing direction from Graciosa to Flores, the main island of the West Azores, 11°WNW (**Fig.9**), and also the 11 islands of the Azores and Madeira. Row VIII has two segments, encoding the approximate sailing distance from Graciosa (Central Azores) to Flores (West Azores), about 2dl= 120 NM. Note that the western segment of Row VIII (Graciosa) is situated closely below the western segment of Row VII (Fayal). This shows us that both islands are considered appropriate starting points for crossing to the West Azores.

Rows VII and VIII have together 25+22= 47 menhirs, again encoding, the important latitude of Cape Race, Newfoundland, at 47°N. However, in view of the long windward distance involved, this cape cannot be reached by sailing west. Only the gods would be able to reach Cape Race by going west, and therefore this is a "Royal Crossing". The Sungod is actually shown doing this crossing in **Fig.11**, a petroglyph from Portugal, and again in the petroglyph of **Fig.12**. All sailors returning from the west will return from Cape Race, Newfoundland, to these west Azores, however, because the Gulfstream and the tradewind patterns of the earth have become understood during the last few thousand years of sailing expeditions. Now everyone at the "other side of the waters, in the land where the Sun sets" will return via the West Azores, using this Royal Crossing with the wind from west to east. This mid-ocean route is shown in **Fig.12**, with the 9 islands of the Azores, shown as the home of the 9-stick figure of the SunGod.

Extend the east segment of Row VIII westerly to point C (the dotted line in **Fig.4**). Line CK now makes an angle of 33° with this segment, showing the terminal sailing direction from Cape Race to the island of Flores, 33°ESE (**Fig.8**). Actually, all the eastern segments of Rows II to X, and the third segments of Rows IV and V, all make an angle of 33° with CK, indicating this sailing direction eleven times (9+2=11) (**Fig.4**). This is the direction the ships, and the new King, will return.

Row IX: Flores
Extending the western segment of Row VII (Fayal) toward the east (**Fig.3**), we pass Row VIII (Graciosa), and we arrive on the baseline at stone #15, the start of Row IX, representing Flores. The eastern menhirs of Row VIII (Graciosa) have been placed slightly above the row. Extending the eastern segment of Row VIII (Graciosa) to the west, we arrive at the west end of Row IX, Flores, the main island of the West Azores. So it is possible to reach the western end of the Azores, Flores, from either Graciosa or Fayal, but going further by the same methodology is not indicated. Row IX has 15 menhirs, supporting the important direction from Kerlescan to the West Azores, 15°WSW (**Fig.8**).

Row X: Corvo
The next Row X represents the last island of Corvo. This row has fewer menhirs than Row IX, because Corvo is smaller than Flores. Rows IX (15) and X (8) have together 23 menhirs (15+8=23), which show the sailing direction from Flores to Corvo, 23°NNE, and the holy Tropic of Cancer, at 23°N, referring to the Sun religion. Row X has 8 menhirs, corresponding to the latitude of the West Azores, 8° below Cape Race and Kerlescan, at 39°N (47-8= 39). Row V has 39 menhirs, confirming this latitude. Row X makes from

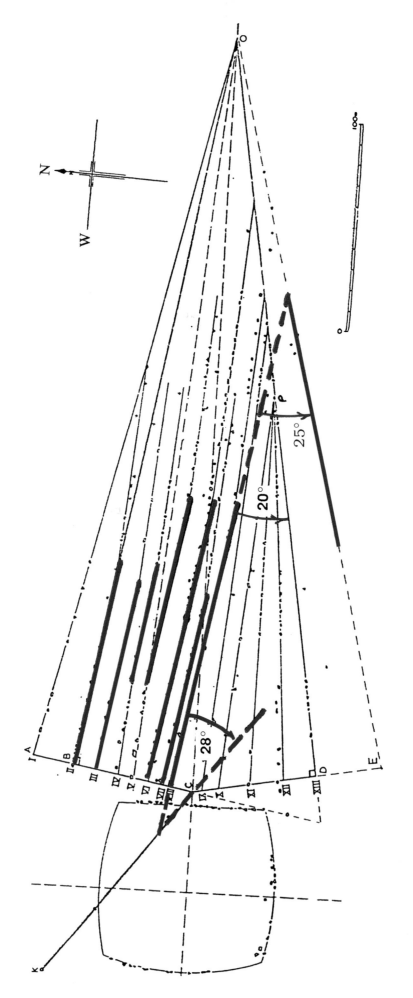

Fig. 5 The seven rows of Kerlescan that are at 28°, the sailing direction (TSD) to the East Azores, the 25° sailing direction from the Central to the West Azores, and the 20° sailing direction (ISD) from Cape Finisterre (NW Iberia), to the East Azores.

point P an angle of 15° with the baseline, confirming the direction from Kerlescan to the West Azores, 15°WSW yet again (**Fig.4**).

Note that Rows IX and X are below the axis, and not bent. It does not appear easy or recommended to sail between these islands, as the two row lines are parallel with one another (not intersecting).

The Other 9 Menhirs, below the rows

Below the big arrow OACD and the 13 stone rows above, are 9 menhirs, roughly along dashed line OE, representing the 9 islands of the Azores. The easternmost menhir on line OE (#9), is in line with the eastern segment of Row VII, representing the island of Fayal. Fayal is located on the usual route to the West Azores, so this easternmost menhir must represent Sao Miguel (East Azores), also on this route. The next menhir on line OE lies on the extended part of the eastern segment of Row VIII, representing the island of Graciosa. Graciosa is not located on the usual route to the West Azores, so this menhir must represent Santa Maria, which in general will not be visited either, except for ships coming from Gibraltar. Close investigation shows that all 9 menhirs from east to west have the same, island-associated meanings as Rows II to X from north to south. So the three menhirs on line OE represent one after the other: Sao Miguel, Santa Maria, and Pico. The most western menhirs (1&2) represent Flores and Corvo, the West Azores. Rows 11, 12, and 13 encode the route to the west, as explained below.

The Voyage to the Realm of the Dead

Kerlescan is situated in Brittany, at the west coast of Western Europe, and the rows of menhirs point to the west. In the west is the ocean. Therefore, the western part of Kerlescan, the U-shaped stone circle, symbolizes the North Atlantic Ocean. The stones along the east side of the U represent the coast of Europe and Africa, the stones in the south side of the U, the coast of South America, and the U stones in the west, the coast of North America.

The vertical row of stones in the east (**Fig.7**) is the straight meridian along the coast of the Old World, where the monument of Kerlescan is situated. This row has 19 menhirs, corresponding to the degree of latitude of the Gulf of Campeche in Central America. This is the center of the Realm of the Dead, at 18-20°N. This is the place where the new King can be found! An important government delegation will travel to that far-off country to accompany the King on his return voyage to the Azores. The enormous arrow OACD points to these 19 menhirs. So this is the main goal of the voyage. The bowed south side of the U represents the long crossing to the Realm of the Dead, along a southern, far-away, curved latitude. Along the curved west side, is where one has to sail to return. This represents a far-away, curved meridian along the coast of the big continent at the other side of the Ocean, North America.

The government delegation sails from the Old World in the east, so from starting point 0. The eastern sections of Rows II to X make an angle of 15° with the baseline OD (Row XIII) (**Fig.4**), nine times corresponding to the latitude of the Southern Cape Verde Islands, at 15°N (**Fig.10**), and the 9 Cape Verde Islands. Angle COE is 15° (**Fig.2**), and the

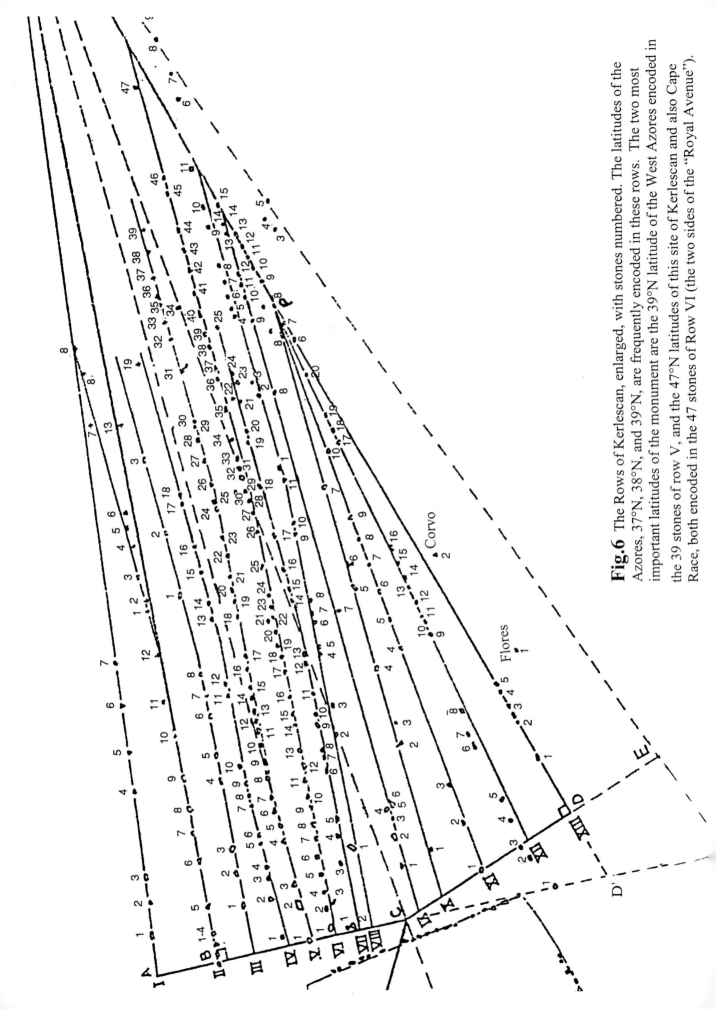

Fig.6 The Rows of Kerlescan, enlarged, with stones numbered. The latitudes of the Azores, 37°N, 38°N, and 39°N, are frequently encoded in these rows. The two most important latitudes of the monument are the 39°N latitude of the West Azores encoded in the 39 stones of row V, and the 47°N latitudes of this site of Kerlescan and also Cape Race, both encoded in the 47 stones of Row VI (the two sides of the "Royal Avenue").

baseline OD has 6+9= 15 menhirs, both confirming this latitude. From these islands one sails across the Ocean to the New World, with the current and the tradewinds.

Point P on the baseline is, like 0, the starting point for some lower rows. The Southern Crossing across the Atlantic is represented by the short piece of line OP. Between points 0 and P are 5 rows, so the length of the crossing is 5HDL x 5 moira/DDL= 25 moira, or 25 moirax60NM/moira= 1500 NM. (One Half Distance Line= 5° of latitude= 5x60 NM= 300 NM). This is the accurate distance from the Cape Verde Islands to Cape Sao Roque, Brazil, so by moving along the row O to P, one has sailed the Southern Crossing to Brazil.

Angle DOE below the baseline is 5°, corresponding to Cape Sao Roque, Brazil at 5°S (**Figs.2,10**). The legs of this angle contain15+3= 18 menhirs, because this cape marks the shortest crossing of the Ocean on the way to the Realm of the Dead, at 18°N. The line OE has 3 menhirs, representing the three islets on this route, St. Paul, and the 2 islets of Fernando de Noronha. Adding ten Cape Verde Islands on the Southern Crossing route, these three form 10+3=13 islands, represented by the 13 rows of Kerlescan.

In practice, ships cut the corner, and disembark higher on the coast of South America (**Fig. 10**). Line PD along the baseline represents the equator at the level of the mouth of the Amazon River, at 0°N. Along this line are 8 menhirs, corresponding to the Orinoco river at 8°N. On the whole line OD are 15 menhirs, corresponding to Cape Gracias a Dios and the culture along the north coast of Honduras at 15°N-16°N, as confirmed by all the 15° angles in Fig.4, and the 16 menhirs at the south side of the U-shaped stone circle. This south side represents the journey to the Realm of the Dead, literally. Some of the menhirs at the bottom of the U-shape may be indicating large islands reported off the coast of Venezuela, along this east-west route, from Isla Margarita to Aruba.

Row XII makes an angle of 5° with the baseline OD (**Fig.2**), corresponding to the coast of French Guyana at 5°N. It is here that ships prefer to land. Row XII contains 18 menhirs (#3 - #20), again corresponding to the center of civilization around the Gulf of Campeche, at 18°N. This is the main goal of the journey. It is the land where the King can be found! Row XII continues to CD', picking up rocks #1 and 2, so now the Row XII totals 20 menhirs, to show that the Realm of the Dead extends to 20°N. Row IV contains 19 menhirs and Row II has 20 menhirs, both confirming these important latitudes. The western and center segments of Rows II to VIII make with the baseline an angle of 20° (as shown in Fig. 5), making with line OD an angle of 20° confirm this again.

The next Row XI runs parallel to the axis of the monument, and makes an angle of 10° with the baseline (**Fig.2**), corresponding to the huge island of Trinidad at 10°N. The ten menhirs of this Row XI confirm this important latitude. This island lies at the start of the northerly island-hopping Antilles Route, which in general, is disuaded (Ref.2), preferring the more direct and safer coastal route to Central America.

Row X makes an angle of 15° with the baseline (**Fig.2**), corresponding to the islands of Martinique and Dominica, at 15°N in the Lesser Antilles. The angle also again confirms the culture along the north coast of Honduras, at 15°N. The Rows IX and X have 10+8=

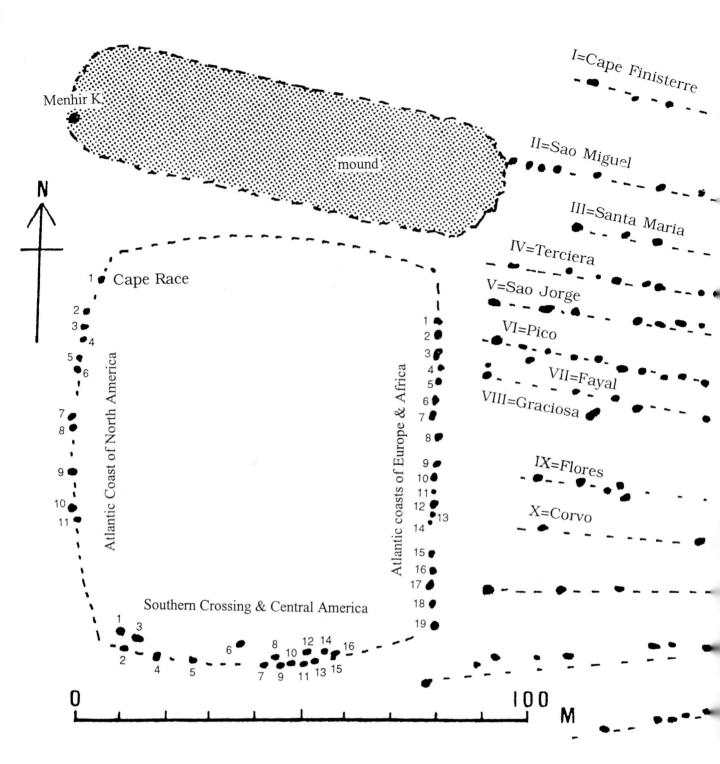

Fig.7 The western U stones of Kerlescan, with the mound on the north side, and the rows of the monument identified by its associated island, as discussed in the text. (Lines and numbers added by the authors.)

18 menhirs, confirming the center of civilization around the Gulf of Campeche, at 18°N. In Egypt this area is called Punt (Refs.1,2). Here the government delegation will join the new King!

The Return Voyage to Newfoundland

The west side of the U-shaped stone circle represents the coasts of Central and North America. This side has 11 menhirs, in agreement with the sailing direction from Cape Catoche, the NE cape of Yucatan, to Cuba, 11°ENE. The legs of the big arrow AOE contain 8+3=11 menhirs, confirming this direction, and Row VIII has 11+11=22 menhirs, corresponding with the latitude of this crossing, at 22°N (**Fig.10**).

The angle of arrow AOD is 23° (**Fig.2**), and the legs of this angle contain 8+15=23 menhirs, both corresponding to the holy Tropic of Cancer along the north coast of Cuba, at 23°N, where the short crossing to Florida starts. Rows IX and X contain 15+8=23 menhirs, confirming this latitude. Row VII contains 25 menhirs, corresponding to the south point of Florida, at 25°N. When Row VIII is extended toward the east to line OE, it also contains 22+3=25 menhirs, confirming this important latitude. The western segments of Rows II to VIII make an angle of 25° withline OE, confirming this seven times (**Fig.5**).

Rows VIII and X contain 22+8=30 menhirs, and Rows XI and XII contain 10+20=30 menhirs, both corresponding with the mouth of the Mississippi River at 30°N. The Mississippi was a major, copper trade corridor via Poverty Point from 2500 BC to 1200 BC copper trade. This trade was going on, and increasing, when this monument was built. The west and south sides of the U have 11+15=26 menhirs, revealing the latitude of Bimini, across the Gulfstream from Florida, at 26°N. When Row VII is extended toward the east to line OE, it contains 25+1=26 menhirs, confirming this latitude. Bimini is of importance for the Bermuda route to the Old World, which was discovered c.2200 BC, as documented by the Devil's Head Petroglyphs (Ref.2).

The west side of the U has 11 stones, corresponding with Cape Hatteras, 11° below Cape Race and Kerlescan, at 47-11=36°N. Rows III and VII contain 11+25=36 menhirs, confirming this latitude. This is also the latitude of the Strait of Gibraltar, at 36°N, at the other side of the Ocean. The west side of the U has 8 stones above the axis, corresponding to Delaware Bay, 8° below Cape Race, at 47-8=39°N. The most important row, Row V of 39 stones, confirms this latitude of 39°N.

Rows IV and VIII contain 19+22=41 menhirs, corresponding to Nantucket, at 41°N. Rows II and VIII have 20+22=42 stones, encoding Cape Cod, at 42°N. Rows I, II, and XIII of enormous arrows AOD and BOD have 8+20+15=43 menhirs, corresponding to America's Stonehenge (N.H.) and the south cape of Nova Scotia at 43°N. This nautical center for crossing the Ocean is the most important megalithic monument of North America (Refs.2,6).

The total number of stones in the U is 46 (11+16+19= 46), a latitude just below Cape Race at 47°N, used for actual departure for the Old World. The enormous arrow AOD

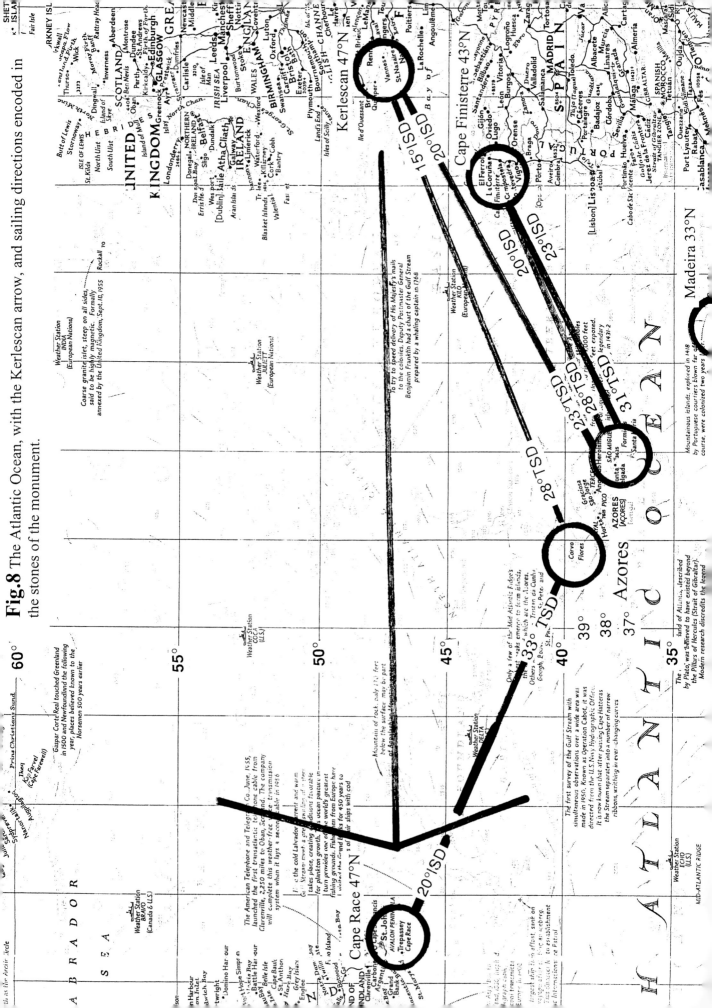

Fig.8 The Atlantic Ocean, with the Kerlescan arrow, and sailing directions encoded in the stones of the monument.

points along the 47° latitude line from Kerlescan to Cape Race (**Fig.8**). The most important row of Kerlescan, Row VI, contains 47 stones, confirming this latitude, and Rows VII and VIII have together 25+22=47 stones, confirming this again. Extending the most important Rows V and VI to the west (**Fig.4**), we arrive at the uppermost menhir of the west side of the U, which represents Cape Race, literally.

The Crossing to the West Azores and Return

Below the enormous arrow to the east, AOD, are nine menhirs, with numbers 5, 8 and 9 on our imaginary line OE, representing the 9 islands of the Azores, as explained before. This positioning of some of the stones, especially 1 &2, above line OE, shows that the crossing of the new King and the government delegation to these islands starts at a higher latitude. Between menhir K and Rows II and III is an oblong burial mound across the full width of the U (**Fig.7**). It is a royal vault, about 75 meters long, 20 meters wide, and nowadays only c.1.5 meters high. In view of its position above the stone circle, this burial mound, and with it the whole monument, deals with the crossing from Newfoundland to the Azores, and as a consequence with the return of the King from the Realm of the Dead.

The west side of the U has above the axis 8 stones, corresponding with the West Azores, 8° below Cape Race, at 47-8= 39°N. The second most important row. Row V, has 39 stones, confirming this latitude. Arrow BOD, symetrical around the axis, points due east, with an angle of 20° (**Fig.2**). This is the initial sailing direction (ISD) from Cape Race to the West Azores, 20°ESE (**Fig.8**), and to its sailing distance of 20dl (20dl=20°=1200 NM). The western segments of Rows II to VIII make an angle of 20° with the baseline (**Fig.5**), and the eastern segments of Rows II to X , as well as the western segments of Rows IV and V (not shown) make an angle of 20° with line OE, confirming this direction 7+9+2=18 times. This is the start of the difficult crossing of the Ocean via the 9 islands of the Azores, the 2 islands of Madeira, and the 2 eastern Canary Islands, represented (9+2+2=13) by the 13 rows of menhirs at Kerlescan. The east and south sides of the U have 15+18=33 stones, encoding Madeira at 33°N, while the south and west sides of the U have 11+18 stones, encoding the Canaries at 29°N.

Because of the curvature of the earth, and the long sailing distance involved, the crossing from Cape Race to the West Azores is complicated.The number of menhirs of the south and east sides of the U are 33, also indicating the terminal sailing direction in the neighborhood of the West Azores, 33°ESE. Rows IX, X, and XI have 15+8+10=33 menhirs, confirming this sailing direction. The east segments of Rows II to X, and the west segments of Rows IV and V all make an angle of 33° with line KC, confirming this sailing direction 9+2=11 times. The line KC symbolizes this crossing from Cape Race to Kerlescan, and the 13 menhir rows of Kerlescan symbolize the 13° difference between the ISD and TSD sailing directions, of 33=20=13°. Angle AOC also is 13°, confirming this again.

The SunGod

In the monument of Kerlescan there are a lot of details about the Azores. Of course, this archipelago was discovered to be on the best return route across the ocean. But there is also a religious reason. Row IX (Flores) has 15 menhirs, corresponding with the culture

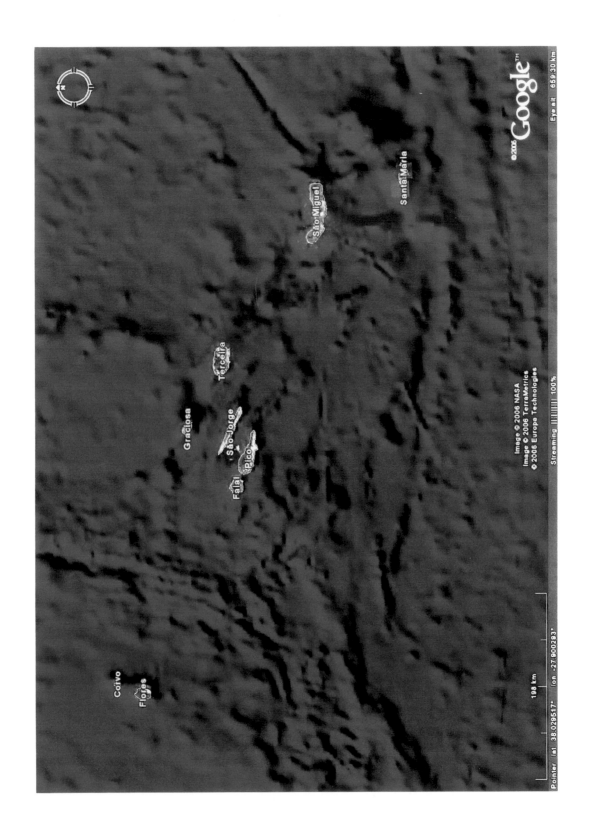

Google 1 Sattelite photo of Azores Islands.

along the north coast of Honduras, at 15°N, confirmed twice by the 15° baseline angles of Rows IX and X. Rows IX and X (Flores and Corvo) together have 15+8=23 menhirs, corresponding to the Tropic of Cancer at 23°N, and pointing to the center of the Southern Egyptian Empire at 23°N. On their portion of the baseline (P-D) are 7 stones, now corresponding to the Nile Delta (23+7=30°N), the center of the Northern Egyptian Empire. Row X combined with the next Row XI, gives 8+10=18 menhirs, the center of Tuat, the Realm of the Dead, at 18°N. Here at Corvo, in the middle of the Ocean, the new King with his princely suite returns. On the main island of Flores (Row IX) he will be awaited by the delegation of his people from the Old World (Refs 1,2).

Belief in the two gods Horus and Osiris, below the SunGod Ra is illustrated in the petroglyph of **Fig.11**, and in the two straight, parallel rows IX and X (the royal islands of Flores and Corvo), which are only connected by the baseline, and also by the two Rows V and VI (SaoJorge and Pico), which contain the most menhirs. These form a true "Royal Avenue" to the upper side of the U, across the large plaza, in front of the royal burial mound.

Dating
Kerlescan was built after the discovery of America via the Atlantic, c.2500 BC (Refs.1,2). The monument uniquely reveals the mouth of the Orinoco River, and the islands of Martinique and Dominica of the Lesser Antilles as suitable, far-off landing points of the Southern Crossing, while including Bermuda, which was discovered c.2200 BC (Ref.2). These and other details suggest a late megalithic construction date of about 1900 BC.

Discussion
It may seem odd to you that all this complexity is embedded in this site design, built at great labor for mnemonic use. It must not be thought beyond their capabilities just because it seems strange to us. No one on earth does this anymore. This monument was built deep in the past, when man could not write his thoughts, and had no computers for calculating routes to the moon. Written languages have only been developed in the last couple of thousand years, so have been a very late development in human experience. These recent forbears of ours were curious about what was on the other side of the planet. They knew the Earth was round, like the moon and the sun, because only on a round surface does the angle (latitude) of the sun and the moon and the stars change as you move north and south. But there was a great ocean to the west, and they fantasized about what might be on the other side of the ocean, and the other side of the planet. We know from their monuments, that the megalithic culture had its homeland along the Atlantic coast of Europe, and these people traveled by water more easily and safely than through the forests. By studying megalithic sites, we have learned that they started exploring their world by sea at nearly the start of the culture, 6000 BC. They had finally understood the tradewind patterns of the Earth, and explored the globe by the end of the culture, at the end of the Bronze Age, 1200, though a bit later, 500 BC, in outlying places. These row sets are the largest megalithic ruins in the world, at their cultural center. To be able to decipher the forgotten meaning of these sites, one must "learn to think like they did". What we have discovered is illustrating the navigational skills and memory processes of this long-gone culture. We all have reason to be proud of these ancestors, the first

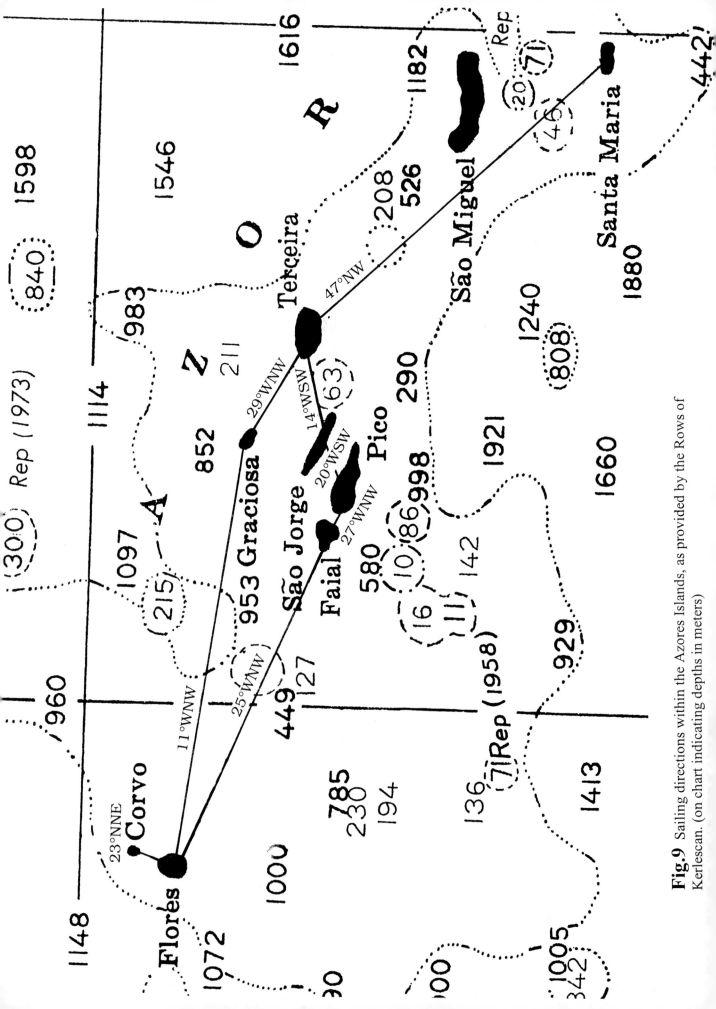

Fig. 9 Sailing directions within the Azores Islands, as provided by the Rows of Kerlescan. (on chart indicating depths in meters)

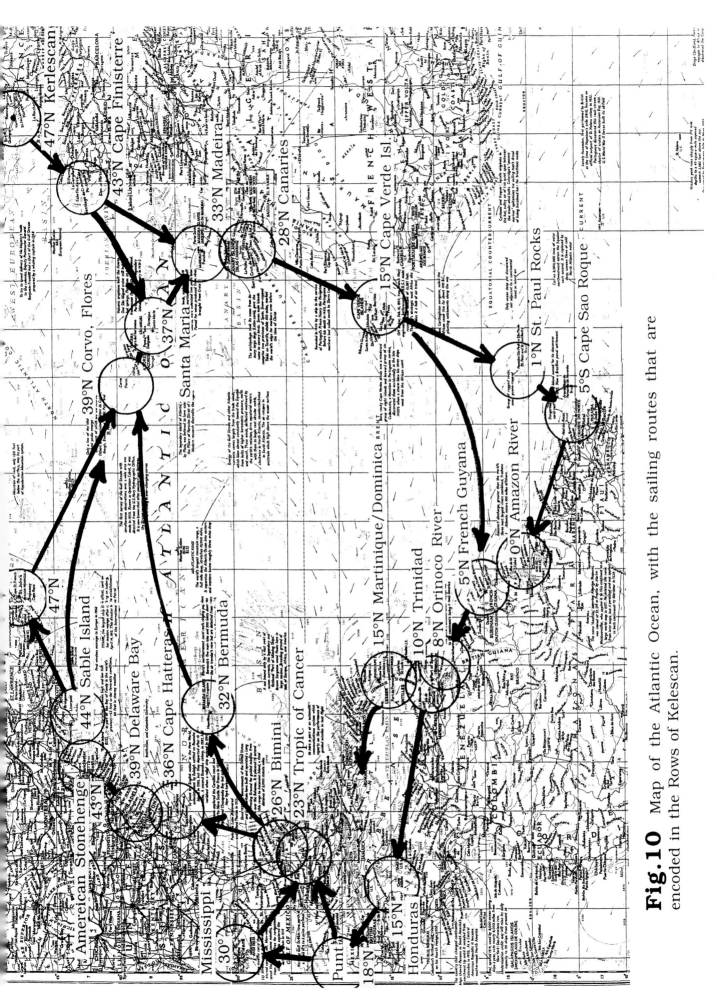

Fig.10 Map of the Atlantic Ocean, with the sailing routes that are encoded in the Rows of Kelescan.

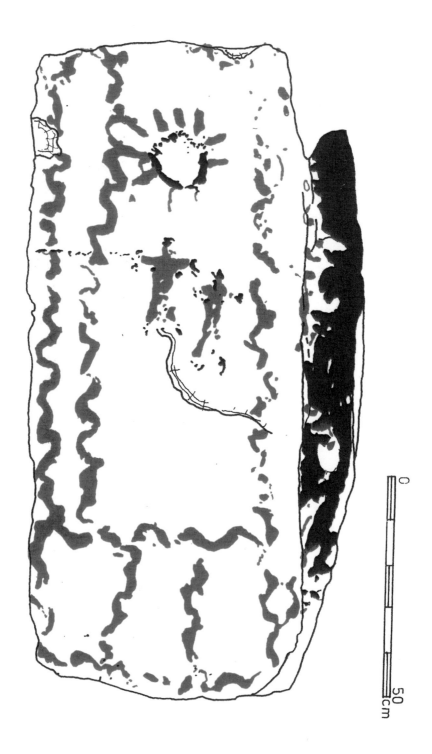

Fig.11 The Atlantic Ocean above the Southern Crossing. Below the SunGod Ra, the Egyptian gods Horus and Osiris are shown in the mid-ocean Royal Crossing on their way to Tuat, the Kingdom of Death, in the west, at the other side of the waters, in the land where the sun goes down. Note the coast of Iberia to Cape Finisterre, probably a natural edge on the stone, below the two figures (in red ochre, Porto University, Portugal, 1900 BC). (From Twohig, Ref. 34.)

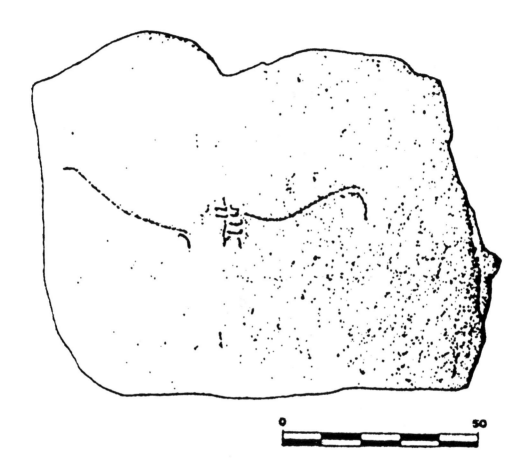

Fig. 12 The SunGod Ra (in the middle, as a 9-stick figure, also the 9 islands of the Azores) involved in the difficult "Royal Crossing" of the Atlantic Ocean. Note the coast of Iberia to Cape Finisterre as a small curve at the right side. (Portillo de las Cortes, Guadalajara, Galica, western Spain, c.2000 BC). (From Twohig, Ref.34)

explorers of the globe. The metals they discovered, and how much they changed the world, is another story.

References

1. De Jonge, R.M., and IJzereef, G.F., De Stenen Spreken, Kosmos Z&K, Utrecht/Antwerpen, 1996 (ISBN 90-215-2846-0) (Dutch)
2. De Jonge, R.M., and Wakefield, J.S., How the SunGod Reached America c.2500 BC, A Guide to Megalithic Sites, 2002 (ISBN 0-917054-19-9). also on CD
3. Website: www.howthesungod.com, De Jonge, R.M., and Wakefield, J.S.
4. De Jonge, R.M., and Wakefield, J.S., "The Discovery of the Atlantic Islands", Migration & Diffusion, Vol.3, No.11, pgs.69-109 (2002)
5. De Jonge, R.M., and Wakefield, J.S., "The Passage Grave of Karleby, Encoding the Islands Discovered in the Ocean, c. 2950 BC", Migration & Diffusion, Vol.5, No.18, pgs.64-74 (2004)
6. De Jonge, R.M., and Wakefield, J.S., "A Nautical Center for Crossing the Ocean, America's Stonehenge, New Hampshire, c.2200 BC", Migration & Diffusion, Vol.4, No.15, pgs.60-100 (2002)
7. De Jonge, R.M., and Wakefield, J.S., "Germany's Bronze Age Disc Reveals Transatlantic Seafaring, c.1600 BC", Ancient American, Vol.9, No.55, pgs.18-20 (2004)
8. De Jonge, R.M., and Wakefield, J.S., "The Three Rivers Petroglyph, A Guide-post for River Travel in America", Migration & Diffusion, Vol.3, No.12, pgs.74-100 (2002)
9. De Jonge, R.M., and Wakefield, J.S., "Ales Stenar, Sweden's Bronze Age 'Sunship' to the Americas, c.500 BC", Ancient American, Vol.9, No.56, pgs.16-21 (2004)
10. De Jonge, R.M., "Great Circle Mound: An Indiana Temple to the Egyptian SunGod?", Ancient American, Issue 60, Vol.9, pgs.31-32, 2004.
11. De Jonge, R.M., and Wakefield, J.S., "The Disc of Nebra, Important Sailing Routes of the Bronze Age Displayed in A Religious Context", Migration and Diffusion, Vol.5, No.17, pgs. 32-39, 2004
12. De Jonge, R.M., and Wakefield, J.S., "The Monument of Ales Stenar, A Sunship to the Realm of the Dead", Migration and Diffusion, Vol.5, No. 19, pgs. 94-106, 2004
13. De Jonge, R.M., and Wakefield, J.S., "The Rings of Stenness, Brodgar, and Bookan, Celebrating the Discovery of South Greenland", Migration and Diffusion, Vol 6, No.24, 2005
14. De Jonge, R.M., and Wakefield, J.S., "The Paintings of Porcellano Cave, The Discovery of Guadelupe, c.3000 BC", Migration and Diffusion, Vol. 6, No. 22, 2005
15. De Jonge, R.M., and Wakefield, J.S., "Mexican Cave Artists, 3000 BC", Ancient American, Vol. 10, No. 62, 2005
16. De Jonge, R.M., and Wakefield, J.S., "Greenland: Bridge between the Old and New Worlds", Ancient American, Vol. 11, No. 67, 2006
17. De Jonge, R.M., and Wakefield, J.S., "The Passage Grave of Karlesby: Encoding the Islands Discovered in the Ocean c.2950 BC", submitted to Ancient American, and accepted for publication
18. De Jonge, R.M., and Wakefield, J.S., "The Discovery of the Islands in the Atlantic, Stone C-8, Cairn T, Loughcrew, Ireland, c.3200 BC", submitted to Ancient American, Vol.13, No.81, January 2009
19. De Jonge, R.M., and Wakefield, J.S., "The Stone Rows of Tormsdale: A Voyage to Central America, The Realm of the Dead; Caithness, NE Scotland, c.1600 BC, Ancient American, Vol.11, No 70, pgs 28-34, 10/2006
20. De Jonge, R.M., and Wakfield, J.S., "A Return Route across the Ocean, encoded in the Tormsdale Rows; Caithness, NE Scotland, c.1600 BC", Ancient American, Vol.12, No.74, pgs 8-12, 8/2007
21. De Jonge, R.M., and Wakefield, J.S, "The Crossing of the Labrador Sea (The Stone Rows of Lagatjar, Brittany c.1600 BC)", Ancient American Vol.12, No.76, pgs 32-37, 12/2007
22. De Jonge, R.M. de, BRES 158, 1993 (Dutch)
23. De Jonge, R.M., de, and Uzereef, G.F., Exhibition, The Megalithic Inscriptions of Western Europe, 1996
24. Twohig, E. Shee, The Megalithic Art of Western Europe, Clarendon Press, Oxford, 1981
25. Burl, A., From Carnac to Callanish, The Prehistoric Stone Rows and Avenues of Britain, Ireland, and Brittany, Yale University Press, 1993 (ISBN 0-300-05575-7)
26. Briard, J., The Megaliths of Brittany. Gisserot, 1991
27. Batt, M., and others, Au Pays des Megalithes. Carnac-Locmariaquer, Jos, 1991 (French)
28. Cartographia Kft., 1:400.000, Budapest, 1995 (ISBN 963-352-9808 Cm)
29. Tompkins, P., Secrets of the Great Pyramid, Harper & Row, London, 1971 (ISBN 0- 06-090631-6) (Portion by Dr. Stecchini)
30. Giot, P.R., La Bretagne des Megalithes, Ed. Ouest France, 1995 (ISBN 27373-1388- 0) (French)
31. Bailloud, G. et.al., Carnac, Les Premieres Architectures de Pierre, CNRS Edition, 1995 (ISBN 2-85822-139-1) (French)
32. Thom, A., "Megalithic Geometry in Standing Stones", New Scientist, Mar.12, 1964
33. An Approach to Megalithic Geography, Association Archaeologique Kergal, Booklet No.20, 1992 (ISSN 0220-5939), (ISBN 2902727.20.8)

THE ROWS OF LEURE
Two Routes for Crossing the Ocean
(St.Jean, Crozon, Crozon Peninsula, Finistère, Brittany, c.1900 BC)

R.M. de Jonge, drsrmdejonge@hotmail.com
J.S. Wakefield, jayswakefield@yahoo.com

Summary
The meaning of the monument on the Crozon Penninsula had been long forgotten, and the monument is now destroyed. However, the groundplan as surveyed clearly shows it was a mneumonic map of sailing routes on the Atlantic Ocean.

Introduction
In West Brittany the district of Finistère is located, and in the far west of this region is the Crozon Peninsula. Here the hamlet of St.Jean is situated close to the town of Crozon, south of Brest, near the base of the French atomic submarine fleet, formerly a base of the Nazi U-Boat fleet. Just to the north of St. Jean were two menhir rows intersecting at right angles, about 10km from the coast of the Atlantic Ocean (**Fig.1**) (Ref.1). The monument is now destroyed. This article is based upon a groundplan provided by Aubrey Burl (Ref.1).

Menhirs of comparable size were located on two straight lines. The SW row had a length of 165 meters, with 5 big stones, and the NW/SE row had a length of 95 meters containing 9 big stones. By labeling the stones in this way, the stone at the junction of the rows is counted in the NW row (**Fig.2**). In the SW/NE the menhirs are placed further apart than the other row. The two rows meet at a 90° angle, and the angles of the two rows are 23° and 67° to the horizontal, adding up to 90°.

The Egyptian Connection
The row SW/NE points 23°ENE, corresponding to the Southern Egyptian Empire at the Tropic of Cancer, located at 23°N. This important number can be found in the design of all important megalithic monuments. The other row points 67°NW, confirming the complementary latitude of 90-67= 23°N, where at midsummer day the Sun is directly overhead. The slow northern movement of the Sun turns into a southern movement, changing the season. Never before, have the authors seen a site where these two "holy" angles are so prominent in the site design. By these angles alone, we know for sure that this is a monument created by the megalithic culture, and the monument is concerned with the navigational problems of crossing the Atlantic Ocean.

These two angles also show that the creators of the monument were involved in the SunReligion. Directly below the SunGod Ra were two very different gods, Horus and Osiris, here represented by the two rows of menhirs at Leuré, intersecting at a right angle. The Kings of Egypt were the official substitutes of both gods. Including the central menhir, the NE/SW row has 5+1= 6 menhirs, corresponding to the Nile Delta, the Northern Egyptian Empire, at 23+6= 29°N. The 6 menhirs of the NW row, situated above

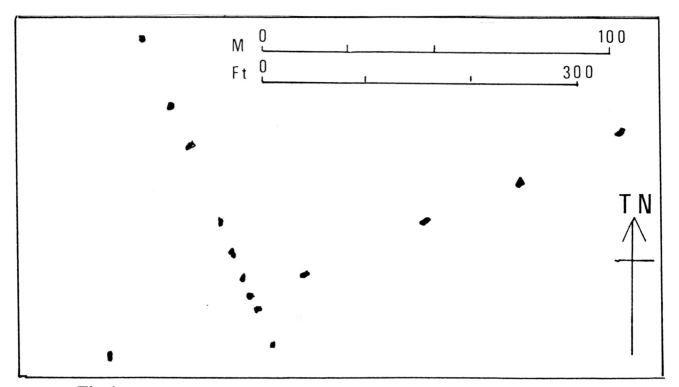

Fig.1
Groundplan of the intersecting menhir rows of Leuré (Ref.1).
(Leuré, Crozon, Crozon Peninsula, Finistère, Brittany, c.1900 BC)

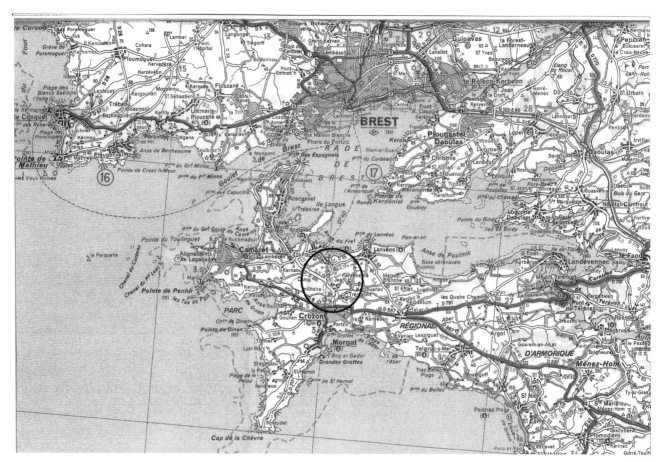

Map 1.   Location of destroyed site. (St.Jean, Crozon Peninsula, Brittany, C.1900 BC)

the NE row (the Tropic of Cancer), confirm the latitude of 23+6= 29°N. The 29 units also agree with the direction from Leuré, Brittany, to the center of the Southern Egyptian Empire, 29°ESE. The 23 units also agree with the direction to the center of the Northern Egyptian Empire, 23°ESE.

The Southern Crossing of the Atlantic Ocean

We know megalithic constructions are almost always mission monuments with religious and geographic meanings. Leuré is located only 10km from the west coast of Western Europe, and both alignments point to the huge Ocean to the west. The effort to discover what might be beyond this Ocean, what might be on the other side of the world, had been going on for thousands of years, as is shown by many megalithic monuments. The most row NE/SW points 23°WSW, also encoding the place where the Tropic of Cancer leaves the continent of Africa, at 23°N. At his latitude these people wanted to cross the Ocean to the Realm of the Dead, in honor of the SunGod (Refs.6-9). The God Ra is recorded in Egyptian Heiroglyphics as saying: "The Realm of the Dead is in the west, at the other side of the waters, in the land where the Sun sets." But crossing the water at this latitude had turned out to be very difficult, because this is the "horse latitudes", with its Sargasso Sea, in the center of circling currents. This is the space between countervailing tradewinds, where the horses died aboard sailing ships, and probably many heroes died in megalithic times, attempting this route.

The NE/SW row (5 stones) and the southern portion of the NW/SE row (6 stones) possess together 5+6= 11 menhirs, corresponding to the Bissagos Islands, at 11°N. From there the Ocean could be crossed. The whole monument has 5+9= 14 menhirs, corresponding to Cape Verde, at 14°N. This is the westernmost point of all continental land. From there it would be possible, too. Counting the central menhir twice, the number of menhirs total to 14+1= 15, corresponding to Brava, the SW Cape Verde island, at 15°N. This is the SW point of the Old World. The formerly mentioned 29 units also agree with the correct sailing direction from Brava to South America, 29°SSW. The NE/SW row has 5 menhirs in total, encoding Cape Sao Roque (the Holy Rock), Brazil, at 5°S, the place where they should arrive. This row represents the Southern Crossing of the Ocean, literally. It points 23°WSW, the direction of the smarter, alternative crossing, cutting the angle. In this context, the NW row represents the NE coast of South America, where the landing place is located.

Central America

The important NE/SW alignment and the south part of the NW row (N1-N6) total 5+6= 11 menhirs, corresponding to the latitude of the entry to the Carribbean, at 11°N. The 9 menhirs of the NW row correspond to the isthmus of Panama, at 9°N. Over this isthmus, people could cross to the Pacific (in the direction of the SW row). Counting the central menhir twice, the number of menhirs of the monument total to 14+1= 15, corresponding to Cape Gracias a Dios, the east cape of Honduras, at 15°N, the south border of the culture along the North Coast of Honduras, Belize, and Guatemala. This was the entry to the Realm of the Dead, the Land of Punt, the goal of the voyage.

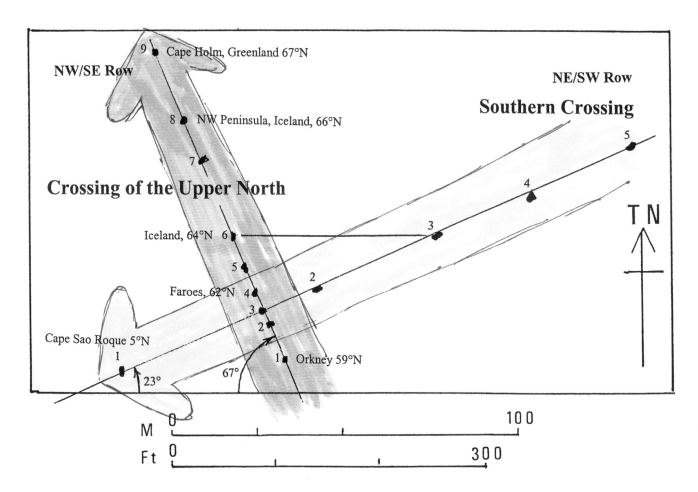

Fig .2
Figure 1 with angles and nomenclature and numbering added, for two Crossing routes to the West.

The Crossing of the Upper North

The north part of the monument, including the central menhir, has 4+7= 11 menhirs. Adding these northern stones to the site latitude of 48°N gives 48+11= 59°N, the latitude of the Orkney Islands. This archipellago is represented by the southern menhir NW1. From there the Ocean could also be crossed. The whole monument possesses 14 menhirs, corresponding to the Faroe Islands, at 48+14= 62°N. Counting the central menhir twice, the number of menhirs total to 15, corresponding to South Iceland, at 48+15= 63 N, NW5. The 67° Arctic Circle, minus 3 stones 1,2&3 gives the latitude of SE Iceland, at 67-3= 64°N, represented by menhir NW6. Menhir NW8 represents the NW peninsula of Iceland, at 64+2= 66°N. The whole row of stones points 67°NW in the direction of the crossing to Cape Holm, Greenland, represented by the last menhir NW9, and encoding its latitude at the Arctic Circle, at 67°N. This is the northernmost line where the Sun still shines at midwinter day. Also at this latitude people are able to cross the Ocean to the Realm of the Dead, in honor of the SunGod. The row points 67°NW, also encoding the shortest crossing from West Greenland to Baffin Island, again at the Arctic Circle, at 67°N. So, the NW row symbolises the complete Crossing via the Upper North. (The EW axis SW4-NW6 suggests an alternative crossing at 64°N, as shown at Lagatjar, and other monuments.)

Note, that the north part of the monument could also represent both coasts of South Greenland, literally. Menhir NW2 could be Cape Farvel, the south cape of Greenland, at 59+1= 60°N, and the central menhir NW3 could be the SW Cape of Greenland, at 59+2= 61°N. The westernmost menhir of the SW row would now represent the coast of Labrador, at 59-1= 58°N. The row itself gives the correct sailing direction of 23°WSW. For all these details to be understood, and incorporated, this monument must date from after the discovery of America, c.2500 BC, and we think probably it dates from c.1900 BC.

The Leure/Newfoundland Connection

The monument of Leuré was built here at 48°N, because there is something special at the other side of the Ocean. The East Cape of North America, Cape Race, Newfoundland is located at 48°N. The SW row can now be seen as the coast from Newfoundland to the south, while the NW row can now be seen as the coast from Newfoundland to the north.

Including the central menhir, the SW/NE row possesses 5+1= 6 menhirs, corresponding to Cape Cod, at 48-6= 42°N. The western menhir SW1 represents Cape Cod, literally. The central menhir NE2 is America's Stonehenge, and the south point of Nova Scotia, at 42+1= 43 N. America's Stonehenge is the most important megalithic monument of North America (Ref.19). It was definitely a "crossing point" for east and west voyages. Many ships depart from here to the West Azores. One prefers sailing via Sable Island, at 44°N (menhir NE3), 150km offshore Nova Scotia. However, one orients on Cape Race, Newfoundland, the East Cape of North America, at 47°N, represented by the last menhir NE6.

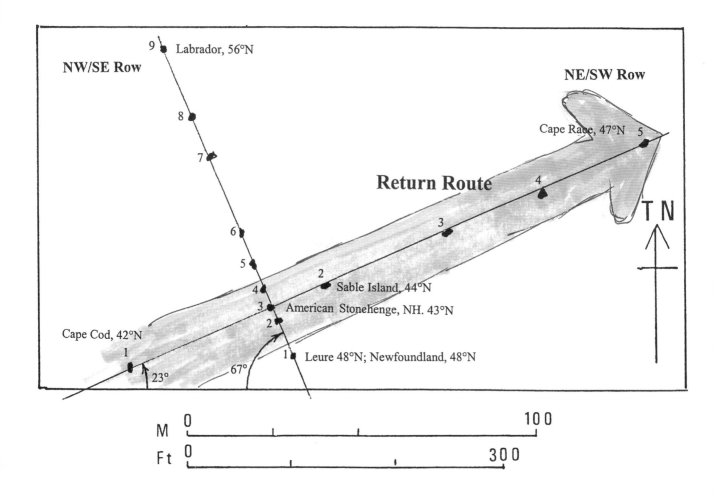

Fig.3
Figure 1 with angles and nomenclature and numbering added, for the Return Route via the Azores.

The Return Crossing via the Azores

The important NE/SW row represents the East Coast of North America, from Cape Cod to Cape Race, Newfoundland. This row points 23°ENE and has 5 menhirs, corresponding to the initial sailing direction from Cape Race to the West Azores, 23-5= 18°ESE, and to the sailing distance, 18dl= 2000km (both corresponding with the center of the Realm of the Dead, at 18°N). This is a long and dangerous crossing! The monument possesses 14 menhirs in total, in agreement with the terminal sailing direction in the neighborhood of the West Azores, 48-14= 34°SE. The difference between both sailing directions is due to the curvature of the surface of the Earth. The NW/SE row has 9 menhirs, encoding the West Azores at 48-9= 39°N, as well as the 9 islands of the Azores.

References

1. Burl, A., From Carnac to Callanish, The prehistoric stone rows and avenues of Britain, Ireland and Brittany, Yale University Press, 1993 (ISBN 0-300-05575-7)
2. Giot, P.R., La Bretagne, des Megalithes, Ed. Ouest France, 1995 (ISBN 2-7373-1388-0) (French)
3. Briard, J., The Megaliths of Brittany, Gisserot, 1991
4. Balfour, M., Megalithic Mysteries, Dragon's World (1992) (ISBN 1-85028-163-7)
5 An Approach to Megalithic Geography, Association Archeologique Kergal, Booklet No.20, 1992 (ISSN 0220 5939)(ISBN: 2902727.20.8)
6. Jonge, R.M. de, BRES 158, 1993 (Dutch)
7. Jonge, R.M. de, and IJzereef, G.F., De Stenen Spreken, Kosmos Z&K, Utrecht/Antwerpen, 1996 (ISBN 90-215-2846-0) (Dutch)
8. Jonge, R.M. de, and IJzereef, G.F., Exhibition: The Megalithic Inscriptions of Western Europe, 1996
9. De Jonge, R.M., and Wakefield, J.S, How the Sungod Reached America, A Guide to Megalithic Sites, MCS Inc., 2002 (ISBN 0-917054-19-9)
10. People of the Stone Age: Hunter-gatherers and Early Farmers, Weldon Owen Pty Limited, McMahons Point, Australia (1995)
11. Old World Civilizations/The Rise of Cities and States, Weldon Owen Pty Limited, McMahons Point, Australia (1995) (ISBN 90 215 2505 4)
12. New World and Pacific Civilizations. The Illustrated History of Humankind, Weldon Owen Pty Limited, Australia (1995) (ISBN 90 215 2512 7)
13. Casson, L., Ships and Seafaring in Ancient Times, British Museum Press, 1994
14. Wachsmann, S., Seagoing Ships and Seamanship in the Bronze Age Levant, College Station, Texas, 1998
15. Heyerdahl, T., The Ra Expeditions, George Allen & Unwin, London, 1971
16. Fell, B., America BC, Pocket Books, Simon & Schuster, 1994
17. Bailey, J., Sailing to Paradise, Simon & Schuster, 1994
18. Thompson, G., American Discovery, Misty Isles Press, Seattle, 1994
19. "Oldest City of America's confirmed, Peruvian complex contemporary with Egypt's pyramids." The Seattle Times, A4, April 27, 2001
20. Wallis Budge, E.A., Osiris and the Egyptian Resurrection, 2 Vol., 1911, Dover Pub., N.Y. 1973 (ISBN 0-486-22780-4)
21. Jairazbhoy, R.A., Ancient Egyptians and Chinese in America, Rowman & Littlefield, Totowa, N.J., 1974 (ISBN: 0-87471-571-1)
22. Gruener, J., The Olmec Riddle, An Inquiry into the Origin of Precolumbian Civilization, Vengreen Publications, 1987, Rancho Santa Fe, Cal. (ISBN 0-9421-85-56-0)
23. Giot, P.R., Prehistory in Brittany, Ed JOS (ISBN 2-85543--123-9)
24. Drier, R.W., Du Temple, O.J., Prehistoric Copper Mining in the Lake Superior Region, A Collection of Reference Articles, published privately, 1961, and reprinted in 2005
25. De Jonge, R.M., "Great Circle Mound: An Indiana Temple to the Egyptian SunGod?", Ancient American, Issue 60, Vol.9, pgs.31-32 (2004)
26. De Jonge, R.M., and Wakefield J.S., "The Discovery of the Atlantic Islands, Migration & Diffusion, Vol.3, No.11, pgs.69-109 (2002)
27. De Jonge, R.M., and Wakefield J.S., "A Nautical Center for Crossing the Ocean, America's Stonehenge, New Hampshire, c.2200 BC", Migration & Diffusion, Vol.4, No.15, pgs.60-100 (2002)
28. De Jonge, R.M., and Wakefield, J.S., "The Passage Grave of Karleby, Encoding the Islands Discovered in the Ocean, c. 2950 BC", Migration & Diffusion, Vol.5, No.18, pgs.64-74 (2004)

Fig.1 Aerial Photo of Menec, showing farm buildings in West Circle. The X cluster is within the lower half circle, and the E&F cluster is in the right circle. The fallen stone "O" is in the upper circle. From www.megalithic.co.uk

The Rows of Menec

The Royal Crossing of the Ocean
(The Rows of Menec, Carnac, Brittany, c.1800 BC)

R.M. de Jonge, rmdejonge@gmx.net
J.S. Wakefield, jayswakefield@yahoo.com
www.howthesungod.com

Summary

The monument of Menec is the most western and best preserved of the three row sets at Carnac, in Brittany, France. When the 1153 stones are seen to represent latitudes, the monument is found to be a mneumonic device that encodes sailing directions to the Azores, and the New World. The 12 rows symbolize the 12 islands on the crossing of the Ocean from NW Africa, via the Azores, to Newfoundland. The East and West Circles of Menec represent the Old and the New Worlds. The monument of Menec has the same shape as this crossing, and is essentially an arrow-shaped stone map of the Royal Crossing of the Atlantic Ocean in the Bronze Age.

Background

Huge stone rows, menhirs, chambers, tumuli and other ruins abound around the Gulf of Morbihan, Brittany, France. The stone rows are among the largest ancient ruins in the world, and cultural treasures. This area is considered the center of the coastal Megalithic Culture of Europe, which extended from Lixus, Morocco, to the Orkney Islands. The town around these ruins is named Carnac. The name of the holy center of southern Egypt is named Karnac. Egyptian ouchtabi figurines were found in Ploungonven Passage Grave in northern Brittany, now on exhibit the Museum in Quimper. We noticed a deeply carved fifteen-inch Egyptian anch carved into a French menhir nearby at the windsurfing site of Point de la Torche. With such considerable evidence for close cultural connections with Egypt, it would not be a surprise if the site of Menec is named for the first Pharoah of United Egypt, Menes, at c.3000 BC.

The best (but brief) description of the Carnac Rows is in the excellent 1993 book by Aubrey Burl, entitled From Carnac to Callanish, the Prehistoric Stone Rows and Avenues of Britain, Ireland and Brittany. Our studies are based upon the meticulous surveys and drawings done by Alexander Thom and his son Archie from 1970-1974, over the sites which stretch for 2 ½ miles. Without this survey work, further analysis could not be done. The meaning of the rows was lost after the end of the Bronze Age (1200 BC), so throughout the Celtic Iron Age and after the Roman Gallic War, the site was as mysterious as it is today. So these enormous ruins have been a tourist site for three thousand years, today drawing visitors from all over the world, every day. Roads and farm buildings have been built around and in the ruins, and today the rows are mostly fenced off, with observation towers built midway along the rows. Burl remarks that "the subject of megalithic rows is still an almost unstudied aspect of European prehistory", and that "Over the centuries interpretations of the rows have been neither numerous nor plausible". Indeed, we know of no scientific explanations to reference. Burl concludes,

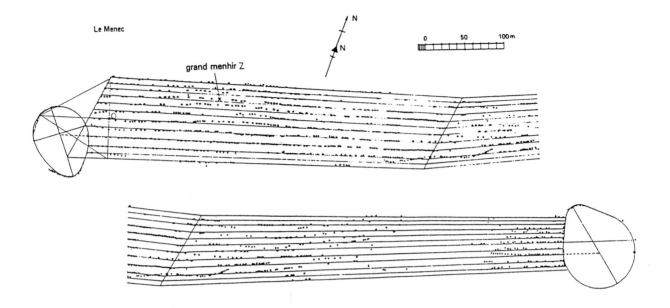

Fig.2 Groundplan of the monument of the Menec by Thom (Ref.5), with some lines added by the authors. It is an Arrow of about a kilometer length, pointing to the west. The Eastern Menhir Rows point to Sao Miguel (East Azores), and the Western Menhir Rows point to Pico (Central Azores). (Menec, Carnac, Brittany, c.1900 BC)

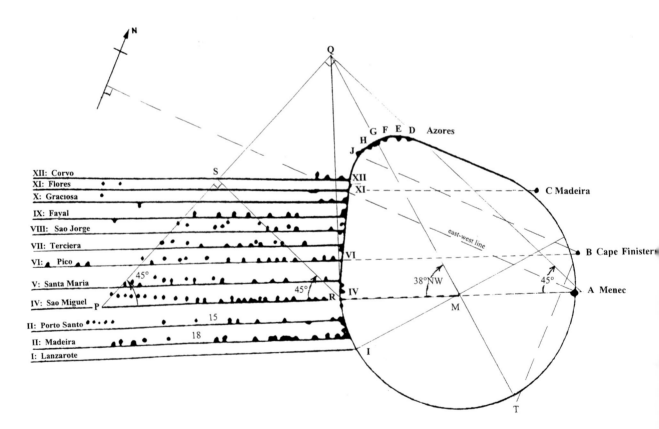

Fig.3 The East Side of Menec. It describes the crossing from the Menec (A) via Cape Finisterre (B), and the crossing via Madeira (C), to the 2 islands of the West Azores (rows XI and XII). (Menec, Carnac, Brittany, c.1900 BC)

however, that "The rows are prehistoric accretions whose successive builders were not obsessed with exactness". We think this is incorrect. Our study of these sites shows that they were very precisely designed, with very clear intentions behind the enourmous labor of their construction.

Site Description

The monument called "Menec" is located in Carnac, Brittany. It has a huge length of about a kilometer, and a tapering width of about 100 meters. It contains 12 almost parallel rows of 1061 menhirs. About in the middle, the rows are all a bit bent. The height of the menhirs increases gradually from less than a meter in the eastern ends of the rows, to more than 2.5 meters high in the western ends. The East Circle has only 13 menhirs, but the more important West Circle has 79 menhirs. East of the bend, the Eastern Rows have 361 menhirs, and west of the bend, the Western Rows have 700 menhirs. About halfway in the Eastern Rows is a gap of 85 meters length without a single menhir. East of it are only 136 menhirs, but in the remaining parts west of it are about 925 menhirs. The total number of granite menhirs in rows and circles of the monument amounts to 1061+13+79=1153.

The pear-shaped East Circle has a long head-axis of 110m, with at right angles a side-axis of 92m. The width of the rows increases from 65 m at the start in the east, to 85m near the bend, and up to102m at the end in the west. The egg-shaped West Circle has a short side-axis of 70 meters, with at right angles a head-axis of 92 meters.

The rows should be counted upward, from south to north, as will be explained, and are labeled with Roman Numerals. Rows I and II have only 20 and 35 menhirs, so they do not appear to be very significant. Row IV has the highest number of menhirs (150), and it connects the centers of both circles. The central row VI (118 menhirs), starts at the first (most easterly) menhir of the East Circle, and finishes at the top of the West Circle.

Geographic Meaning

During the megalithic period, the oceans were being explored, in attempts to learn what was on the unknown backside of the Earth. From our study of many monuments and petroglyphs, we have found that most of these contain geographic information that record these explorations (How the SunGod Reached America, A Guide to Megalithic Sites, 1982). This monument of Menec is situated in Brittany, near the sea. The rows of stones form a huge arrow, pointing to the Azores Islands in the west. So it appears this monument also deals with the crossing of the Ocean.

We study the architecture of megalithic monuments. Nearly all megalithic monuments contain the angle or stone count of 23 in their designs. This is known today as the Tropic of Cancer, the highest latitude reached by the sun in the summer, the most important fact in the science of celestial navigation, which was obviously important to these people. We think offshore explorations of the oceans were probably first undertaken at this latitude. Unfortunately, this led them to the Doldrums, the windless area between the tradewinds. Some followed birds or light winds to the north, which led to their early discovery of the Azores Islands. The 39-stone monument of Gavrinis, with its 23 highly decorated stones,

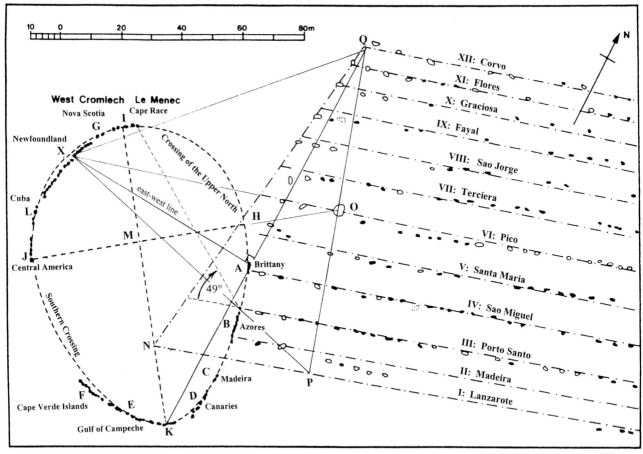

Fig.4 The end of the Western Menhir Rows, and the West Circle of the Menec. At the edge of the Circle are two clusters of menhirs. Group A represents Brittany, and the 3 groups of the western cluster are 'at the other side of the sea'. (Menec, Carnac, Brittany, c.1900 BC)

Fig.5 Photo of fallen Menhir "O", looking east from the West Circle, up row VI (left), and row V (right). (Menec, Carnac, Brittany, c.1900 BC)

also located in Carnac, is the monument built to the discovery of the Azores at 39°N in 3600 BC (for a full explanation of Gavrinis, see How the SunGod Reached America). In this way, the Azores became the most western known land on Earth for nearly the next thousand years.

At the time of the construction of the Menec, the Azores were the famous island group in the middle of the Ocean. The Western Rows have twice as many menhirs as the Eastern Rows, so the western direction is strongly emphasized by the monument. This is confirmed by the height of the menhirs, which slowly increase from less than 1 meter in the east, to 2.5 meters in the west. The Eastern Rows point between 25.5° and 23° WSW, which is the actual direction from the Menec to Sao Miguel, the main island of the East Azores. The Western Rows point between 19° and 17.5° WSW, which is the actual direction from Menec to Pico, the main island of the Central Azores.

From previous work, we suspect that the two stone circles at he ends of the Rows of Menec probably each represent the spherical Earth. It has been thought in the literature, that these were incomplete stone circles, with many stones taken for construction. But this article will show that they make a lot of sense as they are. The huge menhirs on their edges symbolize "land", and "water" where stones are lacking. Both circles have menhirs on their eastern and western sides. So, both circles deal with the crossing of the Ocean, from lands on the east to lands in the west.

When one projects the whole monument of Menec on a chart of the North Atlantic Ocean, the shape of the rows is similar to the crossing of the Ocean. The 12 rows of menhirs represent the crossing via the 1+2+9= 12 islands of the eastern middle Atlantic Ocean, each row representing an island. The southern row I is Lanzarote, the eastern Canary island, rows II and III are the 2 islands of Madeira, and rows IV to XII are the 9 islands of the Azores, which are located more to the north.

Between both circles, the important central row VI has a length of 489 meters in the east, and 453 meters in the west (ratio= 1.080). The distance from NW Africa to the West Azores amounts to 2193km, and the distance beyond to Newfoundland is 2047km (ratio= 1.071). The stone rows show the distances across the Ocean with an error of less than 1%. Note that the latitude of the Menec monument is the same as the latitude of Cape Race, the SE cape of Newfoundland, both at 47° N. The total length of the monument, via the central row, with both circles included, is 1111 meters. This distance exactly equals 0.01 dl= 0.01° of latitude, 1/100 of the Egyptian unit of one moira, the distance of one degree, a very important unit of length among the megalith builders.

The monument of Menec is situated on slightly sloping terrain. The East Circle, the bend, and the West Circle are located more or less on hill tops, and the middles of the rows are lying in shallow valleys in between. Although the height differences do not exceed 5 meters, they can be clearly seen at the site. This situation is clearly illustrated with a special menhir row on the south side of the bend. The shape of this bent row, having a length of 140 meters, provides a height profile of the Menec. It is also the height profile of the crossing of the Ocean from NW Africa, via the West Azores, to Newfoundland.

Fig.6 Photo of Menhirs F and E, of West Circle, the Gulf of Campeche (Mexico), and Cape Verde Islands (Menec, Carnac, Brittany, c.1900 BC)

Fig.7 Photo of Menhirs J,L, and X, of West Circle, Central America, Cuba, and the American coast to Newfoundland (Menec, Carnac, Brittany)

This bent row possesses 39 menhirs, corresponding to the latitude of the West Azores, at 39°N. As said before, this bend represents the location of the West Azores, literally.

Religious meaning

The two lower rows I and II (Lanzarote and Porto Santo in the Canaries) contain very few menhirs. The coastal island of Lanzarote was not considered especially important. For that reason, Menec can be seen to possess not 12, but 11.5 rows. As a consequence, the eastern and western sections of the monument add up to (2 x 11.5 =) 23 rows, corresponding to the Tropic of Cancer, and the Southern Egyptian Empire, at 23°N. The total number of menhirs around the East Circle is 23, and the upper eastern row XII (Corvo) makes an angle of 23°, both confirming this important latitude. This repeated use of the number 23 shows their level of navigational skill, as well as widespread belief in the SunGod religion., which became especially developed in Egypt.

The monument of Menec also resembles a huge, ritual boat, from stem to stern (from West to East Circle) made of planks (rows), seen on the port side. This ritual boat is meant for crossing over the waters to the Realm of the Dead, as shown in so many Egyptian petroglyphs. Since the overall site is a stone map of the Ocean, this is a reasonable double meaning.

Directly below the SunGod Ra were two other gods, Horus and Osiris. In a symbolic way, the East Circle is the Empire of the Living of the Sungod Horus, and the West Circle is the Realm of the Dead of the Moongod Osiris. But the course of these gods over the waters was the important focus of this monument, so the rows have much larger and more stones than the circles. This all was the work of the Earthgod Maat, creator of the East and West Circles. So the many menhirs may also represent the people. As in the army they are all lined up in rows for the Sun, shining daily in the south for the supreme God Ra. The Moongod Osiris is represented by the enormous menhir O. He is the ruler of the Realm of the Dead (the West Circle). The Sungod Horus, the large menhir Z, helps him in his difficult voyage to reach this goal.

The important Western Rows of the Menec represent the long crossing from the West Azores to Newfoundland (c.2050 km). However, this crossing is against the governing winds and currents. The megalith builders could not sail this difficult windward route. They had learned to cross to the west by the Route of the Upper North, or by the Southern Crossing, in accord with the tradewind patterns of the Oceans. In the time period when the Menec was built, their vessels had been returning from Cape Race, Newfoundland by the route of Menec to the Azores for c.600 years. They thought nobody could accomplish this crossing in western direction, except the King. So they believed it was a "Royal Crossing". In this manner he could have directly reached the Realm of the Dead. It is carved into an Egyptian temple that the SunGod Ra has said: "The New King will appear in the Realm of the Dead in the west, at the other side of the waters, in the land where the Sun sets." So basically, the monument of Menec is a rock map of the Royal Crossing to the Realm of the Dead.

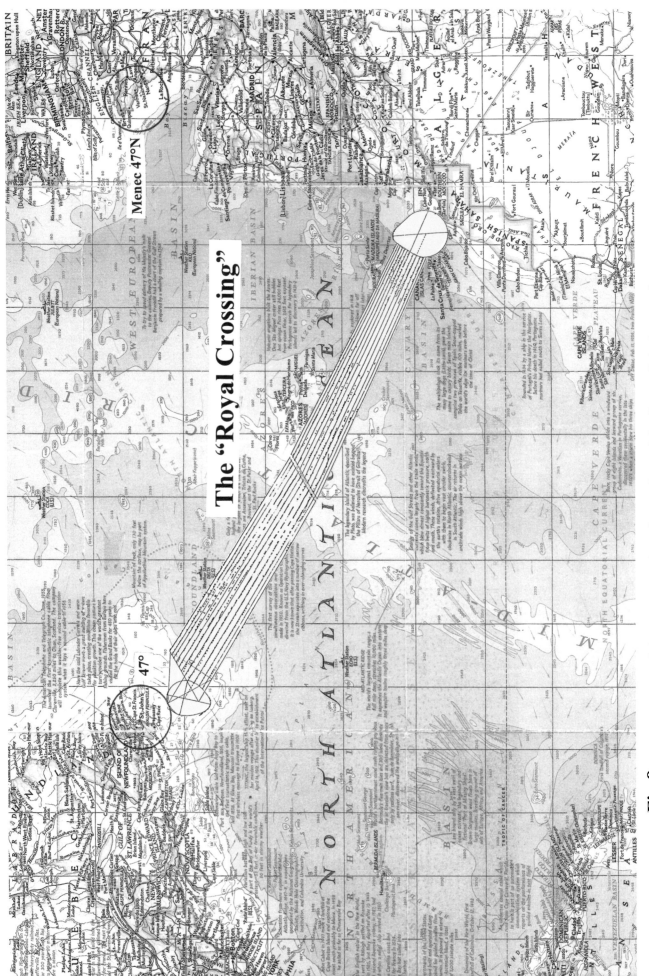

Menec 47°N

The "Royal Crossing"

47°

Fig.8 The monument of the Menec, projected on a chart of the Ocean. It is the crossing
from the Old World (NW Africa), via the bend (the West Azores), to the New World
(Newfoun land), with 12 menhir rows (via 12 islands The bend in the rows of the Menec

The eastern side of Menec

These stones deal with the Crossing of the Ocean to the West Azores, and beyond.The pear shaped East Circle of the has 9 free standing menhirs at the east and north sides, and also a number of menhirs at the start of the rows at the west side. Here, the total n-s width of the rows is 65 meters. The long, eastern rows have a gap of 85 meters. East of the gap and over a length of more than 100 meters is a group of 136 menhirs. The East Circle and this group of menhirs are called the East Side of the Menec.

The East Circle of the Menec symbolizes the spherical Earth with the big ocean in it.. In the east is Western Europe (menhirs A and B), in the west is North America (the start of the rows), and in between are the islands in the Ocean (menhirs C and D-J). In view of the many big menhirs in lowest row II one has an important goal in Central America. This row has 18 menhirs corresponding to the civilization around the south point of the Gulf of Campeche, the center of the Realm of the Dead, at 18°N. Row III has less and smaller menhirs, refering to a less important goal. This row has 15 menhirs, corresponding to the culture along the north coast of Honduras, at 15°N. Row IV possesses 25 menhirs, so it appears people want to reach these goals via the south point of Florida, at 25°N. However, these issues are important for the future. Here, at the East Side of the Menec, the provisional goal is the 9 islands of the Azores. For that reason there are besides rows II and III, 9 other rows IV-XII.

The huge easternmost menhir A represents the site of Menec itself, in Brittany. The menhir is situated at the very start of important row IV. All eastern rows of the Menec with 361 menhirs, and especially row IV, point 25°WSW to the main island of the East Azores, Sao Miguel. That is the first goal of a sailing voyage.

Menhir B is situated at the very start of central row VI. It represents Cape Finisterre, the NW cape of Iberia. It is the most logical point of departure for crossing to Sao Miguel. Cape Finisterre (menhir B) is located more to the west than the Menec (menhir A), and it is closer to the Azores (menhirs D-J). The NS-line from menhir B (Cape Finisterre) cuts the head-axis at the base of the Circle in point T. This head-axis, line TQ, runs through these menhirs D-J, and points 38°NW, encoding the Azores, at 38°N. This is the main goal at the East Side of the Menec. So, in general people sailed from Cape Finisterre toward Sao Miguel, the first island of the Azores.

The isosceles triangle AQP has base angles of 45°, because the direct sailing direction from the Menec to Cape Finisterre is 45°SW. The figure contains the 9 rows IV-XII, confirming that people sail from Cape Finisterre to the 9 islands of the Azores. Menhir C has a special position. This stone represents Madeira, important for travelers coming from the Mediterranean (Egypt). Madeira (menhir C) is located more to the west than Cape Finisterre (menhir B), and closer to the Azores (menhirs D-J).

The Twelve Rows

In view of the absence of any menhirs in row I, people do not bother about Lanzarote, the island close to the shore of NW Africa. Row II possesses more and bigger menhirs than row III. So, row II represents the main island of Madeira, and row III is the side island of

Porto Santo. Row IV running from big menhir A to the west, has more menhirs than row V. So, row IV represents the larger main island of the East Azores, Sao Miguel. Seen from Menec (menhir A), it is the first island of the Azores. Row V is automatically the other and smaller island of Santa Maria. At the very start of central row VI is the first menhir B of the monument (Cape Finisterre). Out of the next five alignments, row VI possesses the highest number of menhirs. So, it symbolizes the main island of the (Central) Azores, Pico. Row VII is the easternmost island of the Central Azores, Terciera. Row VIII represents the neighboring island of Pico, Sao Jorge. Row IX possesses big menhirs, so it represents the westernmost island of this group, Fayal. Row X has only a few menhirs, so it represents the northern and distant island of Graciosa. At the very start of row XI is menhir C. So this row represents the main island of the West Azores, Flores. The last row XII automatically represents the other and smaller island of Corvo.

Menhir A

Huge menhir A (Menec) is an angular point of the large triangle AQP. The 45° angle at A and the 2 menhirs above it, add to 45+2= 47 units, corresponding to the latitude of the Menec, at 47°N. Rows II (Madeira), III (Porto Santo), and V (Santa Maria) possess together 18+15+14= 47 menhirs, confirming this latitude. These are exactly the islands one does not visit, when sailing from Menec to the West Azores. Menhir A is situated at the very start of the most important row IV (Sao Miguel), having the highest number of menhirs. This row points (together with the other eastern rows with 361 menhirs) 25°WSW, directly from the Menec to Sao Miguel, the main island of the East Azores. Row IV (Sao Miguel) possesses 25 menhirs, confirming this direction. This is the first goal. The EW-line from menhir A runs to the start of row XI (Flores). So the final goal from the Menec is this main island of the West Azores. (Sailing directions are illustrated in our campanion article, on the Rows of Kerlescan.)

Cape Finisterre (Menhir B)

The 45° angle at A encodes the sailing direction from the Menec to Cape Finisterre, 45° SW. The important rows II (Madeira) and IV (Sao Miguel) possess together 18+25= 43 menhirs, corresponding to the latitude of Cape Finisterre, at 43°N. (Again, Madeira is the island one does not visit on this route.) Below and beside big triangle AQP are 18+15+8+2= 43 menhirs, confirming this latitude. Menhir B represents Cape Finisterre, literally. This menhir is situated at the very start of central row VI (Pico). Below this alignment are 4 rows of menhirs II-V, again confirming the latitude, 4° south of Menec, at 47-4= 43°N. This row VI possesses 19 menhirs, corresponding to the initial sailing direction (ISD) from Cape Finisterre to Sao Miguel, 19°WSW. The row points (together with the other western rows with 700 menhirs) 19° WSW, strongly confirming this important sailing direction! Rows III (Porto Santo) and V (Santa Maria) have together 15+14= 29 menhirs, in agreement with the terminal sailing direction (TSD) in the neighborhood of Sao Miguel, 29°WSW. (Again, these islands are not visited.) The difference is due to the curvature of the Earth. Within triangle RSP, refering to Cape Finisterre, row VI (main island) has 13 menhirs, corresponding to the sailing distance from Cape Finisterre (menhir B) to Sao Miguel, 13dl= 780 NM (Nautical Miles).

This Menhir B, which represents Cape Finisterre at 43°N, is situated at the very start of central row VI (the main island of Pico). This important row runs all the way to huge Menhir O , close to the West Circle, and beyond it to a menhir on the western side of the West Circle, which will be shown to be the south point of Nova Scotia at 43°N, and also the location of America's Stonehenge at 43°N. (America's Stonehenge, on the coast of New Hampshire, was the largest megalithic structure in North America, and, as we have shown, a teaching center for this return sailing route To the West Azores from the New World.)

Within triangles AQP and RSP are 9 rows, corresponding to the 9 islands of the Azores, and to the latitude of Sao Miguel and the Central Azores, 9° south of the Menec, at 47-9= 38°N. The head-axis of the Circle makes an angle of 38°, confirming this latitude. This angle also equals the sailing direction from Sao Miguel to Terciera, 38°NW. Rows IV (Sao Miguel) and VII (Terciera) possess together 25+13= 38 menhirs, confirming the sailing direction from Sao Miguel to Terciera, and their latitude. The 2 rows IV (Sao Miguel, East Azores) and VII (Terciera, Central Azores) correspond to the sailing distance between these islands, about 2dl = 2moira = 120NM.

Row VII (Terciera) has 13 menhirs, corresponding to the sailing direction to the next island, Sao Jorge, 13°WSW. Row VI (Pico) possesses 19 menhirs, corresponding to the sailing direction from Sao Jorge to this main island, 19°WSW, and further from Pico to Fayal, 19° WNW. Rows VI (main island) and VII (Terciera) possess together 19+13= 32 menhirs, encoding the sailing direction from Terciera to the northern and distant island of Graciosa,32°NW.

Rows VI (Pico) and IX (Fayal) possess together 19+9= 28 menhirs, encoding the sailing direction from Fayal to the West Azores, 28° WNW. Fayal is the western neighboring island of Pico. Rows VII (Terciera) and VIII (Sao Jorge) possess together 13+12= 25 menhirs, corresponding to the sailing direction from Sao Jorge (and Terciera) to the West Azores, 25° WNW. Rows IX (Fayal) and X (Graciosa) possess together 9+4= 13 menhirs, corresponding to the sailing direction from Graciosa to the West Azores, 13° WNW. (On the distant island of Graciosa one appears to orient on Fayal, the westernmost island of the Central Azores.) In all cases the 2 rows involved correspond to the sailing distance from the Central to the West Azores, about 2dl = 120NM.

Rows IV (Sao Miguel) and V (Sta Maria) possess together 25+14= 39 menhirs, corresponding to the latitude of the West Azores, 39°N. These base rows of the Azores provide the latitude of the goal. The East Side of the Menec has 8 rows II-IX with many menhirs, confirming this latitude, 8 south of the Menec, at 47°-8= 39°N. The EW-line from menhir B (Cape Finisterre) runs towards the last and westernmost menhir J of the Circle, Corvo, the goal of the voyage.

Madeira (Menhir C)

Because of the presence of menhir C (Madeira), the route via this island to the Azores will be examined, too. The southern row I represents Lanzarote, the eastern Canary island. This alignment contains 3 menhirs in its eastern part, but east of the gap, the row is empty. So, Lanzarote does not seem to be considered of any importance for the crossing to the Azores. However, the row is present, because the side-axis through the middle M of the Circle starts at this very row at point I. Rows III (Porto Santo) and V (Santa Maria) possess together 15+14= 29 menhirs, corresponding with the latitude of Lanzarote, at 29°N. Both islands are important for the sailing route from Lanzarote.

Rows II (Madeira), IV (Sao Miguel), and V (Santa Maria) contain together 18+25+14= 57 menhirs, in agreement with the sailing direction from Lanzarote to Madeira, 57°NW. Rows II (Madeira) and III (Porto Santo) possess together 18+15= 33 menhirs, corresponding to the latitude of these islands, at 33°N. The sailing distance from Lanzarote to Madeira equals the difference in latitudes, about 33-29 = 4 moira = 240 NM.

Outside the large triangle AQP, rows II (Madeira), III (Porto Santo), and VI (main island of Pico) contain together 18+15+3= 36 menhirs, in agreement with the initial sailing direction (ISD) from Madeira to Sta Maria (East Azores), 36°NW. The latitude of Lanzarote is in agreement with the terminal sailing direction (TSD) in the neighborhood of Sta Maria, 29°NW. In this calculation rows III (Porto Santo) and V (Santa Maria) were involved. There are 8 rows II-IX with many menhirs, and there are 8 menhirs west of the triangles, both corresponding to the sailing distance from Madeira to Santa Maria, 8dl= 480NM.

Rows II (Madeira) and VI (main island of Pico) possess 18+19= 37 menhirs, corresponding to the latitude of Sta Maria, at 37 N. The sailing direction from Sta Maria to Sao Miguel equals that of Lanzarote to Madeira, 57 NW. In the calculation rows IV (Sao Miguel) and V (Sta Maria) were involved. Menhir C (Madeira) is situated at the very start of row XI (Flores), showing that also in this case the goal is to reach the West Azores. Row VI (Pico) has 19 menhirs, also corresponding to the distance from NW Africa to the West Azores, 19dl= 1140 NM.

The Sun Religion
Rows V (Santa Maria) and IX (Fayal) produce together 14+9= 23 menhirs, corresponding to the holy Tropic of Cancer, and the Southern Egyptian Empire, at 23°N. Rows VI (Pico) and VIII (Sao Jorge) of the largest islands of the Central Azores, consist together of 19+12= 31 menhirs, corresponding to the Nile Delta, the Northern Egyptian Empire, at 31° N. Rows II (Madeira) and IX (Fayal) have together 18+9= 27 big menhirs, corresponding to the United Egyptian Empire, at 27°N. This center is located halfway the Tropic of Cancer and the Nile Delta. In the calculations, Madeira and Sta Maria are involved, because these islands are important in the sailing route from Egypt, via Gibraltar, to the Azores. Row IX (Fayal) is twice involved, because it contains big menhirs, as well as big menhir Z near the West Circle (Sungod Horus).

The top row XII (Corvo) makes an angle of 23°, also encoding the Tropic of Cancer, at 23°N. Together with base row II (Madeira) they possess 18+5= 23 menhirs, confirming this latitude. At midsummer day the Sun is directly overhead at 23°N. The slow northern movement of the Sun then turns into a southern movement, and the seasons xhange. The prevalence of these references to 23°, shows that the monument builders were involved in a sunreligion. In an Egyptian tomb it is written that SunGod Ra has said: "The New King will appear in the Realm of the Dead in the west, at the other side of the waters, in the land where the Sun sets."

After the gap, east row IV (Sao Miguel) contains 23 menhirs, also encoding the holy Tropic of Cancer and the Southern Egyptian Empire, at 23°N. The whole east row II (Madeira) with 23 menhirs confirms this latitude. After the gap, east row V (Santa Maria) contains 31 menhirs, encoding the Northern Egyptian Empire, at 31°N. The whole east row X (Graciosa) with 31 menhirs confirms this latitude. After the gap, east row X (Graciosa) contains 27 menhirs, encoding the United Egyptian Empire, halfway the Tropic of Cancer and the Nile Delta, at 27°N. The whole east rows VI (Pico) and VII (Terciera) contain both 39 menhirs, twice emphasizing the importance of the West Azores, at 39°N.

Newfoundland

The East Side of the Menec provides the routes from Cape Finisterre and Lanzarote to the West Azores. Routes beyond these islands are not given here, because the East Circle and the long eastern rows symbolize the Old World and the crossing to the West Azores. However, the start of row XI high in the East Circle represents the east coast of America at a high latitude. Menhir C has been placed at the very start of this row. The EW-line from big menhir A (Menec at 47°N), runs to the start of row XI, now representing Cape Race, Newfoundland, at the same latitude as the Menec, at 47° N.

Rows III (Porto Santo) and VI (main island of Pico) possess together 15+19= 34 menhirs, encoding the initial sailing direction (ISD) from the West Azores to Cape Race, Newfoundland, 34 NW. Row III contains the bent row, symbolizing the West Azores. Important row IV (Sao Miguel) and row IX (Fayal, big menhirs) possess together 25+9= 34 menhirs, confirming this direction. Rows VII, VIII, and IX, the top rows with many menhirs, contain together 13+12+9= 34 menhirs, confirming this direction again.

Row II (Madeira) possesses 18 big menhirs, encoding the terminal sailing direction (TSD) in the neighborhood of Cape Race, 18°WNW, as well as the sailing distance involved, 18dl= 1080 NM. Row VI (main island of Pico) has 19 menhirs, confirming both the approximate terminal sailing direction (TSD), and the distance.

The western side of Menec

The long rows of menhirs (the central one 949 m) finish at the West Circle of Menec. The menhirs in the rows are large, as they approach this circle. Farm buildings now occupy the center of this circle. At the edge of the circle are two clusters of menhirs, an east side cluster of 45 stones, and a west side cluster of 45 stones. The menhirs are of about the same size as those of the East Circle, and about half as big as those in the Western Rows.

As in the East Circle, the authors have added some lines to the surveyed figure by Thom. In the central row VI (main island of Pico) is a surprisingly big menhir O (now fallen). For that reason a line is drawn from menhir O to the lowest menhir J of the western cluster. The piece of line HJ is the side-axis of the egg. The perpendicular line through its center M runs to the head-axis K of the circle. The lowest row I is extended to point N on the head-axis. Line QN coincides with the most western menhirs of rows VIII to XI.

Next we connect the central row to menhir X of the western cluster. The perpendicular of row VI in O is the piece of line PQ across the full width of the rows. Finally, the equilateral triangle PQX is drawn. Now, the monument of the Menec is an enormous Arrow pointing to the islands of Azores in the south west. Finally, line AX is drawn; this is the EW-axis of the circle. Line AK is the NS-axis.

The West Circle: The Azores
The most important row IV (Sao Miguel) finishes at the West Circle at group A of the eastern cluster. Angle POA1 is 49°, corresponding to the latitude of North Brittany, at 49° N. The A group consists of 3 stones, so is representing the 3 latitudes of Brittany at 47°, 48°, and 49°N. The central row VI (main island of Pico), and with it the enormous Arrow of the Menec, finishes at point X of the western cluster. This cluster is situated at the other side of the egg, so in respect to Brittany (group A) at the other side of the sea. So, the whole cluster represents the Azores. As far as the menhirs are concerned, 3 main groups are distinguished, of which the central main group has been placed slightly to the front. So, these menhir groups represent the 3 island groups of the Azores, with in the center the Central Azores. The enormous Arrow of the Menec also points literally to the Central Azores, confirming this, because the west part of row VI points 19° WSW to the main island of Pico. The angle JOX is19°, confirming this direction.

Important row IV (Sao Miguel) points with its eastern part 25° WSW to Sao Miguel, the main island of the East Azores. Angle JOG at the West Circle also is 25°, confirming this. So, the 2 eastern groups of menhirs I and G represent the 2 islands of the East Azores (Sta Maria and Sao Miguel). And also, the 2 western groups of menhirs L and J represent the 2 islands of the West Azores (Flores and Corvo). And finally, the 5 central subgroups around point X, placed to the front, represent the 5 islands of the Central Azores.

The Eastern Cluster, the East Side of the Ocean
The crossing-route from Brittany to the Azores has been indicated at the East Circle. Then at the West Circle, we do not expect the Azores at the west side, but rather at the east side. And indeed, below the 3 menhirs of Brittany (A)is a group of 9 menhirs (B), representing the 9 more southerly located islands of the Azores. The menhirs can be counted correctly as latitudes, to be precisely below 50° N, starting with menhir A1. Menhir A3 (of Brittany) represents the Menec itself, at 50-3= 47°N. Row II (Porto Santo) finishes at menhir B8 (of the Azores). This menhir provides the latitude of the West Azores, at 47-8= 39°N, and the last menhir B9 of this group gives the latitude of the (Central) Azores, at 47-9= 38°N.

Below it is a group of 2 menhirs (C), representing the 2 southerly located islands of Madeira. However, menhir C1 gives the latitude of Santa Maria (East Azores), at 38-1= 37°N, and menhir C2 that of the Strait of Gibraltar, at 38-2= 36°N.

Below it is a group of 7 menhirs (D), representing 7 southerly located Canary Islands. When counting the menhirs, menhir D3 provides the latitude of Madeira, at 36°-3= 33°N, and the last menhir D7 gives the latitude of Lanzarote (the NE Canary island). This is also the latitude of the Nile Delta, the center of the Northern Egyptian Empire, both at 36° -7= 29°N. Most of the menhirs of this group are placed outside the egg, because the majority of the Canary Islands do not play a role in the story of Menec.

At the next group menhir K3, at the lower end of the head-axis, represents the United Egyptian Empire, halfway between the Nile Delta and the Tropic of Cancer, at 29°-3= 26°N. It is the location of the center of government. The last menhir K6 symbolizes the Tropic of Cancer, at 29°-6= 23°N.

At the next group menhir E5 provides the latitude of the center of the Realm of the Dead, at the other side of the Ocean (**Fig.10**), at 23°-5= 18°N. This center of civilization around the south point of the Gulf of Campeche, Mexico, is the focus of this monument. Menhir E7 gives the latitude of the Cape Verde Islands at 23°-7= 16°N, and also the latitude of the culture along the North Coast of Honduras.

The next menhir E8 is situated on the line QN, and is also the last stone on the edge of the egg. This gives the latitude of Cape Verde, the westernmost point of all continental land, of the Southern Cape Verde Islands, and also of Cape Gracias a Dios (Honduras), at 23°-8= 15°N.

The next group F of 10 menhirs represent the ten Cape Verde Islands. The first 6 menhirs are the 6 Northern Cape Verde Islands, the remaining 4 menhirs denote the 4 Southern Cape Verde Islands. These last islands may be used as the start of the Southern Crossing to South America. The total number of menhirs of the eastern cluster, 45, agrees with a possible sailing direction, 45°SW. However, the 10 menhirs of the archipelago are placed outside the egg, because these do not play a role in the story of Menec.

Menhir F2 represents Cape Gallinas, the north cape of South America, at 15°-2= 13°N. Menhir F6 represents the mouth of the Orinoco River, and the isthmus of Panama, both at 15°-6= 9°N. This last location is of great importance for the coastal navigation of the Pacific. The last menhir F10 provides the latitude of the coast of French Guyana (South America), at 15°-10= 5°N. This usually is the most important landing point of the Southern Crossing from the Cape Verde Islands.

The West Circle is symbolic for the southern part of the Ocean. The bottom part of it is narrow, because people knew the Southern Crossing between Africa and South America. The East Circle is symbolic for the northern part of the Ocean. The top part of it is narrow, because people knew the crossing of the Upper North, via Iceland and Greenland. However, both crossings are not as important in the monument, because the Menec is a great Arrow, pointing to the Azores.

The Western Cluster, North America

The 9 menhirs of group B at the east side of the egg represent the 9 islands of the Azores. As a result of this new insight the western cluster at the other side now represents the East Coast of North America, at the other side of the Ocean. Line AX is the EW-axis of the circle. So the enormous Arrow of Menec now points to Newfoundland, at the same latitude as Brittany, at 49°N! Newfoundland is the easternmost landmass of North America, and now it is represented by the central group of menhirs around point X, placed to the front. This all sounds very logical, because the whole monument of the Menec represents the crossing from NW Africa, via the West Azores, to Newfoundland, and the monument was built in Brittany, which is located at the same latitude as Newfoundland.

However, the easternmost group of menhirs of this western cluster is not situated near X, but literally around point I (**Figs.9,10**). When positioning the protractor along important row III, menhir B1, the American East Coast (the western cluster) is being observed from the northernmost island of the West Azores, Corvo. Menhir I at the other side now makes an angle of exactly 49°, so it corresponds to Newfoundland at the other side of the Ocean, at 49°N. So, the 3 menhirs east of the head-axis represent the 3 latitudes of Newfoundland, at 47°, 48°, and 49° N, which are comparable with the 3 menhirs of Brittany (group A). However, the great question is, how do we sail from the West Azores (menhir B1) to Newfoundland (menhir I3)?

The great crossing from Corvo, West Azores, to Cape Race, Newfoundland, against the wind and the current, is the most important subject of the monument of the Menec. This long and difficult voyage is represented by the Western Rows. These contain twice as many menhirs as the Eastern Rows, the menhirs are on the average twice as big, and the end of the rows is about twice as broad as at the start, on the East Side. The Great Secret of how this direct crossing to the west could be done by the Gods, against the winds and currents, is indicated by the enormous Arrow of Menec! This Arrow points to the western cluster, which has 34 menhirs, corresponding to the Initial Sailing Direction (ISD) from the West Azores to Cape Race, 34° NW. The Arrow especially points to the group of 18 menhirs of the central group X, placed to the front. This number agrees with the Terminal Sailing Direction (TSD) in the neighborhood of Cape Race, 18°WNW. The difference between both sailing directions is due to the curvature of the surface of the Earth. The 18 menhirs of group X also correspond to the sailing distance, 18dl= 18 moira (=1080 NM). The uppermost west row XII (Corvo) makes an angle of 18, confirming this terminal sailing direction (TSD), and the sailing distance.

The groups of menhirs of the western cluster represent the important coastal areas of North America. Group I is Newfoundland, group G is Nova Scotia, main group X is the mainland of North America, group L is Cuba, and group J is Central America. Further details of the American coast can be found in the details of the monument, but are too much detail for this article.

Besides huge menhir O in the central row VI (main island of Pico), there is another surprisingly big stone, namely menhir Z in row IX (Fayal). Both great menhirs are located in the Western Rows, but there is a big difference. Menhir O is situated close to the West Circle, and it has clear functions in the construction of the equilateral triangle PQX, and in the explanation of the meaning of the Circle. Menhir Z, situated in the western part of row IX , in a field of small menhirs, gives a confirmation of the whole story by its angles with the West Circle. Our study shows that it emphasizes the important latitude of 18°, the location of the civilization of Central America, and the latitude of 30°, the Mississippi delta, the destinations of these sailing voyages.

Dating

Each stone in the construction of Menec is used to represent one degree of latitude, not multiple latitudes, as was done later at some other sites to save labor. Details of the American Coast and Mississippi which are encoded in this monument, but not the more easterly Kerlescan Row, indicate this was a later monument. The monument of Kermario, between Menec and Kerlescan, is disturbed, so is hard to study. It appears Menec is a "better" monument, which had been built with new energy and new information, closer to the Ocean. In view of the theme of the "Royal Crossing", the most probable date is c.1800BC.

References

1. De Jonge, R.M., and Wakefield, J.S, How the SunGod Reached America, A Guide to Megalithic Sites, MCS Inc., 2002 (ISBN 0-917054-19-9)
2. Batt, M., and others, Au Pays des Megalithes, Carnac-Locmariaquer, Jos, 1991 (French)
3. Briard, J., The Megaliths of Brittany, Gisserot, 1991
4. Giot, P.R., Prehistory in Brittany, Ed JOS (ISBN 2-85543-123-9)
5. Thom, A., "Megalithic Geometry in Standing Stones", New Scientist, Mar. 12, 1964.
6. Burl, A., From Carnac to Callanish, The Prehistoric Stone Rows and Avenues of Britain, Ireland and Brittany, Yale University Press, 1993 (ISBN 0-300-05575-7)
7. Bailloud, G., et.al., Carnac, Les Premieres Architectures de Pierre, CNRS Edition, 1995 (ISBN 2-85822-139-1) (French)
8. Fell, B., America BC, Pocket Books, Simon & Schuster, 1994
9. Bailey, J., Sailing to Paradise, Simon & Schuster, 1994
10. Thompson, G., American Discovery, Misty Isles Press, Seattle, 1994
11. Jairazbhoy, R.A., Ancient Egyptians and Chinese in America, Rowman & Littlefield, Totowa, N.J., 1974 (ISBN 0- 87471-571-1)
12. Cartographia Kft., 1:400.000, Budapest, 1995 (ISBN 963-352-9808 CM)
13. De Jonge, R.M., and Wakefield, J.S., "The Discovery of the Atlantic Islands", Migration & Diffusion, Vol.3, No.11, pgs.69-109 (2002)
14. De Jonge, R.M., and Wakefield, J.S., "The Passage Grave of Karleby, Encoding the Islands Discovered in the Ocean, c. 2950 BC", Migration & Diffusion, Vol.5, No.18, pgs.64-74 (2004)
15. De Jonge, R.M., and Wakefield, J.S., "A Nautical Center for Crossing the Ocean, America's Stonehenge, New Hampshire, c.2200 BC", Migration & Diffusion, Vol.4, No.15, pgs.60-100 (2002)
16. www.megalithic.co.uk/modules/My_eGallery/France?Brittany/Carnac

A "Royal Ship" c.2500 BC, Life Magazine, "History of Egypt", painting by X.Gonzales

Crossing the Labrador Sea
(The Stone Rows of Lagatjar, Brittany, c.1600 BC)

R.M. de Jonge, drsrmdejonge@hotmail.com
J.S. Wakefield, jayswakefield@yahoo.com

Summary

The megalithic monument of Lagatjar is located on the west coast of Brittany, just south of Brest, France. It consists of three rows of large standing stones. It is widely thought that the monument was largely destroyed, with no hope of ever understanding its meaning. In this article it is shown that the rows are almost fully intact, and that the stones (representing degrees of latitude) were carefully placed to create a map of lands on both sides of the Atlantic Ocean. The monument describes the routes for crossing the Ocean via the Upper North. It was built to celebrate a new shortcut route for Crossing of the Labrador Sea, a new sailing route to America. This shortcut to the Realm of the Dead in the West was discovered during the 16th and 17th Dynasties of Egypt. The discovery enabled easier transatlantic shipping of copper, drugs, and other goods from America to the peoples of the Old World.

Introduction

The rows of Lagatjar (groundplan, **Fig.1**) are located on a bluff between a beach and the village of Camaret-sur-Mer on the western tip of Crozon Peninsula, in Western Brittany (**Map 1**). You can see the stone rows in **Photo 1**, from the air (Google Earth). The Crozon Peninsula, with its former Nazi submarine base at Isle Longue, is now home to the French nuclear submarine fleet. The Pointe de Penhir, south of the stone row site, has spectacular sea cliffs that attract young mountain climbers. **Photo 2**, which we took on our trip in May of 2005, shows a beach to the south of the monument. There are Nazi bunkers with a U-boat museum, and an enormous memorial statue of a strong Breton woman breaking the chains of Nazism from her wrists.

Lagatjar consists of three long rows of standing stones (see **Fig.1**): one long row pointing SW (205m, or 216 yds), and, at its west side, roughly at right angles, two shorter rows pointing NW. The stones are not dressed, but are rough and weathered. They are a hard, bright, white quartzite. We have numbered the stones in each row, and beside each stone is the encoded latitude. The long row is divided into three sections. We have labeled these from north to south: A, B, and C, with 18, 16, and 14 stones in them, for a total of 48. On the west side of this row, reaching WNW toward the Ocean, are the two shorter rows with larger stones. We have labeled the north one D, with 13 stones (60m, or 63 yds), and the south one E, with 16 stones (65m, or 68 yds). On the groundplan there are another 5 stones, three huge ones in a southern row (F1, F2, F3), one (G) to the north, and one (H) near row B.

The groundplan of Lagatjar we are using is reproduced from a book by Burl (Ref.3). He says the recorded survey was done by Devoir (Refs.4-7) who claimed "the orientations are exact to one or two degrees". Burl reports that "at the beginning of the century, many of the stones were prostrate, but they were re-erected by Pontois in 1928". In that year,

Photo 1 The Rows of Lagatjar (c.1600 BC) near Camaret, on the west point of the Crozon Peninsula, in West Brittany, France. (Google Earth)

Lagatjar was officially designated a "Historic Monument". We found the site to closely match the survey, though row A is now about half incomplete, and the isolated menhirs G and H have disappeared. ("Menhir" is the French word for a single tall standing stone.) This has been a military neighborhood through two World Wars, and a lot of stone buildings have been built nearby. The stones of row A were close to a road, and most vulnerable being taken for building material. We note that the western menhir of row F is now about ten meters southwest of its position on the groundplan. The original positions of menhirs can be established by surveyors through the identification of the "setting stones", which were stones originally placed in the hole around the base of each menhir, to help hold them upright. We can trust these surveyors not to place a menhir in a position in their groundplan that appears out of place, without finding the setting stones in that position. The best information is to rely on the survey, despite some discrepancies with the site seen today.

Sailing from Brittany to Greenland

The long row ABC of Lagatjar might represent the west coast of Europe. It has 48 menhirs, encoding the latitude of Lagatjar, at 48°N. (As usual with megalithic sites, the latitude of the monument is included in the site design.) The short rows D&E, attached on the west side of long row ABC, have the largest menhirs. They are not completely straight, which makes the exact angles imprecise, but both point c.32°NW, roughly in the direction of the Labrador Sea, at the other side of the Ocean. This Sea can be approached by the "Upper North Sailing Route", which is via the Faroe Islands and Iceland. This direction to the Labrador Sea appears to be the most important meaning of the monument (see **Map 2**). This does not surprise us, because we know this maritime culture was exploring the Ocean (Refs.1,2,27-32), and here is a major monument they constructed on the West Coast of Western Europe, on the western tip of Brittany, close to the Ocean.

The Labrador Sea can be approached via the Upper North route. To do this, people had to sail northward from Lagatjar, to the northwest. So upper row D, with its northwestern orientation,shows the way. Its direction of 32°NW encodes the complementary latitude of the North Coast of Scotland, at 90-32= 58°N, located due north of Lagatjar. From this coast, or its offshore islands, the Hebrides, they set off for the Upper North. The 13 stones of row D, added to the long row, encode the latitude of the sea between the Shetlands and the Faroe Islands, 13° north of Lagatjar, at 48+13= 61°N. Perhaps by this date they skipped the megalithic communities in the Orkneys, a bit east at 59°N. The Faroes are small, and only visited when crossing the Ocean. These islets were considered in the area of East Greenland (see **Map 2**). Note that the entire upper V-shaped portion of the monument resembles the coastal profile of south Greenland (shaded in **Fig.1**). The remainder of this voyage to south Greenland is illustrated in row A (East Greenland).

In row A each stone of the row represents one degree of latitude, with the latitudes getting smaller, as they sail south. The upper, northeastern stone A1 represents the Faroes, at 48° (the starting latitude) +13° (sailed to the north)= 61, +1 (this stone)= 62°N. The second stone A2 represents one degree of latitude at Sea, so 63°N. The 3rd stone A3 is the SE Coast of Iceland at 61+3= 64°N. People sailed around the west coast of Iceland (A4) at 65°N, to the NW peninsula of Iceland (A5) at 66°N. Five small stones follow

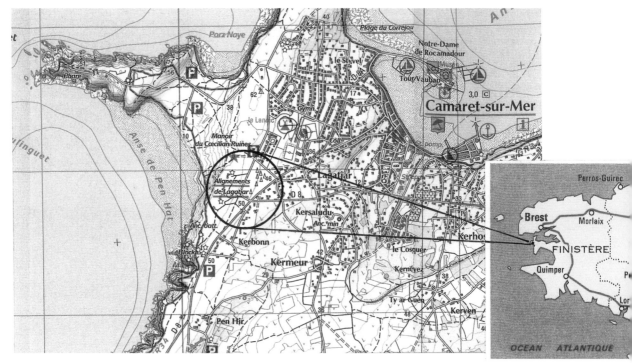

Map 1   Geographic position of the monument of Lagatjar on the west end of the
Crozon Peninsula, in West Brittany (Ref.8). The rows are situated c.1km from the coast,
at the east side of a small bay.
(Camaret, Brittany, c.1600 BC)

Photo 2   A beach south of the site, typical of the area, showing WWII defensive
works in the foreground. (Crozon Peninsula, Brittany, May 2005)

(6,7,8,9,10), five more degrees of latitude, encoding the crossing to Cape Holm, Greenland, a sailing distance of 5 moiras = 5° = 300 NM, which is correct. (The moira is the ancient Egyptian unit of measure of the distance on Earth's surface of an arc of one degree, and the Nautical Mile (NM) is defined as 1/60th of the arc of 1°.) Big Menhir A11 beyond these little stones represents Cape Holm, at 66+1= 67°N, the latitude of the holy Arctic Circle. This is the northernmost line where the Sun still shines at midwinter day. This latitude has a special meaning in the Sunreligion of the Megalithic Culture.

Cape Holm (A11), at 67°N, is the northernmost latitude of the Upper North Route. From here, the east coast of Greenland was then followed to the south, so subtract the remaining seven stones (18-11= 7) when going south, so 67-7= 60°N, the latitude of Cape Farvel, the South Cape of Greenland. This sailing route to Greenland was known prior to 3200 BC, as shown by the monument of Stonehenge I, England, and by the petroglyphs of Loughcrew, Ireland (Refs.1,2, 27-32).

The West Coast of Greenland

As shown on **Fig.1**, row D represents the west coast of Greenland with 13 big stones. Above Cape Farvel (A18, at 60°N), the stones D1 and D2 of this row are the habitable West Capes of Greenland, at 61°N and 62°N. The three megalithic rings in the Orkneys show that these West Capes became more important than Cape Farvel (Refs.30,32). When one sees the progression of these people's seafaring experience in their monuments, it makes it possible to put the monuments in historical sequence, and helps date them. The Vikings later reported finding stone buildings in these fjords, when they rediscovered Greenland about 2500 years later (Ref.20).

The northernmost last stone D13 of the D row may represent the end of the ice-free West Greenland shore, at 60+13= 73°N. The Labrador Sea had been approached by boats via the "Upper North" sailing route since c.3200 BC, as shown by the petroglyphs at Loughcrew, Ireland (see "How the SunGod Reached America", Ref.1). Known as "The Wall" in the great sailing ship days, the Labrador Sea had its worst fogs and icebergs in July of each year. This is because the biggest temperature differences between sea currents in the world occur here between the south-flowing Labrador Current, and the north-flowing Gulfstream. This fearsome "wall" was not crossed by megalithic sailors for more than 700 years (from 3200 BC to 2500 BC) (Refs.18, 24-26). After their discovery of America via the Aleutians in the west (c.2600 BC), as discerned in the petroglyphs of Dissignac, France (Refs.1,2), the Upper North Sailing Route was chosen as the preferred sailing route for extending exploration toward the newly discovered continent. It was apparently always considered to be treacherous, however. The Greek historian Plutarch (90AD) writes that "the sea at this point is difficult to be crossed by great vessels, and the opinion arose in ancient times that it was frozen (Ref.37).

Crossing the Davis Strait at the Arctic Circle

In the middle of row D, on the west side of Greenland, is a big pointed menhir D7, clearly seen in **Photo 3**, on the left. It indicates the sea-crossing at the holy Arctic Circle, at 60+7= 67°N. Previously, as we sailed down the east side of Greenland (row A), stone A6 was part of a distance measure, of the sea between Iceland and Greenland. Now we

Photo 3 View to NW, up row D. It represents the West Coast of Greenland. Dr. De Jonge has his hand on stone A18, the departure point from South Greenland. (Lagatjar, Brittany, c.1600 BC, May 2005)

see that A6 also symbolizes the Arctic Circle, 1° above the NW peninsula of Iceland (A5), at 66+1= 67°N. Line A6-G is at right angles to row A, so menhir G (at the top of **Fig.1**) also represents the East Coast of Greenland, at 67°N. The EW axis from A6 meets the NS line from G at big menhir D10, the latitude of huge Disko Island (West Greenland, row D), which strongly supports this conclusion. Surely the success they had in finding Greenland from Iceland at 67°N, would have led them to first try to cross Davis Strait at this same holy latitude. As their luck would have it, this was the shortest crossing, of only 3 Egyptian moiras (180 NM), as correctly indicated by the 3 stones (G, D13, and E16). The SunGod had shown them the way to the Realm of the Dead in the west (America). Notice that the end of row E bends to the north, just as does the Baffin Island shoreline at Cape Dyer (E16).

The whole southwestern portion of the Lagatjar monument represents North America (the lower colored block in **Fig.1**). Row E, representing the Baffin Island and Labrador coasts, has 16 stones. In the north, this coast ends curved out to Cape Dyer at 67°N. The coast runs southeast 16 stones, or 16 degrees, to stone E1. Note that the largest stone in the row, E9, at 60°N, encodes the most important Cape Chidley, at the northern end of the Labrador coast. Going down row E in **Fig.1**, we find stone E2 at 53°N, the closest Labrador Coast, and the last small stone E1, which is the small island of Belle Isle at 52°N, which marks the end of the Labrador coast, at the entrance to the more protected inland waters behind Newfoundland.

Row C starts with the large stone C14, shown in Photo 4, the big menhir on the left. This is the latitude (51°N) of Belle Isle Strait, the beginning of the east coast of America to the south. Large menhir C10 represents important Cape Race, at 47°N, the easternmost point of land of North America, and the departure point for return voyages across the Gulfstream to the West Azores. Notice this is emphasized by a 90° angle at C10, to the East Azores (F3). Similarly, C9 is perpendicular to the Central Azores (F2) at 38°N. Note the 38° true north line from H to F1, giving the correct latitude of the Central Azores, and C8 is perpendicular to the West Azores (F1), which are at 39°N. Stone C6, down 8 stones at 43°N (51°-8= 43°) is the location of the most important Bronze Age site on the American coast, America's Stonehenge, where mariners learned how to sail the return route, and made sacrifices to ensure their safe passage (Refs.1,28). C4 at 41°N encodes Long Island Sound and the mouth of the Hudson River at that latitude. Note that C1 is at 38°N, the latitude of Chesapeake Bay, while large stone C2 is at 39°N, the latitude of Cape May, and Delaware Bay. The site design reveals a 38° angle from row ABC to the huge stones of the F row, the Azores, which lie in the Ocean at 38°N. Rows E, C, and F total 33 (16+14+3= 33), encoding Madeira at 33°N, which completes the route to the Old World.

The Old Crossing of Davis Strait

We have studied other monuments, which show that these people learned to "cut the corner" by crossing Davis Strait at 65°N (Refs.30-32). We think this was done for a very long time, from c.2500 BC to c.1600 BC, so approximately 900 years! That is why we call this the "Old Crossing". This latitude is indicated by the 25° angle of row A to menhir H, showing the complementary (90-25= 65) 65°N latitude across Davis Strait.

4

Photo 4 View NW, up row E. It represents the coasts of Labrador and Baffin Island. Menhir C14 (left) represents the end of the Crossng of the Labrador Sea (row B to right). (Lagatjar, Brittany, c.1600 BC, May 2005)

Photo 5 View of row C from the south. Note the 3 Azores Menhirs to the right, and the perpendicular rows D&E behind Dr. De Jonge, which run to the west. (Lagatjar, Brittany, c.1600 BC, May 2005)

Notice that A4, representing the West Coast of Iceland at 65°N, is on an east-west axis with D13, so that now a line connecting G, D13, and E16 can also be seen as the crossing line at 65°N. Now E16 can be seen as Cape Mercy, Baffin Island.

It would be nice to explain the monument in a simple way. But we have to note that these monuments were designed with multiple meanings, and are not so simple as we might wish. We have seen so many multiple meanings, that we can only conclude that, to the builders, multiple meanings increase the "holiness" of the monuments. They try to record their stories in "permanent" huge rocks for posterity, and the more clever the sites become, the more special the site becomes. Their culture was thousands of years old. They had no idea that four thousand years later, man would have huge machines and weapons that could ruin their enormous "permanent" monuments.

By re-counting the stones 2° to the south, geographic locations can be identified down the American coast. Big menhir E12 is now the entrance to Hudson Strait at 61°N, E3 is Belle Isle at 52°N, C14 is Cape Freels, Newfoundland, at 49°N, C8 is America's Stonehenge at 43°N, while the line C8-F1 shows the best Return Route, with the wind and current, from America's Stonehenge to the West Azores, F1 (Ref.28). The southernmost menhir C1 is Cape Hatteras North, the East Cape of the US, at 36°N, the same latitude as the Strait of Gibraltar. These latitudes were in common shipboard use at the time.

The New Crossing of the Labrador Sea

Row ABC (48) plus row D (13) also encode their common menhir A18 as the inhabitable fjords of the Southwest Cape at 61°N (48+13= 61). This was important, because this was the actual departure point for the crossing of the Labrador Sea. Note that the tallest menhir (D8) of row D, clearly seen on the left in **Photo 3**, would represent the south point of Disko Island at 61+8= 69°N, known to be an important hunting area, and a reference point for explorations further north.

Row B is the result of a discovery that it was possible to sail this new route from the SW Cape (A18) directly to America (C14) without sailing further north (ship icons, **Fig.1**). This new shortcut route is the reason this monument was built. Note that there are gaps at both ends of row B, that it is not contiguous with the lands, and that it is made of small stones, because here there is no land, only Sea. Row B lies at an angle 29° SSW of true north. Note that this cleverly confirms the departure point of 90-29= 61°N. From the West Cape of South Greenland, the East Cape of Labrador actually lies at an angle of 29° SSW, so the layout of row B is correct on a modern map (**Map 2**). The correct sailing direction from Cape Farvel to Belle Isle Strait is 48°SW, which is perhaps also encoded in the 48 menhirs of row ABC. This row is associated with the large offset menhir H, so it represents the important island of Newfoundland, the most eastern Cape of North America, and important in the return route to the West Azores.

Row B has 16 menhirs, encoding the 16/2= 8 degrees of latitude on this route. Because of the difficult sailing circumstances in the area, and because this is the focus of the monument, half degrees of latitude and half moiras are used here (Refs.1,2). The sailing

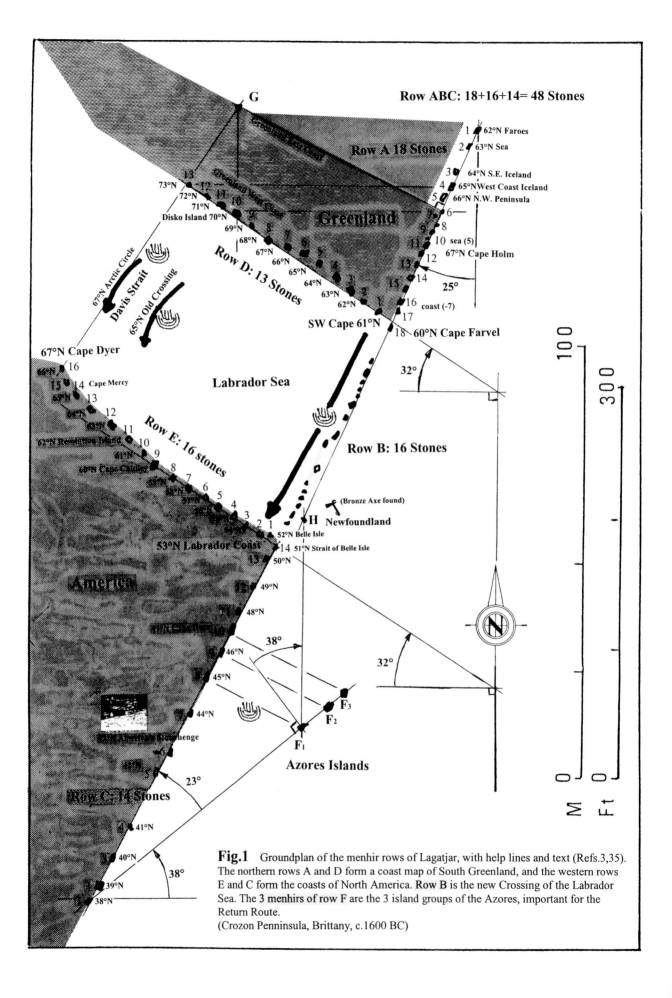

G

Row ABC: 18+16+14= 48 Stones

Row A 18 Stones

1 62°N Faroes
2 63°N Sea
3 64°N S.E. Iceland
4 65°N West Coast Iceland
5 66°N N.W. Peninsula
6
8
10 sea (5)
11
12 67°N Cape Holm
13
14
15 25°
16 coast (-7)
17
18 60°N Cape Farvel

Greenland

73°N
72°N
71°N
Disko Island 70°N
69°N
68°N
67°N
66°N
65°N
64°N
63°N
62°N
SW Cape 61°N

Row D: 13 Stones

67°N Arctic Circle
Davis Strait
65°N Old Crossing
67°N Cape Dyer

66°N
15 14 Cape Mercy
65°N 13
64°N 12
63°N 11
62°N Resolution Island 10
61°N 9
60°N Cape Chidley 8
59°N 7
58°N 6
57°N 5
56°N 4
55°N 3
54°N 2
1
53°N Labrador Coast
13
14 51°N Strait of Belle Isle
50°N

Row E: 16 stones

Labrador Sea

Row B: 16 Stones

32°

(Bronze Axe found)

H Newfoundland
52°N Belle Isle

America

49°N
48°N
47°N
46°N
45°N
44°N
American Stonehenge
43°N
42°N
Row C: 14 Stones
41°N
40°N
39°N
38°N

38°
32°
23°

N

F₃
F₂
F₁

Azores Islands

100
300

M
Ft

Fig.1 Groundplan of the menhir rows of Lagatjar, with help lines and text (Refs.3,35). The northern rows A and D form a coast map of South Greenland, and the western rows E and C form the coasts of North America. Row B is the new Crossing of the Labrador Sea. The 3 menhirs of row F are the 3 island groups of the Azores, important for the Return Route.
(Crozon Penninsula, Brittany, c.1600 BC)

route goes to the protruded coast of Labrador, at 61-8= 53°N. This is the East Cape of the mainland of North America, just north of Belle Isle, which would soon be found upon sailing to the south. Because of the southwestern direction of row B, the sailing distance is slightly longer than the difference in latitudes: together with menhir H, row B has 16+1= 17 menhirs, corresponding to the correct sailing distance of 17 half moiras, or 17x30= 510 Nautical Miles.

Re-counting the stones 2° to the north shows menhir C8 to be Cape Race, Newfoundland, at 47°N, and the line C8-F1 shows the shortest crossing of the Ocean, with the wind and the current, to the West Azores (ship icon, F1). The southernmost menhir C1 becomes the East Coast of the US at 40°N, and when counting is continued to row F, F1 is correctly the West Azores at 39°N, F2 is the Central Azores at 38°N, and F3 is the East Azores at 37°N. These were well-known latitudes at the time, essential stopping points on the voyage home.

Dating

The discovery of America via the Atlantic Ocean dates from c.2500 BC (Refs.1,2), so Lagatjar was built after that date. Devoir reported that a bronze axe was found underneath a 6m menhir in row B, which dates the monument in the Bronze Age (Refs.5,6). Burl states that monuments like this one, with single rows are always late megalithic, almost all of them between 2000 and 1500 BC (Ref.3). Devoir and Lockyer (Refs.5-7) believed Lagatjar contained a direction toward the midsummer sunset (rows D and E) in 1600 BC. Burl (Ref.3) confirms this statement, but in his opinion "1600 BC (is) an improbably late date". However, in our view, this date of 1600 BC may well be correct. The rows of Tormsdale, Scotland, of this date, only indicate the old crossing of Davis Strait at 65°N (Refs.31,36).

Perhaps the stone counts are also indicating Egyptian Dynasties. The Egyptian historian and High Priest of Heliopolis, Manetho (c.300 BC), wrote in Greek a history of Egypt in sequentially numbered Dynasties, which still is the way we organize Egyptian Pharonic history. This appears to have been a common dating methodology. Row B, which symbolizes the important Crossing of the Labrador Sea, has a total of 16 menhirs, which by this method, would date this monument to the 16th Dynasty of Egypt (c.1611-1580 BC). Row E also has 16 menhirs. If you include menhir H in row B, you have 16+1= 17 menhirs, encoding this Crossing in the 17th Dynasty, which ruled almost simultaneously. Rows C and F have 14+3= 17 menhirs too. Thus these row counts may be additional evidence that the monument of Lagatjar dates from c.1600 BC.

Discussion

Megalithic people are widely regarded in the literature as being very sensitive to inclusion of natural landscape features on their site designs (Refs.12-17). Lagatjar is situated between the Pointe du Toulinguet (to NW), and the Pointe de Penhir (to SW), both projecting into the Sea (**Map 1**). The short sea crossing between these points of land appear to be a parallel symbolism to the design of this monument, which is about the sea crossing between two points of land. About 10km further to the west is the Pointe de St. Mathieu in the north, and Pointe du Raz in the south (not shown on **Map 1**). The sea

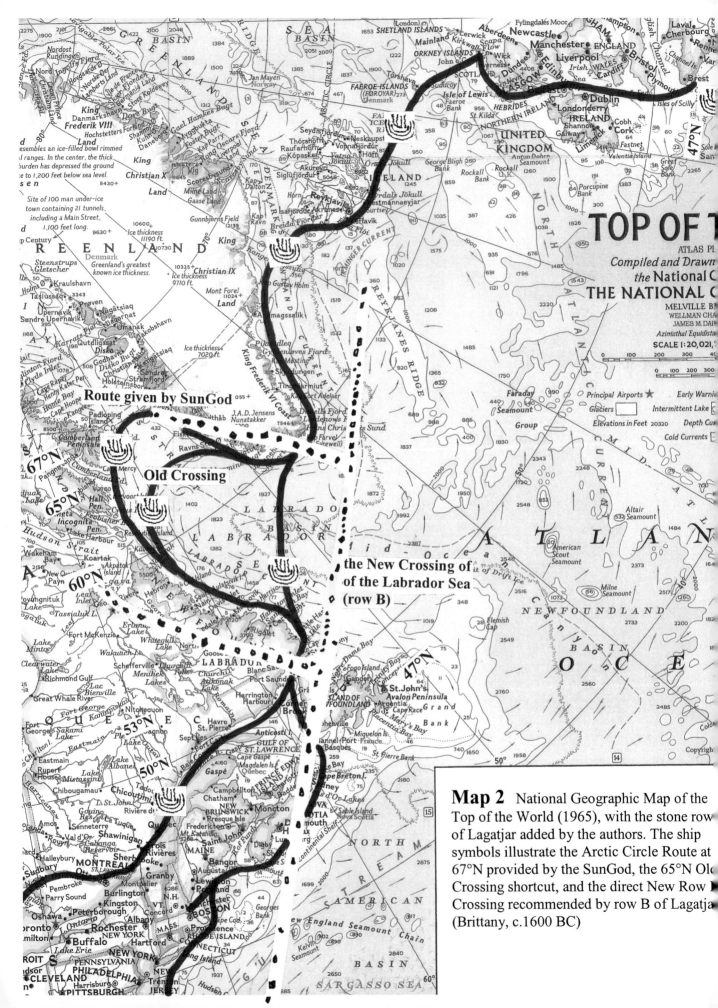

Map 2 National Geographic Map of the Top of the World (1965), with the stone row of Lagatjar added by the authors. The ship symbols illustrate the Arctic Circle Route at 67°N provided by the SunGod, the 65°N Old Crossing shortcut, and the direct New Row B Crossing recommended by row B of Lagatjar (Brittany, c.1600 BC)

crossing between these points is also symbolic of this New Crossing. The name "Crozon" for this peninsula may be related to the word "Crossing", so important in this ancient monument.

In his book Megalithic Brittany (Ref.11), Aubrey Burl claimed that there are "some 100 stones [at Lagatjar], and that there were once perhaps three or four times that many, with the others taken for walls, roads, and buildings nearby". Later, he states that "a little south of the middle of the longest line there had been a 6m (20ft) high pillar, "La Pierre du Conseil", broken up in the mid-nineteenth century. Devoir (who did the survey) stated that "a bronze axe was found underneath it". We do not know if the bottom portion of the pillar remains, or whether Devoir left it off the groundplan, or whether it is missing stone H (which would be the best confirmation). We have not heard of a megalithic pillar consecrated by burial of a bronze axe below it before, but it would be hard to have a more credible witness to the story than Devoir, the surveyor of the site. This burial of a bronze axe is very compatible with a 1600 BC mid-Bronze Age date.

Although many stories have appeared that the menhir rows are heavily disturbed, that does not appear to be true, since the site makes sense as it is. Also, because of the careful restoration by Pontois in 1928 (Ref.4), the monument appears to be almost standing in the original state, except for the missing stones of Row A and at G and H. The speculation (without evidence) that many stones were removed is not justified. Probably, it was thought to be disturbed because of its unusual design that was not understood.

The monument has upper and lower portions, showing two continents, and can also depict the twin-gods of Egypt. In Egypt, below the SunGod Ra were two other gods, Horus and Osiris here dramatized in this monument, which has two parts. Horus was the god of the Old World and the Land of the Living, here represented by the land on the right, South Greenland. Osiris was the god of the New World and of the Realm of the Dead, here represented by the land on the left, America (Refs.1,2). The SunGod Ra has told (hieroglyphs, in Egyptian tombs): "The Realm of the Dead is in the west, at the other side of the waters (row B), in the land where the Sun sets. After death you will reunite there with your ancestors, your family, your relatives, your friends, your acquaintances!"

Trading was also a motivating factor for Egyptian voyages. The cocaine and other New World drugs found in hundreds of Egyptian mummies, were intended to help the deceased persons reach paradise, given their effects when taken by live persons. After extensive study, researcher W.J. Perry (Ref.33) concluded that obtaining these drugs was an important motivation for these sailing voyages to the Americas.

The details of the Lagatjar site show it to be a geographic map, a walk-in map set in stone. We have shown this to be true at some other megalithic sites, notably the Rings of Brodgar, Stenness, and Bookan on the Orkney Islands (Refs.30,32), and America's Stonehenge in New Hampshire (Refs.1,28). These sites have documented astronomic orientations, and Lagatjar has been found to have them too (Refs.3-7).

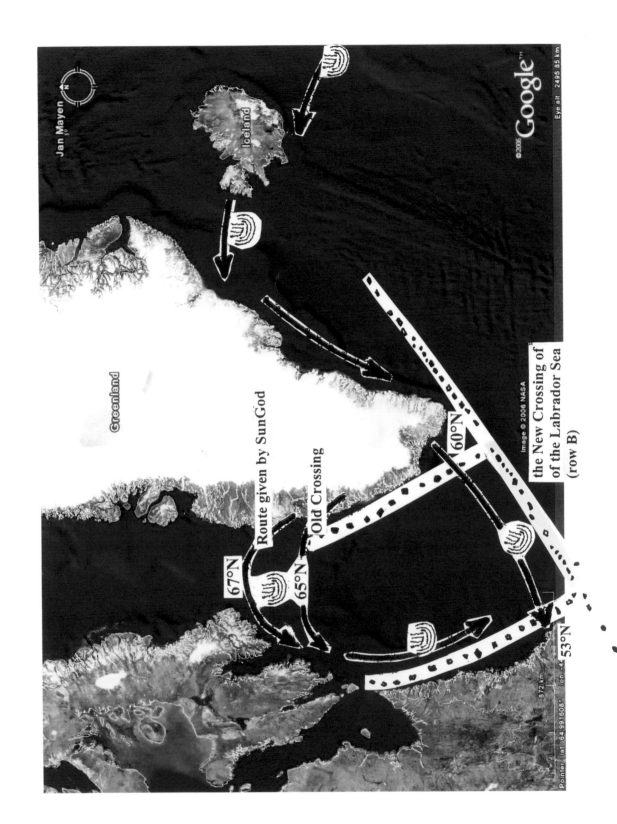

the New Crossing of
of the Labrador Sea
(row B)

The enormous Bronze Age trade in copper (2400-1200 BC) may have been near its height at the date of this monument. The world's primary source of this pure copper was in Lake Superior, the Upper Peninsula of Michigan, at 48°N. An estimated half a billion pounds of pure crystal copper (with crystalized silver or gold in some of it) was mined in thousands of pits during this period and "disappeared" (Refs.19,20,22). The arrival of shiploads of Michigan copper into southern Spain is probably documented by the radiocarbon date of c.2200 BC obtained by archaeologists of the University of Grenada, for the date of the abandonment of the Chalcolithic copper smelting town of Los Millares, near Almeria (date on sign at the site). Smelting of small amounts of copper from ores suddenly became uneconomic. The three latitude coincidences of 48°N (Lagatjar, Newfoundland, Isle Royale) were not lost on these people, who celebrated these coincidences in this long row ABC of 48 stones on this site. The copper routes were so important, that perhaps it is also not an accident that this monument is shaped like a big copper axe facing west (**Fig.1**), or like one of the rock hammers used in mining copper.

It took early man thousands of years to learn the current and tradewind patterns of the Atlantic Ocean. Considering the historical context, and information from other megalithic sites, Lagatjar, which illustrates a new route to America, the Crossing of the Labrador Sea, appears to date about 1600 BC. During the construction of this monument of Lagatjar, huge and valuable quantities of copper were being moved by the sailing routes displayed in this monument, equipping the armies of the Old World with bronze weapons of war, lifting man, for better and worse, from the Stone Age.

We show that the angles and latitude encodings in the site indicate a statistically probable and sensible interpretation of the monument that is consistent with known events and dates in prehistory. The monument is about the sailing routes to and from America via Greenland and the Azores, with emphasis shown regarding a recently-discovered short-cut route across the Labrador Sea. Lagatjar is one of the later megalithic monuments, but it dramatically illustrates the importance of sailing routes and trade routes to these people of the Bronze Age.

References

1. De Jonge, R.M., and Wakefield, J.S, How the Sungod Reached America, A Guide to Megalithic Sites, MCS Inc., 2002 (ISBN 0-917054-19-9) Available: MCS Inc., Box 3392, Kirkland, Wa 98083-3392, also on CD. Website: www.howthesungod.com

2. De Jonge, R.M., and IJzereef, G.F., De Stenen Spreken, Kosmos Z&K, Utrecht/Antwerpen, 1996 (ISBN 90-215-2-846-0) (Dutch)

3. Burl, A., From Carnac to Callanish, Yale University Press, New Haven and London, 1993 (ISBN 0-300-05575-7), groundplan on pg.109

4. Pontois, B., Le, Le Finistere Prehistorique, Paris (1929), pgs.95-121, groundplan on pg.110 (French)

5. Devoir, A., "Les grands ensembles megalithiques de la presqu'ile de Crozon et leur destination originelle", Bull. de la Societe Archeologique Finistere, 38, 3-38 (1911) (French)

6. Devoir, A., "Temoins megalithiques des variations des lignes des ravages armoricans", Bull. Soc. Arch. Finistere, 39, 220-239 (1912) (French)

7. Lockyer, Sir N., Stonehenge and Other British Stone Monuments Astronomically Considered, 2nd Edition, London (1909), pgs 100-4, 485-7

8. IGN Map 0418ET, Website: www.ign.fr

9. Atlantic Ocean, National Geographic Society, 1968, Mercator Projection

10. Burl, A., Prehistoric Stone Circles, Shire Archaeology, 1988 (ISBN 85263-962-7)

11. Burl, A., Megalithic Brittany, A Guide to Over 350 Ancient Sites and Monuments, Thames and Hudson, 1985 (ISBN 0-500-27460-6)

12. Giot, P.R., <u>Prehistory in Brittany</u>, Ed JOS (ISBN 2-85543-123-9)
13. Giot, P.R., <u>La Bretagne des Megalithes</u>, Ed. Ouest France, 1995 (ISBN 2-7373-1388-0) (French)
14. Briard, J., <u>The Megaliths of Brittany</u>, Gisserot, 1991
15. Briard, J., Palmer, T., Bailey, M.E., <u>Natural Catastrophes during Bronze Age Civilizations</u>, BAR International Series 728, Oxford, 1998 (ISBN 0-86054-916-X)
16. Briard, J., et Gautier, M., <u>La Prehistorie de la Bretagne, Vue du Ciel</u>, Ed. Gisserot (ISBN 2-87747-622-7) (French)
17. Michelin Guide, <u>Brittany</u> (ISBN 2-06-538102-7)
18. <u>The Atlantic Crossing Guide</u>, RCC Pilotage Foundation, Ed by Philip Allen, W.W. Norton & Co., New York, 1983 (ISBN 0-393-03283-3)
19. Drier, R.W., and Du Temple, O.J., <u>Prehistoric Copper Mining in the Lake Superior Region, A Collection of Reference Articles</u>, published privately, 1961, and reprinted in 2005
20. Rydholm, C. F., <u>Michigan Copper, The Untold Story</u>, Winter Cabin Books, Marquette, 2006 (ISBN 0-9744679-2-8)
21. Fell, B., <u>America BC</u>, Pocket Books, Simon & Schuster, 1994
22. Bailey, J., <u>Sailing to Paradise</u>, Simon & Schuster, 1994
23. Thompson, G., <u>American Discovery</u>, Misty Isles Press, Seattle, 1994
24. Casson, L., <u>Ships and Seafaring in Ancient Times</u>, British Museum Press, 1994
25. Wachsmann, S., <u>Seagoing Ships and Seamanship in the Bronze Age Levant</u>, College Station, Texas, 1998
26. Heyerdahl, T., <u>The Ra Expeditions</u>, George Allen & Unwin, London, 1971
27. De Jonge, R.M., and Wakefield J.S., "The Discovery of the Atlantic Islands, Migration & Diffusion, Vol.3, No.11, pgs.69-109 (2002)
28. De Jonge, R.M., and Wakefield J.S., "A Nautical Center for Crossing the Ocean, America's Stonehenge, New Hampshire, c.2200 BC", Migration & Diffusion, Vol.4, No.15, pgs.60-100 (2002)
29. De Jonge, R.M., and Wakefield, J.S., "The Passage Grave of Karleby, Encoding the Islands Discovered in the Ocean, c. 2950 BC", Migration & Diffusion, Vol.5, No.18, pgs.64-74 (2004)
30. De Jonge, R.M., and Wakefield, J.S., "The Rings of Stenness, Brodgar, & Bookan, Celebrating the Discovery of South Greenland", Migration & Diffusion, Vol 6, No.24, pgs. 20-40, 2005 (ISSN: 1563-440X)
31. De Jonge, R.M., and Wakefield, J.S., "The Stone Rows of Tormsdale: A Voyage to Central America across the Atlantic", Ancient American, Vol.11, No. 70 (2006)
32. De Jonge, R.M., and Wakefield, J.S., "Greenland, Bridge between the Old and New Worlds", Ancient American, Vol.11, No. 70 (2006)
33. Perry, W.J., <u>The Children of the Sun</u>, Adventures Unlimited Press, Illinois, 2004, originally published in 1923 (ISBN 1-931882-27-4)
34. Hall, G.P. D., <u>Ocean Passages for the World</u>, Hydrographer of the Navy, Ministry of the Navy, Taunton, Somerset, 1973
35. The "sailing ship icon" in Fig.1 is a petroglyph from Loughcrew, Ireland of c.3200 BC (Ref.1)
36. De Jonge, R.M., and Wakefield, J.S., "A Return Route Across the Ocean, Encoded at Tormsdale Rows (Caithness, NE Scotland, c. 1600 BC), Ancient American, Vol.12, No.74, pgs.8-12 (2007)
37. Wall, A., "An Ancient Greek Historian's Sailing Directions to America", Ancient American, Issue #37, pg.20; Plutarch, <u>Morals</u>, Vol.5, circa 90 AD

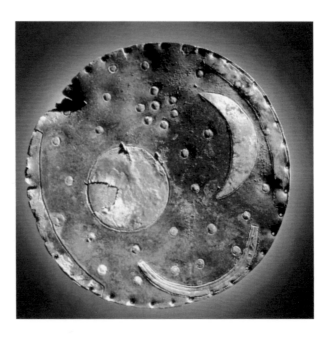

The Disc of Nebra
Important Sailing Routes of the Bronze Age displayed in Religious Context
(Nebra, Sachsen-Anhalt, Germany, c.1600 BC)

R.M. de Jonge, drsrmdejonge@hotmail.com
J.S. Wakefield, jayswakefield@yahoo.com

Introduction
In 1999 a bronze disc was stolen from a prehistoric grave in the neighborhood of Sachsen-Anhalt, in the Harz Mountains, in Germany (Ref.1). Three years later, in 2002, it was recovered. **Figure 1** is reproduced from The New Rotterdam Newspaper, where an article about the Disc appeared on December 7, 2002. It caught our interest, and this article was written to explain the object. Recently (Nov.24, 2003), a color (mostly gold and green) photograph of the disc has appeared in the popular American magazine U.S. News and World Report (Ref.23), and then also the January 2004 issue of National Geographic Magazine.

Though **Figure 1** is much smaller, the actual object is reported to have a diameter of 32cm, and a weight of about 2 kg. The Disc is partially covered with pieces of goldplate, though in some places, the gold plating is gone. Originally, around the edge, there probably were 39 small holes. The backside status is not reported. The grave from which it was taken is located within a circular-shaped wall system of c.200 to 350 meters, on the Mittelberg mountain at Nebra, close to a tributary of the Weser River, at a distance of 250 km from the coast of the North Sea (Atlantic Ocean). The bronze Disc contains a relatively high quantity of arsenic, and the gold is contaminated with other substances. From these content data, as well as the strong corrosion of the bronze surface, and from the depth and type of the original grave, it was deduced that the disc dates from c.1600 BC. This is almost a thousand years after the discovery of America via the Atlantic, c.2500 BC (Refs.2,3).

Astronomic Interpretation
On the front side of the disc we see a large golden sun, with damage to its gold plating, and a crescent quarter moon in the sky, as seen from the earth. On two sides, were strips of gold plating, now obviously gone on one side. Looking at the object astronomically, these could be seen as the eastern and western horizons, usually imaged as land or mountains in ancient pictographs. There is a cup, or bowl-shaped object at the top or bottom, possibly symbolizing the Milky Way, and a number of golden "stars", including a group of seven, that might represent the 7 stars of the 7 star constelation, the Pleiades. There are 23 other stars, so the stars total 30. The Newspaper article says there are two more stars under the gold plating of the edge horizon, but only one is clearly visible in the reproduced photo.

Anthropomorphic Interpretation
The Disc of Nebra might represent the head of a person (**Fig.2**). At one side we see a complete eye, and, beside it, a crescent of the other eye. In Egyptian mythology, Amun-

Fig.1
The bronze Disc of Nebra with pieces of goldplate. On top between the stars is the Milky Way, or an upside down Sunbark sailing to the west. Actual diameter 32cm, weight 2 kg. Reprinted from the New Rotterdam Newspaper (Ref.1).
(Nebra, Sachsen-Anhalt, the Harz Mountains, Germany, c.1600 BC)

Re has the "solar eye", while Amenophis is the "Lunar eye" (Ref.24), these are the two eyes of the SunGod. Below might be a mouth, with a smile. At the sides, might be hair, or ears, or earspools. The Disc of Nebra is late megalithic. Sometimes, petroglyphic images can appear to be faces of the SunGod, but we have shown that such petroglyphs (and also monuments) of this time period often have additional religious, political, and geographic meanings (Refs.2,3).

Religious Meaning

The whole disc is the Realm of the SunGod, and is about the sunreligion which became highly developed in Egypt. In Egyptian images, the sun is usually shown rising from the Eastern horizon, and the moon is shown over the Western horizon, the Land of the Dead. Each day, the Sun traverses the sky to the West, and each evening the God sails west in his Sunbark to the Other Side of the World, the Realm of the Dead. Sometimes this Sunbark is shown as an upside-down boat in the sky (like **Fig.1**), and at other times as an upright Sunboat on water (like **Fig.2**). So there may be no "up" or "down" to this Disc, as it may be intended to be 3-dimensional (the 4 cardinal directions, plus up to the sky, above the earth).

On the Disc are a group of 7 stars, and 23 separate stars. The 23 correspond to the latitude of the Tropic of Cancer, at 23°N. This latitude is holy to the sunreligion because at noon on mid-summer day the Sun is directly overhead at this latitude, having moved up from the south. After staying at this latitude a couple of days, the sun turns, and begins a slow movement back to the south. Most megalithic petroglyphs and monuments contain this holy number of 23, so we are sure the Sunreligion was widely believed, and a prominent feature of the society.

The 23 separate stars also corresponded to the latitude of the Southern Egyptian Empire, at 23°N. This was the geographical center of the sunreligion. So, from the 23 stars, we know the Disc of Nebra represents the face of Ra, and the details of the Disc are about the Sunreligion, centered on Egypt. Together with the group of 7 stars, the total is 30 stars, the latitude of the Nile Delta, the center of the Northern Egyptian Empire, at 30°N. The group of 7 stars may also represent the seven degrees of latitude of the United Egyptian Empire, from 23°N to 30°N, again confirming that the Sunreligion originates in Egypt.

Political Meaning

In Egyptian religious hierarchy, below the SunGod Ra are two other gods, the moongod Osiris, and the sungod Horus, indicated on the Disc by the two eyes of Ra. The Pharaohs (Kings) on earth were considered living personifications of Osiris and Horus (Refs.4,5). On this Disc of Nebra, if one sees the moon as placed close to the eastern (Old World) horizon (**Fig.2**), it might be concluded that this item was fabricated during the reign of an Osiris-King. The complicated Egyptian religion then predicts that this Pharaoh will be succeeded by a Horus-King (the Sun), who rises from the east, while the Osiris-King (the Moon) sinks in the west, the Land of the Dead. The whole political procedure of resurrection and accession is thus symbolized by a voyage around the Earth, across the Ocean. This led to a profound interest in the Realm of the Dead on the west side of the

Fig.2
The Disc of Nebra is the complicated face of the Egyptian SunGod Ra, with the Sun,
Moon, and the Sunbark, sailing to the west. The stars have been numbered by the authors.
The western horizon is the coast of Central America.
(Nebra, Sachsen-Anhalt, the Harz Mountains, Germany, c.1600 BC)

Ocean for thousands of years, as shown by the benevolent expression on the face of Ra on the Disc.

Geographic Meaning

Each day the Sun moves to the west, and each day the God Ra sails in his Sunbark in that direction. So, the round disc, the head of Ra, also represents the spherical Earth, and especially the North Atlantic Ocean, which is located in the west. So the mouth of Ra is also the Sunbark, sailing on the Ocean to the west.

Details of the crossing may be encoded in the placement of the stars on the disc. Let us assume that the "boat" is upright on the Ocean (**Fig.2**), with the moon near the eastern horizon, and the Sun moving to the west. Usually, in megalithic petroglyphs, the center of the eastern horizon is the Strait of Gibraltar, on the coast of the Old World. The Tropic of Cancer leaves the continent of Africa at 23°N, encoded by the 23 stars. This is the historic place they wanted to cross the Ocean in honor of the SunGod Ra (Refs.2,3). Unfortunately this proved to be impossible, due to the contrary winds and currents at that latitude. We are sure some brave people lost their lives in the doldrums of the Sargasso Sea, trying to cross it (Ref.2). These attempts did, however, result in the early discoveries of the Cape Verde Islands and the Azores. After many years, and actual discovery of the Americas from the other side (Ref.2), the wind and current patterns became known. Finally these people had learned how to cross the ocean with the tradewind and the currents at their back, via the Southern Crossing, from the Cape Verde Islands to South America (Refs.2,9-13).

In the bowl, or "boat" image on the Disc of Nebra are 3 stars (#1,2,3) (**Fig.2**), which may represent the 3 island groups of the Cape Verde Islands. The boat actually represents the Cape Verde Islands, literally, which actually have this shape in the Ocean. Below the sun and moon are 10 stars (#1-10), encoding the ten islands of the Cape Verde Archipelago. Below the centers of the sun and the moon are 15 stars (#1-15), the latitude of the most southern Cape Verde Islands (15°N), and the sailing direction from there, 15°WSW, to South America, as well as Cape Gracias a Dios, the east Cape of Honduras, also at 15°N. The 15th star touches the western horizon, so the culture of Central America starts at this Cape. In total there are 30 stars on the Disc, encoding the correct length of the Southern Crossing, 30dl (distance lines), or 30°, equal to 1800 Nautical Miles (NM)(Ref.2). In front of the boat are 2 stars (#4,5), which combined with the 3 in the boat, could indicate a landing target on the shore of British Guyana, at 5°N. The 4 southernmost stars (#1-4) form a line pointing to the southernmost point of the western horizon, so it appears that Cape Caciporee, Brazil, at 4°N may have been a favorite landing spot in this time period.

At the left side of the Sun is another star (#16), for a total of 16 stars, corresponding to the culture along the North Coast of Honduras, Belize, and Guatemala, at 16°N. Above these are two more stars, (#17,18), encoding the center of the Olmec Civilization on the river mouths around the southern basin of the Gulf of Campeche ("Egyptian Gulf") at 18°N (Refs.14-21). Above these, are two more stars, (#19, 20), showing the northern border of this civilization, at 20°N. The center of the western horizon (formerly in gold) corresponds to this southern coast of the Gulf of Campeche, and is clearly situated on the

Disc to the WSW of the center of the eastern horizon, in agreement with the latitudes (Gibraltar is at 36°N). This is confirming of the discovery of America before the c.1600 BC date of this Disc of Nebra, and the importance of ancient Central America (the Land of Punt).

At the top of the Disc is the 21st star, encoding the NE Cape of Yucatan, at 21°N, and the 22nd star gives the latitude of SW Cuba at 22°N. The last two stars (#22,23) could provide the sailing distance from the Cape of Yucatan to the SW Cape of Cuba, 2dl, or 120 NM, at a direction of 10°ENE (#21,22,23 + 7). The total of 23 stars again provide the Tropic of Cancer, this time, along the North Coast of Cuba. The group of 7 stars also represent the areas of South Florida with this shape, 7° above the south point of the Gulf of Campeche, at 18°+7°= 25°N. The 30 total stars of the Disc confirm the importance of the mouth of the Mississippi River, and its Poverty Point trading center for Michigan copper at 30°N, the economic engine of the Bronze Age. Since the Nebra Disc is dated to c.1600 BC, it was made prior to the abrupt ending of the Michigan copper mining at c.1200 BC, coincident with the worldwide catastrophes of that date (Ref.22).

The return route to the Old World runs with the winds and the Gulfstream off Newfoundland (not shown) to the Azores and Madeira (Refs.6-13). The Sun, appearing in the center of the Ocean on the Disc, represents the importance of the Azores on this return route, because following their discovery, c.3600 BC, these islands had been revered as the western home of the SunGod for a thousand years (Ref.2). The edge of the Disc probably had 39 small holes, corresponding with the West Azores at 39°N. The group of 7 stars may also represent the star group called the Pleiades. If so, its appearance in the sky may have indicated the end of the sailing season in the autumn. The group of 7 stars plus two western stars (#17,19) represent the 9 islands of the Azores, illustrating the importance of the western two Azores islands (Corvo and Flores). These islands were the sailing goal for ships leaving Cape Race, Newfoundland, returning with their holds full of copper. The moon here represents Madeira, with two stars near it (#12,13), the actual two islands of Madeira. It is possible that the group of 7 stars might also be representing the 7 Canary Islands. For more graphic megalithic maps of these islands and sailing routes, see the petroglyphs in Ref.2.

The Disc was found in Nebra in a circular wall system, at 52°N, the same latitude as the westernmost point in Europe (Dunmore Head, Ireland). This also is the latitude of Cape St. Charles, the East Cape of mainland North America. The Azores, represented by the Sun on the Disc, are situated at the complementary latitude (90°-52°) of 38°N. If there are two more stars behind the gold eastern horizon, the total stars would then be 32, encoding the latitude of Bermuda, at 32°N, an alternative in late date return routes (after c.1700 BC).

Discussion

Through the use of encoded latitudes, combined with graphic design, the Disc of Nebra indicates routes on the Ocean that are the most common ones in other Bronze Age petroglyphs (Ref.2). The finding of this large, beautiful gold and bronze relic in

Germany is an important piece of confirmatory evidence regarding the religion and trading routes of the Bronze Age.

References

1. The New Rotterdam Newspaper, December 7, 2002
2. Jonge, R.M., and Wakefield, J.S., How the SunGod Reached America, A Guide to Megalithic Sites, MCS Inc., 2002 (ISBN 0-917054-19-9)
3. Jonge, R.M., de and IJzereef, G.F., De Stenen Spreken, Kosmas Z&K, Utrecht/Antwerpen, 1996 (ISBN 90-2152846-0)
4. People of the Stone Age: Hunter-gatherers and Early Farmers, Weldon Owen Pty Limited, McMahons Point, Australia (1995)
5. Old World Civilizations, the Rise of Cities and States, Weldon Owen Pty Limited, McMahons Point, Australia (1995) (ISBN 90-215-2505-4)
6. Lambert, J.D., America's Stonehenge, An Interpretive Guide, Sunrise Publications, Kingston, N.H., 1996 (ISBN 0-9652630-0-2)
7. Ferryn, P., "5000 Years Before Our Era: The Red Men of the North Atlantic", NEARA Journal, Vol. XXXI, No. 2 (1997)
8. Fell, B., America BC, Pocket Books, Simon & Schuster, 1994
9. Bailey, J., Sailing to Paradise, Simon & Schuster, 1994
10. Thompson, G., American Discovery, Misty Isles Press, Seattle, 1994
11. Casson, L., Ships and Seafaring in Ancient Times, British Museum Press, 1994
12. Wachsmann, S., "Seagoing Ships and Seamanship in the Bronze Age Levant", College Station, Texas, 1998
13. Heyerdahl, T., The Ra Expeditions, George Allen & Unwin, London, 1971
14. "Oldest City of Americas Confirmed, Peruvian Complex Contemporary with Egypt's Pyramids", The Seattle Times, A4, April 27, 2001
15. Wallis Budge, E.A., Osiris and the Egyptian Resurection, 2 Vol., 1911, Dover Pub., N.Y. 1973 (ISBN 0-486-22780-4)
16. Jairazbhoy, R.A., Ancient Egyptians and Chinese in America, Rowman & Littlefield, Totowa, N.J., 1974 (ISBN 0-87471-571-1)
17. Peterson, F.A., Ancient Mexico, 1959
18. Stuart, G.E., "New Light on the Olmec", National Geographic, Nov. 1993
19. Bernal, I., The Olmec World, University of California Press, London, 1969 (ISBN 0-520-02891-0)
20. Gruener, J., The Olmec Riddle, An Inquiry into the Origin of Precolumbian Civilization, Vengreen Publications, 1987, Rancho Santa Fe, Cal. (ISBN 0-9421-85-56-0)
21. New World and Pacific Civilizations, The Illustrated History of Humankind, Weldon Owen Pty Limited, McMahons Point, Australia (1995) (ISBN 90-215-2512-7)
22. Joseph, F., The Destruction of Atlantis, Compelling Evidence of the Sudden Fall of the Legendary Civilization, Bear & Co., Rochester, Vt. (2002) (ISBN 0-89281-851-1)
23. "Barbarians get Sophisticated" by Andrew Curry, U. S. News and World Report, November 24, 2003, page 62
24. Wilkinson, R., The Complete Temples of Ancient Egypt, Thames & Hudson, New York, 2000 (ISBN 0-500-05100-3)

Photo 1 ENE view from the west bank of the Thurso River to the Tulach Mor Broch (Iron Age), with new windfarm behind. (Spring, 2003)

THE STONE ROWS OF TORMSDALE

A Voyage to Central America, the Realm of the Dead
(Caithness, NE Scotland, c.1600 BC)

R.M. de Jonge, drsrmdejonge@hotmail.com
J.S. Wakefield, jayswakefield@yahoo.com

Summary

The stone rows of Tormsdale, now buried under peat beside the Thurso River, in NE Scotland, are known from 1982 and 1984 surveys as described by Myatt. The monument consists of two groups of stone rows pointing NW, and a NS row. The stones are shown to encode latitudes, which describe the coastal sailing route via the Upper North to Central America. For the voyage segments with sea-crossings, the sailing directions and sailing distances are encoded. The latitudes of Central America are emphasized. The monument can be dated to c.1600 BC.

Introduction

The megalithic monument of Tormsdale consists of a fan of rows of low stones about 1 meter above the original ground level (**Fig.1**). It is located in the region of Caithness, in the NE corner of Scotland, alongside the small Thurso River, about 15 miles (24km) from both north and east coasts (**Map1**, Ref.1). In the spring of 2003, we tried to visit the site to get an impression of the heights of the individual menhirs, and to take photographs. However, in spite of accurate directions in the literature, we were not able to find the stones. Like a number of other sites in the region, the rows of Tormsdale are buried in the peat.

Photo 4 shows the depth of peat being harvested, off the dirt road north of Tormsdale. The peat layer is more than a meter high. This area on the north coast of Scotland is called the "Flow Country", a blanket bog that developed after the Ice Age. It is claimed to be one of the most important ecosystems of its kind in the world. The authors were astonished by the number of curlews and oystercatchers nesting in the bogs. Formerly, large estate owners employed groundskeepers who burned the heather to the ground in August each year, to provide better feeding for the sheep in the spring. Now there are fewer sheep, the estate owners have died, some of the estates are hotels, and people have moved away. The estate lands of the Tormsdale site have been sold for the windfarm, and for tree farms, which adjoin the site.

The stone rows at Tormsdale were first recorded by the Archaeology Branch of the Ordinance Survey in 1982 (Ref.32), and a subsequent survey was done in 1984, as described by L.J. Myatt (Ref.1). He says: "The stone setting covers an area of approximately 60m x 60m and is on ground which rises very gradually to the SE. The area is grass covered for the most part and has been colonized by soft rushes which make it difficult to identify the full extent of the rows of stones visually, since many of the stones protrude only a small distance above the surface and others appear as small hummocks on the surface where the grass has grown over them". Myatt states that peat cutting had taken place on the northern and western sides of the Rows of Tormsdale,

Map 1

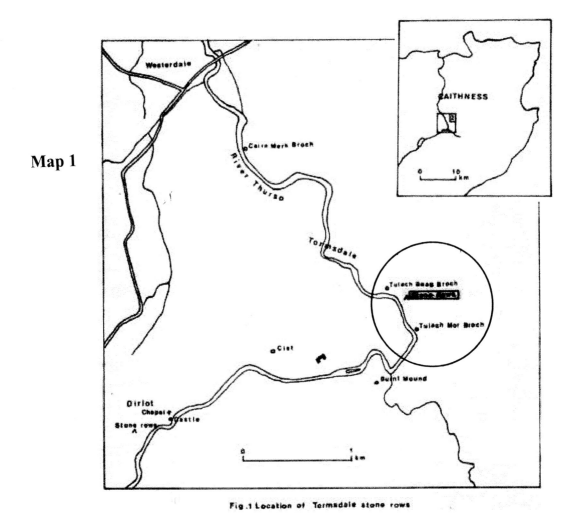

Fig.1 Location of Tormsdale stone rows

Photo 2 View NW across the Sheepfold. The Tormsdale Rows are supposed to be at the right side of the bend of the Thurso River, some 100m NW of the fold.

where he found some stones fallen and displaced. "When plotted on a large scale drawing, the stones were seen to be aligned in fan-shaped rows, with a single isolated row which has an azimuth due north and south… the tallest stones occur at the south end of this single row" (Ref.1).

The site is located between two ruined brochs, once graceful circular drystone towers, dating from the Iron Age (**Map 2**, Ref.31). **Photo 1** provides an ENE view from the west bank of the Thurso River to the Tulach Mor Broch, with the new windfarm nearly completed behind it. The authors found the area open for walking, but marshy. The Broch has intriguing mounds around it, surrounding a pool of the river that is out of the current. It looks like a great place for fishing or netting salmon. The Tormsdale Rows are supposed to be 300m north of this broch. **Photo 2** gives a NW view across the Sheepfold, which is 200m north of the broch. The rows should be at the right side of the bend of the Thurso River, some 100m NW of the fold. **Photo 3** is shot from downriver, looking south across the top of the other broch (Tulach Beag Broch), to Tulach Mor Broch in the distance. The Tormsdale Rows are probably in the weeds, about 100m left of the river bend.

Nearby Sites

From Tormsdale, the Thurso River runs a short distance north to its mouth, going over beautiful small falls at the Westerdale bridge (**Maps 1,2**), where large salmon are occasionally still caught. Ancient ruins are all over the maps of Caithness, so the area has been densely inhabited since the Stone Age. About a mile due west, and upriver from Tormsdale, is the site of the Dirlot Stone Rows. **Map 1** shows these rows, but again they were not to be seen. The heather growth has swallowed them up. What gets your attention (looking downstream) are the ruin heaps of Dirlot Castle, dating from the Iron Age, on a rock spire surrounded by cliffs and a big pool of the river down below, and a 19thC graveyard built of castle stones on the cliff edge. **Photo 5** shows the bucolic view upstream, up the valley of the Thurso.

Photo 6 shows a portion of the rows of Loch Stemster, off the A9, a few miles SSE of Tormsdale. Due to less peat, the stones stick 3-4 feet above the ground. This is also true for the only signposted row site, the famous and easily found "Hill of Many Stanes (Stones)", 15 miles (24km) ESE of Tormsdale, shown in **Photo 7**. The more than 200 stones in 23 slightly fan shaped rows appear to descend the hill, overlooking the seacoast and oil rigs in the bay to the south (Ref.3).

There are a total of 32 multiple stone row sites in the rather flat regions of Sutherland and Caithness, in NE Scotland (Refs.3,7). Similar sites occur in Dartmoor and Exmoor, in SW England, and in Brittany, France. In Brittany, however, the stones and the rows are on average three times as large (Refs.21-25). All the rows in Scotland consist of only small stones, often located along rivers or lochs (lakes). Some of them are reported to be "disturbed, others even removed" during the times of the land clearances, when the tenant farmers were replaced with sheep by their chieftains. However, we find that the condition of most sites is usually better than reported. In the book "From Carnac to Callanish" (Ref.3), author Aubrey Burl classifies the Tormsdale site as "ruined, but

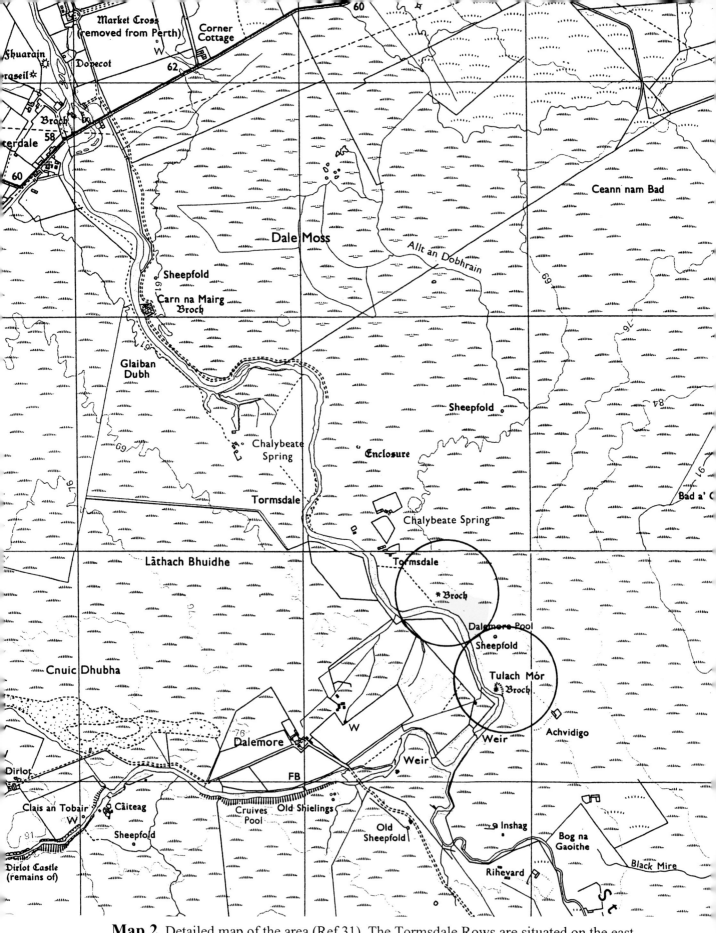

Map 2 Detailed map of the area (Ref.31). The Tormsdale Rows are situated on the east bank of the Thurso River, between Tulach Mor Broch (SE), and Tulach Beag Broch (NW). The grid distance is 1 km.

recognizable". However, since we find that analysis of the groundplan reveals a sensible result, we think the rows are actually not ruined, but are actually in good condition, now buried in peat.

The Rows of Tormsdale

Using the groundplan surveyed by Myatt, we see that Tormsdale consists of rows of low stones, forming two arrows, both pointing NW, which are cut by a NS line (**Fig.1**). The 5 southern rows A-E are directed to one point Y, and form a group, called Group Y. The 7 northern rows B and P-U are focused on distant point Z, and form a group, called Group Z. The important line B is a common row of both Groups Y and Z. In parentheses following the letter labeling of each row is the total number of stones in each row. It is a rather large construction. In total, there are 104 stones, each of them having a length of about a meter, and a width of half a meter, as can be seen using the scale in Fig.1. On the average they are about one meter high. The taller menhirs are placed at the south side of the monument (Refs.1-7).

Like almost all megalithic monuments Tormsdale is a religious construction with a geographic meaning (Refs.8,9). Most of these monuments are located on the west coast of Western Europe. Tormsdale is situated in the NE corner of Scotland, 15 miles upriver from the sea. The rows form two arrows, both pointing northwest. So the monument appears to deal with crossing the Ocean in north-western direction. On a globe, you will see above Scotland, one after the other, the Orkney Islands, the Shetland Islands, the Faroes, Iceland, and Greenland.

This route across the Ocean, "via the Upper North" as we call it, is described in the old megalithic monuments of Stonehenge I (South England), and Loughcrew (Ireland), of c.3200 BC (Refs.8,9). In our previous work, we have shown that this route is illustrated in many early petroglyphs. This monument with its stone rows resembles the Kerlescan rows in Brittany, of c.1800 BC. Kerlescan is dated 700 years after the discovery of America via the Atlantic, c.2500 BC (Refs.8-11). The discovery of this new land on the backside of he Earth brought a lot of excitement, social changes, and many voyages across the sea.

From our previous work, we suspected at the outset of this study, that the Tormsdale rows encoded a description of the crossing of the Ocean to America. Ice core research in Greenland has recently shown that the North Atlantic Ocean had "extreme summertime conditions" prevailing around 2200 BC (Ref.38). This made it easier for these people to explore this route to the Upper North, following the discovery of new lands in the west. Note that the Thurso River flows north from the Tormsdale site to the sea, and upstream, it runs southwest into a beautiful valley (**Maps 1,2**). Perhaps the location of the monument was chosen because here it was easy to visualize a voyage that ran to the north in the sea, then ran southwest into the beautiful Caribbean.

Crossing from Scotland to Greenland

The stones of Tormsdale appear to represent latitudes, so the stones are numbered by us in a pattern that seems to make sense. This is like re-engineering an engine, and seeing if

Photo 3 View South, across the top of Tulach Brag Broch (to Tulach Mor Broch in the distance). The Tormsdale Rows are probably in the grass left of the river bend.

Photo 4 Current peat harvesting along the dirt road north of Tormsdale.

you can get it to work. When studying the western row X carefully, we soon reach the conclusion that the southernmost and tallest menhir X59 represents Tormsdale as well as the Orkney Islands, both at about 59°N (see **Fig.1**). Sailing from mainland Scotland (Tormsdale) to the Orkneys is easy, because they are separated by the Pentland Firth, a narrow strait having a width of only 5 miles (8km). However, to reach the Shetlands at 60°N, represented by the next menhir X60, a very seaworthy boat is needed. With such a boat sailing is also possible via 61°N (X61, sea) to the Faroes, at 62°N (X62). Thus, when we move up the X row of menhirs, to the north, we are sailing north up stones marking the latitudes as we go. In the meantime, arrow Y gives the approximate direction.

The East-West axes from the first three menhirs X59-61 (not drawn) do not touch any stones of the arrows (**Fig.1**). This appears to mean, that crossing from the Orkneys to the Faroes is considered to be simple. It is not necessary to give more details. This is correct, because the latitude of the Orkneys, at 59°N, corresponds to the sailing direction (59°NW) from these islands to the Faroes, and the 4 menhirs X59-62 used so far, encode the sailing distance involved, 4 Moiras= 4°= 240 NM (1 Egyptian Moira= 1 degree of latitude= 60 Nautical Miles). The monument is telling us that they considered the Faroes to be coastal Islands of Europe.

From menhirs X62-67 we drew six horizontal axes ("latitude lines") (**Fig.1**). Menhir X62, representing the Faroes, is placed at the level of axis 1 of the first stone in row A of the big arrow pointing to Y. When sailing NW, the direction arrow Y is pointing, we arrive via 63°N (X63, sea) at the SE coast of Iceland, at 64°N (X64). Axis 1 touches a first group of 2 stones in row A, and axis 3 hits a second group of 6 stones in this row A. To encode high numbers, it appears an encoding convention has been used, where the first stones of each of the arrow rows counts for "tens". So, if the first group represents the tens, and the second group the units, the encoded sailing direction from the Faroes to Iceland would be 20+6= 26°WNW, which is correct. The axis 3 hits stones in rows A (10 stones) and B (16 stones) which contain together 26 stones, confirming it. The first group of 4 stones in row X, up to X62 (the Faroes), determines this first sailing distance, 4 Moiras= 4°= 240 NM, which is correct.

Sailing continues in western direction around Iceland, via 65°N (X65), to the NW Peninsula of Iceland, at 66°N (X66). Axis 5 (Iceland) cuts the 7th mehir of row B. This row has a first group of 1 menhir (the tens) and a second group of 6 menhirs (the units, to the 7th menhir), suggesting a sailing direction of 10+6= 16°WNW, to Cape Holm, Greenland, which is correct. The row involved (B) has a total of 16 menhirs, confirming it. The second group of 5 stones in row X (X63-67) shows the sailing distance to Cape Holm, 5 Moiras= 5°= 300 NM, which is correct. Cape Holm is located at the holy Arctic Circle, at 67°N (X67). This is the northernmost line the Sun still shines at midwinter day (Refs.8-17). Menhir X67 is placed at the left side of row X to highlight the special position of Cape Holm, also because it is the northernmost place that will be visited.

In a geographic sense, row A, pointing NW, symbolizes the whole crossing from the Faroes to Greenland. The first group of stones represents the Faroes, the second group is Iceland, and the third group symbolizes Cape Holm, Greenland (**Fig.1**). Row X now

Photo 5 Bucolic view WSW, up valley of the Trurso River. A few stones are poking through the grass behind the photographer, where the Dirlot Rows are reported to be. (Spring, 2003).

Photo 6 View north of western row, of the Rows of Loch Stemster (see Loch at upper right). The site is a few miles SSE of Tormsdale; branch off A-9 road is at left.

symbolizes the SE coast of Greenland, with the stones of this row representing the descending latitudes along this coast, to the two south capes of Greenland. Menhir X60 represents Cape Farvel, at 60°N, and menhir X61 is the SW Cape of Greenland, at 61°N. The interesting thing is that, again, the EW axes from these points (not drawn) do not cut any stones of the big arrows. This means that crossing from one of these capes to the coast of Labrador (North America) is dissuaded because no details are given. This advice is in agreement with instructions from several other megalithic monuments (Refs.8,9,33-35).

We know from other monuments and petroglyphs that the Faroes and Iceland were discovered c.3400 BC. Greenland was discovered a century later, c.3300 BC. The megalith builders explored the coastal waters around the south coast of Greenland, but they did not succeed in crossing the Ocean. The monuments of Stonehenge I, in South England, and Loughcrew, Ireland, show that they gave up their efforts to cross Davis Strait, c.3200 BC (Refs.8,9,11,16). This is about 1500 years before the construction of the stone rows of Tormsdale. The famous petroglyphs of Dissignac, Brittany, show that America was discovered via the Bering Sea, c.2600 BC. A century later it was reached via the Southern Crossing from Africa to South America, and also from Greenland to Baffin Island. This happened c.2500 BC, which is about a millennium before the construction of the rows of Tormsdale (Refs.8,9,12,13).

Crossing from Greenland to Baffin Island

The crossing of Davis Strait had not been thought possible for a long time. Even in the "Age of Sail", when great clipperships traversed the sailing routes of the world, the Davis Strait was called "The Wall" in Pilot Books. This is because the warm Gulfstream flowing from the Caribbean meets the cold Labrador Current running south with icebergs calved off the west side of Greenland. This is the greatest temperature difference between two currents in the world, with famous fogs, at their peak in the month of July, just when these early sailors would be trying to cross.

So, Tormsdale recommends crossing Davis Strait from the West Coast of Greenland, which is best symbolized by important row B, the common row of both Groups Y and Z. The coast of Baffin Island is now represented by the western row X (see **Fig.2**). The westerly placed menhir C0 seems to show, by its westerly offset, that crossing of Davis Strait is possible at 62.5°N, halfway between the axes at 62°N and 63°N. All sailing directions are due west, parallel to the axes. However, no menhir is shown at this level in row X, which symbolizes the coast of Baffin Island. So apparently by this date, this rather long crossing directly to the Frobisher Bay area was known to be possible, but not advised.

The westerly placed menhir B2 shows that crossing to Baffin Island is advised along axis 3, at 64°N to the south of Cumberland Sound. The double menhir B1,2 shows it is strongly recommended. The 5 rows A-E of the southern GroupY support this crossing, 5° above Tormsdale, at 59+5= 64°N. Axis 3 cuts 5 to 6 menhirs in total, encoding a sailing distance of 5.5 Moiras= 5.5°= 330 NM, which is correct. The same axis cuts the group of

Photo 7 Hill of Many Stanes, Mid Clyth, view uphill to the north. The site is located due east of Tormsdale, in Caithness, with the bay in the south, and the sea in the east. The 23 rows with a maximum length of 44 meters are roughly oriented NS (2500-1500 BC). (Spring 2003)

6 stones of row A, including big stone A22, confirming it. The 6 northern menhirs of row X, having axes parallel to the sailing direction, confirm it again.

The westerly oriented stone B6 shows that crossing Davis Strait is also possible along axis 5, at 66°N to Angijack Island, off the coast of Baffin Island. The 7 rows B and P-U of the northern Group Z support this short crossing, 7° above Tormsdale, at 59+7=66°N. This axis 5 cuts 3 stones, encoding a sailing distance of only 3 Moiras= 3°=180 NM, which is correct. The northernmost group of 3 menhirs of row X, having axes parallel to the sailing direction, confirm it. Note that the two Groups of rows Y and Z of Tormsdale encode the two difficult crossings of Davis Strait.

The coast of Baffin Island, symbolized by row X, can be followed to the south (**Fig.2**). The rather big distance X65-64 represents the crossing of Cumberland Sound, between 65°N and 64°N, and the big distance X63-62 symbolizes the crossing of Frobisher Bay, between between 63°N and 62°N. Finally, the distance X61-60 is the crossing of Hudson Strait, between 61°N and 60°N. The tall menhir X60 is Cape Chidley, the NE Cape of the continent of North America, at 60°N (see Fig.3).

From Labrador to the Caribbean

South of X60 (Cape Chidley, Canada) is big menhir X59 (**Fig.2**). It is placed at the east side of the row, to prevent sailing into the western Ungava Bay. So, this menhir represents the East Coast of Labrador, at 59°N. This is at the latitude of Tormsdale. Latitudes south of it are represented by the menhirs of Group Z. This group of rows B and P-U possesses a total of 58+1= 59 stones, corresponding with the 58 latitudes of the East Coast of America all the way to the Equator (stone B0, **Fig.2**). The numbered stones in the rows are followed from north to south in accord with the geography, so to sail south, we go south through the latitudes (stones) of the arrow. The northernmost menhir U58 represents the East Coast of Labrador, at 59-1= 58°N (Fig.2). This is at the latitude of the south point of Ungava Bay.

The next row T has 4 stones representing places and their latitudes along the Labrador coast. The southern menhir T54 represents Groswater Bay (Hamilton Inlet), at 58-4= 54°N. The eastern position of this stone illustrates the eastern situation of this Bay. Here is the start of the most important waterway to the interior of Labrador. The second menhir of the next row, S52, is the entrance of Belle Isle Strait, at 52°N. The western position of the previous stone, S53, indicates, the west bank has to be followed to find this strait. The eastern position of the stone next to it, S51, shows, that subsequently, the east bank should be followed. This bank runs along the west coast of the island of Newfoundland to the south.

Stone S48 is the SW point of Newfoundland, at 48°N. The opening next to it indicates that one has to cross Cabot Strait to reach Nova Scotia. After this menhir are two groups of stones in row S, the first group of 4 stones (S39-42, the tens), and a second group of 5 stones (S43-47, the units), so the sailing direction appears to be 40+5= 45°SW, which is correct. The width of the opening between 48-47 corresponds with the space of about one stone, so, the sailing distance is 1 Moira= 1°= 60 NM. The capes on both sides of Cabot

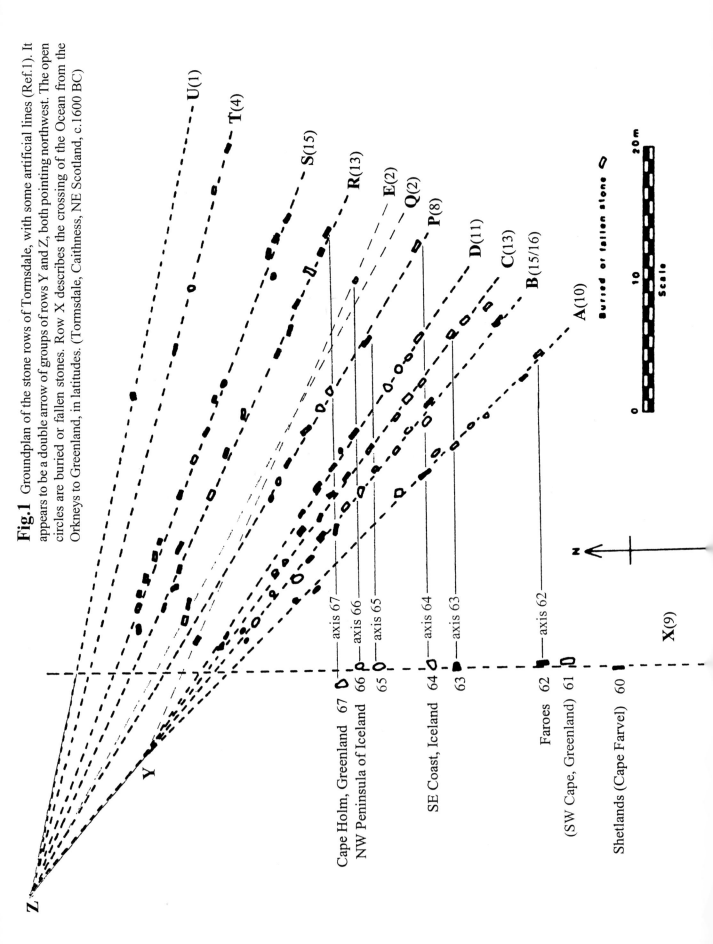

Fig.1 Groundplan of the stone rows of Tormsdale, with some artificial lines (Ref.1). It appears to be a double arrow of groups of rows Y and Z, both pointing northwest. The open circles are buried or fallen stones. Row X describes the crossing of the Ocean from the Orkneys to Greenland, in latitudes. (Tormsdale, Caithness, NE Scotland, c.1600 BC)

Strait were important in the ongoing copper trade down the St. Lawrence River, and leaving Newfoundland through Cabot Strait for the Azores. The eastern position of stone S44 indicates the eastern situation of Sable Island, at 44°N, important when sailing east from the American coast (Refs.8,9,25-27).

Stone S43 is Cape Sable, the south point of the peninsula of Nova Scotia, at 43°N. The opening in the row next to it indicates that one has to cross the Gulf of Maine. Its axis 7 cuts 3 stones (**Fig.2**), corresponding to the westerly sailing distance of 3 Moiras= 3°= 180 NM, which is correct. It leads to America's Stonehenge, New Hampshire, at this latitude, which is the most important megalithic site of North America (c.2300 BC, Refs.8,13,36). This monument illustrates in stone all the return routes across the Atlantic to the Old World, a monument used, we think, to teach these routes to mariners. Note that America's Stonehenge is represented by the intersection of rows X and A on axis 7, which indicates the great importance of this site at 43°N. It was the center of a culture that left behind hundreds of megalithic sites in New England.

The opening in row S has a width of about 3 stones, as shown by the group of 3 stones, S39-41, next to it. Both numbers confirm a westerly sailing distance of 3 Moiras. The western position of S42 confirms the western situation of Cape Cod, at 42°N. On the other hand, it is an east cape, of course, and the eastern position of the next stone S41 illustrates the eastern situation of Nantucket Island, at 41°N. The row finishes with S39, corresponding with Delaware Bay, at 39°N, at the latitude of the West Azores.

The eastern position of R35 in row R corresponds with Cape Hatteras, the East Cape of the US, at 35°N. Stone R32 in this row encodes the mouth of the Savannah River, at 32°N, and also may refer to the island of Bermuda, 550 NM offshore, at this latitude. It had already been discovered by c.2200 BC (Refs.8,9). The openings in the rows after these stones illustrate the importance of the mentioned locations. Other possible meanings can be neglected, because we just follow the East Coast to the south.

Stone R28 has been placed at right angles to the row, to warn for the first coastal islands of the Bahamas, which start above the next latitude of 27°N (R27). Early writings of sailors crossing the Bahama Banks for the first time were mesmerized by the transparent water, and fish visible in the shallow waters that extended for days and days of sailing. No doubt these earlier sailors were mesmerized too, as they are today. The last, easterly placed menhir R26 corresponds with the important island of Bimini, on the edge of the Gulfstream, offshore Florida, at 26°N, where megalithic piers continue to be discovered underwater, and in the shallow water along the Banks to the south. The axis from R26 to the westernmost menhir X67 emphasizes the importance of this latitude (see also Fig.3).

Around the Gulf of Mexico

The top angle of Group Z, between rows B and U, is 29°. The fact that the whole arrow is spread at 29° strongly shows there is something very important at this latitude! The mouth of the Mississippi River, at the south coast of the US, is at 29°N .This means that menhir R29 in this row represents the mouth of the Mississippi, too. This river was a very important outlet for the copper mining in Lake Superior, and just above its delta was

7

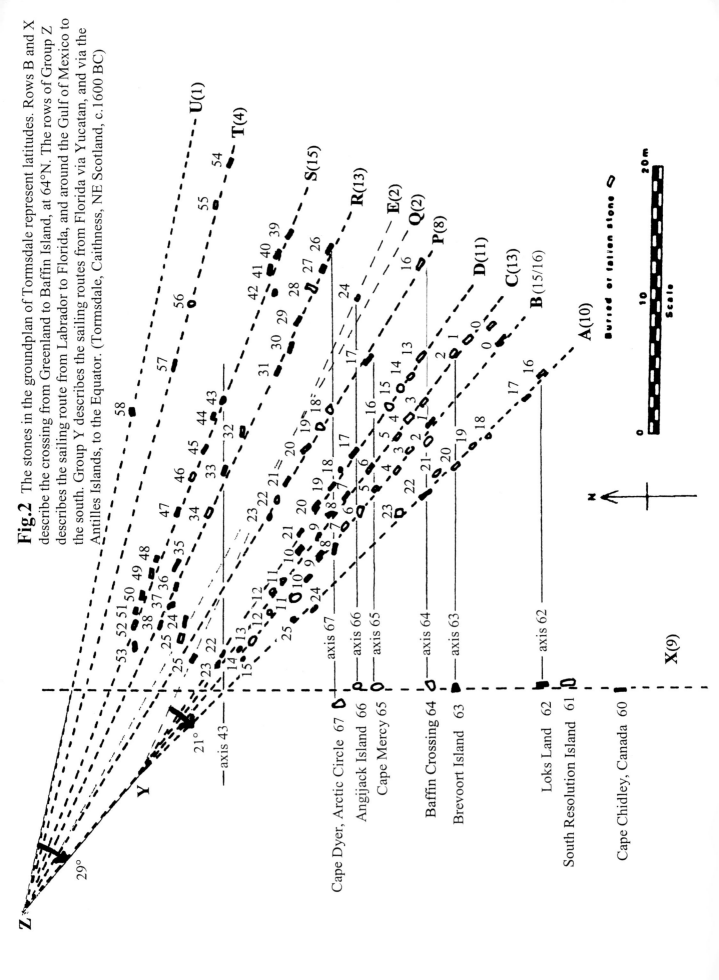

Fig.2 The stones in the groundplan of Tormsdale represent latitudes. Rows B and X describe the crossing from Greenland to Baffin Island, at 64°N. The rows of Group Z describes the sailing route from Labrador to Florida, and around the Gulf of Mexico to the south. Group Y describes the sailing routes from Florida via Yucatan, and via the Antilles Islands, to the Equator. (Tormsdale, Caithness, NE Scotland, c.1600 BC)

located the Poverty Point complex, with its huge semi-circular earthworks, flourishing at this date (Refs.8,9,25-27). Poverty Point is thought to have been full of refugees after the comet disaster of 1628 BC (Ref.40). Copper mining and the copper trade was to end suddenly in the catastrophe of 1200 BC which ended the Bronze Age, but that was to happen 400 years after this Tormsdale monument was built.

The last menhir R26 then represents the mouth of the Rio Grande River, at 26°N. The next rows Q and P also point to Z. They describe the coastal sailing route of Central America, to the south. The last menhir 23 of row P is the holy Tropic of Cancer, at 23°N, and menhir P18 of this row is the south point of the Gulf of Campeche, at 18°N. This stone is situated on axis 67 to the westernmost menhir 67, which emphasizes its importance. Earlier, the westernmost menhir X67 represented the holy Arctic Circle, at 67°N, but it also represents the holy Tropic of Cancer, at the complementary latitude of 90-67= 23°N. The Egyptian SunGod Ra has said: "The Realm of the Dead (menhir X67) is in the west, at the other side of the waters, in the land where the Sun sets." This is the center of civilization in Central America. It is also the famous Egyptian "Land of Punt", described in Queen Hatshepsut's Temple as the goal of ocean voyages lasting 3 years (c.1510 BC).

The last stone P16 of row P corresponds with the culture around the North Coast of Honduras, Belize, and Guatemala, at 16°N. The base row B also points to Z. The northernmost stone B15 gives the south border of this culture, at the level of Cape Gracias à Dios, Honduras, at 15°N (Refs.8,9,25-30). Finally, the westerly oriented menhir B8 represents the Gulf of Panama (Pacific Ocean), at 8°N.This stone points to the 9th, westernmost menhir of row X (X67), because this Gulf can be reached via the Isthmus of Panama, at 9°N.

The Shortest Route to Central America
The monument describes not just one voyage, but a group of routes then in use. These voyages probably took years to complete. Apparently, the monument was a mneumonic tool used as a teaching device, for young folks in Caithness, who wanted to go on the quest for adventure, riches, and fame.

Row Q is directed to the western point Z, but the menhirs Q24 and Q25 of this row are aimed at point Y (**Fig.2**). This means that the western route just described is not preferred, because a better eastern route exists. The next row E is directed to point Y, and possesses two menhirs, too, also numbered 24 and 25 because this is an alternate route. Menhir E25 is the south point of Florida, at 25°N, and the eastern menhir E24 is Florida Strait, at 24°N. The huge gap in the row between E24 and E25 indicates a crossing. The 2 menhirs provide the southerly sailing distance from Florida to Cuba, 2 Moiras= 2°= 120 NM. The 2 menhirs of the previous row Q confirm it.

Row D is also directed to point Y. The northernmost menhir D23 is the north coast of Cuba, at the holy Tropic of Cancer, at 23°N. On midsummer day the Sun is at right angles above this latitude. The slow northerly movement of the Sun then turns into a southerly movement. From the common usage of 23° and counts of 23 in megalithic

8

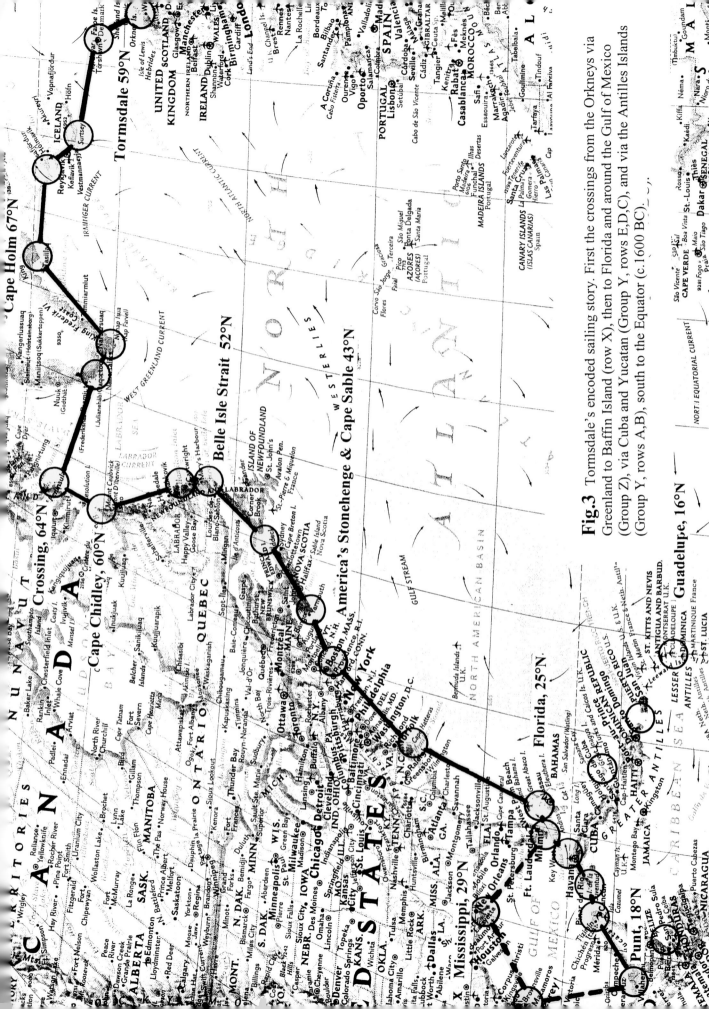

Fig.3 Tormsdale's encoded sailing story. First the crossings from the Orkneys via Greenland to Baffin Island (row X), then to Florida and around the Gulf of Mexico (Group Z), via Cuba and Yucatan (Group Y, rows E,D,C), and via the Antilles Islands (Group Y, rows A,B), south to the Equator (c.1600 BC).

monuments, we can see the movements of the Sun were important to them, and infer that they were involved in SunGod beliefs. This stone D23 also encodes the related latitude of the Southern Egyptian Empire, far in the east, at 23°N, the center of the Sun Religion. The next menhir D22 is the SW Cape of Cuba, at 22°N. The gap in the row D between 22 and 21 is the crossing to Cape Catoche, Yucatan. Row D has a total of 11 stones, showing the sailing direction of 11° WSW. The 2 northern menhirs D23 and D22 provide the sailing distance, 2 Moiras= 2°= 120 NM. The top angle Y, between rows A and E, is to 21°, encoding important Cape Catoche, Yucatan, at 21°N. Menhir D21 represents this Cape, at the end of the crossing. The 2 menhirs of the previous row E confirm the length of the crossing, 2 Moiras. The first group of row E has 1 menhir (the tens), and the second group has also 1 menhir (the units), confirming the sailing direction of 10+1= 11°WSW.

Menhir D19 is the northern area around the Gulf of Campeche, at 19°N. This stone is located on axis 67, to the westernmost menhir, again. Here is the civilization in Central America, which is considered as the "Realm of the Dead" (Refs.25-30). Note, that rows A and X form a triangle, or arrow, containing 18 to 19 menhirs, confirming this pilgrimage to the south point of the Gulf of Campeche, at 18°N and 19°N.

The last menhir D13 of the row is Cape Gallinas, the North Cape of South America, at 13°N. This description of the shortest route to Central and South America was considered to be very important. For that reason row C was constructed, directed to the eastern point Y. Finally, the eastern position of menhir C10 shows, that in spite of the rough tradewind seas, they advised a route (sailing a reach) along the east side of the Island of Trinidad, at 10°N. In this way, the narrow straits at the south side of Trinidad are avoided, where the Trades from the east probably make sailing difficult. Possibly attacks from hostile coastal tribes might have played a role, too.

The Antilles Islands Route

Row A is situated outside the menhirs of group Z. The row has been added, maybe as an afterthought, to the whole construction. This add-on row contains information on an alternative route to South America. The stones of row A had only a modest meaning at the start of the voyage. Now row A describes the less important, eastern Antilles Islands Route. The northernmost menhir A25 is the north coast of Andros Island, at 25°N, or New Providence Island, the site of Nassau. The next menhir A24 is the south coast of Andros Island, at 24°N, or a place along the then-existing edge of the Banks.

The opening next to it is the crossing from Andros to Cuba, SE of Florida Strait. The somewhat westerly placed menhir A24 gives a hint for the most desirable sailing direction, SSW. The 2 menhirs A25 and A24 just mentioned give the sailing distance, 2 Moiras= 2°= 120 NM. Menhir A23 is the holy Tropic of Cancer, at 23°N, and the easterly placed stone A21 refers to the easterly situated island of Great Inagua, Bahamas, still today full of Flamingoes in a huge lake, at 21°N. Finally, menhir A18 provides the latitude of the south coasts of all the islands of the Greater Antilles, at 18°N.

The last menhir A16 of the row is the most important island of the Lesser Antilles,

Guadeloupe, at 16°N. The neighboring row B is also directed to the eastern point Y, and acts as the base line for the Antilles Route. The northernmost menhirs B14 and B15 provide the latitude of Martinique, at 14.5°N. This island is perhaps the center of the Lesser Antilles. Note that the first menhirs of the important base rows B and C both represent the Equator, at the level of the mouth of the Amazon River, at 0°N (see **Fig.3**).

Note, that the stone rows of Tormsdale encode a map in latitudes of the islands of the Caribbean. Along the Windward Islands, because of the easterly Tradewind, it is possible to sail on a beam reach between islands, going either north or south, so by this route it is possible to sail south to the South American coast, and meet other boats arriving from the Cape Verde Islands with the trade wind on the "Southern Crossing" (Ref.8). This Southern Crossing had been in use for 1000 years when these rows of Tormsdale were built.

Dating

The monument of Tormsdale has not been carbon-dated (Ref.3). Its geographic meaning shows it was made after the discovery of America via the Atlantic, c.2500 BC (Refs.8,9). In the 500 years after this date people focused their attention on this new continent, for religious reasons, but also for establishing trade relations. Stonehenge III, the "Sarsen Stone" Circle with the Horseshoe, was built c.2000 BC to celebrate and encode the discovery of America. This date coincides with the start of the strong governments of the 12th Dynasty of the Middle Kingdom (Egypt). Tormsdale, with its rows of small menhirs, is of a completely different design, so, there are reasons to believe that it was built long after 2000 BC. Author A. Burl, who has studied so many sites, states that these types of multiple rows were not constructed after c.1500 BC (Ref.3).

These contemplations provide a time period for this monument. However, possibly, the makers of Tormsdale left a mark for the date. Rows X and A form a right-angled triangle, with axis 1 as a baseline (**Fig.2**). This shape is the Egyptian hieroglyph for "land" (America). Maybe this triangle encodes the date of the rows. It contains 5+10= 15 menhirs, suggesting a date during the 15th Dynasty of Egypt (the Hyksos Dynasty). The outer arrow rows A and T+U contain 10+5= 15 menhirs, also suggesting this. If menhir X67 is included, the triangle has 15+1= 16 menhirs, suggesting a date during the 16th Dynasty. Base row B has 16 menhirs, also suggesting it.

There are reasons to believe that the menhirs of row X represent Dynasties. If counting the Dynasties continues in next row A, big menhir A22, which marks the most important crossing of Davis Strait, would probably represent the date of the site (**Fig.2**). This is the 7th menhir of row A, and would mark the 9+7= 16th Dynasty, again. This dynasty ruled almost simultaneously with the 15th Dynasty. If we accept a date during the 15th and 16th Dynasties of Egypt, it would mean the stone rows of Tormsdale were constructed in the period between 1640 BC and 1580 BC.

The monument of Lagatjar, Brittany, shows the crossing of the Labrador Sea, from SW Greenland to the coast of Labrador, with a sailing direction of about 45°SW (Ref.37). This crossing is more difficult than the crossing of Davis Strait, described in Tormsdale.

Lagatjar dates from c.1600 BC. It appears that Tormsdale cannot be of much later date. For these reasons we assume that Tormsdale dates from the time of the Hyksos Dynasty in Egypt, c.1600 BC.

Discussion

The name of Tormsdale probably stems from to the old Norse version of the Sun Religion. "Tormsdale" literally means "Valley of Thor and Orm". "Thor" is the Norse SunGod, and "Orm" is the Norse earthgod, which is the Norse version of Maat, the Egyptian goddess of law and order in the universe (Refs.8,9,25-28).

We find that the rows of Tormsdale also form a latitude map of the southern return route across the Ocean, when working up the Arrow rows from south to north, the reverse of the process we worked through in this article. Bermuda (latitude 32°N) is seen as an important way-point when this is done. The eleven rows A-U encode the nine islands of the Azores and two of Madeira, "stepping stones" back to the Old World. Hopefully, archaeology students will someday be put to work excavating the site, and these routes will be re-studied after re-confirmation of the accuracy of the groundplan.

The rows of Tormsdale and other megalithic monuments were not built by accident, but were carefully designed by the mind of man. In prehistoric times they were, after all, a lot of work to construct. We believe they were mneumonic devices, used by some members of the community to recall data, and retell encoded stories, prior to the relatively recent development of phonetic writing (Refs.8-20). Maybe the groundplan of the Tormsdale site was burnt in a polished plank of wood, and was carried aboard by sailors for navigational purposes. After a few millennia, the methodology used to interpret the numeric encodings was lost, so later people were unable to read the monuments. However, we think we have rediscovered this methodology, and reading the monument this way makes geographic sense, and cannot be presumed to be beyond the ability of men in the Bronze Age.

Aubrey Burl has probably studied Megalithic Row Monuments more than any other person. He states that "Despite the amazement of visitors amongst the bewilderment of stones, .. the subject of megalithic rows is still an almost unstudied aspect of European prehistory. Over the centuries interpretations of the rows have been neither numerous, profound nor plausible. .. This is no longer acceptable (Ref.3)". This article suggests a method to the understanding of these monuments that utilizes a mathematical analysis, combined with recently understood cultural factors. The result is a new understanding of the longings, abilities, and achievements of man in the Bronze Age.

References

1. Myatt, L.J., "A Survey of the Tormsdale Stone Rows", Caithness Field Club Bulletin, Vol. 4, April 1985. Available at:http://caithness.org/history/articles/stonerowstormsdale/
2. Myatt, L.J., The multiple stone rows of Caithness and Sutherland, I., "Their distribution", Caithness F.C. Bull. 2 (7), 191-5,1980
3. Burl, A., From Carnac to Callanish, The Prehistoric Stone Rows and Avenues of Britain, Ireland and Brittany, Yale UniversityPress,1993(ISBN0-300-05575-7)
4. Myatt, L.J, "The stone rows of northern Scotland", In: (ed. Ruggles, C.L.N. 1988, 277-318).

5. Freer, R., and Myatt, L.J., The multiple stone rows of Caithness and Sutherland, 2, "Their description", 1', Caithness F.C. Bull. 3 (3), 58-63, 1982

6. Freer, R., and Myatt, L.J., The multiple stone rows of Caithness and Sutherland, 2, "Their description", 2', Caithness F.C. Bull. 3 (5), 120-6, 1983

7. "Megaliths in Scotland: Multiple Stone Rows/Avenue", Website of the Megalithic Portal: http:/www.megalithic.co.uk/, Search: Multiple Stone Rows

8. De Jonge, R.M., and Wakefield, J.S, How the Sungod Reached America, A Guide to Megalithic Sites, MCS Inc., 2002 (ISBN 0-917054-19-9) Available: MCS Inc., Box 3392, Kirkland, Wa 98083-3392. (Available: MCS Inc., Box 3392, Kirkland, Wa 98083-3392, also on CD).

9. De Jonge, R.M., and IJzereef, G.F., De Stenen Spreken, Kosmos Z&K, Utrecht/Antwerpen, 1996 (ISBN 90-215-2-846-0) (Dutch)

10. De Jonge, R.M., and Wakefield, J.S., "The Monument of Ales Stenar: A Sunship to the Realm of the Dead (Kaseberga, South Coast of Sweden, c.500 BC)", Migration & Diffusion, Odyssee-Verlag-Wien, Vol.5, No.19, July-September 2004 (ISSN 563-440X)

11. De Jonge, R.M., and Wakefield, J.S., "The Discovery of the Atlantic Islands", Migration & Diffusion, Vol.3, No.11, pgs 69-109, 2002

12. De Jonge, R.M., and Wakefield, J.S., "The Three Rivers Petroglyph, A Guidepost for River Travel in America", Migration & Diffusion, Vol.3, No.12, pgs 74-100, 2002

13. De Jonge, R.M., and Wakefield, J.S., "A Nautical Center for Crossing the Ocean, America's Stonehenge, New Hampshire, c.2200 BC", Migration & Diffusion, Vol. 4, No.15, pgs 60-100, 2002

14. De Jonge, R.M., and Wakefield, J.S., "Germany's Bronze Age Disc Reveals Transatlantic Seafaring", Vol.9, Ancient American, No.55, pgs.18-20, 2004

15. De Jonge, R.M., and Wakefield, J.S., "The Disc of Nebra, Important Sailing Routes of the Bronze Age Displayed in a Religious Context", Migration & Diffusion, Vol.5, No.17, pgs 32-39, 2004

16. De Jonge, R.M., and Wakefield, J.S., "The Passage Grave of Karleby, Encoding the Islands Discovered in the Ocean", Migration & Diffusion, Vol.5, No.18, pgs 64-74, 2004

17. De Jonge, R.M., and Wakefield, J.S., "Ales Stenar, Sweden's Bronze Age Sunship to the Americas", Ancient American, Vol.9, No.56, pgs 16-21, 2004

18. John Tiffany, "Coded Messages of the Megalith Builders", The Barnes Review, Vol.VIII, No.5, Sept/Oct. 2002

19. Ruggles, "Records in Stone, Papers in Memory of Alexander Thom", Cambridge, C.L.N. (1988).

20. Thom, A., "Megalithic Geometry in Standing Stones", New Scientist, March 12, 1964.

21. Batt, M., and others, Au Pays des Megalithes, Carnac-Locmariaquer, Jos, 1991 (French)

22. Briard, J., The Megaliths of Brittany, Gisserot, 1991

23. Giot, P.R., Prehistory in Brittany, Ed JOS (ISBN 2-85543-123-9)

24. Bailloud, G., et.al., Carnac, Les Premieres Architectures de Pierre, CNRS Edition, 1995 (ISBN 2-85822-139-1) (French)

25. Fell, B., America BC, Pocket Books, Simon & Schuster, 1994

26. Bailey, J., Sailing to Paradise, Simon & Schuster, 1994

27. Thompson, G., American Discovery, Misty Isles Press, Seattle, 1994

28. Jairazbhoy, R.A., Ancient Egyptians and Chinese in America, Rowman & Littlefield, Totowa, N.J., 1974 (ISBN 0-87471-571-1)

29. Gruener, J., The Olmec Riddle, An Inquiry into the Origin of Precolumbian Civilization, Vengreen Publications, 1987, Rancho Santa Fe, Cal. (ISBN 09421-85-56-0)

30. New World and Pacific Civilizations, The Illustrated History of Humankind, Weldon Owen Pty Limited, McMahons Point, Australia (1995) (ISBN 90-215-2512-7)

31. Portions of Ordinance Survey Maps, Pathfinder #66 ND 04/14 "Achavanich" and ND 05/15 "Halkirk"

32. Archaeology Branch of the Ordinance Survey, Discovery Excavation Scotland 1982, 49

33. Casson, L., Ships and Seafaring in Ancient Times, British Museum Press, 1994

34. Wachsmann, S., Seagoing Ships and Seamanship in the Bronze Age, Levant, College Station, Texas, 1998

35. Heyerdahl, T., The Ra Expeditions, George Allen & Unwin, London, 1971

36. Lambert, J.D., America's Stonehenge, an Interpretive Guide, Sunrise Publications, Kingston, N.H., 1996 (ISBN 0-9652630-0-2)

37. De Jonge, R.M., and Wakefield, J.S, The Megalithic Monument of Lagatjar (Brittany, c.1600 BC), to be published.

38. Nadis, S., "Ice Man", Archaeology, Nov/Dec 2001 (ISSN 0003-8113)

39. The World, National Geographic, Political, 2003 (modified from a portion of)

40. Joseph, F., Survivors of Atlantis, Their Impact on the World, Bear & Co., Vermont, 2004 (ISBN 1-59143-040-2)

41. The Top of the World, National Geographic Society, 1949 (modified from portion of)

A Return Route across the Ocean, encoded at Tormsdale Rows

(Caithness, NE Scotland, c.1600 BC)

R.M. de Jonge, drsrmdejonge@hotmail.com
J.S. Wakefield, jayswakefield@yahoo.com

Summary

The stone rows of Tormsdale are buried under peat beside the Thurso River, in NE Scotland. The monument consists of two groups of rows, both pointing NW, and a NS row. When the stones are numbered, and interpreted as latitudes, it is possible to read encoded sailing information. In a previous article, we showed that the rows describe the coastal sailing route via the Upper North to Central America. In this article we show that the site also encodes the return route across the Ocean to Scotland.

The Rows of Tormsdale

Tormsdale consists of a fan of rows of low menhirs, about 1 meter above the original ground level (**Fig.1**). It is located in the region of Caithness, in the NE corner of Scotland, alongside the small Thurso River, about 15 miles (24km) from both north and east coasts (Ref.2). Like a number of other sites in the region, the rows of Tormsdale are buried in a layer of peat which is more than a meter high. The stone rows were first recorded by the Archaeology Branch of the Ordinance Survey in 1982. The site covers a surface area of 60m x 60m, and is located between two ruined brochs, once graceful circular drystone towers, dating from the Iron Age (Ref.1). **Photo 1** gives a NW view across a Sheepfold, which is 200m north of the southern broch. The rows should be at the right side of the bend of the Thurso River, some 100m NW of the fold.

Using the groundplan, as labeled for our first article (**Fig.1**), we see that Tormsdale consists of rows of stones forming two arrows, both pointing NW, which are cut by a NS line. The 5 southern rows A-E are directed to one point Y, and form a group, called Group Y. The 7 northern rows B and P-U are focused on distant point Z, and form a group, called Group Z. The important line B is a common row of both Groups Y and Z. In parentheses following the letter labeling of each row is the total number of stones in each row. It is a rather large construction. In total, there are 104 stones, each of them having a length of about a meter, and a width of half a meter, as can be seen using the scale in **Fig.1**. On the average they are about one meter high. The taller menhirs are placed at the south side of the monument (Refs.1-7).

The Sailing Route from Scotland to Central America

First, we will recap the route as described in our previous article (see **Fig.4**). When sailing to the northwest (along row A in **Fig.1**), the latitudes along the stones of row X increase from 59°N (the Orkneys, X59), to 67°N (Cape Holm, Greenland, X67). The double arrow of Tormsdale gives the global sailing direction (NW), via the Faroes and Iceland to Greenland. These three areas are represented by the three groups of stones of row A. Sailing continues along the SE coast of Greenland (which is via row X) to the south.

From the west coast of Greenland (row B, the western stone B2) (see **Fig.2**), we cross at 64°N (along axis 64) due west to Cumberland Sound (X64). Sailing continues along Baffin Island to the south (by going down the latitudes of row X) to the coast of Labrador (X59), at

Photo 1 View NW across the Sheepfold. The Tormsdale Rows are supposed to be at the right side of the bend of the Thurso River, some 100m NW of the fold. (Caithness, NE Scotland)

59°N. The continuation of this route is provided by the stones of Group Z, following the rows U-R from north to south. From Labrador (U58), at 58°N, we sail along the East Coast of North America to the south, all the way to the island of Bimini (R26), offshore Florida, at 26°N.

Tormsdale has a big arrow to western point Z, and a small arrow to eastern point Y (**Fig.2**). Rows Q, P, and B of arrow Z provide the western route from Florida around the Gulf of Mexico, and rows E, D, and C of arrow Y give the shortest, eastern way to Central America. Both sailing routes lead to the south point of the Gulf of Campeche, at 18°N (P18/D18), the center of the Realm of the Dead, and beyond to the south.

The Return Route across the Ocean

The target of the voyage described in the Tormsdale rows was the south point of the Gulf of Campeche in Mexico, at 18°N (Refs.22,30-38,41). So, for the return route this will be the point of departure, shown in **Fig.3**. The southernmost menhir X18 now represents this point, literally, the Gulf of Campeche, at 18°N (Fig.4). Menhir X21 is Cape Catoche, Yucatan, at 21°N. Here we have to cross to Cuba. Axis 21 leads to the first stone of row A. This row contains a total of 10 stones, corresponding with the correct sailing direction to Cuba, 10°ENE. The group of 2 menhirs 20 and 21 of row X provide the sailing distance, 2 Moiras= 2°= 120 NM.

Note that the stones of the rows in **Fig.3** are changed by one number, compared to **Figs.1 and 2** used in the previous article to encode the route west. They now end at 59, on the top row, not 58. It appears that the monument was designed this way, because when this is done, and the same methodology is employed in "reading" the monument, return latitudes are obvious, and indicated correctly. We do not know if the stones ever had painted numbers on them. They may have just been mneumonic devices, that required counting to be used. They may have been copied from dots in boards, or other navigating devices. In any case, after the invention of writing, the ability to use these devices was no longer useful, and so forgotten.

Along the coast of Cuba we continue to sail to the northeast. X23 is the north coast of Cuba, at the holy Tropic of Cancer, at 23°N. On midsummer day the Sun is here at right angles above. The slow northerly movement of the Sun then turns into a southerly movement. This is also the latitude of the Southern Egyptian Empire, far in the east. It is the center of the Sunreligion (Refs.8,9). (Note, that menhirs X23 and A23 are located at the ends of axis 23, which previously, at the way there, indicated the important crossing of Davis Strait (**Fig.2**).

From Cuba, we cross due north to Florida. The group of 2 menhirs 22 and 23 of row X provide the sailing direction and sailing distance, 2 Moiras= 2°= 120 NM. X25 is the south point of Florida, at 25°N. The last, special menhir X26 is the island of Bimini, offshore Florida, at 26°N. This is the important departure point of the long voyage across the Ocean (**Fig.4**).

Rows C, D, and E also describe this short route from the Gulf of Campeche to Bimini. They have together 13+11+2= 26 stones, confirming Bimini (E26), at 26°N. Rows B, P, and Q of Group Z describe the western route around the Gulf of Mexico. They possess together 16+8+2= 26 stones, again confirming Bimini (Q26). Rows B and A describe the easterly Antilles Route. They contain together 16+10= 26 stones, once again confirming Bimini

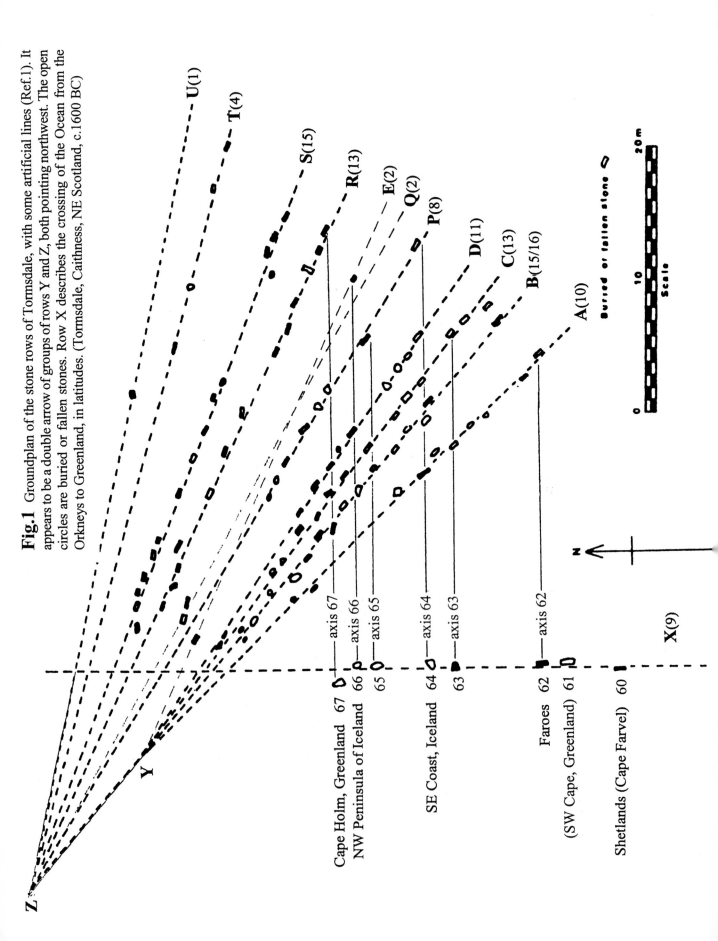

Fig.1 Groundplan of the stone rows of Tormsdale, with some artificial lines (Ref.1). It appears to be a double arrow of groups of rows Y and Z, both pointing northwest. The open circles are buried or fallen stones. Row X describes the crossing of the Ocean from the Orkneys to Greenland, in latitudes. (Tormsdale, Caithness, NE Scotland, c.1600 BC)

(A26). In our previous article these rows were shown to encode the three routes from Bimini to the south (Ref.41).

From Bimini (X26) we sail (along the upper axis) to the neighboring island of Great Abaco (R27), Bahamas, at 27°N. From here we set a course to Bermuda (R32), at 32°N. This small island was discovered c.2400 BC (Refs.8,9,12,13). Probably the island was visited briefly, as a welcome place to take a break and refresh. Certainly it was important for emergencies. The first group of 3 stones (usually the tens) finishes with a stone at right angles to the row. So, the initial sailing direction (ISD) to Bermuda is 3x10= 30°NE.

After R27 (Great Abaco) we see a group of 2 stones (the tens), and after this a second group of 3 stones (the units), finishing with R32 (Bermuda). So, the terminal sailing direction (TSD) in the neighborhood of Bermuda is 20+3= 23°NE. The difference between both sailing directions is caused by the curvature of the Earth. After R27, Great Abaco, there are 12 stones in row R, corresponding with the sailing distance to Bermuda, 12 Moiras= 12°= 720 NM, which is correct.

From Bermuda (R32), at 32°N, we sail to the West Azores (R39, the last stone of row R), at 39°N. The Azores (R37-39), at 37, 38, and 39°N were discovered c.3600 BC (Refs.8-12). They form an archipelago which can be easily found (**Fig.3**). Accurate instructions are not needed now. We are sailing with the wind and the current to the northeast. The first group of 3 stones (R33-35, the tens) shows the correct initial sailing direction, c.30°NE. The second group of 4 stones (R36-39, the units) gives the terminal sailing direction in the neighborhood of the West Azores, c.4°ENE. The rows R (13 stones) and S (15 stones) possess together 28 stones, providing the sailing distance, 28 Moiras= 28°= 1680 NM. Row R points to the top angle Z of 29°, confirming it, about 29 Moiras, which is correct. The eastern stone R36 illustrates the eastern situation of the Strait of Girbraltar, at 36°N.

From the West Azores (R39) we sail to the west coast of Ireland (S52-54, the last stones of row S), at 52, 53, and 54°N. Again, we are sailing with the Gulf Stream. The first group of 4 stones in row S gives the initial sailing direction, c.40°NE, the second group of 5 stones gives the sailing direction halfway, c.50°NE, and the last group of 6 stones gives the terminal sailing direction, c.60°NE. Row S (15 stones), row T (4 stones), and row U (1 stone) provide the sailing distance to Ireland, about 15+4+1= 20 Moiras= 20°= 1200 NM. The western stone S43 indicates Cape Finisterre, NW Spain, at 43°N. S48 is the west point of Brittany, France, at 48°N.

Finally, the last stone 58 of row T is the island of Lewis of the Outer Hebrides, Scotland, at 58°N, and U59 represents both the Orkney Islands and Tormsdale, at 59°N. So, in this way people were sailing back, with the wind and the current, to the Old World (see **Fig.5**).

The rows of Tormsdale form a numerically-encoded map of this southern return route (via Bermuda) across the Ocean. Row X symbolizes the western island of Bermuda, rows A-E and P-S form a group of 9 rows, representing the 9 islands of the Azores, and the last group of 2 rows, T and U, encode the 2 British Isles. All these islands represent the "stepping stones" to the Old World. This route across the waters had a special religious meaning. In antiquity, the Old World was considered as the "Land of the Living".

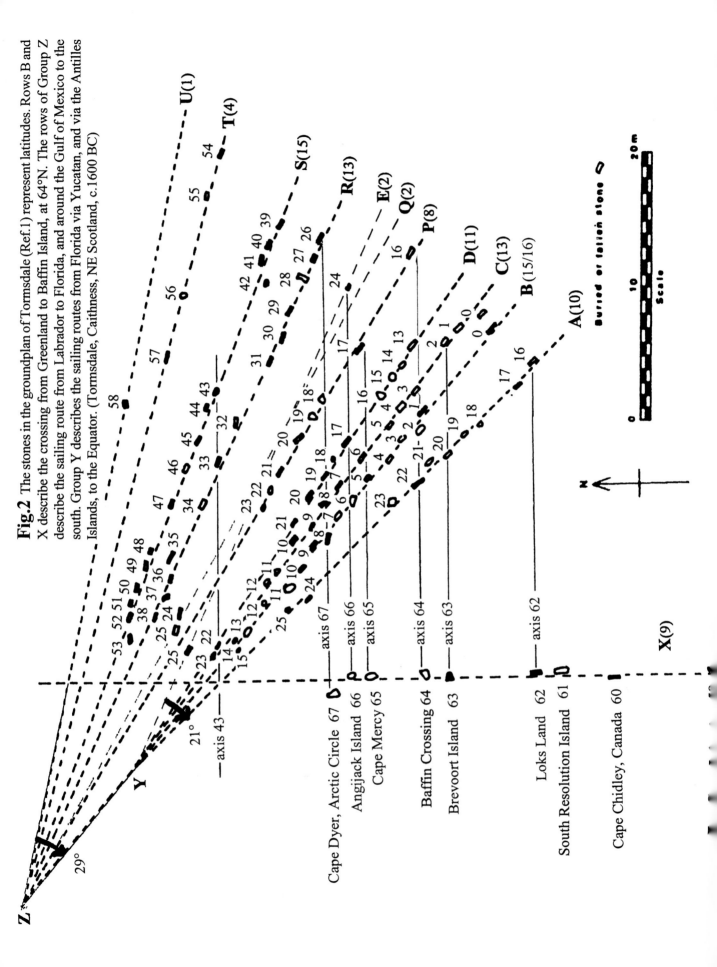

Fig.2 The stones in the groundplan of Tormsdale (Ref.1) represent latitudes. Rows B and X describe the crossing from Greenland to Baffin Island, at 64°N. The rows of Group Z describe the sailing route from Labrador to Florida, and around the Gulf of Mexico to the south. Group Y describes the sailing routes from Florida via Yucatan, and via the Antilles Islands, to the Equator. (Tormsdale, Caithness, NE Scotland, c.1600 BC)

Discussion

The rows of Tormsdale and other megalithic monuments were not built by accident, but were carefully designed by the mind of man. In prehistoric times they were, after all, a lot of work to construct. We believe they were mneumonic devices, used by some members of the community to recall data, and retell encoded stories, prior to the modern development of phonetic writing. Maybe the groundplan of the Tormsdale site was burnt in a polished plank of wood, and carried by sailors for navigational purposes. After a few millennia, the methodology used to interpret the numeric encodings was lost, so later people were unable to read the monuments. However, we think we have rediscovered this methodology, and reading the monument this way makes geographic sense, and cannot be presumed to be beyond the ability of men in the Bronze Age.

References

1. Burl, A., From Carnac to Callanish, The Prehistoric Stone Rows and Avenues of Britain, Ireland and Brittany, Yale University Press, 1993 (ISBN 0-300-05575-7)

2. Myatt, L.J., "A Survey of the Tormsdale Stone Rows", Caithness Field Club Bulletin, Vol.4, April 1985. Available at website: http://caithness.org/history/articles/stone rowstormsdale/

3. Myatt, L.J., "The multiple stone rows of Caithness and Sutherland, I, Their distribution", Caithness F.C. Bull. 2 (7), 191-5, 1980

4. Myatt, L.J, "The stone rows of northern Scotland", In: (ed. Ruggles, C.L.N. 1988, 277-318).

5. Freer, R., and Myatt, L.J., "The multiple stone rows of Caithness and Sutherland, 2, Their description", 1', Caithness F.C. Bull. 3 (3), 58-63, 1982

6. Freer, R., and Myatt, L.J., "The multiple stone rows of Caithness and Sutherland, 2, Their description", 2', Caithness F.C. Bull. 3 (5), 120-6, 1983

7. "Megaliths in Scotland: Multiple Stone Rows/Avenue", Website of the Megalithic Portal: http:/www.megalithic.co.uk/, Search: Multiple Stone Rows

8. De Jonge, R.M., and Wakefield, J.S., How the SunGod Reached America c.2500 BC, A Guide to Megalithic Sites, 2002 (ISBN 0-917054-19-9). (Available: MCS Inc., Box 3392, Kirkland, Wa 98083-3392, also on CD)

9. De Jonge, R.M., and IJzereef, G.F., De Stenen Spreken, Kosmos Z&K, Utrecht/Antwerpen, 1996 (ISBN 90-215-2-846-0) (Dutch)

10. De Jonge, R.M., and Wakefield, J.S., "The Discovery of the Atlantic Islands (4500-2900 BC)", Migration & Diffusion, Vol.3, No.11, pgs 69-109, 2002

11. De Jonge, R.M., and Wakefield, J.S., "The Passage Grave of Karleby, Encoding the Islands Discovered in the Ocean (c.2950 BC)", Migration & Diffusion, Vol.5, No.18, pgs 64-74, 2004

12. De Jonge, R.M., and Wakefield, J.S., "A Nautical Center for Crossing the Ocean, America's Stonehenge, New Hampshire, c.2200 BC", Migration & Diffusion, Vol. 4, No.15, pgs 60-100, 2002

13. Tiffany, J., "Coded Messages of the Megalith Builders", The Barnes Review, Vol.VIII, No.5, Sept/Oct. 2002

14. Ruggles, "Records in Stone, Papers in Memory of Alexander Thom", Cambridge, C.L.N. (1988).

15. Thom, A., "Megalithic Geometry in Standing Stones", New Scientist, March 12, 1964.

16. Varen, Vechten en Verdienen. Scheepvaart in de Oudheid, Allard Pierson Museum, Amsterdam, 1995 (Dutch)

17. Siliotti, A., Egypt, Temples, People and Gods, Bergamo, Italy, 1997

18. Kemp, B.J., Ancient Egypt, Anatomy of a Civilization, London, Routledge, 1991

19. Adams, B., and Cialowicz, K., Protodynastic Egypt, Shire Egyptology, Princes Risborough, 1997

20. Tompkins, P., Secrets of the Great Pyramid, Harper & Row, London, 1971 (ISBN 0-06-090631-6)(Dr. Stecchini)

21. Hart, G., A Dictionary of Egyptian Gods and Goddesses, Routledge, London, 1986 (ISBN 0-7102-0167-2)

22. Breasted, J.H., Ancient Records of Egypt, Vol.2: "The Eighteenth Dynasty", London, 1988

23. Wallis Budge, E.A., Osiris and the Egyptian Resurrection, 2 Vol., Dover Pub., N.Y., 1973 (ISBN 0-486-22780-41)

24. Gruener, J., The Olmec Riddle, An Inquiry into the Origin of Precolumbian Civilization, Vengreen Publications, 1987, Rancho Santa Fe, Cal. (ISBN 09421-85-56-0)

25. New World and Pacific Civilizations. The Illustrated History of Humankind, Weldon Owen Pty Limited, McMahons Point, Australia (1995) (ISBN 90-215-2512-7)

26. Fell, B., America BC, Pocket Books, Simon & Schuster, 1994

27. Bailey, J., Sailing to Paradise, Simon & Schuster, 1994

28. Thompson, G., American Discovery, Misty Isles Press, Seattle, 199429

29. Wachsmann, S., Seagoing Ships and Seamanship in the Bronze Age Levant, College Station, Texas, 1998

30. Heyerdahl, T., The Ra Expeditions, George Allen & Unwin, London, 1971

31. Archaeology Branch of the Ordinance Survey, Discovery Excavation Scotland 1982, 49

32. The World, National Geographic, Political, 2003 (modified from a portion of)

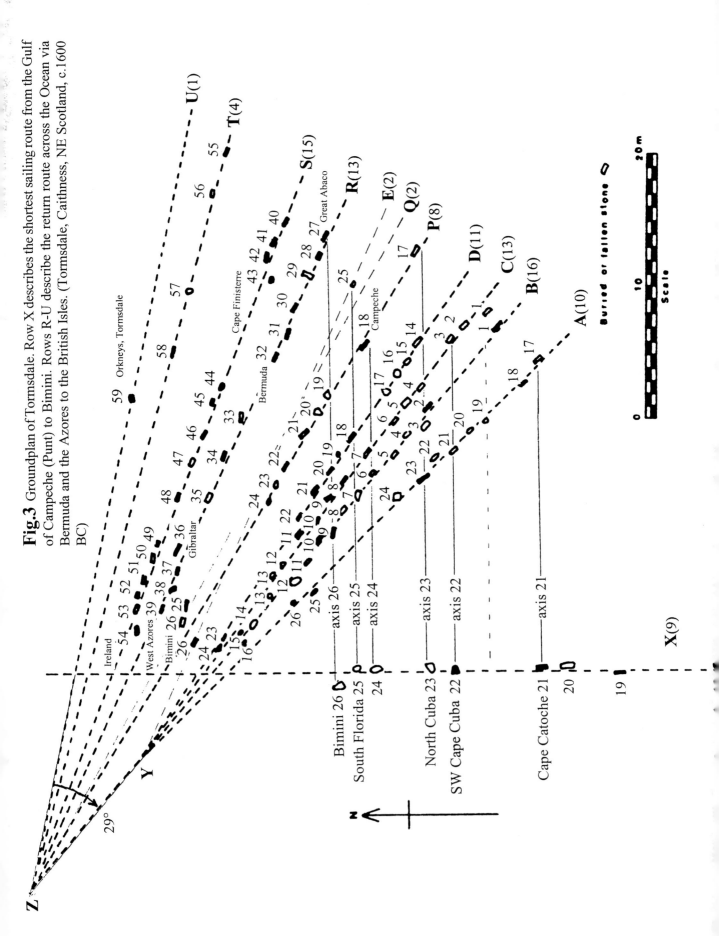

Fig.3 Groundplan of Tormsdale. Row X describes the shortest sailing route from the Gulf of Campeche (Punt) to Bimini. Rows R–U describe the return route across the Ocean via Bermuda and the Azores to the British Isles. (Tormsdale, Caithness, NE Scotland, c.1600 BC)

Fig.4 Tormsdale's encoded sailing story (Ref.39). First the crossings from the Orkneys Via Greenland to Baffin Island (row X), then to Florida and around the Gulf of Mexico (Group Z), via Cuba and Yucatan (Group Y, rows E,D,C), and via th Antilles Islands (Group Y, rows A,B), south to the Equator (c.1600 BC).

Fig.5 Tormsdale's encoded sailing story (Ref.40). First the sailing route from the Gulf of Campeche (Punt) to Bimini (row X), then the return route across the Ocean via Bermuda and the Azores to the British Isles (Group Z, rows R–U). (c.1600 BC)

POVERTY POINT
Bronze Age Town & Gulf Ports on the Copper Trail
Open-fire manufacturing of Copper Oxhides
(Epps, NE Louisiana, c.2000-700 BC)

J.S. Wakefield, jayswakefield@yahoo.com

Summary

The "Late Archaic" Poverty Point earthworks in Louisiana are the earliest and largest monuments in prehistoric North America. The site that remains covers a square mile, features six concentric segmented semi-circular walls, surrounded by six large mounds. The site is shown to be a prehistoric town, and a manufacturing and trading center which was a part of the worldwide megalithic culture. The site design reveals encoded latitudes of transatlantic sailing routes, and evidence of multicultural involvement in the manufacturing of copper oxhide ingots.

Introduction & Dating

The Poverty Point complex is a Louisiana State Commemorative Area, open to the public, and has been a National Historical Landmark since 1962. Collectors have been picking up artifacts since the 1870's, but it was not recognized as such a huge site until the ring pattern was recognized in a 1938 aerial photograph (**Fig.2, right**). The American Museum of Natural History dug at the site in 1942/3 and 1955, and showed "how large and unusual [the site] was" (Ref.1). Today, there is a road built through the rings, and 15,000 visitors a year pass through the site's museum. Some of the illustrations used in this article are from the book (The Ancient Mounds of Poverty Point, Place of the Rings) and website of John L. Gibson, previously employed as the site archaeologist, who devoted his career to the study of Poverty Point.

The site is located in the northeastern corner of Louisiana, northwest of Vicksburg, Mississippi at 33°N (**Fig.1**). Poverty Point is built on Maçon Ridge, a plateau 90 miles long, and five miles wide, in the swampy floodplains of the Mississippi River. Gibson reports 38 radiocarbon dates, all between 2278 BC (2470-2040) and 650 BC, with most between 1500 and 1300 BC. Gibson says that while the land and waters were biologically rich, the richest asset was the location. "This was one of the few places in the entire Mississippi valley where a departing pirogue could have been paddled without portages"(Refs.1,2).

The River and the Bayou

The huge ring complex is on a bluff above the west bank of Bayou Maçon. Other abandoned river channels and the route of the Bayou Macon indicate an active branch of the Mississippi flowed against the site in the past. Gibson's reconstruction drawing of the site (**Fig.3**) shows the steepness of the "precipitous bluff" on the east side of the site. The water of the bayou below is still, with fall maple leaves floating on the surface (**Fig.4**). This is the Bayou Macon, which originates near another isolated oxbow bend of the Mississippi in Arkansas, now called Chicot Lake. This valley bottom of the Mississippi

1

Fig.1 Top, State map of Poverty Point, located on the plateau of Maçon Ridge, about 10 miles west of the Mississippi, in the northeastern corner of Louisiana, at 33°N. **Below**, regional map of Mississippi River floodplain, locating Poverty Point. (Ref.1).

today contains many "bayous", which once were river channels, and vast swamps, with 29 Wildlife Refuges and Wildlife Management Areas. By air, the valley shows hundreds of old oxbows, and bayous. The Mississippi is a powerful river that spills a "half a million tons of sediment a day" into the Gulf of Mexico. The Chandeleur Islands in the Gulf (east of New Orleans, south of the State of Mississippi) "are remnants of a delta that vanished 1800 years ago (200 AD), when the river shifted its channel – something it has done six times in the last 9,000 years" (Ref.50).

"Precipitous bluffs" that are not rock are quickly eroded to a lesser slope unless they are being eroded at the bottom by active water. This "precipitous" bluff must have been made by a meandering branch of the Mississippi in relatively recent geologic times. Was Poverty Point built in a "C" shape as we see it in Gibson's **Fig.3?** Probably not. It was a trading center, where it was visited by people carrying heavy goods, including rock and metal, by water. These people would not have wanted to portage these goods in and out of bayous and swamps, and so would have chosen a site easily accessible by boat. Surely boats would have had direct access to the Poverty Point site. Four thousand years ago, prior to levees on the Mississippi, there was an annual flood season. The glacial meltwater from the Great Lakes and ice dam collapses at the southern end of Lake Superior brought major flooding events.These were times of fast flow. Then there were times of slow flow, when it is said a canoe could have been paddled up the Mississippi. When coming upriver from the Gulf, the Macon Ridge may have been the first high ground suitable for a settlement and trading site.

The site had been inhabited for more than a thousand years, but suffered a huge setback with the catastrophe of 1200 BC. Archaeologist Kidder says: "the elaborate trade and mound building abruptly ceased. Research has shown evidence for catastrophic flooding and global climate change c.1200-400 BC. The evidence comes from geological and soils mapping, archaeological and stratigraphic investigations, and an extensive program of coring. The greatly increased flood frequencies and magnitudes are associated with the demise of Poverty Point culture" (Ref.26).

The huge plexiglass panel display (**Fig.5**) hanging in the Visitor Center (contradicting Gibson) shows the "abandoned" and "new" channels (in black lettering on the plexiglass) of the Mississippi at "1000 BC" when it changed its channel. The River moved against the bluff, eroding almost half the rings, but when it meandered back the other way, it left the isolated bayou as we see it today.

That the site was originally circular is confirmed by the evidence reported by J.A. Ford and C.H. Webb following their excavations for the American Museum of Natural History in 1955 (Ref.49). They found the "distinguishing reddish brown clay soil [iron salts] of the Arkansas river" in the natural levees of the Bayou Macon and a layer of it in the trenches they dug across some of the rings. This layer "contrasted markedly with the gray soils deposited by the Mississippi". "The Braided Mississippi did much, but not all, of the final cutting into the eastern edge of Macon Ridge ... the meandering course of the Arkansas River ... carved the bluff and appears to have destroyed about half of the large geometrical earthworks" (Ref.49).

2

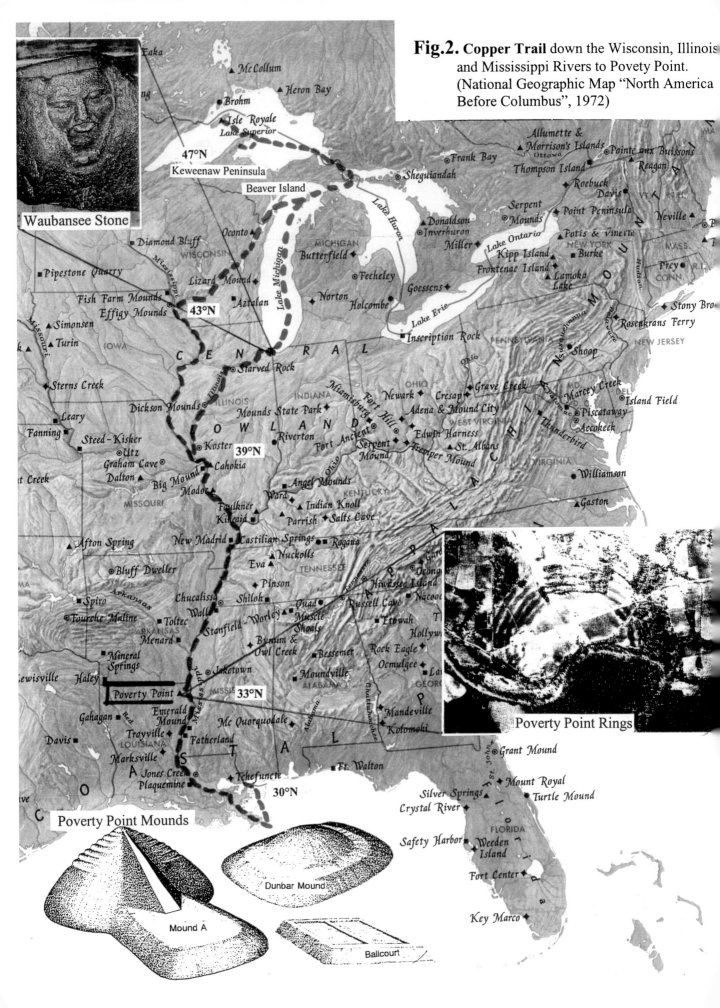

Fig.2. Copper Trail down the Wisconsin, Illinois and Mississippi Rivers to Povety Point. (National Geographic Map "North America Before Columbus", 1972)

Waubansee Stone

Poverty Point Rings

Poverty Point Mounds

Mound A

Dunbar Mound

Ballcourt

The original structure as a circular ring design is illustrated in **Figure 5.** Between 2500 BC and 1200 BC a thousand stone circles were built in the British Isles, showing a paradigm change in thinking when the other side of the world was discovered, and the world was confirmed to be round. This new conception of the world brought continued repetition of the representation of the Earth as a sphere. Many actual stone spheres are found. The most well known examples are in the Costa Rican Disquis Delta, but they are also found in Brittany and other places. The Bronze Age city of Atlantis was designed in circular shape. Stonehenge III was a circular site, also built at about 2,000 BC, the same time as Poverty Point.

The Earthworks: The Circular Rings

Poverty Point has "11.2 miles of artificial ridges", at one point about 7 feet high. A few of these were trenched by the American Museum in 1955, and were thought to support dwelling sites (Ref.49). These rings can be shown to have a geometric plan **(Fig.6)**. From north to south, the mounds B, A, L, and J are situated on a straight line, called the western North-South axis. (The site axes are not true N-S lines, but point 8° NNW, called "Poverty Point North" ("PPN"). This is similar to Olmec La Venta, on the south side of the Gulf of Mexico, designed at about the same time, both oriented opposite their sites' (magnetic) deviation of 8° east.) The line through the mounds M and D, called the eastern North-South axis, runs parallel to it. The 90° right angle intersection of the east axis with line A-C from Mound A will be called point C, and the line A-C we call the horizontal axis. Apparently, this point C is considered the "center of the plaza. The line connecting mound B and the center C makes angles of 45° with the horizontal and vertical lines. The line L-D, from Ballcourt Mound to Dunbar Mound, is at right angles, or near to right angles to B-C. These lines are the baselines of the complex.

There are 5 aisles which connect the central plaza with the area outside the rings. They divide the figure into segments of comparable size. The plaza was found to be "free of trash", but numerous filled-in holes up to 3 feet diameter were found "where posts had been set" on the western side. The SW segment possesses a special wall, parallel to the corridor beside it, which is called the Causeway. This Causeway continues to run beyond the rings in southwestern direction over a distance of 800 feet. No burials have yet been identified at Poverty Point.

The circular rings of Poverty Point model the planet Earth more accurately than you would expect. The rings are symbolic for the "Wheel of the Law", dedicated to Maat, the Egyptian goddess of law and order in the universe. The 6 walls in 10 segments of the full circle form 6 x 10= 60 units, showing the sailing route below Cape Farvel at 60°N. The 6 mounds X 6 rings = the latitude of Gibraltar at 36°N, and with 10 segments of the rings, may also show the size of the Earth, at 360°. Since a moira is the Egyptian distance unit for 1°, and our unit is the Nautical Mile (1°= 60 NM), they probably indicate the circumference of the Earth to be 360 moira, which would be 360 X 60= 21,600 NM, which is correct..

Gibson shows 38 radiocarbon date tests, with results running from 2300 BC (possibly 2470), to 650 BC (possibly AD 70). These radiocarbon datings put the site in the Late

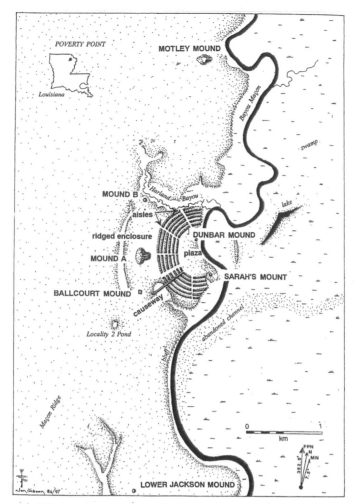

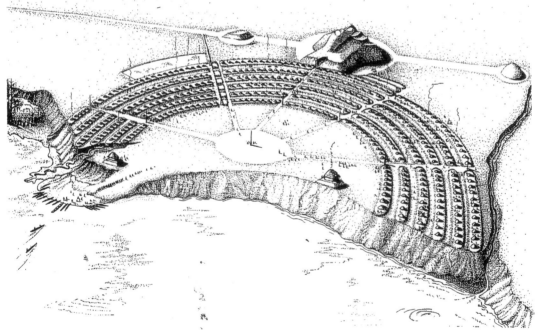

Fig.3 **Above:** Reconstruction drawing by Gibson, Poverty Point, c.1350 BC; **Below:** Groundplan of the earthworks of Poverty Point, as drawn by Gibson (Ref.1).

Archaic period in North America. The massive earthworks and tons of "exchange rocks" were considered incompatible with the Archaic "hunter-gatherer" period. But no agriculture, and very little pottery could be found, which has been very troubling to archaeologists. When one finds corn agriculture, earthworks and pottery, the culture is called "Woodland", and these sites are one or two thousand years more recent than early Poverty Point. There are no large rocks at Poverty Point, so the site features earthworks, not huge stone monuments. The whole complex of mounds has a North-South length of 3.5 miles, and a width of nearly a mile. At the center of the site are the 6 concentric, semi-circular walls around a wide plaza. The 5-8 foot tall rings are now reduced to one foot by plowing. Following its 1950's work, the American Museum of Natural History in New York reported dark middens (old debris) on the fore and aft slopes of the rings, and postholes on the rings, suggesting occupied buildings on the rings. Their work consisted of test holes, not excavated areas, so no patterns of construction have been seen. Gibson reports that "less than 3/10 of 1% of the area of the rings has been excavated" (.3%).

The Site Design and encoded latitudes

We have found that the site latitude is usually encoded clearly in the site design at Bronze Age sites. The line LC points 33° from the horizontal axis. This is the latitude of Poverty Point, 33°N. The angles between the major axes of the site and the mounds, show many of the latitudes frequently found in megalithic sites on both sides of the Atlantic. The angle of the Causeway is 39°, the latitude of the West Azores (39°N), the focus of safe return trips to the Old World. The junction of the Illinois with the Mississippi on the Copper Trail, and the Serpent Mound of Ohio are also at 39°N. Its reciprocal, 51°, is the latitude where the Belle Isle Strait joins the Gulf of St. Lawrence, and is also the site latitude of Stonehenge, in England. Stonehenge had been enlarged by adding the large Sarcen Stones in its center at about 2000 BC, commemorating the discovery of the New World (Ref.3), its development probably slowed by the comet disaster of 2347 BC. This famous monument, also built in a circular design, was probably known to the builders of Poverty Point.

The angle between L-D and the axis, could be 45°, depending on just where the measurements were taken. This would add symmetry to the design, since B-C is at 45°. If not intentionally replicating this angle, it is likely that the intended angle is 43°, which shows the important Nautical Center of America's Stonehenge, at 43°N, north of Boston. This is the largest megalithic stone monument in North America, where sailors with shiploads of copper were taught how to sail back to Europe (Ref.3). This is also the latitude on the Copper Trail where the Wisconsin River joins the Mississippi. The reciprocal angle of line L-C is 47°, the latitude of Cape Race, the eastern Cape of North America. The latitude of the Keweenaw copper mines is also 47°N. Other angles important to sailing the Atlantic are indicated, 45°N (Nova Scotia), 35°N (Cape Hatteras), 55°N (Hamilton Inlet), 21°N (Yucatan), 15°N (Cape Gracias a Dios, Honduras), and 13°N (Barbados, and Mid Caribbean Islands).

The Mounds

Ford and Webb calculated that 980,000 cubic yards of earth were moved in the construction of the mounds and rings, equal to "40 million basket loads" (Ref.49).

Fig.4 Two photos down the steep bank behind the Visitor Center to the Bayou Macon at the north end of the rings. Erosion along the bank is a problem for Park Staff. Clearly, the River, or a branch of it, was running against this bank in the not-too-distant past. (Photo by Wakefield, October, 2006)

The "Bird Effigy" **Mound A** is often described as having the shape of a bird flying to the west **(Fig.2)**. Supporting this interpretation is a potsherd in the site museum that has an eagle image on it. The mound has a two-story flat platform facing the rings on the east, and a ramp up to its western top, at 70 feet. Excavations have shown that at least several of the mounds were built in separate stages, with platforms being used for an unknown period before being covered with more earth (Ref.22). This height is second only to the original height of upriver Monk's Mound at Cahokia, considered the largest in the USA, which was built two thousand years later.

In Greek mythology, eagles were symbols of Zeus. In Egypt, the falcon was the image of heavenly power, an image of Ra, the Sungod, who was also imaged as a circular golden disc, rising each morning between the horns of Taurus, the bull in the Zodiac. The Benu Bird of Ra was the bird of solar creation, that undergoes death and is a symbol of regeneration (Ref.32). Professor Covey, Emeritus Professor of History, Wake Forest College, states that "both mounds apparently modeled after the gigantic flying-bird effigy at San Lorenzo" (near La Venta, Mexico) (Ref.28). A similar-looking spread wing eagle effigy 32 feet wide was found inside a mound in Ohio, which was surrounded, in European style, by standing slabs of stone, now reburied (Ref.23). Milner, author of *The Moundbuilders*, says "These works without question reflect the northern Native American cosmological theories of 'Thunderbirds' and 'snakes', which reflect the fear of comets, tied to the appearance of Comet Enecke in 1628 BC, and tied to its climate collapse. An early form of priest-kings were functioning in these massive 'thunderbird' mounds, trying to emulate the thunderbirds, and protect the people against the impacts" (Ref.22).

In Egyptian hierarchy, below the SunGod Ra, were two other important gods, the sungod Horus and the moongod Osiris. In an Egyptian temple, it is recorded that the SunGod Ra has said: "The Realm of the Dead is in the west, at the other side of the waters, in the Land where the Sun sets." In Poverty Point the two big Mounds may represent these gods. The somewhat smaller **Motley Mound (M)** is located at the end of the north axis, fenced off on private property, covered by trees. It symbolizes Horus, also the god of the North Star. The Bird Mound A is located at the end of the west axis. It symbolizes Osiris, the god of the Underworld, the West. The river symbolizes the "waters", and the ring walls are "the setting Sun". The site is the partially explored "Heavenly Empire in the Underworld", located at the west side of the river, just as the tombs of Egypt were built on the west side of the Nile, the direction of the Underworld.

Conical shaped Mound B has had quite a bit of excavation. Gibson reports that Mound B did not contain burials, but was raised over the ashes of a huge bonfire, which had consumed at least one person. It was conical, two stories high, built in four major stages. Interestingly, "in Egyptian temple art, Anubis (the black dog with ears standing up) is usually paired with a conical pyramid" (Ref.15). Remember the 6" polished black statue of Anubis reported found while digging for water in a 10' trench on a small island off the northeast coast of Haiti (Ref.43). Note that the early Olmec pyramid at La Venta is a conical pyramid. The Canaries have a high perfectly conical volcanic mountain (Pico), and conical pyramid structures. Mt Atlas was described as a conical volcanic mountain.

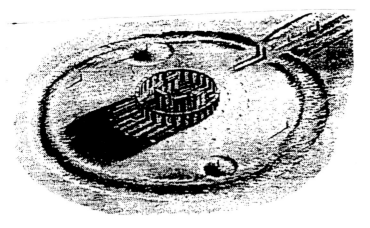

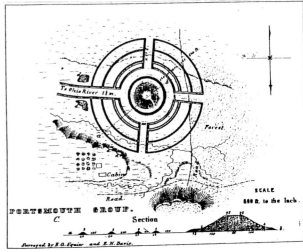

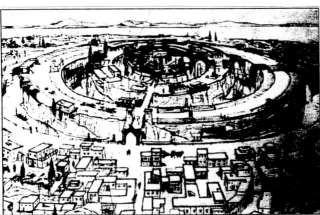

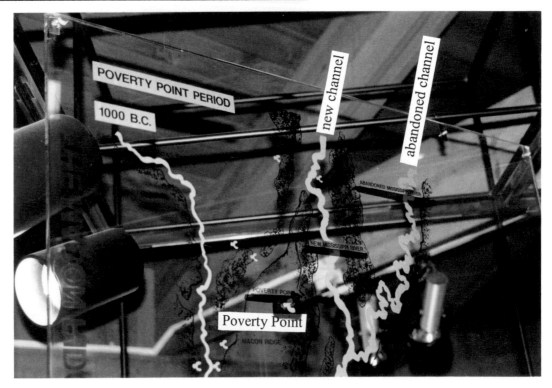

Fig.5 **Below:** Photo of a plexiglass panel in Visitor Center shows the new and abandoned channels of the Mississippi River at 1000 BC (Wakefield photo, October, 2006).
Above right: Circular Monument called the "Portsmouth Group", on the Ohio River, by Squier & Davis (Ref.47); **Left lower:** illustration of the circular capital city of Atlantis, as described by Plato in Kritias (Ref.45); **Left upper:** drawing of Stonehenge (Ref.3).

Probably, conical mounds were simulating the volcanic conical mountains, perhaps symbols of the West.

The rectangular double-decked **Dunbar Mound (D),** (now called "Mound C" by the Site Archaeologist) was found to have postmold patterns on several of the building stages. The long side of the mound was lined up with the N-S axis. Today sloughing of the bluff has cut what remains of the mound in half. Large quantities of hematite, magnetite, slate, quartz crystals, galena, kaolinite, red ochre, and granite scraps were left on floor layers in the mound, indicating that mound-top activities included preparation of pigments for ceremonial face and body painting, according to Gibson.

The smaller, rectangular **Ballcourt Mound (L)** in the southwest is 300 feet on a side, and 9 feet high. It may have been the foundation for large wooden structures. (The Archaeologist at Poverty Point is now calling this Mound E.) In the south is the **Lower Jackson Mound (J),** which is thought to be older than the big mounds, because objects found, including loess blocks and Evans Points. It is located outside park property.

Small **Sarah's Mound (Fig.3,top)** was a flat-topped rectangular platform, believed to have been built 1,000 years after the decline of the Poverty Point Culture. It is named for Sarah, one of the owners of Poverty Point Plantation, who is buried on the mound. Its long axis pointed toward magnetic north (almost 8° east of true north), not "Poverty Point north". Since it was built so late, it is omitted from **Fig. 6**, which shows the site at its earlier time of use. (The Site Archeologist is now calling this "Mound D".)

Population / Food
Poverty Point was an unusual thing: a pre-historic, pre-agricultural manufacturing town, made possible by the immense biological richness of the area. Habitation areas have been identified around the site, especially on the north side, covering more than a square mile, though Gibson states "only a handful have received more than passing attention". Sixty encampments encircling the core complex are known. No descendants can be traced to any historic tribe or group, despite estimates that many thousands of people were living here, who did not depend upon agriculture, over a thousand year period. Fruits, acorns, pecans, and other nuts were important in the diet, but the superabundant food, available all year long, was fish. Gibson writes "in the 500 square mile swamp around the Poverty Point encampments, there were between 30,000 and 1,000,000 pounds of fish per square mile!" Gibson thinks it was a hunter-gatherer town, a place of residence, a trading center. This puts Poverty Point outside the classical "Late Archaic" archaeological model of hunter-gatherer life. Ford and Webb conclude that "the ruling class probably were invaders from the north, early Hopewellian people" (Ref.49).

Artifacts / Excavations
The old ground beneath the rings was "midden veneered", according to both Ford and Gibson, showing that people were already living or working on the ground before building started. Little pottery has been found, but numerous steatite stone bowls have been found. The steatite had to come from Michigan or the Piedmont Area. These stone bowls are ½"+ thick, and not practical to cook in over a fire, so cooking was done by

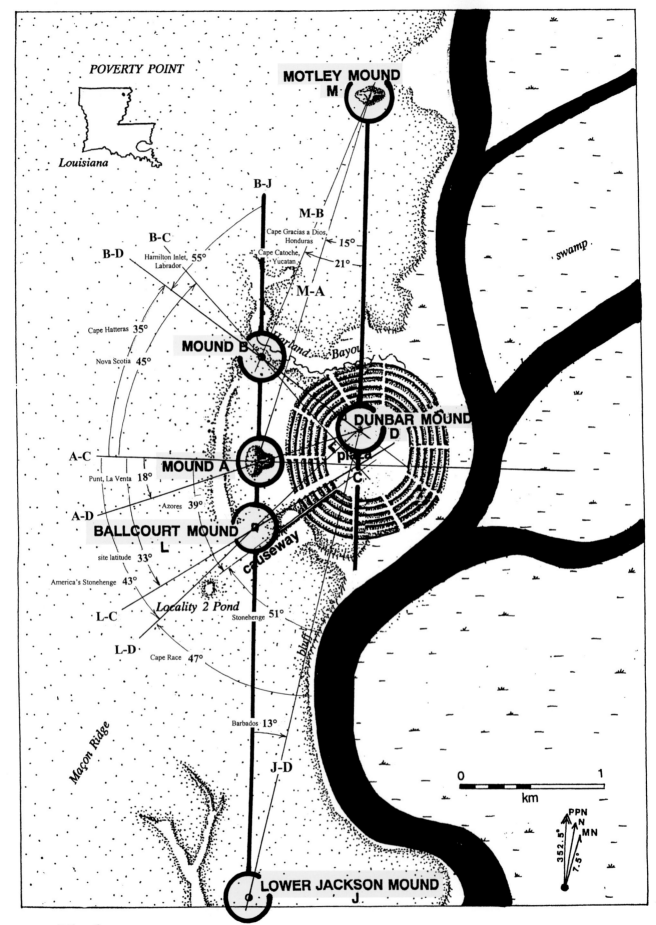

Fig.6 Baselines of the complex, with Rings, mounds, and waterways restored to probable original (c.2000-1200 BC). Site angles added, with corresponding latitude locations noted.

dropping hot clay balls into the soup. Bi-conical cooking-ball fragments (called "Poverty Point Objects", or PPO's) "dominated the trash in the rings". Ford calculated that "associated with small fireplaces scattered throughout the soil, were a minimum of 2200 tons, or 24,000,000 PPOs" (Ref.49). Among the engraved ones, "bird representations were most prevalent", including the horned owl, hungry nestling, songbirds, and crow figures. Turtles, opossum, and panther also occurred, along with strange glyphs, and unique motifs. The trash also included whole and broken, and incomplete, resharpened, and recycled tools, manufacturing debris, fire-cracked rock, caches of projectile points, baked human figurines, plummets, copper beads, a copper bead-maker's kit (copper nuggets hammered into thin sheets, for winding around the copper wire), ornaments, both finished and unfinished, and most of all, exchange rock. In fact, Gibson estimates that "over 71 tons of foreign flint occurrs on the site, an astonishing amount...Millions of items were left on the ground before the rings were built; they were left in the rings while under construction and during breaks in construction; and they were left atop the rings after construction was finished." The Ford report discusses 33 types of Archaic arrowheads over 20 pages, noting that there were thousands in various collections". Most of the plummets were hematite, 1/3 magnetite, one of copper. Ford says that "when the large number of plummets that have been gathered and sold to collectors over the last 50 years is considered, it is apparent that [hematite] was brougt here by boat loads". Gibson says it is estimated that there remain 75-100 tons of exotic rock at the site, and there are hundreds of thousands of "perfectly good tools". He states: "expect the unusual, and it is likely to show up... If I had to sum up Poverty Point's gear and appliances in a single word, it would be abundant. If I could use two words, I would say abundant and rich."

Gibson reports that hundreds of post-molds and firepits were scattered across the rings. In excavating hearths and pits, some were found that "raised questions that can not be answered at present ... one burned area was 4' across ... seven superimposed hearths were dug on successive building layers, in the third upper western ring segment. Each was about 3' in diameter. ... An excavation on the first NW ring revealed an average of one pit for every compact-car sized area."(Ref.1). The rings had caches and deposits of objects. Perforators used to drill stone were concentrated in just the 3rd southwestern ring, and the fifth southern ring, yet the cores from which the perforators were made were primarily found on the other segments. Thus, the distribution of tools is very uneven, revealing divisions of labor, and manufacturing specialization. For example, Gibson writes "no tools described as 'women's culinary' were found in the western three ring groups, but were 10-20% of the finds nearer the Bayou. The west and Northwest ring sets were very low in all finds...over half of the little specialized drills were surface-collected from just two segments" (Ref.1).

Copper
Routes for the extraction of Michigan's copper have been traced downstream from Isle Royale and the Keweenaw Peninsula (Fig.2). These routes run past storage pits with corroded copper in them, past Beaver Island, with its ancient raised garden beds and huge 39-stone circle. In the Great Lakes, water levels fluctuated widely, as ice dams retreated, and the land rebounded from the glacial weight. At 2300 BC there was a high water stage, called the "Nipissing Stage" (Refs.19,21,39). Dr. Jim Schertz, Professor Emeritus with

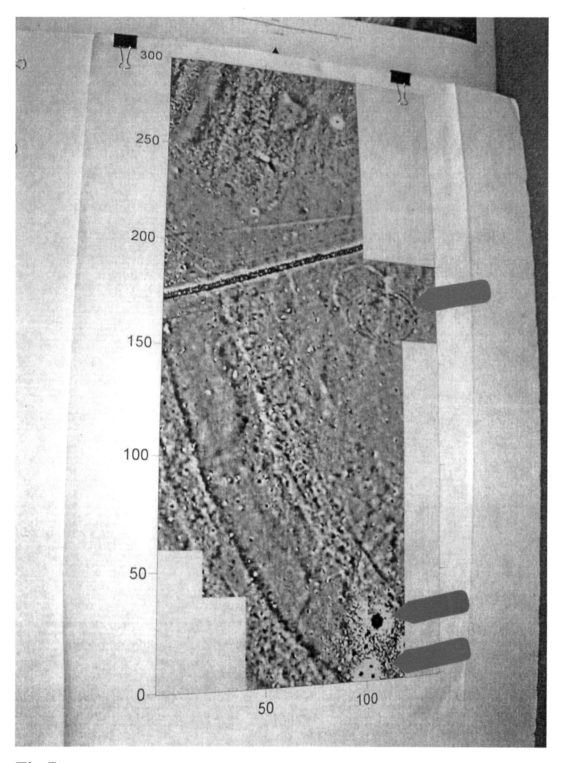

Fig.7 The first Magnetic Gradiometry Study, done by archeologists Mike Hargrave and Burley Clay early in 2006. The State Archaeologist on site, Dianna Greenlee, explained that the dark spots are metal "hits". The large spots at the bottom are particularly interesting. She later reported some of these were "core tested", and showed dark "midden" material or hearths. Note the interesting overlapping circles mid-photo, which were explored by university students in June of 2009 (Photo by Wakefield, October, 2006).

the Ancient Earthworks Society, says that when the water rose 40 feet above present levels, an outlet opened into the Illinois River, through the present chicago Ship Canal. On the south bank, where the river started, stood a 3,000 pound stone block, overlooking Lake Michigan. Known as the Waubansee Stone (top, **Fig.2**), now in the hall of the Chicago Historical Society. It is carved with the face of a man with a beard and holes connecting the bowl at the top to the mouth of the face. It appears to be the face of Moloch on a Phoenician Tophet, where sacrifices were made prior to the perilous voyage, loaded with copper, down the rivers to Poverty Point (Ref.40). Ships then entered the Chicago River, and then ran down the Illinois River, to the Mississippi, or from Green Bay, down the Wisconsin and the Mississippi to Poverty Point. Some copper went east, down the Ottawa River, and the Trent/Severn Waterway to the St. Lawrence River, and some went further south, and down the Chaudiere River from Quebec to Lake Megantic, then down the Kennebec river to the Maine coast (Ref.3). Nevertheless, most of the half billion tons of missing copper (Ref.10) must have gone down the Mississippi.

Jean Hunt, then President of the Louisiana Mounds Society, wrote in 1993 in Ancient American Magazine that "the Poverty Point archaeologist or curator talked about traces of large "spots" of copper on the surface, which he thought might have represented places where raw copper from the Michigan mines was placed while awaiting trans-shipment" (Ref.37). Metals would not be a normal surface finding. Daniel Wood also stated in Ancient American that "as many as 20 copper storage pits have been located at Poverty Point, measuring 15-20 feet in diameter (Ref.38). There was no visual evidence of these pits when I was there in 1996, but it appears they may show in the magnetic gradiometry **(Fig.7)**. Wood describes a 20 x 50 foot Torch Lake (Keweenaw) pit that was found to contain 20 tons of carbonate of copper, that was dated c.1800 BC (also Ref.10), and other pits as far east as Sault Ste Marie, and others in southern Wisconsin.

The big unanswered question at this point is where the raw copper was heated on wood fires and poured into oxhide molds. No site has ever been identified. We know it was done with multiple pours, with enough moisture present to create voids in the oxhides, creating "blister copper" (see article on Michigan Copper in this book). Poverty Point is well forested land, and very humid, being on the Gulf Coast. The melting of the rough copper from the mines into standardized 60 pound one-Talent Oxhides would have required very hot fires. Multiple pourings into the clay moulds in the humidity of the Gulf Coast would have made the workers sweat profusely. Perhaps the sweat and humidity alone, or maybe wet "fresh" wood might have been enough to cause the gas voids that characterize the fragile "blister copper" oxhides. The carrying handles and flat shape of standardized oxhides would have been very helpful for shipping, carrying and selling the copper. With 99.7% of Poverty Point unexcavated, it may be this was the most important activity at Poverty Point, and clay or dirt molds should be watched for in future excavations.

Early in 2006, a magnetic gradiometry study done by Mike Hargrave and Burley Clay **(Fig.7)** shows large dark spots that were described as metal "hits", or "something in the dirt that makes it magnetically different". The State Site Arhaeologist, Dianna Greenlee says that by the end of May 2009 they have surveyed the entire plaza and the first two

pots, Poverty Point

European Beaker Pots

Fig.8 **Above**, two pots on display in the Museum of Poverty Point, Louisiana, which show similarities with European Beaker Pots. The left pot was excavated, the right pot is a simulation based upon unearthed potsherds. (photos by Wakefield, October 2006).
Below, left, two Beaker Pots on exhibit in the Devises Museum, Devises, England.
Below, right, a Beaker Pot in the collection of the Salisbury & South Wiltshire Museum, England (photos by Wakefield, May, 2008).

rings. She reports that the dark spots were tested with "pulled cores", which showed dark midden material/hearths. They are especially interested in the circle patterns (see center of **Fig.7**). They have found many more of them, especially in the south Plaza, with larger circles in the east, smaller in the west. They are 50cm to 1 meter deep, in "good soil, so they are definately prehistoric". A Joint Field School excavation was scheduled for June 3 to July 2, 2009, with 3 staff, and 23 students from the University of Louisiana, and Mississippi State University. The students dug 1 x 2 meter holes over four of the circle patterns. Greenlee reported that the circles were found to be circles of filled postholes, where the posts were supported by PPO's crammed next to them, producing the vertical stacks of PPO's found by the students. In Europe, where stone is available, posts were similarly surrounded by "setting stones", and these rings of stones reveal old post locations. Greenlee thought that more excavations will be helpful in determining whether the post circles were roofed, but thinks some were too large to roof. One radiocarbon date has come back at 1440-1280 BC. No copper objects or hearths were noticed by the students in these four locations in June/July 2009.

Pots

The Poverty Point Visitor Center exhibits include a steatite (soapstone) stone pot, and a few clay pots. Ford recovered "almost 3000 steatite vessel fragments, but only 32 potsherds". He reports that one steatite bowl hit by a plow in 1925 was stated to weigh 16 pounds ... It is possible that the use of clay for pottery was known to them only in the form of finished vessels" (Ref.63). Greenlee says that most of the pottery found at the site has been thick and untempered, "from late occupations", as though they were just learning to make it. By phone (7/22/09), she reported that "none of it is on display". However, she said that the university students doing last month's dig, found a little pottery that is thin, and "looks different". She said she plans to ask some pottery experts about it. **Figure 8** shows a thin pot that is on exhibit in the Visitor Center, the dark one on the upper left. It has a pattern like the English Beaker Pot below it. The upper right pot is modern, a replica patterned on pot shards unearthed at Poverty Point. The two English Beaker Pots below it have considerable resemblance. Analysis should be done on the clay of the Poverty Point pot to acertain where it was made. The "thin" pots may have been introduced into this Archaic date community as shipping containers.

The shape of the upper pot in **Figure 9** is Caddoan, typical of pots of 700 to 1200 AD, a culture in the Red River Valley, west of Poverty Point. Archaeologist Greenlee says it is on exhibit in the Poverty Point Museum to illustrate the later Caddoan Culture. The pot below it, which shares a similar design, and shares the same 1500 BC date as Poverty Point, is Minoan, located in the Iraklion Museum in Crete. Why does the Caddoan pot made 2000 years later, show a Minoan design? Surprisingly, other Caddoan pots are engraved with megalithic-style concentric circles, "lozenge" (diamond) patterns, and sun symbols (Ref.45). It appears that early Woodland pottery in the Red River Valley continued patterns introduced on overseas pots.

The creation story of the Caddo people starts: "In the beginning darkness rules. Man comes, and soon there is a village with thousands of people. Man disappears; returns with seeds. He says the sun is coming and will be given power... the Caddo had conical grass

Caddoan pot (Poverty Point)

Minoan pot (Crete)

Fig.9 **Above**, excavated pot on exhibit in the Poverty Point Museum. (Wakefield photo 2006) **Below**, Minoan pot found at Phaistos, in the Archaeological Museum in Herakleion, Crete (Ref.44). Both pots share the same design element, showing Minoan involvement in the Copper Trade.

lodges up to 60 feet in diameter, were fond of tatooing, and had a calendrical sequence of ceremonies and had temples with a central fire, from which the domestic fires were obtained"(Ref.48). All these cultural features are in keeping with cultural traditions probably obtained from Poverty Point and its visitors.

Gulf Ports

Figure 10 shows the Claiborne and Cedarland Rings, contemporary with Poverty Point, which Gibson calls the "oddest Poverty Point community of all". These mound-rings, in their tools and styles, resembled Poverty Point. They sat on the first high ground rising above the marsh at the Gulf entrance to the Mississippi River, along its Pearl River branch. He states that "since radiocarbon dates have shown these two rings were occupied at the same time, but the artifacts in them were so distinctly different, it was concluded that they were inhabited by two independent, ethnically separate groups, who lived side by side".

Cedarland

The paper of Bruseth, an archaeologist with the Texas Historical Commission, is most interesting: "Cedarland, located in 1957, mapped in 1970, has been extensively damaged by indiscriminate digging by relic seekers and by construction activities related to development of a port and harbor facility. The site was occupied for several centuries prior to 2000 BC, at the confluence of the Mississippi River and the Gulf of Mexico. During the 3rd millenium BC the Mississippi would have been in relatively close proximity, and it is probable that the site was the highest ground (5m) near the mouth of the river... The ring is a large oyster shell and earth midden overlooking the mouth of the Pearl River...This site seems to have formed by accretion, without planning or site layout... No burials have been found" (Ref.24).

Field inspections by Bruseth during bulldozing revealed debris consisting of bone, stone, and clay artifacts... He says "numerous clay-lined, basin-shaped hearths have been uncovered, but few have been carefully excavated ... Raw materials at the site include red jasper, black and white and grey chert, quartz crystal, various quartzites, and Great Lakes copper needles and sheet copper. The lithic materials are rare at Claiborne. Cedarland has 3 and 4 sided drills, while Claiborne posesses only bifacially-formed drills...[beautiful 3-sided points are a feature of the Danish neolithic at this time]. One to 2 meters of deposits indicate intensive utilization,...and re-use of hearths, but few have been carefully excavated (Ref.24).

Bruseth continues: "The hearths varied in diameter from 50 to 65 cm [20-26 inches, the size of oxhide ingots], were basin shaped, and occurred on a common horizontal plane. The walls consisted of oxidized orange soil. However, the tops were found at variable depths below the surface. This factor is interpreted to be the result of digging in and around the hearths after their initial use. As neither ash nor charcoal was observed within the features, they may instead have served as earth ovens rather than hearths. Under this interpretation, the oxidised soil of the features would represent prepared clay walls that became fired from heating in the oven. Numerous amorphous fired clay lumps surround the hearths and are commonly found throughout much of the midden. The author has

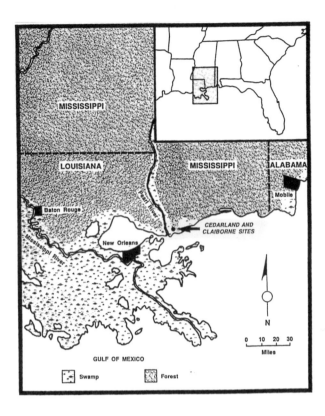

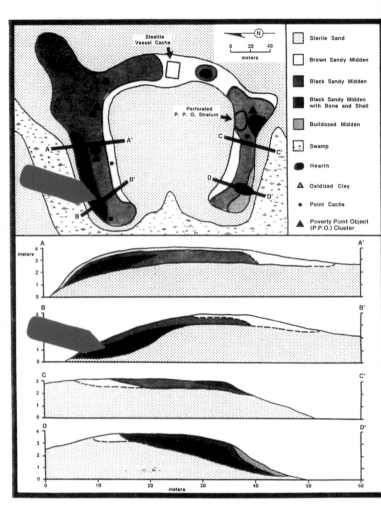

Fig.10 Claiborne and Cedarland, built near the Pearl River mouth, Mississippi. **Upper right**, details of Claiborne (Ref.36).

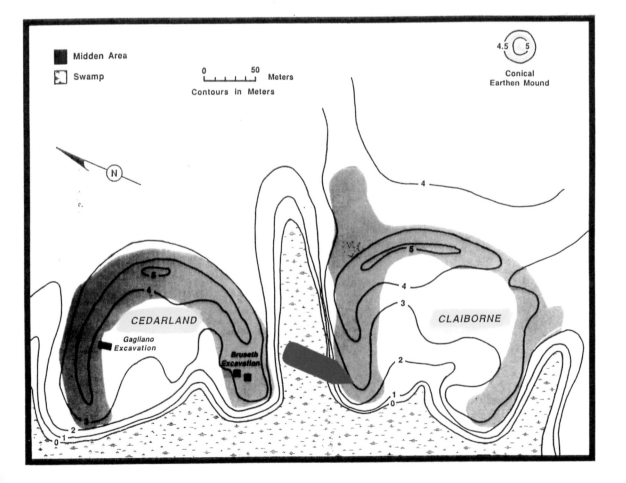

examined several examples for evidence of deliberate shape, but in all instances they were found to be amorphous and unintentionally formed. It was initially thought that these might be baked clay objects used in conjunction with the clay-lined hearths. However, it is probable, based on their small size and lack of clear form, that they are fragments from other clay-lined hearths. Extensive digging and reuse of the hearths evidently scattered burned clay wall fragments throughout the midden" (Ref.24).

Claiborne

Radiocarbon dates for Claiborne, discovered in 1967, range from 2040 BC to 1150 BC. Bruseth says "Claiborne appears to have been a well-structured village throughout much of its history. A conical mound is directly east of the site [as shown in the lower illustration of **Fig.10**]. No clay-lined hearths have been found, but a huge hearth 25m x 3-5m wide was opened by successive bulldozer cuts, a feature which apparently moved upslope by accumulation from use. Smaller hearths of 4m, and 2m x 1.5m were also found. Claiborne plummets are made of magnetite and hematite, while plummets at Cedarland are only made of other materials. Bruseth describes other materials revealed that the "inhabitants of both rings were involved in long-distance exchange, but did so differently, despite being side-by-side. Of special note are the effigy forms, such as locusts, owls, and bivalves, which are not found at Cedarland. There are ceramics... fiber tempered pottery, but none at Cedarland. The two sites are distinctive in layout, feature type, and artifact content, and present a perplexing problem. ...Other sites are known, which most likely represent support camps, to these 'specialized activity areas'. These sites flourished well before the earthwork construction at Poverty Point....Perhaps the monumental earthworks [at Poverty Point] have caused us to underestimate the importance of pre-earthwork occupation." Bruseth concludes the report of his excavation by writing that "the two sites were inhabited by two independent groups who lived side by side" (Ref.24).

Sailors will understand that small sailboats of 30-50 feet, now circling the globe by the multitude, or small ships in prehistory of 70-200 feet, would be heading for a "port". They would not be likely to attempt to sail directly up the huge, muddy, and treacherous Mississippi when in its fast flood stage, but would seek a nearby landing spot, where they could drink fresh water, bathe, and secure and repair their vessels for awhile. Along the shallow beaches of the Gulf Coast, the Pearl River mouth provided the needed deep water entrance. Two separate ports developed. We know there were several different cultures involved in the copper trade. Gibson states that "like any busy place, especially where traders and visitors from strange lands congregated, Poverty Point was exposed to many foreign influences ... many of Poverty Point's basic raw materials came from lands inhabited by strangers". We know the Egyptians and Minoans were involved in copper trading, because paintings of them are on Egyptian tomb walls, carrying copper oxhide ingots. Bruseth says Barry Fell has reported that the language of the Atakapas, the Tunicas, and the Chitimacha tribes of Louisiana had striking similarities with Nile Valley languages involving words one would associate with Egyptian trading communities. Quoting the archaeologist Bruseth again: "Extensive surveys of sites along the Pearl River with similar projectile point types, appear occupied by different groups. We know that trade was crossing ethnic boundaries and probably crossing language boundaries.

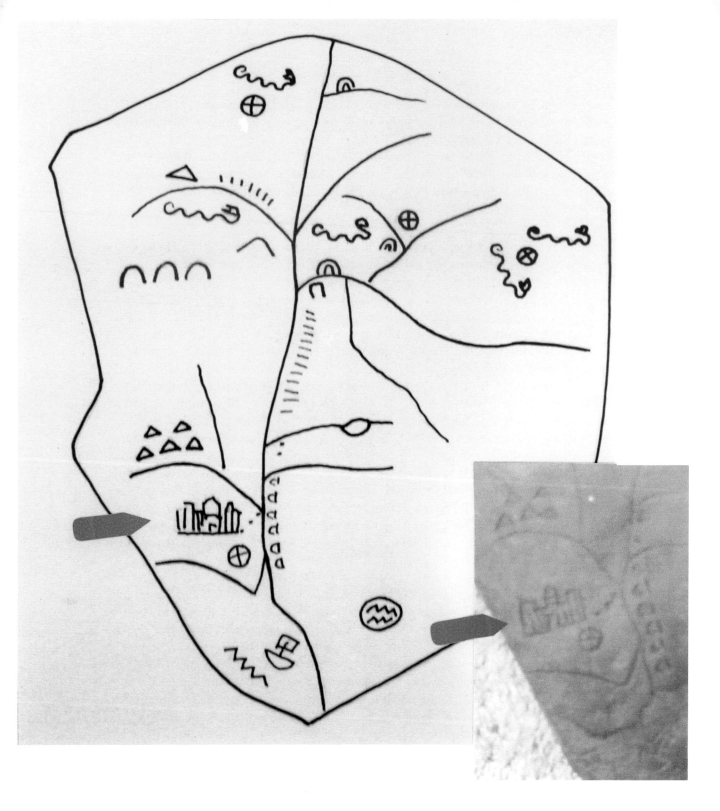

Fig.11 A drawing of a Burrows Cave mapstone, by graphic artist Beverly Mosely, Fellow of the Midwest Epigraphic Society. The stone is thought to have been created by refugees to America, early in the first century AD. The small image is a close-up photo of a corner of the stone, showing another view of the two or three story building, accessed by a trail from junction of the Arkansas and Mississippi Rivers. Apparently, Poverty Point continued to be occupied and its wooden buildings maintained for a long time after the river shifted away from the site. Note the large villages upriver in the Spiro area. (Photos by Wakefield, 2007)

These are certainly groups of people that operate mostly unto themselves most of the time. There are strangers involved" (Ref.24).

Claiborne, with its conical mound, like those in the Canaries, may well have been an outstation of the Atlantean culture. Early written history, Plato principally, tells about the Atlantean culture, which grew rich on trading in "orichalcum", a pure copper, across the Atlantic Ocean, which is named for them. Their principal city of Atlantis was designed with circular rings. The population of Poverty Point is thought to have increased increased greatly after 1200 BC, a date when a comet impact caused all the cities in the Mediterranean to be destroyed in earthquakes and fire, and submerged the Atlantean city, after the eruption of Mt. Atlas (Ref.14). Despite the flood of refugees to the west, the comet disaster ended the Michigan mining, the Atlantic trade, the mound building at Poverty Point, and the European Bronze Age, all at the same time.

Climatologists call the following cold (2° fall) and wet period (1250-1000 BC) the "Plenard Period". So many sites are now underwater, we have lost grasp of how big the trade in copper was in prehistory. The underwater breakwater of Bimini in the Bahamas is well known. (Bimini = Ba [soul] min [Egyptian god of travelers] nini [homage]= "homage to the soul of Min"(Ref.44). Less well known are the enormous walls of 8m x 6m blocks at a depth of 14m that run for several miles on the coast of Morocco, and the old megalithic coastal cities of Lixus and Mogador (Ref.37).

Archaeologist Bruseth's midden cross-sections of the Claiborne site appear to provide evidence for copper oxhide manufacture. **Fig.10**, upper right, shows a hearth as long as a football field: 6' deep, 300' long, in a midden twice as long. "Numerous amorphous fired clay lumps surround the hearths, and are commonly found ...A typical cluster of 86 clay objects... The author has examined several examples for evidence of deliberate shape, but in all instances they were found to be amorphous and unintentionally formed ...A radiocarbon date of 1425 +/- 140 BC ... the stratum seems to represent an activity area where perforated varieties of baked clay objects were being fired. This interpretation is based on the nearly total absence of complete baked objects, and the abundance of charcoal concentrations... Artifact types in the stratum are almost exclusively fragmented baked clay objects... The broken clay objects are interpreted to represent specimens that fragmented during the firing process" (Ref.24). The clay fragments were probably hammered off the copper oxhides when they cooled. Bruseth notes that "the predominant artifact categories included lithic debris and cobbles wth battered ends" (Ref.24). So it appears stone hammers were used to break off the molds.

Burrows Cave Maps
Several mapstones (**Figs.11,12**) from Burrow's Cave (Ref.41) show two story buildings that seem to be at the Poverty Point site. No other site is known that may have had two-story buildings. These mudstones are believed to have been carved in the first century AD, so more than 1200 years after the comet disaster and the end of the copper mining, and even 700 years after the end of the life of the site, according to the archaeologists. Apparently there was a long continued use of the site, since two-story wooden buildings require a lot of maintenance. We see no remains today, other than unexplained postholes,

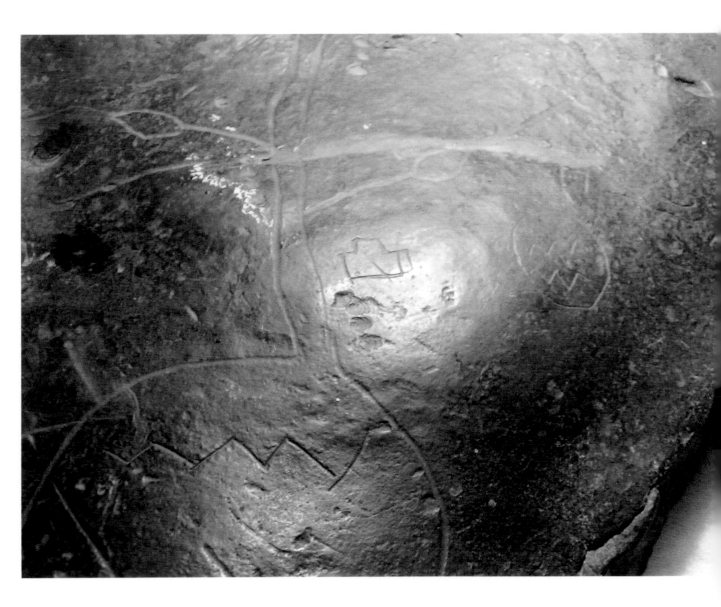

Fig.12 Closeup of another Burrows Cave mapstone of the Mississippi River, showing what appears to be a two-story building on the east side of the Mississippi River. It appears that since the Mississippi had changed its course to the East by the time of these mapstones. This mapmaker apparently had only heard about the place, and put it on the wrong side of the river. (Photo by Wakefield, May, 2009)

because the buildings were not built of stone. Note that the site could no longer be seen from the river (which had moved), as it is accessed by a trail from the junction of the Arkansas River in **Figure 11**. Note a 2-story building placed on the wrong side of the river, and without a trail, in **Figure 12**. Mistakes happen, when you sail by, and only hear of a place, without seeing it. **Figure 13** shows a ship, with some turbaned sailors in it, and **Figure 14** shows they carried Old World mythological beliefs with them. **Figure 15** shows a figure unique among the stones, perhaps a contemporary religious figure, which may help with the dating of the maps.

Timeline context

Time is a hard concept to comprehend, given that the United States has been a nation for only 230 years. We forget that it was a colony for 156 years before that (1620 to 1776). Between the founding of Poverty Point (2400 BC) and Columbus (1492 AD) is a period of almost 4000 years, and Poverty Point at its height (1500 BC) was 3000 years earlier than Columbus! Understanding these time spans, and what might have been acomplished in them, is one of the major stumbling blocks to our understanding of prehistory.

America on the Atlantic side was discovered from Europe by the Megalithic peoples c.2500 BC (Ref.3). By "discovered" we do not mean the first sailors who were blown across the sea, unable to return, and might have been "culture bearers" and disease and parasite carriers. The Mayan calendar starts on August 11th, 3114 BC. By "discovery" we mean the period when people first understood the tradewind and current patterns, so that roundtrips were accomplished. Peru's Pyramid of the Sun and Egypt's Great Pyramid were both built at c.2500 BC, and both with the same base dimension of 758 feet, which was the dimension given by Plato for the Citadel at the center of Atlantis (Ref.14). It is interesting that the earliest Archaic mounds, at Watson Brake, on the Ouachita River, 6 miles west of Poverty Point, on private property near Monroe, have been dated within 200 years of 3,180 BC (Ref.17). Watson Brake consists of a large circular ring, 853 feet across, with one large mound to 25', and "9 or 10" smaller ones over 3' raised atop the ring. Native myths suggest that the mounds were an earthen model of the Earth, and contained elements of ancient creation stories. So earthworks in the Mississippi Valley developed very early, perhaps from the influence of early visitors (Ref.17).

The Michigan copper mining by "red haired white-skinned 'marine men' who came from across the sea" (American Indian myth) soon followed the 2500 BC discovery (Ref.10). From wood timbers preserved anaerobically under water in ancient mine pits, the mining has been radiocarbon dated to 2400 BC to 1200 BC, a period of more than a thousand years. One of the more interesting finds in digging out one of these old mine holes, was a Walrus skin bag (Ref.10), showing the miners had been traveling on salt water in the north. Extensive study of the Ontario Serpent Mound site, on Rice Lake, Petersborough Co. Ontario, another copper shipment route, reported on 33 skulls intact enough for racial identification: 8 Negro, 2 White, and 23 Indian (Ref.25). Carbon dating of one of the graves gave AD 128, a later Viking-Age date.

The Olmec civilization of Mexico is recognized at 2000 BC, with the Jaguar cult forming there, and major construction at 1500 BC, simultaneously with Poverty Point

Fig.13 Burrows Cave stone with sailors who would probably have made the mapstones, thought to be first century AD. Note fellow in the crow's nest! (Background item: the CD with the yellow title "Ancient Mariners in America" can be obtained from Beverly Mosely, via www.midwesternepigraphic.org). (Wakefield photo, May, 2009)

development. Some researchers think Poverty Point has resemblance to the layout of La Venta and Caral. The Olmec built up over a longer time, with the start of San Lorenzo dated at 1200 BC again coincident with the diaspora from Atlantis. While the first known Egyptian voyages to Punt were launched by Pharaoh Neferkare, in the 5th Dynasty of the Old Kingdom (c.2500 BC) (Ref.12) into the "inverted waters" (Southern hemisphere). It is the ships sent on their 3 year voyage to Punt by Pharoah Hatshepsut early in the New Kingdom (1473-1458 BC) that are so well documented, by being carved in her temple. So her voyages were coincident with the prime development of Poverty Point.

This is also considered the time of the development of the Minoan Palace complex of Knossos, which is thought to have had a huge fleet controlling the copper trading of the Bronze Age in the Mediterranean., with most of the early ports of Crete now under water. The Uluburun Shipwreck, which contained 354 copperoxhide ingots (c.10 tons), and 40 tin ingots off the Turkish coast was dated by dendrochronology to 1316-1305 BC (Ref.21), simultaneous with the peak of moundbuilding at Poverty Point.

The Atlanteans were famous for growing wealthy on the trading in copper. Plato reports the temple of Atlantis walls and flooring were made of oricalcum (copper), and the exterior was covered with silver and gold. The innermost circle wall was coated with tin, and the acropolis itself was coated with oricalcum. For the destruction of Atlantis, Plato says he was given a date of "9,000 years ago" by the priests of Sais in Egypt. When we put this date into lunar months, the early Egyptian time system, (divide 9000 months by 12 mos/yr= 750 yrs BC, add 536 BC for Plato's time, = 1286 BC), we get a number close to the cataclysmic events of the 50 year period of 1200 BC. Plato also said the Atlantis destruction was close to the founding of Athens, which is thought to be around 1400 BC.

Ramses III first repulsed the Sea Peoples (Atlanteans and their allies) in 1220 BC, and then again in 1186 and 1070, as documented in his victory temple.. The destruction of Atlantis in 1198 BC led to an abrupt cessation of the mining (perhaps the sky went dark everywhere at once), and is thought to have led to a second diaspora to Poverty Point. Unfortunately so much was lost during the catastrophic events of 1200 BC, when the cities were burned, populations collapsed, the leaders and inteligentsia died, that civilization suffered an enormous setback, and entered a "dark" period. This allowed the Celts to flood unchallenged over Western Europe with chariots, and iron techology, themselves driven west from the forests of Germany, known to have been consumed by fire in the cataclysm. This ushered in a new culture, which developed a large ocean-going fleet, and colonies with hundreds of stone chambers built in New England. The 1200 BC catastrophe caused the ending of the Middle Kingdom in Egypt, ushering in the Hyksos takeover, and the Second Intermediate Period. With the collapse of the Atlantean empire, the Phoenicians expanded westward, and founded Carthage in 814 BC.

The Phoenicians learned the routes of the Atlanteans, and succeeded them, still keeping their routes secret, to protect the rich trade sources. Following their conquest of Spain in 530 BC, they eradicated the ancient city of Tartessus so thoroughly that excavators have been unable to locate the city. Tarshish vanished, and with it all the lore of the Great Western Sea, which Tartessians had sailed for a thousand years. Demons, erie darkness,

Fig.14 Another Burrows Cave carving, showing the Greek myth of the annual Death of Adonis, who has lost his left leg to a boar. "At the festivals of Adonis, which were held in Western Asia and in Greek lands, the death of the god was annually mourned, with bitter wailing, chiefly by women…In the Phoenician sanctuary of Astarte at Byblus the death of Adonis was annually mourned, to the shrill wailing notes of the flute, with weeping, lamentation, and beating of the breast; but the next day he was believed to come to life again and ascend up to heaven in the presence of his worshippers." (Ref.48) This stone shows the cultural origin of the Mapstone makers. (Photo by Wakefield, May, 2009)

mudflats, immense fields of seaweed from which no ship could free itself, horrible monsters and a ghastly death awaited the seafarer beyond Gibraltar was all the Phoenicians allowed to be glimpsed. They were believed, so the competition was finally eliminated. It is known that a Phoenician (Carthaginian) skipper who discovered he was being followed by a Roman vessel, scuttled his ship, to avoid disclosing his route, and was rewarded at home with a rich new vessel. It was Carthaginian policy to throw overboard the crew from any captured ship. The Punic Wars, and complete destruction of Carthage by the Romans, combined with Caesar's defeat of the becalmed Veneti (Celtic) Ocean fleet off the Gulf of Morbihan (Brittany), extingushed the overseas trade routes to the Carribbean, only to be later re-discovered by Columbus.

The Five Nation's (Iroquois) account of their wars with the copper-trading giants concludes that they "ceased to exist". Legends of the Menomini and Hochunk also tell of combat, and killing them (c.600 BC) (Ref.51). Actually, it appears the remnants of the copper miners and traders moved west and south to Ohio, their culture no longer called the "Old Copper Culture", but renamed the "Adena". Grondine continues that "at about the time of the Celtic emigrations in Europe, say about 200 BC or so, a massive revolt took place through most of the area that the descendants of the copper traders controlled. Single-circle astronomically oriented earthen structures were replaced by rings paired with square enclosures. 'Hopewell' has been adopted to describe these societies" (Ref.51).

Conclusions

Although big stones are totally lacking, the Poverty Point site should be considered as part of the wordwide Megalithic Culture in the Bronze Age because of its circular design, conical pyramids, latitude encodings, multiculturalism, and the pottery found at the site. Poverty Point on the Mississippi is contemporary with other Bronze Age population centers in hot climates with big rivers that flooded each year, such as the Olmec, and the Egyptians. It has "ports" on the Gulf, where middens show it is likely that the copper oxhides were made, which fueled the Bronze Age in Europe

References

1. Gibson, J.L., The Ancient Mounds of Poverty Point, Place of the Rings, University Press of Florida, 2001 (ISBN 0-8130-2551-6), pgs 3, 82
2. Gibson, J.L., "Poverty Point, A Terminal Archaic Culture of the Lower Mississippi Valley", University of Southwestern Louisiana (1996). Website: www.crt.state.la.us/crt/ocd/arch/poverpoi/mapopo.htm
3. De Jonge, R.M., and Wakefield, J.S, How the Sungod Reached America c.2500 BC, A Guide to Megalithic Sites, 2002 (ISBN 0-917054-19-9). Available: MCS Inc., Box 3392, Kirkland, Wa 98083-3392, also on CD
4. Kennedy, R.G., Hidden Cities: The Discovery and Loss of Ancient North American Civilization, Penguin Bks, NY 1994 (ISBN 0-14-02.5527-3)
5. Martin, P.S., Quimby, G.I., Collier, D., Indians Before Columbus, Twenty Thousand Years of North American History Revealed by Archaeology, University of Chicago Press, Cuicago, 1947.
6. Hunt, J., "Louisiana's Sacred Site", Ancient American, Vol. 3, Issue 15.
7. Wood, D.J., "Bronze Age Michigan", Ancient American, Vol. 8, Number 51.
8. Joseph, F., The Destruction of Atlantis, Compelling Evidence of the Sudden Fall of the Legendary Civilization, Bear & Co., rochester, Vt., 2002, (ISBN 0-89281-851)
9. Fox, H., Stairway to the Sun, Rediscovering the Origins of New World Culture, Permeable P., San Francisco, 1996
10. Drier, R.W., Du Temple, O.J., Prehistoric Copper Mining in the Lake Superior Region, A Collection of Reference Articles, published privately, 1961, and reprinted in 2005
11. Sullivan, D., Ley Lines, The Greatest Landscape Mystery, Green Magic, Somerset, 2004 (ISBN 0-9542-9634-6)
12. Caroli, K., "Looking for Punt", Ancient American, Issue No. 8.

Fig.15 Burrows Cave religious stones which help with the early AD dating of the mapstones, thought to have been carved by refugees from Roman Judea and Mauritania. Some other Burrows Cave stones shown in very reduced size on the right (Ref.60.)

13. Woodward, S.L., McDonald, J.N., Indian Mounds of the Middle Ohio Valley, A Guide to the Mounds and Earthworks of the Adena, Hopewell, Cole, and Fort Ancient People, Mcdonald and Woodward Publishing Co, Blacksburg, Va., 2002 (ISBN 0-939923-72-6)

14. Joseph, F., Survivors of Atlantis, Their Impact on the World, Bear & Co., Rochester, Vt., 2004, (ISBN 1-59143-040-2)

15. Drews, R., The End of the Bronze Age, Changes in Warfare and the Catastrophe c.1200 BC, Princeton University Press, Princeton, N.J., 1993. (ISBN 0-691-04811-8)

16. Baillie, M., Exodus to Arthur, Catastrophic Encounters with Comets, B.T. Batsford Ltd, London, 1993 (ISBN 0-7134-8681-3)

17. Frank, D., "OCR Carbon Dating of the Watson Brake Mound Complex", 53rd Annual Meeting of the Southwestern Archaeological Conference, Birmingham, Alabama, 1997.

18. May, W., and Joseph, F., "Egyptian Mortuary Statuette Found in N. Illinois", Ancient American, Vol.10, No.64

19. Schertz, J., Old Water Levels and Waterways during the Ancient Copper Mining Era, Dept. Of Civil & Environmental Engineering, Madison, Wis, 1999

20. Mertz, H., The Mystic Symbol, Mark of the Mound Builders, Hayriver Press, Wisc., 2004

21. Jewell, R., Ancient Mines of Kitchi-Gummi, Cypriot/Minoan Traders in North America, Jewell Histories, Pa 2004 (ISBN 0-9678413-3-X)

22. Milner, G., The Moundbuilders, Ancient Peoples of Eastern North America, Thames & Hudson, London, 2004 (ISBN 0-500-28468-7). Wood, D., "Bronze Age Michigan", Ancient American, 2004, #51

23. Joseph, F., "The Discovery and Loss of Ohio's 'Hopewell Age Mound'", Ancient American, 2004, #51

24. Byrd, K., The Poverty Point Culture, Local Manifestations, Subsistence Practices, and Trade Networks, incl: Bruseth, J., "Poverty Point Development as Seen at the Cedarland and Claiborne Sites, Southern Mississippi", Geoscience Publications, Louisiana State University, Baton Rouge, La, 1990 (ISBN 0-938909-50-9)

25. Anderson, J., "The Serpent Mounds Site Physical Anthropology", Occ. Pap 11, Royal Ontario Mus., Toronto, 1965

26. Kidder, T., "Climate Change and the Archaic to Woodland Transition (1000-500 BC) in the Mississippi River Basin", American Antiquity, 71-22, April 2006, pg. 195

27. Toye, D., "The Emergence of Complex Societies: A Comparative Approach", http//worldhistoryconnected.press.uiuc.edu/1.2/toye.html

28. Covey, C., "Poverty Point to Mississippian", Midwest Epigraphic Journal, Vol 18/19, 2004-5, Pgs 35-46

29. Zapp, I., Erickson,G., Atlantis in America, Adventures Unlimited P., Kempton, Ill., 1998 (ISBN 0-932813-52-6)

30. Morris, E., Charlot, J., Morris, A., The Temple of the Warriors at Chichen Itza, Yucatan, Carnegie Institution of Washington, May 21, 1931

31. Fitton, J., The Minoans, The Folio Society, London, reprint 2004

32. Quirke, S., The Cult of Ra, Sun-Worship in Ancient Egypt, Thames & Hudson, N.Y., 2001, (ISBN 0-500-05107-0)

33. Squier, E., & Davis, E., The Ancient Monuments of the Mississippi Valley, 1848; Lithography Of Saxony & Major, Eastern National, 2003, xxviii, face p. 78

34. Frazer, J., The Golden Bough, Oxford

35. White, J., "Mystic Symbol Deity Yahu Appears to be a SunGod", Midwestern Epigraphic Newsletter, 2-14-09/V.26, No.1 (ISSN 1932-5711)

36. Rydholm, F., Michigan Copper, The Untold Story, A History of Discovery, Winter Cabin Books, Marquette, Mich., 2006 (ISBN 0-9744679-2-8)

37. Childress, D., Lost Cities of Atlantis, Ancient Europe, and the Mediterranean, 1996 (ISBN 0-932813-25-9)

38. Childress, D., Lost Cities of North & Central America, Adventures Unlimited P., Ill. 1998 (ISBN 0-932813-09-07)

39. Schertz, J., "Ancient Trade Routes in America's Copper Country", Ancient American, #35, pg.31

40. Joseph, F., "Chicago's Great Stone Face", Ancient American, #19/20, pg.54

41. Covey, C., "Burrows Cave", Ancient American

42. Schoenherr, N, "Hunter-gatherers more sophisticated than once thought?", U. Comm., Washington U., St. Louis

43. Joseph, F., "The Riddle of Haiti", Ancient American, #11, pg.55

44. Joseph, F., "Mysteries of the Deep", Ancient American, #3, Nov/Dec 1993, P.3.

45. Bonde, J. Ed., Art of the Ancient Caddo, Grove Hill Publishing, Leonard, Texas, 2006 (ISBN 0-9776339-0-X)

46. White, J., "Discussion of Mystic Symbol Colonies Prompted by a Burrows Cave Ship Artifact", Midwestern Epigraphic Journal, Vol. 21, 2007

47. Byers, D., & Joseph, F., "A Minoan Pendant found in Ohio", Ancient American, Vol 13, #83, July, 2009, p.6.

48. Dorsey, G., Traditions of the Caddo, University of Nebraska Press, Lincoln, 1997, (ISBN 0-8032-6602-2)

49. Ford, J.A., and Webb, C.H., "Poverty Point, a late Archaic Site in Louisiana" Vol.46: part 1, Anthropological Papers of the American Museum of Natural History, New York, 1956

50. Atlas of North America, Space Age Portrait of a Continent, National Geographic, USA, 1985

51. Grondine, E., Man and Impact in the Americas, 2005, E.P. Grondine

What did the Olmec "Skywatcher's" See?
(Comet Figurines, c.1200 BC)

Jay S. Wakefield jswakefield@comcast.net

The Photos:
Surrounded by a garden, the six foot tall statue is among similar ancient artwork on public display at Mexico's La Venta Park of Olmec Statuary, in the city of Villahermosa. It is officially known as the "Skywatcher", and its companion pieces were rescued from nearby La Venta, prior to construction of an oil refinery on much of the site. Other photos presented here show smaller Olmec jade or greenstone figurines from private collections. They, too, are gazing upward, sometimes with terrified or apprehensive facial expressions. Note that the bird on one figure is also looking up. The thin figures are drilled at the back, apparently for hanging from around someone's neck, similar to small heads or masks often worn on the chests of shamans.

Dating:
What are these figures trying to express? Stone, being non-organic, is difficult to date. Yet, these small figures are clearly Olmec in style, as evidenced by their down-turned mouths. Having been removed from their unknown, original context, they cannot, unfortunately, be dated by context. The Olmec Culture, after an earlier period of development, first flourished circa 1500 B.C., persisting for about another 1,100 years. Olmec florescence coincided with the Late Bronze Age, which suddenly collapsed in the wake of an enormous natural catastrophe. If, as we surmise, this event inspired the creation of the Olmec figures, they may be dated to the cometary cataclysms known to have taken place about 1200 B.C.

The Catastrophes:
With recent advances in scientific understanding of comets --- their nature and history --- potential for their future impact on our world is better appreciated by the public than ever before. A case in point is today's enfeebled Encke Comet with its traveling companion, Oljato, an unusual rock one mile across. Although it appears to be an asteroid, Oljato is actually the severed head of another, dead comet, probably Encke's close predecessor.

In the years preceeding1200 B.C., the ominous comet must have been visible for years, gradually drawing closer to Earth with each pass. When it did come, the catastrophe probably consisted not of a single asteroid colliding with Earth, but an almost regular barrage of extraterrestrial debris varying in magnitude from showers of fireballs, most of which burned up in their descent. The celestial attack, which resumed every summer and autumn for almost a century, made collisions with our planet inevitable. But not until 1997 did the scientific community generally concede that a killer comet was indeed responsible for the demise of Bronze Age Civilization.

As the Earth turned on its axis below, the proto-Encke comet, Oljato, bombarded everything from above the equator to below the Arctic Circle, depending on the comet's inclining angle toward Earth. Passing over the Caribbean, it fired down an object one mile across. Moving a hundred times the velocity of a 9mm bullet, the asteroid plunged through the water and exploded with a force equal to one million megatons, excavating a 900-foot deep crater on the seafloor, perhaps sinking the coast and an island city

Fig.1 The large Olmec statue called "Skywatcher",
is standing in La Venta Park, in Villahermosa, Mexico.
The two small flat figurines have string holes in back,
probably for hanging from the neck. Note the bird.
The impacts must have been extremely noisy.

off Cuba. The resulting 1,000 foot-tall wall of water swept far inland across Alabama, killing everything in its path. The explosion set off volcanoes from the Antilles to El Salvador. Over North America, the comet let loose a barrage that created a nuclear bomb-like event in the Ohio Valley, then triggered a hellish series of volcanic outbursts in Washington, Oregon and Wyoming. Cosmic bombs falling across the Pacific Ocean raised roaring walls of water that obliterated whole island populations. In the Hawaiian Islands alone, a towering wall of water placed coral nearly a thousand feet above sea level .

But Europe and the Near East, the cradles of Western Civilization, were especially hard hit by Oljato. A veritable deluge of flame descended in waves of thunder from out of the sky. Hattusas, capital city of the mighty Hittite Empire, erupted in a fiery holocaust. Hundreds of cities and towns with hundreds of thousands of their residents all across Asia Minor were abruptly incinerated. The worst was yet to come. Leaving the continent in flames, Oljato dispatched a salvo of cosmic bombs hurtling toward the ocean at 20,000 miles per hour. As each broke the sound barrier, they filled the air with reverberating thunder. The celestial war is described in the Mahabharata of India.

At least one meteorite hit the geologically sensitive Mid-Atlantic Ridge. It awoke like the enraged Midgaard Serpent of Norse myth. Seaquakes caused five hundred foot high tsunamis. Volcanoes roared in furious choruses of steaming magma and piling cloudbanks of ash from Ascension and Candlemass Islands in the South Atlantic, to Iceland's Hekla in the North. The Canary Island volcanoes of Gran Canaria, Fuerteventura, and Lanzarote exploded in flames, as the nearby coast of North Africa writhed in seismic anguish. Geologic violence shot along the length of the Mid-Atlantic Ridge, and across the fault boundary where Plato's Atlantis was allegedly situated. Unable to vent the sudden force of so much erupting magma, one wall of the Mt Atlas volcano blasted out laterally. An inconceivable wall of seawater rushed into the gaping wound, where water and fire combined to destroy the entire island.

"Southern Europe grew suddenly colder and wetter, while the Mediterranean became arid. The Earth's cold phase peaked around 1100 B.C., and lasted for roughly the next four hundred years. Climatologists have long recognized the worldwide conditions resulting from the worldwide fall of two degrees Celsius as conditions of the "Plenard Period", from 1250 to 1000 B.C."

British anthropologist Richard Desborough said of the Plenard Period, "the changes that came about were little short of fantastic. The craftsmen and artists seem to have vanished almost without a trace: there is little new stone construction of any sort, far less any massive edifices; the metal workers' techniques revert to primitive, and the potter, except in the early stages, loses his purpose and inspiration; and the art of writing is forgotten. But the outstanding feature is that by the end of the twelfth century B.C., the population appears to have dwindled to about one-tenth, of what it had been a little over a century before". This period of reduced sunlight and plummeting temperatures caused by a massive dust-veil event almost perfectly coincides with the appropriately termed Dark Ages that separated the end of the Bronze Age from the beginning of the Classical Period. Literature, the arts, monumental construction, city planning, medicine, organized religion, mathematical sciences, manufacturing, physics, astronomy, commerce, and everything else characteristic of high civilization vanished practically overnight. For the next 400 years, (1200 BC to 800 BC), humans groped through a dark age so black that these former accomplishments were forgotten or relegated to myth.

In the opening pages of Richard Drews' 1993 book, *The End of the Bronze Age*, he offers a map of the Eastern Mediterranean, showing the Bronze Age cities that burned to the ground, all at the same time. The list of these incinerated cities fills the page. Simultaneously, the New Kingdom ended in Egypt, the

Fig.2 Above right: Alabaster Olmec comet figurine. **Above left:** The flat figurine standing on a stairway has string holes in back, for hanging as a pendant. **Below:** Beautiful 5" jade reclining figure, on his elbows.

Hittite Empire collapsed, the Shang Dynasty ended in China; the Mycenaean States, the Rigvedic Period in India, and the Atlantean Empire all came to an end.

A 2002 book by Frank Joseph, *The Destruction of Atlantis*, describes the situation in detail: "All these kingdoms were economically prosperous, militarily vigorous, artistically rich, and at the height of their powers. Of the 320 Greek cities and towns standing in 1200 B.C., perhaps forty were still inhabited ten years later. Settlements were reduced to metropolitan-sized cauldrons of flame, the very masonry melted. Magnificent Tiryns, its formidable bulwark recently erected against some major threat from the sea, was blasted so severely that the metropolis and everything in its immediate vicinity, including the neighboring city of Midea, were virtually atomized by the heat. The ruins were then swamped by a devastating flood. "The Ipuwer Papyrus in Egypt reads, "Gates, columns, and walls are consumed by fire. The sky is in confusion." The inscriptions of Ramses III's Upper Nile Victory Temple at West Thebes describe even worse conditions in Libya, which until then was considered a relatively fertile, prosperous country: "Libya has become a desert. A terrible torch hurled flame from heaven to destroy their souls and lay waste their land. Their bones burn and roast within their limbs." ...Pollen analysis has revealed that the entire Black Forest region of southwest Germany, predominantly pine until around 1200 B.C., was wrapped in flames. Precisely how many people perished in the catastrophe is impossible to estimate. Some idea of the loss of life may be gathered from the fact that thirty-two centuries ago, Anatolia, Greece, and even Britain were almost entirely depopulated."

In his 1998 book, *Man and Impact in the Americas*, Ed Grondine reviews Indian legends of meteoric impacts in the Americas. Peoples on the East Coast of North America were carried away by a "Great Atlantic Mega-Tsunami" that swept far inland from the beaches. Many of the Olmec remains at La Venta were found buried under about twenty feet of marine sediment. After the event the more inland city of San Lorenzo became the leading Olmec Center, until the resurgence of La Venta, about 900 BC. The Skywatcher statue and the figurines must have been created before the Caribbean impact, or perhaps carved after resettlement. Obviously, the possibility of recurring, celestial catastrophes was in the uppermost of people's thoughts for some period of time. Not only were the Olmec responsible for these statues and figurines, but many ancient peoples, especially the Maya of Yucatan, dedicated enormous resources to their astronomers, observatories, and calendar development. It would seem the people who survived had great fear of cosmic events destructive enough to end the Bronze Age. As perhaps should we.

References:

1. Joseph, F., *The Destruction of Atlantis, Compelling Evidence of the Sudden Fall of the Legendary Civilization*, Bear & Co., Vermont, 2002 (ISBN 1-59143-019-4)
2. Drews, R., *The End of the Bronze Age, Changes in Warfare and the Catastrophe Ca. 1200 BC*, Princeton University Press, N.J., 1993 (ISBN 0-691-04811-8)
3. Grondine, E., *Man and Impact in the Americas*, 1998, (ISBN: 0-9776152-0-0)
4. Donnelly, I., *The Destruction of Atlantis*; Ragnarok: The Age of Fire and Gravel, R. Steiner Publications, New York, 1971 (ISBN: 0-8334-1718)
5. Firestone, R., West, A., Warwick-Smith, S., *The Cycle of Cosmic Catastrophes: Flood, Fire, and Famine in the History of Civilization*, Bear & Co., Vt., 2006 (ISBN 159143061-5)
6. Peiser, B., Palmer, T., Bailey, M., *Natural Catastrophes During Bronze Age Civilizations, Archaeological, geological, astronomical and cultural perspectives*, Hadrian Books Ltd., Oxford, 1998 (ISBN: 0-86054 916 X)
7. "Asteroid darts by, "darn close" to Earth", www.seattletimes.nwsource.com/html/nationworld/2008814689_asteroid05.html, 3/5/2009

Photo 1
Ales Stenar from the SE, showing the big
SE menhir (1) on the axis. The photo
illustrates the big size of the menhirs,
compared to Dr. de Jonge.
(Kaseberga, South Coast of Sweden,
August, 2003)

Photo 2
Ales Stenar from the SE, showing the big
SE menhir (1), and the small keelstone
(59) in front of it, at the right side below.
(Kaseberga, South Coast of Sweden,
August 2003)

The Monument of Ales Stenar
A Sunship to the Realm of the Dead
(Kaseberga, South Coast of Sweden, c.500 BC)

R.M. de Jonge, drsrmdejonge@hotmail.com
J.S. Wakefield, jayswakefield@yahoo.com

Summary

The huge megalithic ship monument of Ales Stenar, overlooking the Baltic Sea on the South Coast of Sweden, is shown to be a Sunship to the Realm of the Dead. The quadrants of the ends of the ship both contain 23 menhirs at 23° angles, encoding the 23° Tropic of Cancer, a holy latitude of the Sunreligion that is a numeric feature of all megalithic monuments. Latitudes encoded in the monument, often based upon the site latitude, show the sailing route used on voyages to Central America, located at the other side of the waters, and symbolizing the Land of the Dead. Ales Stenar turns out to be one of the last megalithic monuments of Europe, dated c.500 BC.

Introduction

The huge monument of Ales Stenar is located near Kaseberga, 15 km east of Ystad, obliquely overlooking the sea on the south coast of Sweden (the port side, or SW quadrant, faces the sea) (Refs.1-4). There are hundreds of ship-like formations in southern Scandinavia, but this is reported to be the largest one. It may be considered the most important megalithic monument in Sweden (**Fig.1**). It is a formation of 58 big menhirs, having a length of 67 meters, and a width of 19 meters. (In reality only 57 menhirs are present, because menhir #46 is missing, but the foundation is still there.) The axis of the ship points exactly 45° northwest of true north. Fifty six of the menhirs have average diameters of about 1 meter, and heights of 1.5m, and the remaining two menhirs on the axis are larger, with heights of about 3 meters (**Photos.1-4**). On the average, the menhirs are placed about 2.5 meters apart.

At least four menhirs of white sandstone, among these the two big menhirs on the axis, are thought to have been brought a considerable distance, some 40km, down the coast from the northeast, near the town of Simrishamn. The other boulders could have been collected at different spots in south Skane at comparable distances, probably not close to the site. Most of the menhirs have nice smooth surfaces, but they are not dressed. The smoothness is from the working of the ice sheets during the Ice Ages in Scandinavia. Inside the NW end, and beside the axis, is a small stone. It is highly probable that it was moved from an original position behind the big NW menhir (shown as #60 in Fig.1), making this part of the ship symmetrical with the other end. These two stones (59 and 60, Fig.1) are called "keelstones", at each end of the ship. Their diameters and heights are only about half a meter. Adding these two small posts to the 58 menhirs gives a total of 60 stones.

The monument is situated on a flat hilltop, a 37 meter high ridge, about 100 meters from the sea. The latitude of the site is 55.5°N, or rounded off to 56°N. Some scientists believe

Groundplan of Ales Stenar

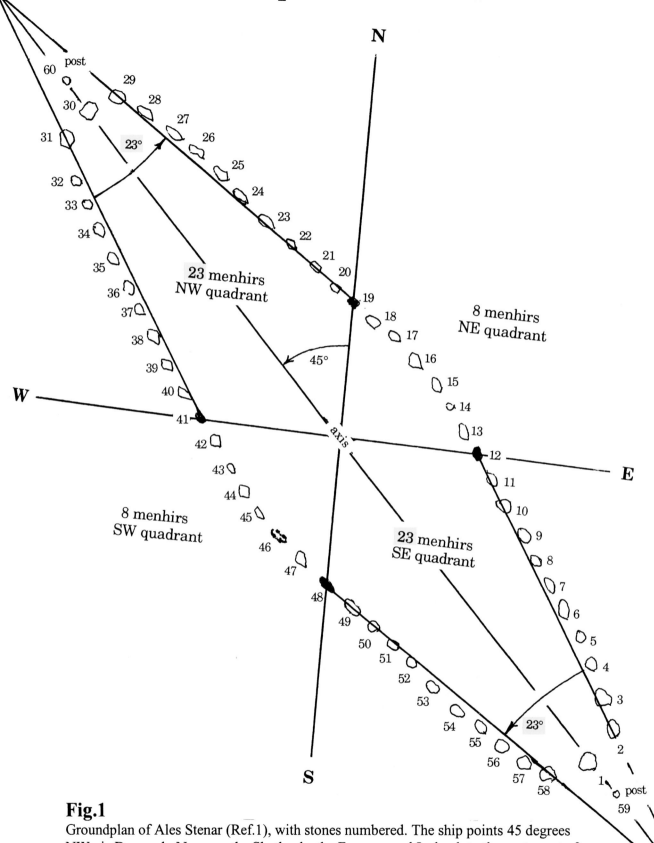

N

post
60
29
30
28
27
31
23°
26
32
25
33
24
34
23 menhirs
NW quadrant
35
23
36
22
37
21
38
20
19
39
18
45°
17
40
16
W
15
41
axis
14
42
13
43
12
E
44
11
8 menhirs
SW quadrant
45
10
46
23 menhirs
SE quadrant
9
47
8
48
7
49
6
50
5
51
52
4
53
3
54
55
23°
2
56
1
57
post
58
S
59

8 menhirs
NE quadrant

Fig.1

Groundplan of Ales Stenar (Ref.1), with stones numbered. The ship points 45 degrees NW via Denmark, Norway, the Shetlands, the Faeroes, and Iceland, to the east coast of Greenland. The 58 big menhirs encode the north coast of Scotland, at 58 degrees N. The 23 menhirs in the NW end, (or 23.5 including the keelstone), encode the holy Arctic Circle, at 90-23= 67 degrees N. In total there are 58+2= 60 stones, encoding the south cape of Greenland, at 60 degrees N. (Kaseberga, South Coast Sweden, c.500 BC)

the monument dates from c.700 BC (late Bronze Age), while others believe a date from c.600 AD (late Iron Age). The site was partially excavated in 1916, and again in 1956, when mainly sand that had blown over the site was removed.

Egypt & the Sun Religion

Ales Stenar is basically a Sunship, with its destination in the west. The symbol of the Sunship was of central importance in the religion of Egypt. The cosmic Sunship is still seen today carrying the SunGod Ra across the ceilings of the tombs which dot the west bank of the Nile River. The name "Ales" (or "Als") means "Sanctuary" in old Nordic, while "Stenar" means "of stone". Seen from the center of the monument, the four cardinal points are occupied by menhirs: N (stone #19), S (#48), E (#12), and W (#41) (see **Fig.1**). Perhaps these four stones were originally painted, or perhaps were decorated when the monument was still in use. Like the rectangle of the four Stationstones at Stonehenge, these four "cardinal" stones, here in a perfect square, help mark the equinoxes and solstices observed at the site. Including the cardinal stones, there are 23 menhirs in both ends of the ship. These menhirs also form 23° angles in both ends, as shown on **Fig.1**.

Our globes today still show the 23° Tropic of Cancer, a holy latitude of the Sunreligion. This latitude is as far north as the sun appears overhead in summer. Also at the latitude of 23°N was located the center of the Southern Egyptian Empire, the geographic center of the Sunreligion. Where the Tropic of Cancer crosses the coast of Africa, at 23°N, was of course an early focus for ocean explorations (Refs.5-7). The Egyptian Sun-God Ra has said: "The Realm of the Dead is in the west, at the other side of the waters, in the land where the Sun sets. After death you will reunite there with your ancestors, your family, your relatives, your friends, your acquaintances!" This Sunship monument memorializes the sailing route that was used to reach the west.

Extending the axis of the monument to the SE at 45° on a globe, you see it points to the delta of the River Donau, at 45°N. By sailing the rivers Wista (in Poland) and Dnister (in Ukraine) to this delta, traders accomplished the first half of the shortest route from the Baltic to the Black Sea and the Eastern Mediterranean. The direction from Ales Stenar to the Nile Delta, the center of the Northern Egyptian Empire, is 60°SE (60 stones), and the complementary angle (90°-60) = 30°, is the latitude of the Nile Delta at 30°N. (Complementary angles are used in megalithic sites to encode large numbers, because this was easier than moving large numbers of stones. Think of the labor involved.) The two halves of the ship each contain 30 menhirs, confirming the 30° latitude of the Delta. If you exclude the 3 bow and 3 stern menhirs, which are slightly taller, the sides of the ship each contain 52/2= 26 menhirs, the 26° latitude of the United Egyptian Empire, halfway between the Tropic of Cancer and the Nile Delta. This latitude marks the center of government in Egypt.

The Crossing Via the Upper North

The axis of the monument points 45°NW via the northern tip of Jutland (Denmark), the southern tip of Norway, the northern tip of the Shetland Islands and the Faeroes, to the SE and West Coasts of Iceland, and the East Coast of Greenland (at 65°N.) The 58 big

Photo 3

Ales Stenar from the NW, showing the big
NW menhir (30) on the axis, and a number
of northern menhirs of the monument.
(Kaseberga, South Coast of Sweden,
August, 2003)

Photo 4

The main NW menhir (30) of Ales Stenar
from the NE, with Dr. de Jonge behind it.
In the background the Baltic Sea in the SW.
(Kaseberga, South Coast of Sweden,
August, 2003)

menhirs of Ales Stenar correspond to the north coast of Scotland at 58°N, which is very important (Refs.8,9). From this location, it is a 45° angle to sail via the SW coast of Iceland to Cape Holm, Greenland, on the Arctic Circle, at 67°N. From megalithic monuments, such as Stonehenge, and Loughcrew, Ireland, we have shown that Greenland was found by explorers from Iceland at the latitude of 67° (Refs.5-7). The complementary angle of 23° (90°-23°) = 67 degrees, provides this other holy latitude, the Arctic Circle, which was holy to the Sunreligion, because it is the northernmost latitude where the Sun shines at midwinter. Seen from the center of the monument on the winter solstice, the Sun rises exactly behind the big SE menhir on the axis (Refs.1-4).

In total, Ales Stenar consists of 60 stones, which encode the S and SW Capes of Greenland, at 60°N. The sailing direction from the SW Cape to the coast of Labrador is 45°SW, which appears to them as they reach the latitude of 56°N, the same latitude as Ales Stenar, as shown by the 58-2= 56 menhirs in the two sides of the ship. The SW side of the central part of the ship, including the cardinal stones, contains 8 stones (#41-#48), encoding the sailing distance of 8dl= 8°= 8 Egyptian Moira= 480 Nautical Miles (NM). Significant sites always contain their latitudes encoded in the site design, and it is done here by the 60 stones minus the 4 cardinal stones. These stones simultaneously encode the 56° latitude where a big new land was found on the other side of the Ocean, which is one of the main reasons why this monument was built, and why it is located where it is. (Note that there are significant parallels with Stonehenge, such as the 56 Aubrey Holes inside the circular wall of this monument.) By dropping off the 3 bow and 3 stern menhirs, we find the latitude of important Belle Isle Strait, at 58-6= 52°N. So the sailing route west of Newfoundland is shown to be preferred. The sailing direction from the SW Cape of Newfoundland to Cape Breton Island is 45°SW, again shown by the orientation of the ship at 45°.

Central America

Sailing continues to the south along the East Coast of the US. The 2 big menhirs on the axis encode the south cape of Florida, 2 degrees above the Tropic of Cancer, at 23°+2= 25°N (see also **Table 1**). The same 2 menhirs provide the sailing distance to Cuba, 2dl= 2°= 120 NM. The four sides at the ends of the ship each contain 11 menhirs (**Fig.1**), encoding the sailing direction from Cuba to Yucatan, 11°WSW. Again, the 2 big menhirs on the axis provide the sailing distance involved, about 120 NM.

The 16 menhirs in the central part of the ship provide the latitude of the culture of the North Coast of Honduras, Belize and Guatemala, at 16°N. Adding the 2 big menhirs on the axis again, gives us the latitude of the civilization around the Gulf of Campeche ("Egyptian Bay"), at 18°N. This is the center of the Realm of the Dead, called "the Land of Punt". These two latitudes are common in late megalithic monuments and petroglyphs (Ref.5). The complementary angle of the monument's 60 stones (90°-60= 30°) reveals the Mississippi River Delta at 30°N, gateway to the Poverty Point complex. It was of importance for the copper trade with the hinterland.

The visits to Punt took place in the so-called Formative Period in Central America, which lasted from about 1500 BC to 200 AD. In this period the most striking characteristics of

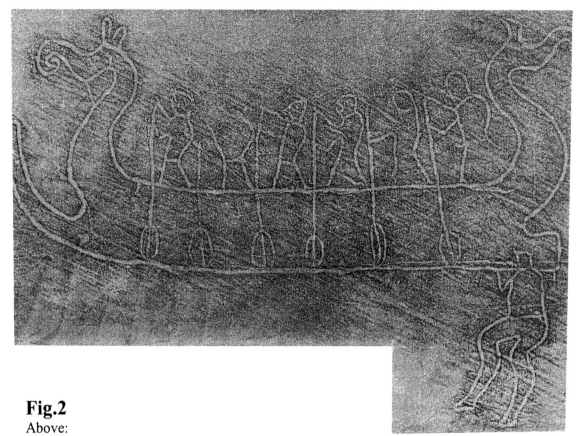

Fig.2

Above:
Petroglyph of a ritual boat (with a length of 4.13m) which is carried to the Realm of the Dead in the west (America), via the holy Arctic Circle, at 67 degrees N. Rickeby, at 60 degrees N, Uppland, north of Stockholm, Sweden, c.500 BC (Ref.11).

Below:
Petroglyph of ritual boat from Namforsen in Angermanland, near the east coast of Central Sweden. It is a huge fantasy boat (with a length of 2.4m), containing 67 rowers, showing the latitude of the holy Arctic Circle, at 67 degrees N. Above the crew are carvings of features of the newly discovered coast of Greenland. (Namforsen, Noton Island, Angermanland, Sweden, c.3200 BC (Ref.11).

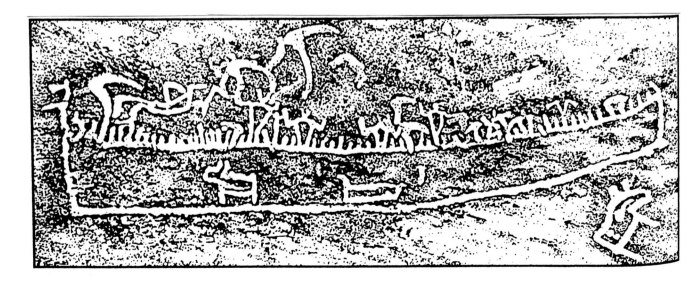

the civilization developed. Around 500 BC the first towns and states are in evidence, in several places, more or less at the same time. The mouth of the Motagua River, at 16°N, leads south to the Old Maya Culture, which developed from about 2000 BC, and flourished after c.1600 BC, when permanent villages appeared along the river valleys. The main center formed around Copan, Honduras. Around 500 BC, the time of these visits, a gradual expansion of these settlements took place, and the growing town of Tikal began to develop. The Zapotecs lived further west, and ruled the valley of Oaxaca from a town on Monte Alban ("the hill of the jaguar"), which had at least 5000 inhabitants in this time period, and possesses interesting petroglyphs indicating cultural diffusion. The Olmec culture flourished from c.1200-300 BC, famous for their unique art, and their religion and calendar. The colossal Negroid stone heads with Egyptian-style helmets found around the ceremonial plazas date from before 500 BC (Refs.15-20).

The Southern Crossing

Central America could also be reached via the Southern Crossing of the Ocean (see Ref.5). The departure point is the Cape Verde Islands, at 16°N, again encoded by the 16 menhirs in the central part of the ship. The sailing direction from the Cape Verde Islands to the closest Brazilian shore is 60°SW, again encoded by the 60 stones. The two ends of the ship each contain 23 menhirs, corresponding to the sailing distance, 23dl= 23°= 1380 NM, which is correct. The big SE menhir on the axis corresponds with the southern Atlantic island of St. Paul at 1°N. The 4 menhirs of the cardinal directions correspond with the two islands of Fernando de Noronha, at 4°S, and together these 5 correspond with Cape Sao Roque (the "Holy Rock"), Brazil, at 5°S.

The Return Routes

An alternative return route from Central America to Europe proceeded via the isolated island of Bermuda. The 3 bow menhirs (#29,#30,#31) correspond to Bimini near Florida, 3 degrees above the Tropic of Cancer, at 23°+3= 26°N. The 2 big menhirs on the axis encode Bermuda, 2° above the Nile Delta, at 30°+2= 32°N, as well as the initial sailing direction (ISD) from Great Abaco to Bermuda, 32°NE. Between the cardinal stones in the center quadrants are 6+6= 12 menhirs, corresponding to the sailing distance involved, 12dl= 12°= 720 NM. Bermuda was discovered from the American coast, about 2200 BC, as shown by the Devil's Head petroglyphs in Harmony, Maine (Ref.5). However, from Bermuda to the West Azores is a long sailing distance.

For that reason, most ships sailed along the East Coast of the US to the north. The 3 bow and 3 stern menhirs encode Cape Hatteras, the East Cape of the US, 6° above the Nile Delta, at 30°+6= 36°N. It is located at the same latitude as the famous Strait of Gibraltar, at the entrance of the Mediterranean. The main departure point for returning, with the winds and currents, was the east coast of Nova Scotia, at 45°N, again encoded by the 45° axis angle. They oriented on Cape Race, Newfoundland, 2° higher, encoded by the 2 big menhirs on the axis, at 45°+2= 47°N. It is the East Cape of North America. The sailors focused upon finding the West Azores, in mid-ocean at 39°N, encoded by adding together the 23 menhirs of the south end of the ship, with the 16 central menhirs (23+16= 39). The mathematical encoding is beautiful in its simplicity. Other encodings are of course possible, but are less likely.

Table 1

The Sailing Route to Central America, The Realm of the Dead
(The Important latitude encodings of Ales Stenar)

The list below illustrates the beauty of the methodology used to encode large numbers. Rather than construct a huge, laborious monument of a great many stones, they used a few combinations repeatedly, as an encoding convention. These rules of encoding in this monument used the 60 total stones, 1 end post stone, the 2 end post stones, the 4 cardinal stones, the 8 stones of each of the side quadrants, the 23 stones of the end quadrants, and complementary numbers (from 90). Clearly, the most important encodings of the monument are the 23° Tropic of Cancer, and the 60° Cape Farewell of South Greenland. Using these numbers (60,23,8,4,2, and 1), all these encodings were done:

Locations:	Latitude:	Menhirs of Encoding:
Ales Stenar, site	56°N	60-4 (total-cardinal)
Nile Delta	30°N	60/2
Tropic of Cancer	23°N	23 (each end of ship)
North Scotland	58°N	60-2
Faeroe Islands	62°N	60+2
SE Iceland	64°N	60+4
NW Iceland	66°N	Scotland (58)+8
Cape Holm	67°N	90-(23) Tropic of Cancer
Arctic Circle	67°N	90-(23) Tropic of Cancer
South Greenland	60°N	60 (total stones)
SW Greenland	61°N	South Greenland (60)+1
Labrador	56°N	South Greenland (60)-4
Belle Isle Strait	52°N	South Greenland (60)-8
Mississippi Delta	30°N	60/2 (=Nile Delta)
South Florida	25°N	Tropic of Cancer (23)+2
North Cuba	23°N	Tropic of Cancer (23)
NE Yucatan	21°N	Tropic of Cancer (23)-2
Honduras	16°N	8+8 (sides of ship)
Gulf of Campeche	18°N	Honduras (16)+2

The ship is sailing SE from Newfoundland. So the 3 bow menhirs (#1,#2,and #58) symbolize the 3 island group of the Azores, which had been discovered by 3600 BC, as shown in the Tumulus of Gavrinis, in the Gulf of Morbihan, Brittany (Ref.5). Excluding these 3 bigger stones, the end of the ship has 9 stones on each side of the end, symbolizing the 9 islands of the Azores. The 9 menhirs on each side add together to the initial sailing direction (ISD) from Cape Race to the important West Azores, 18°ESE, and the sailing distance of 18dl= 18°= 1080 NM, which is correct. The 3 stern menhirs and the 30 stones at the SE half of the ship encode the terminal sailing direction (TSD) in the neighborhood of the West Azores, 30+3= 33°ESE. The difference between the sailing directions is due to the curvature of the Earth. The image is striking, the lonely stones of Ales Stenar on the high ridge overlooking the Baltic is like a small ship sailing the endless ocean!

From the West Azores they sailed along the other islands to the East Azores. The big SE menhir on the axis encodes Sta Maria, East Azores, 1 degree above Gibraltar, at 36+1= 37°N. The latitude of the Eastern Canaries (at 29°N) corresponds to the ISD from Sta Maria to Madeira, 29° ESE. Half the 16 menhirs in the center correspond to the sailing distance to Madeira, 8dl= 8° = 480 NM. The latitude of Gibraltar (at 36°N) corresponds to the terminal sailing direction (TSD) in the neighborhood of Madeira, 36°SE. The 3 bow menhirs encode the latitude of Madeira, 3° above the Nile Delta, at 30°+3= 33°N.

All the 58 menhirs of the ship correspond to the sailing direction to the eastern Canary Islands, 58°SE. The 29 menhirs of the SE half of the ship encode the Eastern Canaries, at 29°N. This is the end of the religious voyage to Central America, the Land of Punt. The whole ship of Ales Stenar symbolizes the pilgrimage to the west. The northern menhirs (#2-#29), represent the northern route, which is from the Old World (stern menhir) to the New World (the bow menhir), while the southern menhirs (#31-#58) represent the main southern return route.

Dating and Discussion

Dating the monument of Ales Stenar poses a real problem. It is surely after the discovery of America via the Atlantic, c.2500 BC, because of the encodings we see in the monument (Refs.5-7). It describes the crossing of the Labrador Sea from South Greenland to mainland North America, which points to a date after c.1600 BC. Ales Stenar is a highly stylized ship, telling a story by reference latitudes, and these show a very late megalithic date, after c.1000 BC. The article clearly shows a relation with the Egyptian SunGod religion, so it was probably built before the Second Persian Rule of Egypt, which lasted from 341 BC to 333 BC. Surely it was built before the Hellenistic Period, which lasted from 332 BC until 642 AD. During the Hellenistic Period in Egypt, Greek was the official language in Egypt.

The fact that cup marks have been found on many of the menhirs (Refs.1-4), points to the Bronze Age, which ends in Scandinavia c.500 BC. However, it has been observed that some of these marks were carved in strange places, some hardly visible. The idea was put forth that these menhirs were taken from old Bronze Age monuments in the neighborhood. We doubt this, since the stones are thought to have been brought large distances, and in general sanctuaries were not built by demolishing older sanctuaries. Usually, megalithic monuments were only seriously disturbed in recent centuries. But Ales Stenar is a Scandinavian ship-setting, and these kinds of structures, though generally much smaller, usually date from the Iron Age, or even later. For all these reasons we think Ales Stenar dates from the very end of the Late Bronze Age, which is c.500 BC. However, a strong relation with the Egyptian SunGod religion is a typical megalithic tradition. The date of c.500 BC implies that Ales Stenar is by far the latest megalithic monument of Europe! The megalithic culture officially ends c.1500 BC.

The biggest carved rock petroglyph of a ritual boat in Sweden (**Fig.2**), having a length of 4.13 meters, has the same date, c.500 BC (Ref.11). It is from Rickeby in Uppland (north of Stockholm), which is situated at the latitude of Cape Farvel, Greenland, at 60°N. It contains 6 full sized and dressed rowers, encoding the NW peninsula of Iceland, at 60°+6= 66°N. The whole boat is carried by another man, the SunGod, encoding Cape Holm, Greenland, at the holy Arctic Circle, at 66°+1= 67°N. He carries the ship to the Realm of the Dead in the west (from Greenland to America). The lower petroglyph in Fig.2, dated from c.3200 BC, is a ship with 67 rowers, showing that it too, sailed to Cape Holm at the Arctic Circle. Note the long time span of this Megalithic, religious tradition.

Beneath one of the Ales Stenar menhirs (#6) a piece of birch charcoal was found, and carbon-dated to c.600 AD (Ref.4). This result is definitely not in line with the previous arguments. We have to presume this sample was not representative. We recommend further research in this field, if possible, to clarify these conflicting indications. The Danish island of Als (meaning "sanctuary" again) is 270 km west of this monument. On this island a now famous ship of 19m length has been excavated, which has been dated from the Iron Age, c.150 BC. The remains contained tens of iron shields, spears and swords, but also Roman beakers and dishes, which points to trade with the Roman Empire. Compare this with the monument of Ales Stenar, with its religious orientation on Egypt; the Ales Stenar monument is clearly of a much earlier date.

Table 1 shows the menhir encodings for the sailing route to Central America. The Table illustrates the beauty of the methodology used to encode large numbers. Rather than constructing a huge, laborious monument of a great many stones, they used a few combinations repeatedly, as an encoding convention. These rules of encoding in this monument used the 60 total stones, 1 end post stone, the 2 end post stones, the 4 cardinal stones, and the 8 stones of each of the side quadrants, the 23 stones of the end quadrants, and complementary numbers (from 90). Clearly, the most important encodings of the monument are the 23° Tropic of Cancer, and the 60° Cape Farvel of South Greenland. All the encodings of **Table 1** were done using these numbers: 60,23,8,4,2, and 1.

This description of the pilgrimage to Central America, the Realm of the Dead, is confirmed by the menhir distances within the monument. This is a particular feature of this late megalithic construction, and important to mention. As an example, we will illustrate the main goal of the voyage. The width/length ratio of Ales Stenar, at 56°N, confirms the latitude of the North Coast of Honduras, at (19.1m/67.0m) x 56= 16°N. This and similar results of other distance/length ratios contribute to the beauty of this ancient, sacred monument.

The numbers of the huge menhirs in these monuments is not happenstance, but carefully designed by the human mind. As in other megalithic sites, astronomic and calendrical meanings appear to have been also built into the monument (Ref.2). This complex entwining of encodings is particularly clear at Stonehenge in England, and at America's Stonehenge in New Hampshire (Ref.5). Given their known level of astronomic expertise, the encoding of their adventures and commercial routes in numbers and petroglyphs should have been expected. Remember that these people could not write their spoken language, but they lived outdoors much of the time, and must have been very capable of physical exploits, in a world full of wildlife, prior to commercial fishing. That so much information, both astronomic and geographic, could be encoded in so few stones must have seemed holy, or special to them, as it seems amazing to us.

References

1. Ales Stenar, Lind, B.G., 10 page booklet (ISBN 91-631-3736-4) (Swedish and English)
2. Website: www.alesstenar.com, Lind, B.G.
3. Ales Stenar, Pamphlet by Riksantikvarieambetet. Website: www.raa.se
4. Kobos, Andrew, M., "Ales Stenar, When? Who? What For?" Website: www.fermi.phys.ualberta.ca/~amk/as/aleseng.html
5. De Jonge, R.M., and Wakefield, J.S., How the SunGod Reached America c.2500 BC, A Guide to Megalithic Sites, 2002 (ISBN 0-917054-19-9). Available: MCS Inc., POB 3392, Kirkland, Wa 98083-3392, also on CD
6. De Jonge, R.M., and IJzereef, G.F., De Stenen Spreken, Kosmos Z&K, Utrecht/Antwerpen, 1996 (ISBN 90-215-2846-0) (Dutch)
7. Website: www.howthesungod.com, De Jonge, R.M., and Wakefield, J.S.
8. Ekornavallen, the prehistoric enclosure of, B. Hjohlman, Svenska Fornminnesplatser 52, 1977 (ISBN 91-7192-376-4)
9. Silent Messengers from a Distant Epoch: Falbygden Area Passage Tombs, Hugin & Munin Kulturinformation AB, Lansstyrelsen, Vastra Gotaland, Sweden
10. Coles, J., Images of the Past, A Guide to the Rock Carvings of Northern Bohuslan, Bohuslans Museum, 1990 (ISBN 91-7686-110-4)
11. Evers, D., Felsbilder, Botschaften der Vorzeit, Urania, Berlin, 1991 (ISBN 3-33200482-4) (German), pgs.58,85
12. Fell, B., America BC, Pocket Books, Simon & Schuster, 1994
13. Bailey, J., Sailing to Paradise, Simon & Schuster, 1994
14. Mallery, A.H., and Harrison, M.R., The Rediscovery of Lost America, The Story of the Pre-Columbian Iron Age in America, Dutton, NY, 1979 (ISBN 0-525-47545-1)
15. Thompson, G., American Discovery, Misty Isles Press, Seattle, 1994
16. Jairazbhoy, R.A., Ancient Egyptians an Chinese in America, Rowman & Littlefield, Totowa, N.J., 1974 (0-87471-571-1)
17. Tedlock,D., trans., Popol Vuh, The Definitive Edition of the Mayan Book of the Dawn of Lfe and the Glories of Gods and Kings, Simon & Schuster, New York, 1985 (ISBN 0-671-61771-0)
18. Coe, M.D., (Principal), Mysteries of the Ancient Americas, Reader's Digest General Books, 1986, USA (ISBN 0-8957-7-183-7)
19. Zapp, I., and Erikson, G., Atlantis in America, Navigators of the Ancient World, Adventures Unlimited Press, 1998 (ISBN 0-932-813-52-6)
20. Mertz, H., Atlantis, Dwelling Place of the Gods, Box 207 Loop Sta., Chicago, 60690, 1976 (ISBN 0-9600952-3-3)

Left, six inch tall Phoenician marble tablet of the god Horus, of 300 BC, excavated in the old Phoenician city of Tyr, on the eastern shore of the Mediterranean. The winged hawk is the Egyptian symbolism for the living god Horus, embodied by the pharaoh in Egypt (Wakefield photo, 8/2009). **Above,** portion of New Kingdom painting, Tomb of Unsou, East Thebes (Louvre). **Right,** rock carving of Assyrian King Assurnasirpal II (Intro. Ref.45). **Opposite page,** monument found when the airstrip was constructed at La Venta, Mexico. This appears to be a "culture bringer", holding in a seed bag, the gift of agriculture. Note the upside-down boat to the Underworld in the West, with the square royal deckhouse (photo by Wakefield, in Olmec Park, in Villahermosa, Mexico).

Olmec head, located in Olmec Park, villahermosa, Mexico. These fellows must have been running things. There are now 17 heads found, each different. (Wakefield photo, 3/19/02)